THE BLUE HELMETS

P9-CDV-575

A Review
of United Nations Peace-keeping

United Nations

Department of Public Information
New York, 1985

Note

This comprehensive account of the peace-keeping operations of the United Nations has been compiled on the occasion of the Fortieth Anniversary of the Organization in an attempt to make available in easily accessible form the main facts about these operations. It is intended as an information paper for general use and is not a formal report of the United Nations.

ISBN: 92-1-100275-3

UNITED NATIONS PUBLICATION
Sales No. E.85.I.18

00895

October 1985

Contents

Foreword by the Secretary-General

Like many political institutions, the United Nations has been faced, virtually throughout its existence, with a deep gulf between theory and practice, between the principles and objectives of the Charter and the political realities of our time. The effort to bridge this gulf has been the main theme of the first forty years of the United Nations.

Nowhere has the gulf between theory and practice been so evident as in the primary function of the United Nations, the maintenance of international peace and security. The Charter's provisions for this purpose, based primarily on the activity of the Security Council and the unanimity of its permanent members, have never yet been permitted to function fully. Being unable to exercise the magisterial but relatively simple powers prescribed in the Charter, the Council has had, time and again, to fall back on less well-defined measures—good offices, conciliation, mediation and delegation of responsibility to the Secretary-General.

Of these less well-defined measures, the form of conflict control which is now known as peace-keeping is perhaps the most original and most ambitious. Peace-keeping is a technique not mentioned, let alone described, in the Charter. In fact it is in many ways a reversal of the use of military personnel foreseen in the Charter. It has been developed for situations where there is no formal determination of aggression. Its practitioners have no enemies, are not there to win, and can use force only in self-defence. Its effectiveness depends on voluntary co-operation.

It may seem strange that the United Nations has turned to various forms of this technique no less than 13 times and that peace-keeping is widely regarded as one of the Organization's most successful innovations. The reason presumably lies in the nature of international relations in our time. There are now many conflicts which neither side can hope to win but in which peaceful settlement remains elusive. Peace-keeping offers a dignified and inexpensive escape from such situations. In the present relationship of the most powerful nations, it is usually impossible for the Security Council to reach more drastic decisions for putting an end to threats to or breaches of the peace.

In a time of nuclear armament, it is more than ever important that regional conflicts in sensitive areas should be kept out of the sphere of possible great-Power nuclear confrontation. In this context, peace-keeping operations are one important means of conflict control, working, as they usually do, in partnership with the efforts of the Security Council and the Secretary-General to gain time and to promote just and peaceful settlements of international disputes. It is worth noting that peace-keeping operations tend to be established for conflict control in particularly sensitive areas of the world where the danger of escalation is high.

I believe that this novel but still fragile creation is an important addition to the armory of peace in the nuclear age. I hope that the lessons of the past will contribute to a strengthening and wider employment of the peace-keeping technique in the future. In the particular international conditions of our time, I believe that the institution and technique of United Nations peace-keeping is an indispensable, and potentially highly effective, weapon in the struggle for world peace.

Javier Pérez de Cuéllar

Part One:
An overview

A holding action

The evolution of international relations after the Second World War, the process of decolonization and differing concepts among the membership about the use of United Nations machinery quickly affected the functioning of the world Organization founded in 1945. It became apparent that since all international disputes were not at once to be resolved by peaceful means, some way had to be found to stop or contain those which escalated into armed conflict. Out of that need, United Nations peace-keeping operations evolved as, essentially, a holding action. They do not purport to replace the means of voluntary settlement of disputes which are set out in Chapter VI of the United Nations Charter, nor the enforcement action envisaged in Chapter VII, but rather seek to supplement the purposes and intent of those two Chapters. As Secretary-General Dag Hammarskjöld put it, they could take the place of a new Chapter of the Charter—to be numbered "Six and a Half".

As suggested by that comment, peace-keeping operations were not originally envisaged in the Charter as among the measures to preserve world peace; they are a purely empirical creation born of necessity. The term "peace-keeping operation" gained currency in the 1960s, not only well after the Charter was drawn up but also, in effect, after the pragmatic use of this novel concept had already been established within the strict limits set by the essentially voluntary nature of dispute resolution, the burden of resolution resting with the parties themselves.

Characteristics

The definition of a peace-keeping operation followed in the Secretary-General's reports is that of an operation involving military personnel, but without enforcement powers, established by the United Nations to help maintain or restore peace in areas of conflict.

Such an operation falls broadly into two main categories: the observer missions and the peace-keeping forces. In either form they operate under the same basic principles. They are normally established by the Security Council (two were exceptionally authorized by the General Assembly), and they are directed by the Secretary-General. They must have the consent of the host Governments and, normally, also of the other parties directly involved. The military personnel required are provided by Member States on a voluntary basis. The military observers are not armed and, while the soldiers of United Nations peace-keeping forces are provided with light defensive weapons, they are not authorized to use force except in self-defence. A further key principle is that the operations must not interfere in the internal affairs of the host country and must not be used in any way to favour one party against another in internal conflicts affecting Member States. This latter point, together with the non-use of force, demands exceptional restraint but is fundamental not only on grounds of principle but to ensure the operations' effectiveness. The United Nations operations cannot take sides or use force without becoming part of the problems at the root of the dispute.

Another requirement of peace-keeping is a broad political consensus among the membership for its mandate, not only at the creation of the operation, but in its continuing functioning.

The most important element in that consensus is the Security Council, whose continuing support is essential. Also fundamental is the need for the continuing support not only of the countries or parties principally concerned in the conflict but also of the States contributing troops to the peace-keeping operation.

Besides support, there must be co-operation. Since the peace-keepers have little or no capacity for enforcement and their use of force is limited to self-defence—as a last resort—any determined party can effectively defy a peace-keeping force.

There should be a clear mandate, or one as clear as possible given the probable consensus nature of the decisions taken by the Security Council. A clear mandate, based on specific agreement by the parties, means that the peace-keeping operation should encounter few difficulties. An unclear or ambiguous mandate means that the operation will face recurrent difficulties and become involved in actions likely to be viewed as controversial. Nevertheless, there are times when the mandate is not as clear as could be wished, e.g. when the Security Council has decided that the prime requirement of international peace and security requires creation of an operation even in the face of the obvious fact that the operation will not easily achieve the objectives set.

A final characteristic is the general improvisational nature of most peace-keeping operations. The United Nations has no sovereignty of its own and can undertake peace-keeping operations only by specific mandate from the Security Council, and exceptionally from the General Assembly. The present political, constitutional, administrative and budgetary arrangements of the United Nations are such that no permanent establishment can be maintained for peace-keeping.

Normally, peace-keeping operations deal with regional conflicts that potentially threaten international peace and security and where, often, power vacuums have resulted from the decolonization process. They have become tested devices for maintaining the delicate balance of international peace when that peace is threatened by a regional conflict in which there is the likelihood of great-Power involvement. Characteristically they fulfil the role of an impartial and objective third party to help create and maintain a cease-fire and form a buffer zone between conflicting States. They have become an important instrument in preventing local or regional conflicts from escalating to encompass much wider areas and in precluding the introduction of outside forces.

Charter provisions

As mentioned earlier, it is almost necessary to imagine a new bridging "Chapter Six and a Half" of the United Nations Charter when considering peace-keeping operations. But while the Charter sheds little light on the nature of these operations, since it contains no specific reference to them, the maintenance of international peace and security, to which United Nations peace-keeping operations are closely related, is, of course, prominently mentioned in the Charter.

The first of the purposes of the United Nations listed in the Charter is "To maintain international peace and security, and to that end: to take effective collective measures for the prevention and removal of threats to the peace, and for the suppression of acts of aggression or other breaches of the peace, and to bring about by peaceful means, and in conformity with the principles of justice and international law, adjustment or settlement of international disputes or situations which might lead to a breach of the peace".

The concrete measures to be taken by the United Nations to achieve this purpose are set out in Chapters VI and VII of the Charter. Chapter VI provides for disputes to be brought to the attention of the Security Council or the General Assembly and for the former to call on the parties to settle their disputes by peaceful means and to recommend appropriate procedures or methods of adjustment. The action of the Security Council in this context is limited to making recommendations; essentially, the peaceful settlement of international disputes must be achieved by the parties themselves on a voluntary basis.

If the peaceful means outlined in Chapter VI should prove insufficient and the dispute should develop into a conflict endangering the maintenance of international peace and security, then Chapter VII may come into play. This Chapter provides that when the Security Council determines "the existence of any threat to the peace, breach of the peace or act of aggression", it may take certain measures of an enforcement character in order to maintain or restore international peace and security. In this connection, the Council may first take, under Article 41, measures not involving the use of armed force, including "complete or partial interruption of economic relations and of rail, sea, air, postal, telegraphic, radio, and other means of communication, and the severance of diplomatic relations".

Should the Security Council consider the measures provided for in Article 41 to be inadequate, it may then take, in accordance with Article 42, "such action by air, sea and land forces as may be necessary to maintain or restore international peace and security". Such action may include "demonstrations, blockade, and other operations by air, sea, or land forces of Members of the United Nations". Plans for the application of armed force as an enforcement action are to be made by the Security Council with the assistance of a United Nations Military Staff Committee. All Members of the United Nations undertake to make available to the Security Council, on its call and in accordance with special agreements, armed forces, assistance and facilities "necessary for the purpose of maintaining international peace and security".

The measures outlined in Articles 41 and 42, which must be decided by the Security Council acting on behalf of the international community as a whole, constitute the core of the system of collective security envisioned by the Charter to ensure the maintenance of international peace and security.

A basic feature of this system is the determining role reserved for the five major Powers, namely, China, France, the Union of Soviet Socialist Republics, the United Kingdom of Great Britain and Northern Ireland and the United States of America. These Powers are permanent members of the Security Council and can block any of its substantive decisions by their veto. They also control the activities of the Military Staff Committee, which is made up exclusively of their military representatives. Consequently, the United Nations collective security system, and especially its key provision concerning the use of armed force, can work only if there is full agreement and co-operation among the major Powers. But this essential condition has never been met as, shortly after the establishment of the United Nations, the co-operation that had existed during the Second World War rapidly collapsed.

The inapplicability of Chapter VII in its most important provisions created a vacuum, which had to be filled somehow, and hence the development of peace-keeping operations. These operations can be considered as based on Article 40 of the Charter, which provides that before resorting to the action provided for in Articles 41 and 42, the Security Council may take provisional measures to prevent the aggravation of a conflict situation without prejudice to the rights, claims and position of the parties concerned.

Peace-keeping and peace-making

Peace-keeping is only part of a large machinery for attempting to maintain international peace and security. This machinery includes the Security Council, the diplomatic role of the Secretary-General and bilateral efforts of Member States. Chapter VI of the United Nations Charter, dealing with the "Pacific Settlement of Disputes", says the parties to the dispute "shall, first of all, seek a solution by negotiation, enquiry, mediation, conciliation, arbitration, judicial settlement, resort to regional agencies or arrangements, or other peaceful means of their own choice". Each of the methods mentioned has been used in conjunction with the peace-keeping process, together with specific mandates for the Secretary-General to use his good offices, directly or through appointment of a Special Representative.

Essentially, United Nations peace-keeping operations are provisional measures which the Organization may take to prevent aggravation of a conflict situation. They can stop and contain hostilities but cannot resolve the political problems underlying the conflict. They can, and do, create the climate, buy the time, and promote the minimum goodwill necessary for settlement through negotiations or other peaceful means. Thus peace-keeping operations and peace-making efforts are closely interrelated. The first promotes the second by creating conditions conducive to negotiations. The second helps the first since, when peace-making efforts give hope for a peaceful solution of the conflict, the parties will be more inclined to observe a cease-fire and to co-operate with the peace-keeping operation.

Conversely, when peace-making fails, or is not pursued vigorously, one or both parties may give up the possibility of a peaceful settlement and resort to force.

The operations

The first use of the military by the United Nations was in 1947, in two United Nations bodies: the Consular Commission on Indonesia and the Special Committee on the Balkans. Since the small officer groups worked as members of the national delegations comprising those bodies, and were not under the Secretary-General's authority, they cannot be considered as United Nations peace-keeping operations as the term has come to be used.

The international force in Korea was also not a United Nations peace-keeping operation in the current sense of the term since it was not under the control of the United Nations, it was not based on the consent of the parties, and it used force.

The first peace-keeping operation established by the United Nations was an observer mission, the United Nations Truce Supervision Organization (UNTSO), set up in Palestine in June 1948. Later, other observer missions were set up according to the same principles as UNTSO: the United Nations Military Observer Group in India and Pakistan (UNMOGIP) in 1949, the United Nations Observation Group in Lebanon (UNOGIL) in June 1958, the United Nations Yemen Observation Mission (UNYOM) in 1963, the United Nations India-Pakistan Observation Mission (UNIPOM) in 1965 and the Mission of the Representative of the Secretary-General in the Dominican Republic (DOMREP) in 1965. Of these, UNTSO and UNMOGIP are still in operation.

There have been, in all, seven peace-keeping forces. The first was the First United Nations Emergency Force (UNEF I), which was in operation in the Egypt-Israel sector from November 1956 until May 1967. The United Nations Force in the Congo was deployed in the Republic of the Congo (now Zaire) from July 1960 until June 1964. The United Nations Security Force in West Irian was in operation from its establishment in September 1962 until April 1963, while the second United Nations Emergency Force (UNEF II) functioned from October 1973 until July 1979. The other three forces, which are still in operation, are the United Nations Peace-keeping Force in Cyprus (UNFICYP), established in March 1964; the United Nations Disengagement Observer Force (UNDOF) established in the Syrian Golan Heights in May 1974; and the United Nations Interim Force in Lebanon (UNIFIL), established in March 1978.

Part Two:
The Arab-Israeli conflict

General review

No other international issue is more complex and more potentially dangerous for the maintenance of international peace and security than the Arab-Israeli conflict in the Middle East. No other issue has claimed more of the Organization's time and attention. It is also the issue out of which the concept of United Nations peace-keeping evolved. The first such operation, in the form of an observer mission, was created in the Middle East in 1948; the first of the United Nations peace-keeping forces was also created in the Middle East, in 1956.

The Arab-Israeli conflict has its origin in the problem of Palestine which arose from the conflicting claims of the Arab and Jewish communities over the future status of that territory. In 1947 Palestine was a Territory administered by the United Kingdom under a Mandate from the League of Nations, with a population of about 2 million, two thirds of whom were Arabs and one third, Jews. Both communities laid claims to the control of the entire Territory after the United Kingdom Mandate ended. Unable to find a solution acceptable to both communities, the British Government brought the matter before the General Assembly in April 1947. A Special Committee appointed by the Assembly to make recommendations for the future status of Palestine proposed in a majority plan the partition of the Territory into an Arab State and a Jewish State, with an international régime for Jerusalem. The partition plan was adopted by the Assembly in November. A United Nations Palestine Commission was to carry out its recommendations, with the assistance of the Security Council. The plan was not accepted by the Palestinian Arabs and Arab States, and the Commission's efforts were inconclusive.

As the impasse continued, violent fighting broke out in Palestine, and the Security Council on 23 April 1948 established a Truce Commission for Palestine, composed of the consular representatives of Belgium, France and the United States, to supervise a cease-fire the Council had called for. The Assembly on 14 May decided to appoint a United

Nations Mediator for Palestine who would promote a peaceful adjustment of the future situation of Palestine. On the same day, the United Kingdom relinquished its Mandate over Palestine, and the Jewish Agency proclaimed the State of Israel (which became a United Nations Member a year later, on 11 May 1949) on the territory allotted under the partition plan. The next day, the Palestinian Arabs, assisted by Arab States, opened hostilities against Israel. The war ended with a truce, called for by the Security Council, which was to be supervised by the United Nations Mediator with the assistance of military observers. The first United Nations peace-keeping operation, the United Nations Truce Supervision Organization (UNTSO), came into being as a consequence.

Since 1948, there have been six full-fledged wars directly connected with the Arab-Israeli conflict, and five United Nations peace-keeping operations have been established in the region. Of these, three are still active—the overall UNTSO operation, an observer force on the Golan Heights and a peace-keeping force in southern Lebanon. The other two operations, now discontinued, were the first and second United Nations Emergency Forces, both in the Egypt-Israel sector.

In addition to the peace-keeping operations, the United Nations has undertaken a series of peace-making efforts, which included the Palestine Commission and the United Nations Mediator (leading to General Armistice Agreements), the United Nations Conciliation Commission for Palestine and the Special Representative of the Secretary-General under the Security Council's resolution 242(1967) of 22 November 1967. In December 1973, a Peace Conference on the Middle East was convened under the auspices of the United Nations and the co-chairmanship of the United States and the USSR. There were also a number of peace initiatives by interested Governments, some of which relied on United Nations machinery to implement agreements arrived at.

Besides the specific peace-keeping and peace-making efforts of the United Nations, humanitarian assistance for refugees began with the United Nations Relief for Palestine Refugees in December 1948. The following year, the Assembly created the United Nations Relief and Works Agency for Palestine Refugees in the Near East (UNRWA) whose mandate has been continuously extended.

Chapter II

UN Truce Supervision Organization

A. Introduction

The first peace-keeping operation in the Middle East was the United Nations Truce Supervision Organization (UNTSO), which continues to operate in the Middle East. It initially came into being during the Arab-Israeli war of 1948 to supervise the truce called for in Palestine by the Security Council. In 1949 its military observers (UNMOs) remained to supervise the Armistice Agreements between Israel and its Arab neighbours which were for many years the main basis of the uneasy truce in the whole area. A unique feature of UNTSO is that its activities have been and still are spread over territory within five States, and therefore it has relations with five host countries (Egypt, Israel, Jordan, Lebanon, Syrian Arab Republic).

Following the wars of 1956, 1967 and 1973, the functions of the observers changed in the light of changing circumstances, but they remained in the area, acting as go-betweens for the hostile parties and as the means by which isolated incidents could be contained and prevented from escalating into major conflicts.

UNTSO personnel have also been available at short notice to form the nucleus of other peace-keeping operations and have remained to assist those operations. The availability of the UNMOs for almost immediate deployment after the Security Council had acted to create a new operation has been an enormous contributory factor to the success of those operations. Rapid deployment of United Nations peace-keepers has always been essential to the success of any operation, since their actual presence becomes the initial deterrent to renewed fighting.

In the Middle East, groups of UNMOs are today attached to the peace-keeping forces in the area: the United Nations Disengagement Observer Force (UNDOF) in the Golan Heights and the United Nations Interim Force in Lebanon (UNIFIL). A group remains in Sinai to maintain a United Nations presence in that peninsula. There is also a group of observers in Beirut, Lebanon.

The body of experienced and highly trained staff officers and its communications system were invaluable in setting up the first United Nations Emergency Force (UNEF I) at short notice during the time of the Suez crisis, as well as for the United Nations Operation in the Congo (now Zaire) in 1960, the observer group in Lebanon during the crisis of 1958, the United Nations Yemen observer group in 1963, UNEF II in Sinai in 1973, UNDOF the following year, and UNIFIL in 1978. They are used today in Iran and Iraq.

At the present time, the following countries provide military observers to UNTSO: Argentina, Australia, Austria, Belgium, Canada, Chile, Denmark, Finland, France, Ireland, Italy, the Netherlands, New Zealand, Norway, Sweden, the USSR and the United States. UNTSO's authorized strength in 1985 was 298 observers.

As of early 1985, the total number of fatal casualties suffered by UNTSO since its inception was 24—both observers and civilian supporting personnel. Of the observers who died, one was assassinated (with the Mediator) and nine were killed in incidents involving firing or mines.

B.   Supervision of the truce

The first observer group

In early May 1948, the Truce Commission established by the Security Council the previous month brought to the Council's attention the need for control-personnel for effective supervision of the cease-fire which the Council had called for when it created the Commission. As the situation worsened, the Commission, on 21 May, formally asked the Council to send military observers to assist it.

On 29 May, the Security Council, in calling for a four-week cessation of all acts of armed force and non-introduction of fighting personnel or war material into Palestine and Arab countries involved in the fighting, decided that the Mediator (Count Folke Bernadotte, of Sweden), in concert with the Truce Commission, should supervise the truce and be provided with a sufficient number of military observers for that purpose. Resolution 50(1948) formed the basis of what would become UNTSO.

After intensive discussions in the area, the Mediator reported a truce agreement, which went into effect on 11 June 1948.[1] Ralph J. Bunche, the then Personal Representative of the Secretary-General with the Mediator, was instrumental in putting into effect the arrangements for the group of military observers. These arrangements had to be made without previous guidelines and implemented within a period of less than two weeks between adoption of the Council's resolution and the effective truce.

The question of the nationality of the observers was resolved by the Mediator's requesting 21 observers each from the States members of the Truce Commission (Belgium, France and the United States), with a further five colonels coming from his own country (Sweden), to act as his personal representatives in supervising the truce. The Mediator appointed one of them, Lieutenant-General Count Thord Bonde, as his Chief of Staff. The United States supplied 10 auxiliary technical personnel such as aircraft pilots and radio operators. The Secretary-General made available 51 guards, recruited from the Secretariat's security force at Headquarters, to assist the military observers.

While these arrangements were being made, the beginnings of what were to become different positions on the question of authority became discernible. The Soviet Union made known its views that selection of military observers should be decided by the Security Council, and expressed the hope that Soviet observers would be appointed. This view was not supported by the Council.

Administratively, the observers remained under their respective army establishments, receiving their normal remunerations from their Governments but getting a daily subsistence allowance from the United Nations, which also met extra expenses resulting from the mission. National uniforms were worn with a United Nations armband. (The distinctive blue beret with United Nations badge was not used until November 1956.) During their assignments with the Organization, the observers were to take orders only from the United Nations authorities. The parties to the conflict were required to co-operate with the observers, to whom the Convention on the Privileges and Immunities of the United Nations applied, and ensure their safety and freedom of movement.

The first group of 36 observers arrived in Cairo between 11 and 14 June and were immediately deployed in Palestine and some of the Arab countries. The number of observers was subsequently increased to 93—31 from each of the States members of the Truce Commission. Their activities, under the general control of the Secretary-General, were directed in the field by the Chief of Staff on behalf of the Mediator. For political and practical reasons, the Mediator clearly separated the truce operation from his mediation mission, with Haifa becoming the temporary headquarters for the former and the island of Rhodes remaining the base for the latter. Close liaison was maintained between the Commission, which supervised the truce in Jerusalem, and the Mediator, who supervised the remainder of the operations area. The functions of the observers and the operating procedures were laid down by the Mediator in consultation with the Secretary-General.

Method of operation

These observers were, and remain today, unarmed. They operated then, as they still do, with the consent of the parties and were dependent on the co-operation of the parties for their effectiveness. Thus they had no power to prevent a violation of the truce or to enforce any decisions. There was no element of enforcement in their functioning, although their very presence was something of a deterrent to violations of the truce and, acting on the basis of United Nations resolutions, they exercised a degree of moral suasion. In the case of any complaint or incident where they could not achieve a settlement between the parties on the spot, their only recourse was to report the matter to their supervisors and ultimately to the Mediator, who, in turn, at his discretion, could report to the Secretary-General and, through him, to the Security Council. Complaints from local civilians or from troops of the parties concerned were dealt with by observers on the spot, those from military commanders by an area commander or the Chief of Staff, and those from Governments by the Mediator himself. In cases requiring investigation, the inquiries were carried out by observers at the scene whenever possible.

The four-week truce expired on 9 July 1948. While the provisional Government of Israel accepted the Mediator's proposal for an extension, the Arab Governments did not. As soon as the truce expired, large-scale fighting erupted again between Arab and Israeli forces. On 15 July, in response to an appeal by the Mediator, the Security Council ordered a cease-fire, with a clear threat of applying the enforcement procedures of Chapter VII of the Charter if necessary (resolution 54(1948)). The Mediator set the time for commencement of the cease-fire at 1500 GMT on 18 July. Both parties complied with the Council's cease-fire order and all fighting stopped by the appointed time.

The second group

Since the new truce was of indefinite duration and was to remain in force until a peaceful adjustment of the situation in Palestine was reached, a more elaborate system of truce supervision was required. As the observers for the first truce and their equipment had already left the area, the new operation had to be created and equipped from scratch. However, profiting from the experience gained earlier, the Mediator was able to set up a larger and more effective operation in a relatively short time.

The Mediator requested the Governments of Belgium, France and the United States each to place at his disposal 100 observers for the supervision of the truce. By 1 August 1948, 137 of those observers had arrived in the mission area. Subsequently, a total of 682 observers and auxiliary technical personnel was requested by the Mediator, of which 572 were actually provided. Major-General Aage Lundström of the Swedish Air Force was appointed Chief of Staff, and he and nine other Swedish officers formed the Mediator's personal staff. The headquarters of the operation remained in Haifa and the general principles and rules devised for the first truce continued to apply. However, the deployment of observers underwent important changes. Observers were now divided into a number of groups assigned to each Arab army and each Israeli army group. One group was assigned to Jerusalem, one to cover the coast and ports of the truce area, one to control convoys between Tel Aviv and Jerusalem and, later, an additional group was set up to cover airports in the truce area. The Chief of Staff was assisted by a Central Truce Supervision Board, presided over by him and consisting of a senior officer from each member of the Truce Commission, together with the Chief of Staff's political adviser, who was a member of the United Nations Secretariat.

On 17 September 1948, the Mediator was assassinated in Jerusalem by Jewish terrorists said to belong to the Stern Gang. Ralph Bunche took over the Mediator's duties and was appointed Acting Mediator. Increased tension led to renewed fighting in October in Jerusalem, the Negev and, to a lesser extent, the Lebanese sector. The Security Council adopted a series of decisions and resolutions to restore the cease-fire and strengthen the observation operation.

The decisions and resolutions of the Security Council between October and December 1948 were the following: on 19 October, a call for an immediate and effective cease-fire in the Negev, to be followed by negotiations through United Nations intermediaries to settle outstanding problems in the area; also on 19 October, a call to the Governments and authorities concerned to grant United Nations observers freedom of movement and access in their areas of operation, to ensure their safety and to co-operate fully with them in their conduct of investigations into incidents; on 4 November, a call to Governments concerned to withdraw their troops to the positions they had occupied on 14 October and to establish truce lines and such neutral or demilitarized zones as desirable; and on 16 November, a request to the parties to seek agreement directly or through the Acting Mediator with a view to the immediate establishment of an armistice.

Acting Mediator's efforts

With the full support of the Security Council and the General Assembly, the Acting Mediator resumed his mediating efforts, concentrating first on arranging indirect negotiations between Egypt and Israel. But his efforts were momentarily interrupted in late December, when hostilities erupted again between Egyptian and Israeli forces in southern Palestine.

Upon receipt of the Acting Mediator's report on this subject, the Security Council adopted another resolution on 29 December (resolution 66(1948)), by which it called upon the Governments concerned to order an immediate cease-fire and to facilitate the complete supervision of the truce by United Nations observers. An effective cease-fire was established by the Acting Mediator soon afterwards.

C. General Armistice Agreements

Four General Armistice Agreements

The Acting Mediator's efforts led to the conclusion of four General Armistice Agreements between Israel and the four neighbouring Arab States—Egypt, Jordan, Lebanon and Syria—in early 1949. On 11 August 1949, the Security Council assigned new functions to UNTSO in line with these Agreements (resolution 73(1949)). The role of Mediator was ended. While the resolution made no reference to the Truce Commission, this body had become inactive since the armistice and had in fact been abolished, although the Council took no formal decision to that effect.

With the termination of the role of the Mediator, UNTSO became an autonomous operation, officially a subsidiary organ of the Council, with the Chief of Staff assuming command of the operation. The functioning was radically altered, since UNTSO's main responsibility now was to assist the parties in supervising the application and observance of the General Armistice Agreements. In two cases, the Israel-Egypt and Israel-Syria sectors, demilitarized zones were established and UNTSO became responsible for ensuring that the parties excluded their armed forces from these zones.

In addition to its functions relating to supervision of the Armistice Agreements, UNTSO had responsibility for observing and maintaining the cease-fire ordered by the Security Council in 1948, which had no time-limit.

Untso's main responsibilities related to the work of the Mixed Armistice Commissions (macs) set up by the Armistice Agreements. The Egypt-Israel General Armistice Agreement provided for a mac of seven members, three from each side and the Chief of Staff (or a senior officer designated by him) as Chairman. The Commission was empowered to employ observers which, if they were to be United Nations military observers, would remain under untso command. The other General Armistice Agreements were similar, except that the respective macs were composed of five members, two from each party and the Chairman.

Structural changes

After the departure of the Mediator, the Chief of Staff assumed command of the operation. He reported to the Secretary-General and was responsible to him. Although the title of Chief of Staff was no longer fully suitable, it was maintained since it was specifically mentioned in the Armistice Agreements and also in Security Council resolution 73(1949). Until 1951, the Chief of Staff had, administratively, the same status as the observers. This was changed in that year when he was given an appointment as a senior official of the United Nations Secretariat with the grade of Principal Director (later Assistant Secretary-General). This arrangement, which greatly strengthened the control of the Secretary-General over untso, was applied to the heads of subsequent peace-keeping operations.

Demilitarized zones

In two cases, armistice arrangements included the establishment of demilitarized zones. One of these zones was established in the El Auja area on the Israeli side of the Armistice Demarcation Line between Egypt and Israel. The Egypt-Israel General Armistice Agreement provided that both Egyptian and Israeli armed forces should be totally excluded from the demilitarized zone and that the Chairman of the Egypt-Israel Mixed Armistice Commission and the observers attached to the Commission should be responsible for ensuring the full implementation of this provision. The Israel-Syria Armistice Agreement contained similar provisions concerning the demilitarized zone established near Lake Tiberias. In this case, the Chairman of the Israel-Syria Mixed Armistice Commission was also empowered to authorize the return of civilians to villages and settlements in the demilitarized zone and the employment of limited numbers of locally recruited civilian police in the zone for internal security purposes.

Mixed Armistice Commissions

The main task of the Commissions was the investigation and examination of the claims or complaints presented by the parties relating to the application and observance of the Armistice Agreements. These claims or complaints concerned, mainly, firing across the Armistice Demarcation Line, crossing of the Line by persons or animals, overflights on the wrong side of the Line, the presence of troops or equipment in demilitarized zones or defensive areas and illegal cultivation contrary to agreements. Occasionally, the Commissions also gave attention to special problems of common interest to the parties.

The observers assigned to each Commission carried out the investigations of complaints submitted to the Commission. They assisted in the handing over of people who had crossed the Armistice Demarcation Line, as well as the handing over of animals and property, and they witnessed the work done by the parties under anti-malaria, anti-rabies and anti-locust agreements. They also participated in rescue and search missions when such missions were undertaken by UNTSO at the request of one of the parties. The Chief of Staff was given special responsibilities for the protection of Mount Scopus, in Jerusalem.

Cease-fire supervision

In addition to its functions relating to the supervision of the General Armistice Agreements, UNTSO had the responsibility of observing and maintaining the cease-fire, since the unconditional cease-fire ordered by the Security Council in its resolution 54(1948) continued to be in force. When an outbreak of violence threatened, the Chief of Staff of UNTSO would, on his own initiative, seek to prevent it by appealing to the parties for restraint, and when a firing incident actually occurred, he would arrange for an immediate cease-fire. In serious cases, the Chief of Staff could bring the matter to the attention of the Security Council through the Secretary-General.

Government House, UNTSO headquarters

On 25 May 1949, the headquarters of UNTSO was transferred from Haifa to Government House in Jerusalem. Government House had been the seat of the British Mandatory Administration during the Mandate period. On the departure of the British authorities from Palestine, and at their request, the International Committee of the Red Cross took over Government House in trust for any successor administration and, during the early fighting in Jerusalem, it established a neutral zone in the area where the building and its grounds were located. On 7 October 1948, following renewed fighting, during which the status of the neutral zone was violated by both Israeli and Jordanian forces, the International Committee transferred Government House and the surrounding grounds to United Nations protection. Both States parties were informed of these arrangements and did not raise any objections.

The cease-fire agreement of 30 November 1948 for the Jerusalem area left intact Government House and the security zone. The General Armistice Agreement concluded between Israel and Jordan on 3 April 1949 provided that in the Jerusalem sector the Armistice Demarcation Lines should correspond to the lines defined in the cease-fire agreement of 30 November 1948, and therefore the status of the Government House area and the neutral zone remained unaltered. Shortly after the conclusion of the Armistice Agreement, Government House became the headquarters of the United Nations Truce Supervision Organization.

On 5 June 1967, after fighting broke out in Jerusalem, Israeli forces occupied Government House and escorted UNTSO staff out of its premises. Following this event, the Secretary-General at United Nations Headquarters and the Chief of Staff of UNTSO in Jerusalem repeatedly pressed the Israeli authorities for the return of Government House to UNTSO. Following lengthy negotiations, the Israeli Government agreed on 22 August 1967 to return Government House and most of its surrounding grounds.[2] The headquarters of UNTSO was immediately re-established at Government House and has remained there until today.

Commission headquarters

The reorganization of UNTSO after August 1949 was geared to the activities of the four Mixed Armistice Commissions. Each Commission had a headquarters and such ancillary installations as it decided to establish. The headquarters of the Israel-Jordan Mixed Armistice Commission was set up in the neutral zone in Jerusalem. The Israel-Lebanon Mixed Armistice Commission (ILMAC) was headquartered in Beirut with a substation located at Naqoura near the Armistice Demarcation Line, the Israel-Syria Mixed Armistice Commission (ISMAC) was established in Damascus with a control centre at Tiberias on the Israeli side of the Armistice Demarcation Line. Finally, the Egypt-Israel

Mixed Armistice Commission (EIMAC) was established in the demilitarized zone of El Auja and was later transferred to Gaza.

Implementation of the Armistice Agreements

The 1949 General Armistice Agreements were meant to be temporary arrangements to be followed by the conclusion of peace treaties. But that was not to be. Two major obstacles appeared soon after the signing of the Armistice Agreements. Israel, for security reasons, refused to let the many Palestinian Arab refugees who had fled their homes during the hostilities return to the areas it controlled, and the Arabs continued to refuse to recognize the existence of Israel and to enter into peace negotiations with it. Thus, the basic issues remained unresolved.

Because of constant disagreement between the parties concerned, the Chief of Staff and the UNTSO observers assigned to the Commissions came to play an increasingly important role. In each Commission, sensitive issues were often deadlocked and resolutions had to be decided by the casting vote of the Chairman. Most investigations into incidents and violations of the Armistice Agreements were carried out by UNTSO observers alone, since the military representatives of the parties could not work with each other. To smooth over difficulties and avert incidents, UNTSO personnel often had to exercise good offices or act as mediators. But, however active and important their functions were, the ultimate responsibility for the observance and application of the provisions of the Armistice Agreements rested with the parties themselves, and without their co-operation and goodwill the Agreements steadily eroded.

Egypt-Israel Mixed Armistice Commission

The difficulties encountered in the implementation of the General Armistice Agreements and the relationships between the parties varied from one Mixed Armistice Commission to another. The most difficult Commission was the Egypt-Israel Mixed Armistice Commission. From the start, Egypt strongly protested against Israel's expulsion of thousands of Palestinians to the Gaza Strip. The matter was brought before the Security Council, which, in its resolution 89(1950) of 17 November 1950, requested EIMAC to give urgent attention to the Egyptian complaint and reminded both Egypt and Israel, as Member States of the United Nations, of their obligations under the Charter to settle their outstanding differences. But despite the Council's decision, the problem remained unresolved. In 1951 Egypt decided to impose restrictions on the passage of international commercial shipping and goods destined for Israel through the Suez Canal. Despite the request contained in Security Council resolution 95(1951) of 1 September 1951, Egypt maintained these restrictions, and indeed extended them to the Strait of Tiran in 1953. By early 1955, Palestinian *fedayeen* undertook, with increasing frequency, commando raids into Israeli territory which were followed by harsh retaliation from Israel. In reaction to the establishment of Egyptian military positions in the El Quseima–Abu Aweigila area, near the border, the Israeli forces occupied the demilitarized zone of El Auja on 21 September 1956 and, shortly thereafter, the Commission became paralysed as Israel prevented the Egyptian delegates to the Commission from entering the area. Following the outbreak of the October 1956 war, Israel denounced the Armistice Agreement with Egypt.

Israel-Syria Mixed Armistice Commission

Great difficulties were also experienced by the Israel-Syria Mixed Armistice Commission. Two of the most frequent disputes concerned the cultivation of disputed lands by Israeli farmers in the demilitarized zone and the activities of Israeli patrols and fishermen on the eastern side of Lake Tiberias next to the Armistice Demarcation Line. These Israeli activities were considered to be illegal by the Syrians and often led to intense exchanges of fire between Israeli and Syrian forces. In addition, there was the unending cycle of violence marked by Palestinian commando raids and Israeli reprisals in the border areas.

In order to ease the situation, the Chief of Staff of UNTSO decided, with the agreement of the parties, to establish in the 1950s a number of observation posts along the Armistice Demarcation Line. These served to reduce tension to some extent in the sensitive areas, but incidents nevertheless continued to occur frequently. On 19 January 1956, after a particularly violent Israeli attack against Syrian forces, the Security Council adopted resolution 111(1956), by which it condemned the attack and called once again on the parties to implement the General Armistice Agreement and to respect the Armistice Demarcation Line and the demilitarized zone. But despite the call of the Security Council, the situation was not improved. As of 14 October 1966, there were 35,485 Israeli complaints and 30,600 Syrian complaints pending before the Commission. The Commission was completely paralysed by the large number of complaints and constant disputes between the parties. It held its last regular meeting in 1951 and its last emergency meeting in February 1960. From 1966 onwards, relations between Israel and Syria deteriorated sharply. At the beginning of 1967, the Secretary-

General succeeded in arranging a series of "extraordinary emergency meetings" of the Commission in order to discuss the cultivation problem in the demilitarized zone which at the time had led to many incidents. But these meetings ended in failure, and on 7 April a serious incident occurred during which Israeli aircraft attacked Damascus itself and shot down six Syrian aircraft. This incident created a new situation and marked the beginning of a new escalation which eventually led to the June 1967 war.

Israel-Jordan Mixed Armistice Commission

The Israel-Jordan Armistice Agreement was subject to different pressures. The West Bank and the Old City of Jerusalem formed part of the Holy Land and were of special importance. They contained large numbers of Palestinian Arabs, many of whom were uprooted and displaced from the area held by Israel. A narrow strip of neutral zone supervised by the United Nations separated the Israeli and Jordanian sectors of the Holy City. The Armistice Agreement created two enclaves: an Israeli enclave on Mount Scopus in Jerusalem and a Jordanian enclave in Latrun on the road from Jerusalem to Tel Aviv. The West Bank was a staging area for the activities of Palestinian *fedayeen*. These factors led to many disputes and problems, which often resulted in exchanges of fire across the Line between the two opposing armies. Despite the difficulties, the Commission continued to meet in emergency sessions until June 1967, and sub-committee meetings were held regularly, on a weekly basis, in an effort to resolve outstanding problems.

Israel-Lebanon Mixed Armistice Commission

Unlike the other Commissions, that for Israel-Lebanon functioned smoothly and often effectively from 1949 until 1967. The main difficulties arose in connection with the activities of Palestinian commandos. However, the Lebanese authorities acted firmly to stop or contain those activities and there were few incidents along the Armistice Demarcation Line. Problems of common concern were discussed and resolved in regular meetings of the Commission, which functioned until the June 1967 war, when Israel denounced the Armistice Agreement with Lebanon as it did the others, although no hostilities took place along the Israel-Lebanon Armistice Demarcation Line.

Observer strength

As for the personnel involved, in 1948 there were 572 observers and auxiliary technical personnel, but with the entry into force of the

General Armistice Agreements, UNTSO's observer strength was reduced to between 30 and 140 according to prevailing circumstances. There were 128 observers at the outbreak of the June 1967 war.

Maintenance of armistice supervision machinery

Following its denunciation of the Armistice Agreement with Egypt in November 1956, the Israeli Government refused to take part in EIMAC. The Secretary-General did not accept this unilateral denunciation as valid, and consequently UNTSO continued to maintain the machinery of the Mixed Armistice Commission. The Commission's headquarters was transferred from El Auja to the town of Gaza in Egyptian-controlled territory. The Commission continued to examine complaints submitted by Egypt, and UNTSO observers continued to conduct patrols on the Egyptian side of the Armistice Demarcation Line. But without Israel's co-operation, these activities were largely symbolic and the real peace-keeping functions were carried out by the United Nations Emergency Force (UNEF I), which was established in the wake of the war and with which UNTSO co-operated closely (see following chapter).

Eleven years later, when UNEF I was withdrawn at the request of the Egyptian Government, the Secretary General pointed out in his report of 19 May 1967 to the Security Council[3] that EIMAC remained in existence and could, as it had done prior to the establishment of UNEF, provide a limited form of United Nations presence in the area. With this in view, the number of observers assigned to the Commission was brought up from 6 to 20 towards the end of May and their patrol activities along the Armistice Demarcation Line were markedly increased. The Government of Israel, while maintaining its position on the Armistice Agreement, raised no objection to this action, and the additional observers sent from Jerusalem to Gaza passed through the Israeli check-point on the coastal road without difficulty. But this emergency measure was not enough and, soon after the withdrawal of UNEF, tension in the area reached the crisis level and war erupted again between Israel and Arab States.

After the June 1967 war, Israel denounced the other three Armistice Agreements and the Secretary-General again refused to recognize the validity of this unilateral action. In the introduction to his annual report to the twenty-second (1967) session of the General Assembly,[4] which was submitted shortly after that war, the Secretary-General explained his position in the following terms:

". . . there has been no indication either in the General Assembly or in the Security Council that the validity and applicability of the

Armistice Agreements have been changed as a result of the recent hostilities or of the war of 1956; each Agreement, in fact, contains a provision that it will remain in force 'until a peaceful settlement between the parties is achieved'. Nor has the Security Council or the General Assembly taken any steps to change the pertinent resolutions of either organ relating to the Armistice Agreements or to the earlier cease-fire demands. The Agreements provide that by mutual consent the signatories can revise or suspend them. There is no provision in them for unilateral termination of their application. This has been the United Nations position all along and will continue to be the position until a competent organ decides otherwise.''

The machinery for the supervision of the four Armistice Agreements was symbolically maintained. The headquarters of the Israel-Lebanon Commission and the Israel-Syria Commission remained in Beirut and Damascus, respectively, with reduced staffs. That of the Israel-Jordan Commission, which was located in Jerusalem, could no longer operate there, but UNTSO established a liaison office in Amman and the Chief of that office served nominally as Chairman of the Commission. The headquarters of EIMAC in Gaza was closed down in July 1967 and the Officer-in-Charge of the Ismailia Control Centre, which had just been established for the observation of the cease-fire in the Suez Canal sector, was assigned, symbolically, the additional function of Chairman of the Commission. This arrangement continued until the conclusion of a peace treaty between Egypt and Israel in March 1979.

D. Cease-fire observation operations, 1967

Background

UNTSO played a crucial role in helping to bring the June 1967 war to an end.

The war started in the early morning of 5 June between Israeli and Egyptian forces and quickly spread to the Jordanian and Syrian fronts. On 6 June, the Security Council adopted resolution 233(1967), calling upon the Governments concerned to take forthwith, as a first step, all measures for an immediate cease-fire. As hostilities continued, the Council met again on 7 June and, by resolution 234(1967), demanded that the Governments concerned should discontinue all military activities at 2000 hours GMT on the same day. Fighting stopped on the Egyptian and Jordanian fronts on 8 June, but it went on unabated between the Israeli and Syrian forces on the Golan Heights. On 9 June, the Security Council adopted resolution 235(1967), by which it confirmed its previous resolutions for an immediate cease-fire, demanded that hostilities should cease forthwith and requested the Secretary-General "to make immediate contacts with the Governments of Israel and Syria to arrange immediate compliance with the above-mentioned resolutions, and to report to the Security Council not later than two hours from now".

On instructions from the Secretary-General, the Chief of Staff of UNTSO, Lieutenant-General Odd Bull of Norway, contacted the Israeli and Syrian authorities on 10 June and proposed to them, as a practical arrangement for implementing the cease-fire demanded by the Security Council, that both sides cease all firing and movement forward at 1630 hours GMT on the same day. He also proposed that the observers, accompanied by liaison officers of each side, be deployed along the front lines as soon as possible in order to observe the implementation of the cease-fire. Those proposals were accepted by both sides and the UNMOs were deployed accordingly in the combat area in the early morning of 11 June.

Israel-Syria sector

On the following days, UNTSO observers demarcated the cease-fire lines on each side. The two cease-fire lines, which included a buffer zone approximately one to three miles wide, were agreed to by the two sides in indirect negotiations conducted by the observers. In signing the map demarcating the cease-fire lines, the Syrian representative stressed that the lines were a purely practical arrangement for the specific purpose of facilitating the observation of the cease-fire by the United Nations and should not affect or prejudice the claims and positions of the Syrian Government.

With the demarcation of the cease-fire lines, UNTSO set up a number of observation posts on each side of the buffer zone. There were, by the end of 1967, seven observation posts on the Israeli side and nine on the Syrian side. Those on the Syrian side were under the control of the headquarters of ISMAC in Damascus and those on the Israeli side reported to the Control Centre at Tiberias. General direction was assumed by the Chief of Staff of UNTSO. The observers, all of whom were drawn from the existing establishment of UNTSO, performed their duties by manning the observation posts and by conducting patrols along the lines as necessary. The two parties were notified by the Chief of Staff of UNTSO that all firings, movements forward of the cease-fire line on each side and overflights would be considered as breaches of the cease-fire.

Arrangements made by the Chief of Staff were endorsed by the

Security Council, which, in resolution 236(1967) of 11 June 1967: affirmed that its demand for a cease-fire and discontinuance of all military activities included a prohibition of any forward military movements subsequent to the cease-fire; called for the prompt return to the cease-fire positions of any troops which might have moved forward subsequent to 1630 hours GMT on 10 June 1967; and called for "full cooperation with the Chief of Staff of the United Nations Truce Supervision Organization and the observers in implementing the cease-fire, including freedom of movement and adequate communications facilities".

After the adoption of the resolution, the observers submitted regularly to the Security Council, through the Secretary-General, reports on the cease-fire situation in the Israel-Syria sector. These arrangements continued until the October 1973 war.

Suez Canal area

When the cease-fire went into effect in the Egypt-Israel sector on 8 June 1967, no observation machinery was set up in that area. At that time, the Israeli forces had reached the eastern bank of the Suez Canal, except for a small area around Port Fuad on the northern tip of the Canal. The situation in the Suez Canal sector was generally quiet during the last part of June but, from early July on, tension began to rise. On 8 July, heavy fighting broke out between Egyptian and Israeli forces at various locations along the Canal, with each side accusing the other of violations of the cease-fire. When the Security Council met on that day, the Secretary-General expressed regret that he was unable to provide the Council with information about the new outbreak of fighting since no United Nations observers were stationed in the area. In this connection, he indicated that as early as 4 July he had decided to take the initiative towards a possible alleviation of this situation and had undertaken exploratory talks with the representatives of Egypt and Israel about the stationing of United Nations military observers in the Canal sector.

On 9 July, the Security Council approved a consensus statement in accordance with which the Secretary-General requested the Chief of Staff of UNTSO to work out with the Governments of Egypt* and Is-

---

*Documents of these years refer to Egypt as the United Arab Republic. Egypt and Syria, separate Members of the United Nations since 1945, joined together in February 1958 to form the United Arab Republic. In September 1961, the Syrian Arab Republic resumed its status as an independent State and its separate membership in the United Nations. Egypt retained the title of the United Arab Republic, reverting to the name of Egypt, or Arab Republic of Egypt, in 1971. For convenience, the title of Egypt is used in this book wherever possible.

rael, as speedily as possible, the necessary arrangements to station observers in the Suez Canal sector. Two days later, having received the agreement of both parties, the Secretary-General instructed the Chief of Staff to work out with the local authorities of both sides a plan for the actual stationing of military observers.

The Chief of Staff proceeded in much the same way as for the observation operation on the Golan Heights. The problem of demarcation of the cease-fire lines was much simpler in this case since, except for the Port Fuad area, the Suez Canal itself constituted a natural buffer zone. The observers made an attempt to demarcate a line of separation in the Port Fuad area, but no agreement could be reached. This question, therefore, remained a subject of controversy, but because of the marshy terrain in the area there were few incidents.

The observation operation began on 17 July when seven observation posts were established along the Canal. This number was eventually increased to 15: eight on the eastern side of the Canal under the Control Centre at Qantara and seven on the western side under the Control Centre at Ismailia. At the beginning, military observers drawn from the existing UNTSO establishment were assigned to the Suez Canal. However, the nationalities of the observers gave rise to some difficulty, as certain countries were not acceptable to Israel, and others not acceptable to Egypt. Finally, after lengthy discussions, agreements were reached on six countries from which observers might be drawn: Austria, Burma, Chile, Finland, France and Sweden. The original observers were then replaced by 90 new observers from those six countries.

The main task of the observers was to observe and report on breaches of the cease-fire, including firings, overflights and movements forward which, in this case, meant movement of boats and craft in the Canal. An understanding was reached on 27 July whereby the two parties agreed to stop all military activities in the Suez Canal, including the movement in or into the Canal of boats or craft for one month, it being understood that the Canal authorities would continue to revictual and secure the safety of the 15 ships stranded in the Canal. This agreement was later extended indefinitely.[5]

With these arrangements, the situation in the Suez Canal sector became stabilized and, although there were occasional exchanges of fire, the cease-fire generally held. This lull lasted until early 1969, when fighting suddenly broke out again. From that time until August 1970, there were extremely intense exchanges of artillery fire across the Canal between the Egyptian and Israeli positions every day, with occasional air strikes by one side or the other. This period of fighting, which lasted nearly 20 months, was known as the "war of attrition". It was full-fledged warfare except that the positions of the opposing armies did not move forward. During the entire period of hostilities, the Secretary-General reported in detail to the Security Council on all the developments monitored by the observers, and appealed on several occasions for an end to the hostilities, but his efforts were inconclusive. Egypt stated that it refused to continue to observe the cease-fire, which it regarded as in effect perpetuating the Israeli occupation of its sovereign territory, while Israel asserted that it would observe the cease-fire only if the other side were willing to do so. Neither side brought the matter before the Security Council and, largely because of the opposing positions taken by two of the permanent members, the Council did not attempt to take up this problem.

The fighting came to an end on 7 August 1970 under a proposal initiated by the United States Government. Under the proposal, Egypt, Israel and Jordan agreed to designate representatives to discussions to be held under the auspices of the Special Representative of the Secretary-General for the Middle East, Ambassador Gunnar V. Jarring of Sweden.[6] In order to facilitate the Ambassador's task of promoting agreement in accordance with Security Council resolution 242 (1967) of 22 November 1967 (containing general principles for a Middle East settlement), they undertook strictly to observe the cease-fire resolutions of the Security Council as from 7 August. On that day, fighting stopped in the Suez Canal sector and the situation there remained quiet until 6 October 1973, when hostilities once again broke out between Egyptian and Israeli forces.

Israel-Jordan sector

No cease-fire observation was established in the Israel-Jordan sector. At the end of the June 1967 war, Israeli forces had occupied the entire West Bank up to the Jordan River. The situation in that sector was generally quiet until the end of 1967 but there was increasing tension in 1968 and 1969, mainly because of the activities of Palestinian commandos operating from the east side of the Jordan Valley and retaliatory action by the Israeli forces. The Secretary-General sounded out the Israeli and Jordanian authorities about the possibility of stationing United Nations observers in the Jordan Valley but could not secure an agreement. On several occasions, the Security Council met to consider serious incidents in the Israel-Jordan sector, and the Secretary-General drew attention to the fact that in the absence of agreements from the parties or of a decision by the Security Council, it was not possible to establish a machinery for the observation of the cease-fire in the sector.

The situation in the Israel-Jordan sector, however, became much quieter after September 1970, when the bulk of the Palestinian armed elements moved to Lebanon.

Israel-Lebanon sector

During the June 1967 war, no fighting took place between Israel and Lebanon, and the Armistice Demarcation Line between the two countries remained intact. Nevertheless, the Israeli Government denounced the Armistice Agreement with Lebanon after the war, as it did the other Armistice Agreements, on the grounds that during the hostilities Lebanese authorities had claimed that they were at war with Israel. The Lebanese Government, however, denied this and insisted on the continued validity of the Agreement. Since the Secretary-General held the view that the Armistice Agreement could not be denounced unilaterally, UNTSO continued to maintain the headquarters of ILMAC at Beirut, as well as a substation at Naqoura in southern Lebanon. But the Commission had few activities and the number of observers assigned to it was considerably reduced.

Following the 1967 war, the Palestinian population in Lebanon markedly increased with the influx of a sizeable number of displaced persons from the occupied West Bank and Gaza, and the Palestine Liberation Army stepped up its training activities in the country, especially in the south. As a result, anti-Israeli raids by Palestinian commandos from Lebanon and reprisals by Israeli forces became more frequent. The situation deteriorated further following the departure of Palestinian armed elements in 1970 from Jordan to Lebanon.

In early 1972, tension heightened in the Israel-Lebanon sector as a result of increasing activities by Palestinian commandos based in southern Lebanon and severe reprisal attacks by Israeli forces. On 29 March, the Permanent Representative of Lebanon to the United Nations submitted the following request to the Security Council:

> "The Lebanese Government, because of repeated Israeli aggression against Lebanon and because the work of the Lebanon-Israel Mixed Armistice Commission has been paralysed since 1967, wishes the Security Council to take necessary action to strengthen the United Nations machinery in the Lebanese-Israeli sector by increasing the number of observers, on the basis of the Armistice Agreement of 1949."[7]

On 30 March, the members of the Security Council decided that the request of the Lebanese Government should be met, and the

Secretary-General was asked by the Council to make the necessary arrangements to this effect. In a memorandum dated 4 April,[8] the Secretary-General informed the Council that, following consultations with the Lebanese authorities, the Chief of Staff of UNTSO had recommended the establishment of three observation posts on the Lebanese side of the Armistice Demarcation Line, together with an increase in the number of observers assigned to the Armistice Commission from the existing seven to 21. On 19 April 1972, the members of the Security Council, in informal consultations, agreed with the proposed plans.

The cease-fire observation operation in the Israel-Lebanon sector commenced on 24 April 1972 with the establishment of the three proposed observation posts, all on Lebanese territory. Two additional observation posts were later set up and the total observer strength was increased to 34. Those observers, who were all drawn from the existing establishment of UNTSO, manned the five observation posts and conducted patrols along the Armistice Demarcation Line as necessary. Their responsibility was to observe and report on violations of the Demarcation Line.

Unlike the previous cease-fire observer operations, the one in Lebanon was established without the agreement of Israel. However, Israel did not seek to obstruct the operation, and the additional observers and their equipment which were transferred from Jerusalem to southern Lebanon passed through the Israeli border check-point without hindrance.

From establishment in April 1972 until the Israeli invasion of Lebanon in March 1978, the observers assigned to the Israel-Lebanon sector reported regularly to the Security Council, through the Secretary-General, on the situation along the Armistice Demarcation Line. These reports dealt mainly with violations of the Line by the Israeli forces, since no such violations were committed by the Lebanese forces. The Israeli violations included firings across the Line, overflights and the establishment of some six positions on the Lebanese side of the Line.

Civil war situation, Lebanon

Severe difficulties were experienced by the UNTSO operation following the outbreak of civil war in Lebanon in 1975. Since United Nations observers are never armed, their protection must be ensured by the host Government. When the five observation posts were set up along the Demarcation Line in 1972, the Lebanese army established a check-post next to each of them. At the beginning of the civil war, the Lebanese army disintegrated and the United Nations observers manning the posts were left on their own in an increasingly danger-ous situation. The Secretary-General had three choices at the time: suspend the operation, arm the observers for their protection, or ask them to continue to operate as before in spite of the changed condi-tions. After careful consideration, the last-mentioned solution was adopted, after consulting the contributing countries and with their agreement. On a number of occasions, observers' vehicles were hijacked and their observation posts forced into by one faction or another. But there were few serious incidents and, on the whole, the fighting factions respected the status of the UNMOS.

Another problem facing the operation after the outbreak of the 1975 civil war concerned the reporting procedure. Fighting involving various Lebanese armed groups as well as Palestinian forces occurred sporadically in the areas where the United Nations observation posts were located. However, it was decided that the reports submitted by the Secretary-General to the Security Council during that period should continue to be limited to developments along the Armistice Demarca-tion Line. In this connection, a footnote in each report explained that no reference was made to fighting inside Lebanon since, in accordance with the consensus reached by the members of the Security Council on 19 April 1972, the observers were concerned only with the cease-fire between Israel and Lebanon called for by the Council.

E. UNTSO assistance to other operations

Assistance to UNEF II

The cease-fire observation operation in the Suez Canal sector was terminated shortly after the outbreak of the October 1973 war at the request of the Egyptian Government. On 6 October, in a surprise attack, the Egyptian force crossed the Canal and soon advanced be-yond the UNTSO observation posts on the eastern bank of the Canal, while, in a co-ordinated move, Syrian troops attacked simultaneously the Israeli positions on the Golan Heights. The first days of the war were marked by heavy air and ground activity, which was fully report-ed to the Security Council by the Secretary-General on the basis of information received from the observers. In the course of the hostili-ties, two United Nations observers were killed.

On 8 October, the Egyptian Permanent Representative informed the Secretary-General that, since the United Nations observers were now behind the Egyptian lines, which put them in physical danger and made their presence unnecessary, the Government of Egypt requested the Secretary-General to take measures for their transfer to

Cairo for their security.[9] The Secretary-General immediately brought this request to the attention of the Security Council, which agreed that it should be acceded to.[10] By 9 October, all the United Nations observation posts on both sides of the Canal were closed and the observers were withdrawn to the Cairo area.

Following the closure of the observation posts, the United Nations no longer had direct information on the hostilities between Egypt and Israel which were raging in the western part of the Sinai.

The situation is considered in greater detail in the chapter below regarding UNEF II. As far as UNTSO is concerned, in accordance with Security Council resolution 340(1973) of 25 October 1973, the number of UNTSO observers in the Egypt-Israel sector was increased and they were given the task of assisting and co-operating with the second United Nations Emergency Force in the fulfilment of the Force's mandate. During the initial phase, the observers manned certain check-points and observation posts in the area controlled by UNEF II. They also assisted in exchanges of prisoners of war and undertook searches for bodies of soldiers killed during the hostilities. In addition, some observers were assigned as staff officers at UNEF II headquarters. After the conclusion of the disengagement agreement of January 1974, they conducted patrols in the buffer zone established in the Sinai in accordance with that agreement and carried out inspections of the areas of limitation of forces and armament on both sides of the buffer zone. While the observers remained administratively attached to UNTSO, they were placed under the operational control of the Commander of UNEF II.

At the end of October 1973, additional observers (three from Sweden and 10 from Finland), were provided at the request of the Secretary-General to strengthen the observer group in the Egypt-Israel sector. Thus, the total strength of UNTSO was increased to 225 observers, from 16 countries. In November 1973, the Governments of the United States and of the Soviet Union, in a joint approach to the Secretary-General, offered to make available observers from their countries for service with UNTSO. The Soviet Union would provide 36 observers and the United States 28—who, with the eight Americans already assigned to the mission, would bring the number of United States observers also to 36. The Secretary-General accepted these offers with the informal concurrence of the Security Council.

Assistance to UNDOF

During the October 1973 war, the central part of the buffer zone established by UNTSO on the Golan Heights was the scene of fierce fighting. In the first days of the war, Syrian forces attacked and over-ran several Israeli positions along the cease-fire lines. However, by 11 October, the Israeli troops had counter-attacked and in turn crossed over to the eastern side of the buffer zone around the Quneitra–Damascus road. As the battle see-sawed, some of the United Nations observation posts had to be evacuated, but others continued to operate.

When the cease-fire called for by the Security Council took effect on 25 October 1973, Israeli forces had occupied a pocket around the village of Saassa on the eastern side of the buffer zone, some 40 kilometres west of Damascus. The United Nations observers set up temporary observation posts around that pocket and, with these changes, the cease-fire observation operation was resumed.

UNTSO's observation in the Israel-Syria sector was discontinued on 31 May 1974 when the United Nations Disengagement Observer Force was established (see chapter V below), and the United Nations ob-servers of the Israel-Syria sector were incorporated into UNDOF and formed an integral part of that Force. The tasks they were assigned included the manning of observation posts and check-points in the UNDOF buffer zone, and patrolling and inspection of the areas of limi-tation of forces and armament. Selected observers were appointed to staff posts at UNDOF headquarters in Damascus. In addition, the ob-servers assigned to ISMAC in Damascus were asked to assist UNDOF in non-operational matters as occasion required. These arrangements have continued to this day.

Assistance to UNIFIL

Following the invasion of Lebanon by Israeli forces, the Security Council decided on 19 March 1978 to set up the United Nations In-terim Force in Lebanon (UNIFIL) (see chapter VI below). As in the Sinai and on the Golan Heights, the cease-fire observation operation in the Israel-Lebanon sector was discontinued with the establishment of the new peace-keeping force, but the observers of the sector remained in the area and were given the task of assisting UNIFIL in the performance of its mandate. Those observers, who were constituted as the Observ-er Group Lebanon, were placed under the operational control of the Commander of UNIFIL. They continued to man the five observation posts along the Armistice Demarcation Line. In addition, they conduct-ed patrols and performed liaison duties with the parties concerned in and around the UNIFIL area of operation. In this connection, observer teams were set up at Tyre, Château de Beaufort and Marjayoun, and also at Metulla in Israel. The headquarters of ILMAC in Beirut func-tioned as a liaison office for UNIFIL. In the principles governing the functioning of UNIFIL, which were approved by the Security Council on 19 March 1978, it was stipulated that ". . . The termination of the mandate of UNIFIL by the Security Council will not affect the continued functioning of the Israel-Lebanon Mixed Armistice Commission, as set out in the appropriate Security Council decision".[11]

Special missions in the Middle East

Observer Group in the Sinai. When UNEF II ended, the Secretary-General, after consultations held by the Security Council, issued a statement on 24 July 1979 in which he indicated that in view of the fact that the withdrawal of UNEF was without prejudice to the continued presence of the UNTSO observers in the area, he intended to make, in accordance with existing decisions of the Security Council, the necessary arrangements to ensure the further functioning of UNTSO.[12]

In accordance with the above statement and with the agreement of the Egyptian Government, five observation posts were established in the Sinai and manned by UNTSO observers, as was also the liaison office in Cairo. This arrangement has continued to this day.

Observer Group in Beirut. The headquarters of ILMAC in Beirut has been maintained and, since 1978, has functioned also as a liaison office for UNIFIL. Ten observers were assigned to the Commission in Beirut in early 1982. When, in the wake of the Israeli invasion of Lebanon that year, Beirut was subjected to intense air bombings, the headquarters of ILMAC was badly damaged and the Chairman of the Commission established temporary offices at Yarze, a suburb of Beirut where the headquarters of the Lebanese National Army was located.

At the beginning of August 1982, after incursions of Israeli forces into West Beirut, a new observation operation was set up in the area. Although that operation was relatively modest in size and its functions were limited, it encountered unusual difficulties because of the opposition of the Israeli authorities in the initial stage.

On 1 August, the Security Council had adopted resolution 516 (1982) by which, after taking note of the latest massive violations of the cease-fire in the Beirut area, it confirmed its previous demands for an immediate cease-fire and authorized the Secretary-General "to deploy immediately, on the request of the Government of Lebanon, United Nations observers to monitor the situation in and around Beirut".

The Secretary-General immediately instructed the Chief of Staff of UNTSO to make the necessary arrangements to this effect in consultation with the parties concerned. The Lebanese authorities, as well as the Chairman of the Palestine Liberation Organization, promised to co-operate fully with the observers in accordance with the Security Council's resolution. The Israeli authorities informed the Chief of Staff that this was an important matter which had to be decided by the Israeli Cabinet itself.

On 3 August,[13] upon learning that the Israeli Cabinet would take up this matter only on 5 August, the Secretary-General decided, as a purely temporary and practical arrangement, to instruct the Chief of Staff to take immediate steps to set up observation machinery in the Beirut area in territory controlled by the Lebanese Government. In accordance with these instructions, the 10 observers already in Beirut were constituted into the Observer Group Beirut (OGB) and began to carry out observation duties in the area. On 4 August, the Security Council, in resolution 517(1982), expressed its appreciation for the steps taken by the Secretary-General and authorized him, as an immediate step, to increase the number of observers in and around Beirut.

The Israeli Cabinet met on the next day and issued a statement which amounted to a rejection of the new observation operation. Despite another demand of the Security Council, contained in resolution 518(1982) of 12 August 1982, the Israeli authorities refused to co-operate with UNTSO. No additional observers could be sent to Beirut, since they could not reach the area without going through Israeli checkpoints, and the 10 observers in Beirut were denied access to areas controlled by Israeli troops. Nevertheless, OGB was able to monitor and report on the main developments in the Beirut area, such as the arrival of the (non-United Nations) multinational force and the evacuation of the Palestinian and Syrian armed forces, the departure of the multinational force after the evacuation of Palestinian forces was completed, the occupation of West Beirut by Israeli forces after the assassination of Lebanese President-elect Bashir Gemayel and, in the morning of 17 September, the massacre of Palestinian refugees that had occurred in the Sabra and Shatila refugee camps in Beirut.

In the early morning of 19 September, the Security Council adopted resolution 521(1982), by which it condemned the criminal massacre of Palestinian civilians in Beirut, authorized the Secretary-General as an immediate step to increase the number of observers in and around Beirut from 10 to 50, and insisted that there be no interference with the deployment of the observers. The Council also insisted that all concerned permit the observers and forces authorized by the Council to be deployed and to discharge their mandates, and called attention to the obligation of all Member States under Article 25 of the Charter of the United Nations to accept and carry out the decisions of the Council.

On 20 September, the Israeli Cabinet concurred with the proposed dispatch of additional observers, and on the same day 25 observers proceeded to Beirut, followed by another 15 during the next two days. The 40 additional observers passed through Israeli check-points without hindrance and the total observer strength of OGB was thus raised to 50.

The UNTSO observers in the Beirut area carry out their duties by means of observation posts and mobile patrols. Their task is mainly to monitor the situation in and around Beirut, with emphasis on developments involving the Israelis and the Palestinians. As a rule, the United Nations observers will not concern themselves with matters which are essentially within the domestic jurisdiction of Lebanon, since it is a fundamental principle of United Nations peace-keeping operations that they should not be involved in such matters.

Following the withdrawal of the Israeli forces from the Beirut area, the tasks of the Observer Group were reduced and its total strength had been brought down to 18 as of October 1985.

Other assistance. While UNTSO's assistance to some other United Nations operations are not connected with the Arab-Israeli conflict, they may conveniently be mentioned here in pointing to the pool of experienced military personnel which UNTSO has been able to provide, as an *ad hoc* arrangement, at almost immediate notice for other operations, particularly in the initial stages.

Thus, at the outset of the United Nations Operation in the Congo (now Zaire) in July 1960, a group of UNTSO observers was detailed to Leopoldville (now Kinshasa) to form the nucleus of the headquarters staff of the United Nations Force. Others were assigned with UNEF personnel to the United Nations Yemen Observation Mission in 1963.

On 12 June 1984,[14] the Governments of Iran and Iraq, in response to an appeal by the Secretary-General, undertook to refrain from initiating military attacks on purely civilian population centres in either country. In this connection, the Secretary-General, with the agreement of the two Governments, set up two observer teams, based in Teheran and Baghdad respectively, each composed of three military observers and a civilian political adviser, for the purpose of verifying compliance with the above undertakings. UNTSO provided, and continues to provide, the military elements of the two teams.

Chapter III

First UN Emergency Force

A. Creation

Background

In October 1956, the United Nations faced a major crisis. The 1949 General Armistice Agreement between Egypt and Israel—concluded under the auspices of and supervised by the United Nations—collapsed when Israel and two major Powers occupied large portions of Egyptian territory. The Organization reacted to the crisis with speed and firmness and, to overcome it, conceived a new form of peace-keeping and set up its first peace-keeping force. This historic development was made possible mainly through the vision, resourcefulness and determination of Secretary-General Dag Hammarskjöld and Lester Pearson, who was at the time Secretary for External Affairs of Canada.

Since the summer of 1955, relations between Egypt and Israel had been steadily deteriorating, despite the efforts of the Chief of Staff of UNTSO and the Secretary-General himself. Palestinian *fedayeen*, with the support of the Egyptian Government, had been launching frequent raids against Israel from their bases in Gaza, and these had been followed by increasingly strong reprisal attacks by Israeli armed forces. The decision taken by Egypt in the early 1950s to restrict Israeli shipping through the Suez Canal and the Strait of Tiran at the entrance to the Gulf of Aqaba, in contravention of a decision of the Security Council, remained a controversial and destabilizing issue. In the heightening tension, the control of armament—which the Tripartite Declaration of France, the United Kingdom and the United States, of May 1950, had sought to achieve in the Middle East—had broken down, and Egypt and Israel were engaging in an intense arms race, with the East and the West supplying sophisticated weapons and equipment to the opposing sides.

On 19 July 1956, the United States Government decided to withdraw its financial aid for the Aswan Dam project on the Nile River. President Gamal Abdel Nasser announced the nationalization of the

Suez Canal Company a week later and declared that Canal dues would be used to finance the Aswan project.

On 23 September 1956, the Governments of France and the United Kingdom requested the President of the Security Council to convene the Council to consider the "situation created by the unilateral action of the Egyptian Government in bringing to an end the system of international operation of the Suez Canal, which was confirmed and completed by the Suez Canal Convention of 1888".[15] On the following day, Egypt countered with a request that the Security Council consider "actions against Egypt by some Powers, particularly France and the United Kingdom, which constitute a danger to international peace and security and are serious violations of the Charter of the United Nations".[16]

The Security Council first met on 26 September to consider both items. At the same time, private negotiations were being carried out between the Foreign Ministers of the three countries with the good offices of the Secretary-General. By 12 October, Hammarskjöld was able to work out six principles on which there seemed to be general agreement. These principles were incorporated in a draft resolution which the Security Council unanimously adopted on the next day. This became resolution 118(1956), by which the Security Council "agrees that any settlement of the Suez question should meet the following requirements:

"(1) There should be free and open transit through the Canal without discrimination, overt or covert—this covers both political and technical aspects;

"(2) The sovereignty of Egypt should be respected;

"(3) The operation of the Canal should be insulated from the politics of any country;

"(4) The manner of fixing tolls and charges should be decided by agreement between Egypt and the users;

"(5) A fair proportion of the dues should be allotted to development;

"(6) In case of disputes, unresolved affairs between the Suez Canal Company and the Egyptian Government should be settled by arbitration with suitable terms of reference and suitable provisions for the payment of sums found to be due."

Following the adoption of this resolution, Hammarskjöld announced that he would pursue his efforts to promote an agreement based on the principles laid down by the Security Council. However, a new situation developed in late October 1956, when Israel, in co-operation with the British and French Governments, launched an all-out attack on Egypt.

The Israeli forces crossed the border on the morning of 29 October, advancing in three columns towards El Arish, Ismailia and the Mitla Pass. In the early hours of 30 October, the Chief of Staff of UNTSO, Major-General E.L.M. Burns of Canada, called for a cease-fire and requested Israel to pull its forces back to its side of the border. In the afternoon of the same day, the British and French Governments addressed a joint ultimatum to Egypt and Israel calling on both sides to cease hostilities within 12 hours and to withdraw their forces to a distance of 10 miles on each side of the Suez Canal. They also requested Egypt to allow Anglo-French forces to be stationed temporarily on the Canal at Port Said, Ismailia and Suez for the purpose of separating the belligerents and ensuring the safety of shipping. The ultimatum was accepted by Israel whose troops in any case were still far from the Suez Canal, but it was rejected by Egypt. On 31 October, France and the United Kingdom launched an air attack against targets in Egypt, which was followed shortly by a landing of their troops near Port Said at the northern end of the Canal.

General Assembly's first emergency special session

The Security Council held a meeting on 30 October at the request of the United States, which submitted a draft resolution calling upon Israel immediately to withdraw its armed forces behind the established armistice lines.[17] It was not adopted because of British and French vetoes. A similar draft resolution[18] sponsored by the Soviet Union was also rejected. The matter was then transferred to the General Assembly, on a proposal by Yugoslavia, in accordance with the procedure provided by Assembly resolution 377(V) of 3 November 1950 entitled "Uniting for peace". Thus, the first emergency special session of the General Assembly called under that resolution was convened on 1 November 1956.

In the early hours of the next day, the General Assembly adopted, on the proposal of the United States, resolution 997(ES-I), calling for an immediate cease-fire, the withdrawal of all forces behind the armistice lines and the reopening of the Canal. The Secretary-General was requested to observe and report promptly on compliance to the Security Council and to the General Assembly, for such further action as those bodies might deem appropriate in accordance with the United Nations Charter.

The resolution was adopted by 64 votes to 5, with 6 abstentions. The dissenters were Australia and New Zealand, in addition to France, Israel and the United Kingdom. In explaining Canada's abstention, Lester Pearson stated that the resolution did not provide for, alongside with the cease-fire and a withdrawal of troops, any steps to be taken by the United Nations for a peace settlement, without which a cease-fire would be only of a temporary nature at best.

Before the session, Pearson had had extensive discussions with Hammarskjöld and he felt that it might be necessary to establish some sort of United Nations police force to help resolve the crisis. Pearson submitted to the General Assembly, when it reconvened the next morning, a draft resolution on the establishment of an emergency international United Nations force.

Enabling resolutions of the United Nations Force

The Canadian proposal was adopted by the General Assembly on the same morning and became resolution 998(ES-I) of 4 November 1956, by which the Assembly:

> "*Requests*, as a matter of priority, the Secretary-General to submit to it within forty-eight hours a plan for the setting up, with the consent of the nations concerned, of an emergency international United Nations Force to secure and supervise the cessation of hostilities in accordance with all the terms of the aforementioned resolution [997(ES-I)]."

The voting was 57 to none, with 19 abstentions. Egypt, France, Israel, the United Kingdom and the Soviet Union and Eastern European States were among the abstainers.

At the same meeting, the General Assembly also adopted resolution 999(ES-I), by which it reaffirmed resolution 997(ES-I) and authorized the Secretary-General immediately to arrange with the parties concerned for the implementation of the cease-fire and the halting of the movement of military forces and arms into the area.

On the same day, the Secretary-General submitted his first report on the plan for an emergency international United Nations Force,[19] in which he recommended certain preliminary steps, including the immediate setting up of a United Nations Command. All his recommendations were endorsed by the General Assembly and included in resolution 1000(ES-I) adopted on 5 November 1956, by which the Assembly:

> —Established a United Nations Command for an emergency international Force to secure and supervise the cessation of hostili-

ties in accordance with all the terms of General Assembly resolution 997(ES-I) of 2 November 1956;

—Appointed, on an emergency basis, the Chief of Staff of UNTSO, Major-General (later Lieutenant-General) E.L.M. Burns, as Chief of the Command;

—Authorized the Chief of the Command immediately to recruit, from the observer corps of UNTSO, a limited number of officers who were to be nationals of countries other than those having permanent membership in the Security Council, and further authorized him, in consultation with the Secretary-General, to undertake the recruitment directly, from various Member States other than the permanent members of the Security Council, of the additional number of officers needed;

—Invited the Secretary-General to take such administrative measures as might be necessary for prompt execution of the actions envisaged.

The resolution was adopted by 57 votes to none, with 19 abstentions. As with resolution 998(ES-I), Egypt, France, Israel, the United Kingdom, the Soviet Union and Eastern European States abstained.

Concept and guiding principles

On 6 November, the Secretary-General submitted to the General Assembly his second and final report on the plan for an emergency United Nations Force.[20] In this report, Hammarskjöld defined the concept of the new Force and certain guiding principles for its organization and functioning. The main points:

(a)　At the outset, Hammarskjöld observed, an emergency international United Nations Force could be developed on the basis of three concepts. In the first place, it could be set up on the basis of principles reflected in the constitution of the United Nations itself. This would mean that its chief responsible officer should be appointed by the United Nations itself and in his functions should be responsible ultimately to the General Assembly and/or the Security Council. His authority should be so defined as to make him fully independent of the policies of any one nation and his relations to the Secretary-General should correspond to those of the Chief of Staff of UNTSO. A second possibility would be for the United Nations to charge a country, or a group of countries, with the responsibility to provide independently for an international Force serving for the purposes determined by the United Nations. In this approach, which was followed in the case of the Unified Command in Korea, it would obviously be impossible to achieve the same independence in relation to national policies as would be established through the first concept. Finally, as a third possibility, an international Force might be set up in agreement among a group of nations, later to be brought into an appropriate relationship to the United Nations. This approach was open to the same reservation as the second concept and possibly others. Hammarskjöld noted that in deciding on 5 November 1956 to establish a United Nations Command, on an emergency basis, the General Assembly had chosen the first type of international force.

(b) Hammarskjöld set out certain guiding principles for the organization and functioning of the Force:

—The decision taken by the General Assembly on the United Nations Command recognized the independence of the Chief of Command and established the principle that the Force should be recruited from Member States other than the permanent members of the Security Council. In this context, the Secretary-General observed that the question of the composition of the staff and contingents should not be subject to agreement by the parties involved since such a requirement would be difficult to reconcile with the development of the international Force along the course already being followed by the General Assembly.

—The terms of reference of the Force were to secure and supervise the cessation of hostilities in accordance with all the terms of the General Assembly's resolution 997(ES-I) of 2 November 1956. It followed from its terms of reference that there was no intent in the establishment of the Force to influence the military balance in the current conflict, and thereby the political balance affecting efforts to settle the conflict. The Force should be of a temporary nature, the length of its assignment being determined by the needs arising out of the current conflict.

(c) Guidelines on the functions to be performed were outlined:

—The General Assembly's resolution of 2 November 1956 urged that "all parties now involved in hostilities in the area agree to an immediate cease-fire and, as part thereof, halt the movement of military forces and arms into the area", and further urged the parties to the Armistice Agreements promptly to withdraw all forces behind the armistice lines, to desist from raids against those lines into neighbouring territories and to observe scrupulously the provisions of the Agreements. These two provisions combined indicated that the functions of the United Nations Force would be, when a cease-fire was established, to enter Egyptian territory with the consent of the Egyptian Government, in order to help maintain quiet during and after the withdrawal of non-Egyptian forces and to secure compliance with the other terms established in the resolution.

—The Force obviously should have no rights other than those necessary for the execution of its functions, in co-operation with local authorities. It would be more than an observer corps, but in no way a military force temporarily controlling the territory in which it was stationed; nor should the Force have functions exceeding those necessary to secure peaceful conditions, on the assumption that the parties to the conflict would take all necessary steps for compliance with the recommendations of the General Assembly. Its functions could, on this basis, be assumed to cover an area extending roughly from the Suez Canal to the Armistice Demarcation Lines established in the Armistice Agreement between Egypt and Israel.

(d)   The Secretary-General indicated that the question as to how the Force should be financed required further study. A basic rule, which could be applied provisionally, would be that a State providing a unit would be responsible for all costs of equipment and salaries, while all other costs should be financed by the United Nations outside its normal budget. It was obviously impossible to make any estimate of the costs without knowledge of the size of the Force and the length of its assignment. The only practical course therefore would be for the General Assembly to vote on a general authorization for those costs on the basis of general principles such as those suggested in the report.

(e)   The Secretary-General stated that, because of the time factor, he could discuss the question of participation in the Force with only a limited number of Member Governments. The reaction so far led him to believe that it should be possible to meet quickly at least the most basic need for personnel. It was his hope that broader participation would be possible as soon as a plan was approved so that a more definite judgement might be possible concerning the implications of participation. Noting that several matters had to be left open because of the lack of time and the need for further study, the Secretary-General suggested that those matters be submitted to exploration by a small committee of the General Assembly. Such a committee might also serve as an advisory committee to the Secretary-General for questions relating to the operation.

Advisory Committee

After considering the report of the Secretary-General, the General Assembly adopted, on 7 November, resolution 1001(ES-I)—approving the guiding principles for the organization and functioning of the emergency international United Nations Force as expounded in the Secretary-General's report; concurring in the definition of the functions of the Force in the report; and approving provisionally the basic rule concerning the financing of the Force laid down in that report. The Assembly established an Advisory Committee composed of Brazil, Canada, Ceylon (now Sri Lanka), Colombia, India, Norway and Pakistan. It requested the Committee, whose Chairman was the Secretary-General, to undertake the development of those aspects of the planning for the Force and its operation not already dealt with by the General Assembly and which did not fall within the area of the direct responsibility of the Chief of Command. It authorized the Secretary-General to issue all regulations and instructions essential to the effective functioning of the Force, following consultation with the Committee, and to take all other necessary administrative and executive action. The Committee was to continue to assist the Secretary-General in his responsibilities, and it could request the convening of the General Assembly if necessary. Finally, the Assembly requested all Member States to afford assistance as necessary to the United Nations Command in the performance of its functions, including arrangements for passage to and from the area involved.

This resolution, which, with resolution 998(ES-I) of 4 November, formed the basis for the establishment of the United Nations Emergency Force, was adopted by 64 votes to none, with 12 abstentions. France and the United Kingdom voted this time with the majority. Egypt and Israel remained with the abstainers, together with South Africa and the Soviet Union and Eastern European States. The representatives of France and and the United Kingdom indicated that the resolution was acceptable to their Governments because it provided, as they had urged, for an effective international Force in the area. In explaining his abstention, the representative of the Soviet Union stated that the establishment of the Force under General Assembly resolution 1000(ES-I) and the plan for its implementation in resolution 1001(ES-I) were contrary to the Charter, and that the only reason for abstaining rather than voting against the proposal lay in the hope of preventing any further extension of the aggression against Egypt.

Further General Assembly resolutions

On the same day, 7 November, the General Assembly also adopted resolution 1002(ES-I), by which it called once again upon Israel immediately to withdraw all its forces behind the armistice lines, and upon France and the United Kingdom immediately to withdraw all their forces from Egyptian territory.

The voting was 65 to 1, with 10 abstentions. Israel cast the lone negative vote. France and the United Kingdom abstained, together with Australia, Belgium, Laos, Luxembourg, the Netherlands, New Zealand, Portugal and South Africa. The representatives of France and the United Kingdom indicated that an immediate withdrawal of their forces could lead to a power vacuum between Egyptian and Israeli forces and that withdrawal could only be effected subsequent to proof of the effective operation of UNEF.

The first emergency special session of the General Assembly ended on 10 November 1956. Before closing the session, the Assembly adopted resolution 1003(ES-I), by which it decided to refer the matter to its eleventh regular session which was then about to convene.

During the first emergency special session, the General Assembly had adopted a total of seven resolutions. By these resolutions, the Assembly gave the Secretary-General the authority and support he required to bring about the cessation of hostilities in Egypt and the withdrawal of foreign troops from Egyptian territory with the assistance of a new type of peace-keeping machinery, the United Nations peace-keeping force. The idea of such a force initially, which was to have such an impact on the work of the United Nations for the maintenance of international peace and security, came from Lester Pearson. Dag Hammarskjöld, through his untiring efforts and extraordinary diplomatic and administrative skill, made it a practical reality.

Initial stages of UNEF

The United Nations Emergency Force was the key element in the United Nations efforts to resolve the crisis arising from the military action of the Israeli and Anglo-French forces against Egypt. It was a pre-condition for securing the cease-fire and a pre-condition for bringing about the withdrawal of the invading forces. Therefore, a priority objective of the Secretary-General, after the adoption of the enabling resolutions, was to assemble a usable Force and land it in Egypt as rapidly as possible.

The establishment of this first peace-keeping Force in the United Nations history was a task of great complexity. The concept had no real precedent. The nearest parallel was UNTSO, which also had peace-keeping functions but was a much simpler operation and did not provide much help as regards the many organizational and operational problems involved.

Immediately after the Assembly authorized the Force, the Chief of Command, General Burns, who was in Jerusalem at the time, selected a group of UNTSO observers who began planning the organization of the new Force. Hammarskjöld approached the Governments of the potential participating countries to obtain the required military personnel. He also initiated negotiations with the Egyptian Government to secure its agreement as the host country for the entry and stationing of the Force in Egypt.

Negotiations with the Egyptian Government

A key principle governing the stationing and functioning of UNEF, and later of all other peace-keeping forces, was the consent of the host Government. Since it was not an enforcement action under Chapter VII of the Charter, UNEF could enter and operate in Egypt only with the consent of the Egyptian Government. This principle was clearly stated by the General Assembly in adopting resolution 1001(ES-I) of 7 November 1956 concerning the establishment of UNEF.

Immediately after the adoption of that resolution, Hammarskjöld instructed General Burns to approach the Egyptian authorities in Cairo in order to prepare the ground for the prompt implementation of the resolution. The Government of Egypt had already accepted the terms of resolution 1000(ES-I) on the establishment of a United Nations Command, and this was considered by the Secretary-General as an acceptance in principle of the Force itself.

However, before consenting to the arrival of the Force on its territory, Egypt wished to have certain points in the Assembly resolution clarified. In particular, it wanted to know in clearer terms the functions of the Force, especially in regard to whether, when the Force reached the Armistice Demarcation Line, the Governments concerned would agree to the areas to be occupied by it, how long the Force would stay, whether it was supposed to have functions in the Suez Canal area apart from observing the withdrawal of the Anglo-French forces and whether it would stay in the Canal area after the Anglo-French withdrawal.

Firm assurance was given to the Egyptian authorities that co-operation with the United Nations would not infringe Egyptian sovereignty, detract from Egypt's power freely to negotiate a settlement on the Suez Canal or submit Egypt to any control from the outside. The Secretary-General impressed upon those authorities that the Force provided a guarantee for the withdrawal of foreign forces from Egypt and that, since it would come only with Egypt's consent, it could not stay or operate in Egypt if that consent were withdrawn.

On the basis of the General Assembly's resolutions as interpreted by the Secretary-General, the Government of Egypt gave its consent on 14 November to the arrival of UNEF in Egypt, and the first transport of UNEF troops took place on the next day.

While the exchange of views that had taken place was considered sufficient as a basis for the sending of the first units of UNEF to Egypt, the Secretary-General felt that a firmer foundation had to be laid for the presence and functioning of the Force in Egypt and for the continued co-operation with the Egyptian authorities. He also considered it essential to discuss personally with the Egyptian authorities, at the highest level, various questions which flowed from the decision to send the Force to Egypt, including the selection of national contingents.

Hammarskjöld therefore visited Cairo from 16 to 18 November. During this visit, he reached agreement with the Egyptian Government on the composition of the Force. President Nasser had first opposed the inclusion of the Canadian, Danish and Norwegian units because they belonged to the North Atlantic Treaty Organization (NATO) and because, in his view, Canada and the United Kingdom were too congeneric. But on the insistence of Hammarskjöld, this opposition was withdrawn. The basic discussions centred on the stationing and functioning of the Force.

The good faith agreement

On this essential matter, a "good faith agreement" was worked out and included in an aide-mémoire which served as the basis for the .stationing of UNEF in Egypt. It noted that the Assembly, by resolution 1001(ES-I) had approved the principle that the Force could not be requested "to be stationed or operate on the territory of a given country without the consent of the Government of that country".[21] It then went on to say:

> The Government of Egypt and the Secretary-General of the United Nations have stated their understanding on the basic points for the presence and functioning of UNEF as follows:
>
> 1. The Government of Egypt declares that, when exercising its sovereign rights on any matter concerning the presence and functioning of UNEF, it will be guided, in good faith, by its acceptance of General Assembly resolution 1000(ES-I) of 5 November 1956.
>
> 2. The United Nations takes note of this declaration of the Government of Egypt and declares that the activities of UNEF will be guided, in good faith, by the task established for the Force in the aforementioned resolutions; in particular, the United Nations, understanding this to correspond to the wishes of the Government of Egypt, reaffirms its willingness to maintain UNEF until its task is completed.
>
> 3. The Government of Egypt and the Secretary-General declare that it is their intention to proceed forthwith, in the light of points 1 and 2 above, to explore jointly concrete aspects of the functioning of UNEF, including its stationing and the question of its lines of communciation and supply; the Government of Egypt, confirming its intention to facilitate the functioning of UNEF, and the United Nations are agreed to expedite in co-operation the implementation of guiding principles arrived at as a result of that joint exploration on the basis of the resolutions of the General Assembly.[22]

The Secretary-General brought this aide-mémoire to the attention of the General Assembly in a report of 20 November 1956.[23] In so doing, he stated that ". . . The aide-mémoire, if noted with approval by the General Assembly, with the concurrence of Egypt, would establish an understanding between the United Nations and Egypt on which the co-operation could be developed and necessary agreements on various details be elaborated." No objection was raised by the Assembly in this connection.

Other Hammarskjöld/Nasser memoranda and agreements

In addition to the good faith agreement, two other memoranda were agreed upon between Hammarskjöld and President Nasser. One of them set out the understanding that the area to be occupied by UNEF after the Israeli withdrawal would be subject to agreement and that the Force would have no function in the Port Said and the Suez Canal areas after the withdrawal of the Anglo-French troops. UNEF could not stay or operate in Egypt unless Egypt continued its consent. The other memorandum specifically separated the question of the reopening of the Suez Canal from the functions of UNEF. Hammarskjöld brought these memoranda to the attention of the Advisory Committee.

With these agreements, UNEF was set up. Subsequent discussions were continued between the Secretariat and the Egyptian authorities to work out more detailed and comprehensive arrangements on the status of the Force in Egypt. These arrangements were set out in a letter dated 8 February 1957 from the Secretary-General to the Minister for Foreign Affairs of Egypt and were accepted by the latter in his reply of the same date to the Secretary-General.[24] This exchange of letters constituted the agreement on the status of the United Nations Emergency Force in Egypt which the General Assembly noted with approval in its resolution 1126(XI) of 22 February 1957.

Status of the Force agreement

The status of the Force agreement covered a wide range of problems, including the premises of the Force and the use of the United Nations flag, freedom of movement, privileges and immunities of the Force, civil and criminal jurisdiction and settlement of disputes or claims. Two of the key provisions concerned freedom of movement and criminal jurisdiction. Members of the Force were to enjoy full freedom of movement in the performance of their duties. They were to be subject to the exclusive jurisdiction of their respective national Governments in respect of any criminal offences which they might commit in Egypt.

The agreement on the status of UNEF was the first document of this kind. It provided a pattern which was followed for the subsequent peace-keeping forces in the Congo and Cyprus. No agreements of this kind could be worked out for later forces for various political reasons but the status of the Force agreement for UNEF has been used as a precedent to deal with various problems arising from the operations of UNEF II, UNDOF and UNIFIL.

Negotiations with the participating countries

The principles of consent applied not only to the host Government but also to the participating countries. In accordance with the principles approved by the General Assembly, the Force was to be composed of national contingents accepted for service by the Secretary-General from among those voluntarily offered by Member States. Troops from the permanent members of the Security Council or from any country which, for geographical and other reasons, might have a special interest in the conflict would be excluded. In selecting the contingents, the Secretary-General had to take due account of the views of the host Government and such other factors as their suitability in terms of the needs of the Force, their size and availability, the extent to which they would be self-contained, the undesirability of too great a variation in ordnance and basic equipment, the problem of transportation and the goal of balanced composition.

The size of the Force was to be determined by the Commander in consultation with the Secretary-General and in the light of the functions to be performed. The original estimate by the Force Commander of the manpower needs to perform those tasks was the equivalent of two combat brigades, or about 6,000 men. It was decided that the national contingents should be sufficiently large to be relatively self-contained and that the Force should have adequate support units, including a light air-unit. From the point of view of balance, it was desirable that the differences in the size of the units should not be so great as to lead to excessive dependence on any one State.

The Secretary-General sought certain assurances from the participating countries. He pointed out that the effective functioning of UNEF required that some continuity of service of the participating units should be assured in order to enable the Force Commander to plan his operations. He also insisted that the Commander of each national contingent should take orders exclusively from the Force Commander and should be in a position to exercise the necessary disciplinary authority with the members of his contingent.

The arrangements between the United Nations and the contributing countries were expanded and set out in formal agreements in the form of an exchange of letters between the Secretary-General and the respective participating Governments.

By 5 November 1956, Canada, Colombia, Denmark, Finland, Norway, Pakistan and Sweden had replied affirmatively. In the following days, Afghanistan, Brazil, Burma, Ceylon, Chile, Czechoslovakia, Ecuador, Ethiopia, India, Indonesia, Iran, Laos, New Zealand, Peru, the Philippines, Romania and Yugoslavia also offered to provide contingents. In addition, the United States Government informed the Secretary-General that it was prepared to help as regards airlifts, shipping, transport and supplies. Italy agreed to place at the disposal of the United Nations the facilities of Capodichino Airport at Naples for the assembly and transit of UNEF personnel and equipment and to help in the airlift of personnel and equipment from Italy to Egypt. The Swiss Government, a non-member State, offered to defray part of the cost of Swissair charter planes.

UNEF's composition

In consultation with the Force Commander and after discussions with the Government of Egypt, Hammarskjöld accepted contingents from 10 countries: Brazil, Canada, Colombia, Denmark, Finland, India, Indonesia, Norway, Sweden and Yugoslavia. The offers of assistance from the United States, Italy and Switzerland were also accepted. With the agreement of Egypt, an air base at Abu Suweir near Ismailia was used as the central depot for the early contingents.

The extent of the area to be covered by UNEF called for highly mobile reconnaissance. This need was met by Yugoslavia, which provided a complete reconnaissance battalion. Canada later supplied a fully equipped, light-armoured squadron. Supporting units were obtained and assigned with the same urgency as those engaged in patrolling. The Indian contingent was given responsibility for the supply depot and the service institute; Canada and India provided units for transport, the Provost Marshal and signals; Norway and Canada covered the medical needs. The Canadian contingent was also made responsible for the ordnance depot and workshop, the base post office, engineering, the dental unit, movement control and air support.

General Burns and his group of UNTSO military observers arrived in Cairo on 12 November 1956 and set up a temporary headquarters there. The first UNEF units, composed of Colombians, Danes and Norwegians, flew to Egypt on 15 and 16 November. They were followed by other contingents. The target strength of about 6,000 men was reached in February 1957 after the Brazilian battalion had arrived at Port Said by sea. With the appointment of staff officers selected from the participating countries, the UNTSO military observers returned to their normal duties in Jerusalem.

The Governments of Indonesia and Finland, which had agreed to participate in the Force only for a limited period, withdrew their contingents in September and December 1957, respectively. The Colombian Government withdrew its contingent in December 1958. The other contingents continued to serve with UNEF until the withdrawal of the Force in 1967. The deployment and assignment of the contingents were changed from time to time according to the requirements of the operation.

The strength of the Force remained at the authorized level of about 6,000 until the end of 1957. In the following years, it was gradually reduced because the situation in the area of operation remained quiet and also because of financial difficulties. There were 5,341 all ranks with the Force in 1960, 5,102 in 1963, 4,581 in 1965 and 3,959 in 1966. In November 1965, a survey team was sent to the area to examine the possibility of further reductions. In accordance with its recommendations, the strength was further brought down to 3,378 at the time the Force began its withdrawal in May 1967.

UNEF's organization

The United Nations Emergency Force, established by the General Assembly, was a subsidiary organ of the Assembly under Article 22 of the Charter. It was directed by the Secretary-General under the general authority of the General Assembly.

The Secretary-General was authorized to issue all regulations and instructions which might be essential to the effective functioning of the Force and to take all other necessary administrative and executive actions. To assist him in these matters, Hammarskjöld set up an informal military group at Headquarters composed of military representatives of participating countries and headed by his military adviser— Major-General I.A.E. Martola of Finland, during the formative period. The Secretary-General was also assisted by the Advisory Committee established under Assembly resolution 1001(ES-I).

The command of the Force was assumed in the field by the Force Commander (originally designated as the Chief of Command), who was appointed by the General Assembly on the recommendation of the Secretary-General. The Commander was operationally responsible for the performance of all functions assigned to the Force by the United Nations and for the deployment and assignment of the troops placed at the disposal of the Force. He had direct authority for the operation of the Force and also was responsible for the provision of facilities, supplies and auxiliary services. He reported to the Secretary-General and was responsible to him. He was normally a general officer seconded by a Member State at the request of the Secretary-General, and during his assignment with the United Nations received an appointment as a senior official of the United Nations Secretariat with the rank of Assistant Secretary-General (Under-Secretary during Dag Hammarskjöld's time).

The Force Commander was authorized to appoint the officers of his command in consultation with the Secretary-General. In selecting the officers, the Commander was required to give due consideration to the goal of a balanced composition and to the importance of contributions made by the participating countries. The national contingents were under the command of the contingent commanders, who were appointed by their respective Governments. These contingents remained part of their respective national armed forces but, during their assignment to UNEF, they owed international allegiance and were placed under the operational control of the United Nations. This control was exercised through the contingent commanders, who received their instructions from the Force Commander. Changes in contingent commanders were made by the Governments of participating countries in consultation with the Force Commander.

The officers and soldiers of each contingent continued to wear their national uniforms but with United Nations insignia. The blue beret and helmet were created by Hammarskjöld during the formative days of UNEF.

Responsibility for disciplinary action in national contingents rested with the contingent commanders. Reports concerning disciplinary action were communicated to the Force Commander, who might consult with the contingent commanders and, if necessary, with the authorities of the participating Governments concerned.

Military police were provided by the Force Commander for all camps, establishments and other premises occupied by the Force and for such areas where the Force was deployed in the performance of its functions. Elsewhere, UNEF military police might be employed in so far as such employment was necessary to maintain discipline and order among members of the Force, subject to arrangements with the authorities of the host country and in liaison with those authorities.

B.   Cease-fire and withdrawal of foreign forces

Establishment of the cease-fire

The first objective of Secretary-General Hammarskjöld was to secure a cease-fire in accordance with the call of the General Assembly
contained in resolution 997(ES-I) of 2 November 1956.

During the meeting at which this resolution was adopted, the
representative of Israel stated that his Government agreed to an immediate cease-fire, provided that a similar answer was forthcoming
from Egypt. On the same day, the Egyptian Government informed the
Secretary-General that it would accept the call for a cease-fire on the
condition that military actions against Egypt were stopped. The
Secretary-General immediately notified Israel, France and the United
Kingdom of Egypt's position and called upon all four parties to bring
hostilities to an end.[25]

On 4 November, Hammarskjöld requested all four parties concerned to bring to a halt all hostile military action by 2400 hours GMT
on the same day. In identical messages addressed to the Governments
of France and the United Kingdom,[26] he pointed out that in the light
of the replies received from Egypt and Israel, it was obvious that the
positions of France and the United Kingdom would determine whether
or not it would be possible to achieve a cease-fire between Egypt and
Israel. He urged the two Governments to give him a definitive acceptance on his cease-fire call at the earliest possible moment. On 5 November, France and the United Kingdom informed the Secretary-General
that as soon as the Governments of Egypt and Israel signified acceptance of, and the United Nations endorsed a plan for, an international
force with the prescribed functions, they would cease all military
action.[27]

Later in the day, the British representative announced that a cease-
fire had been ordered at Port Said. Orders had also been given to cease
all bombing forthwith throughout Egypt, and other forms of air action would be limited to the support of any necessary operation in the
Canal area. Also on the same day, Egypt accepted the Secretary-
General's request for a cease-fire without any attached conditions and
Israel informed the Secretary-General that in the light of Egypt's declaration, it confirmed its readiness to agree to a cease-fire.

In an aide-mémoire dated 5 November,[28] the Secretary-General
informed France and the United Kingdom that, since on that date the
General Assembly had taken a decisive step towards setting up the
international Force by establishing a United Nations Command, and

since Egypt and Israel had agreed, without conditions, to a cease-fire, the conditions for a general cease-fire would seem to be established.

In their replies of 6 November,[29] the two Governments announced that their forces were being ordered to cease fire at midnight GMT on the same day, pending confirmation that Egypt and Israel had accepted an unconditional cease-fire and that there would be a United Nations Force competent to secure and supervise the attainment of the objectives of resolution 997(ES-I). The Secretary-General promptly informed Egypt and Israel that the cease-fire would become effective at midnight. He noted that the Assembly had not made the cease-fire dependent on the creation or the functioning of UNEF, since its call for a cease-fire and its decision to establish the Force were in separate resolutions.

The cease-fire was established at midnight GMT on 7/8 November and, except for isolated incidents, generally held.

Withdrawal of the Anglo-French force

At the same time as the Secretary-General was taking urgent steps to set up the new Force, he was pressing France and the United Kingdom for an early withdrawal of their forces from the Port Said area.

The two Governments told him that their troops would be withdrawn as soon as the proposed United Nations Force was in a position to assume effectively the tasks assigned to it and, in particular, to ensure that hostilities would not be resumed in the area.

Hammarskjöld therefore endeavoured to move the first units of UNEF to Egypt and build up its strength as rapidly as he could. But the establishment of this first United Nations peace-keeping force was not an easy job, and it took time to obtain the required units from the various contributing countries, transport them to the area of operations and make them fully operational. The first units from the Colombian, Danish and Norwegian contingents arrived in the area on 15 and 16 November and were immediately deployed in the Suez Canal area.

On 24 November, the General Assembly adopted resolution 1120(XI), by which it noted with regret that two thirds of the French forces and all of the British forces remained in Egypt, and it reiterated its call to the British and French Governments for the immediate withdrawal of their forces.

In messages dated 3 December,[30] the British and French Governments noted that an effective United Nations Force was currently arriving in Egypt, that the Secretary-General had accepted the responsibility for organizing the task of clearing the Suez Canal as expeditiously as possible, that free and secure transit would be re-established through the Canal when it was cleared and that the Secretary-General would promote as quickly as possible negotiations with regard to the future régime of the Canal on the basis of the six requirements set out in the Security Council's resolution 118(1956) of 13 October. The two Governments confirmed their decision to continue the withdrawal of their forces from the Port Said area without delay.

The Secretary-General immediately instructed General Burns to get in touch with the Anglo-French Commander and work out with him arrangements for the complete withdrawal of the Anglo-French forces without delay, ensuring that UNEF would be in a position to assume its responsibilities in the Port Said area by the middle of December.[31]

On 22 December, the withdrawal of the Anglo-French forces was completed and UNEF took over the Port Said area.

Initial withdrawal of the Israeli forces: November 1956—mid-January 1957

The negotiations undertaken by Hammarskjöld to achieve the withdrawal of the Anglo-French forces required nearly two months; those regarding the withdrawal of Israeli forces took much longer. By resolution 997(ES-I) of 2 November 1956, the General Assembly had urged the parties to the Armistice Agreements promptly to withdraw all forces behind the armistice lines, to desist from raids across those lines into neighbouring territory and to observe scrupulously the Armistice Agreements. In resolution 1002(ES-I) of 7 November, the Assembly, after noting its decision to establish a United Nations Command for an international force, called once again upon Israel immediately to withdraw its forces behind the armistice lines.

On 7 November, the Prime Minister of Israel, David Ben Gurion, in a statement to the Israeli Knesset (Parliament), stated that the armistice lines between Egypt and Israel had no validity and that "on no account will Israel agree to the stationing of a foreign force, no matter how called, in her territory, or in any of the areas occupied by her". On hearing of this statement, the Secretary-General immediately wrote to the Minister for Foreign Affairs of Israel, Golda Meir, to inform her that this position was in violation of the resolutions of the General Assembly and, if maintained, would seriously complicate the task of giving effect to those resolutions.

On 21 November,[32] in reply to queries by the Secretary-General, the Government of Israel stated that there had already been a with-drawal of its forces for varying distances along the entire Egyptian frontier. It reiterated its position regarding the withdrawal of the Is-raeli forces and indicated that the satisfactory arrangements it sought were such as would ensure Israel's security against the recurrence of the threat or danger of attack and against acts of belligerency by land or sea. Noting that it had not yet had an opportunity to discuss the question of satisfactory arrangements to be made with the United Na-tions in connection with UNEF, it stated that it was awaiting informa-tion on the proposed size, location and stationing arrangements of the Force and on the methods proposed for the discharge of its functions as laid down in the General Assembly's resolutions of 2, 5 and 7 November. It was also awaiting a clarification by Egypt on its policy and intention with respect to belligerency or peace with Israel which must influence Israel's dispositions on matters affecting its security.

At a meeting held on 24 November, the General Assembly adopted resolution 1120(XI) by which, after noting that the Israeli forces had not yet been withdrawn behind the armistice lines, reiterated its call to Israel to comply forthwith with its resolution. On the same day, the representative of Israel informed the Secretary-General[33] that the equivalent of two infantry brigades had been withdrawn from Egyp-tian territory into Israel.

In a letter dated 1 December,[34] the representative of Israel ad-vised the Secretary-General that on the morning of 3 December, Is-raeli forces would be removed from a wide belt of territory (about 50 kilometres) in proximity to the Suez Canal along its entire length. Ele-ments of UNEF immediately entered the evacuated area, although progress in this process was slowed down because of minefields and destroyed roads. On 11 December, Israel announced that it was ready to effect further withdrawal of troops in the Sinai peninsula in order to enable UNEF to extend its occupation eastward.

General Burns met with General Moshe Dayan, the Israeli Com-mander, on the morning of 16 December. They agreed on specific ar-rangements for a first phase of withdrawal, and UNEF troops moved forward to within five kilometres of new Israeli positions.

Regarding further withdrawals, General Dayan informed the UNEF Commander that according to his instructions, the Israeli forces were to withdraw from the remainder of the Sinai at an approximate rate of 25 kilometres each week during the next four weeks. This plan was considered by General Burns to be inadequate. Consequently, at his request, a new withdrawal proposal was submitted by the Israeli

Government on 21 December. The new proposal envisaged that the remaining Israeli withdrawal would take place in two phases. The second phase would involve a full Israeli withdrawal behind the armistice lines at an unstated date.

In accordance with this proposal, a further withdrawal of Israeli forces took place on 7 and 8 January 1957 to a north-south line roughly following meridian 33 degrees, 44 minutes, leaving no Israeli forces west of El Arish. On 15 January, the Israeli forces withdrew eastward another 25 to 30 kilometres, except in the area of Sharm el Sheikh. This phase involved the entry into El Arish and St. Catherine's Monastery of the United Nations Emergency Force, which had closely followed the withdrawing Israeli troops.

Sharm el Sheikh and the Gaza Strip

A day earlier, on 14 January, the Government of Israel had informed the Secretary-General that by 22 January the Sinai Desert would be entirely evacuated by Israeli forces with the exception of the Sharm el Sheikh area, that is "the strip on the western coast of the Gulf of Aqaba which at present ensures freedom of navigation in the Strait of Tiran and in the Gulf". Reporting on this matter to the General Assembly,[35] the Secretary-General stated that under the terms of the Assembly's resolution, the Israeli forces should be withdrawn also from that area.

In this connection, he observed that the international significance of the Gulf of Aqaba might be considered to justify the right of innocent passage through the Strait of Tiran and the Gulf in accordance with recognized rules of international law. He did not consider that a discussion of the various aspects of this matter and its possible relation to the action requested in the General Assembly on the Middle East crisis fell within the mandate established for him in resolution 999(ES-I) of 4 November. Like the cease-fire, withdrawal was a preliminary and essential phase in the process through which a viable basis might be laid for peaceful conditions in the area. The General Assembly, in giving high priority to the cease-fire and withdrawal, in no way disregarded all the other aims which must be achieved in order to create more satisfactory conditions than those prevailing during the period preceding the crisis. The basic function of UNEF, which was to help maintain quiet, gave the Force great value as a background for efforts towards resolving such pending problems, although it was not in itself a means to that end.

On 19 January 1957, the General Assembly adopted resolution

1123(XI) by which, after recalling its resolutions of 2, 4, 7 and 24 November 1956, requested the Secretary-General "to continue his efforts for securing the complete withdrawal of Israel in pursuance of the above-mentioned resolutions, and to report on such completion to the General Assembly, within five days".

In pursuance of that resolution, Hammarskjöld held further discussions with Israeli representatives on 20 and 23 January. On 23 January, Israel presented its views in an aide-mémoire on the Israeli position on the Sharm el Sheikh area and the Gaza Strip.[36] Its position on each of the two areas was:

(a)   For the Sharm el Sheikh area, Israel's aim was the simultaneous reconciliation of two objectives: the withdrawal of Israeli forces from that area and the guaranteeing of permanent freedom of navigation by the prevention of belligerence. In this matter, Egyptian compliance with the decision of the Security Council—resolution 95(1951) of 1 September 1951—had a legal and chronological priority over Israel's duty to fulfil recommendations in which Egypt had an interest. Accordingly, Israel formally requested the Secretary-General to ascertain Egypt's intentions with respect to the Council's 1951 resolution concerning the Suez Canal.

(b)   For the Gaza Strip, Israel, after questioning the legality of the Egyptian occupation of Gaza from 1948 to 1956 and criticizing its actions during this period, proposed a plan under which the Israeli military forces would be withdrawn but an Israeli civilian administration would remain to deal with security and administrative matters; the United Nations Emergency Force would not enter and be deployed in the Gaza area, but Israel would co-operate with the United Nations Relief and Works Agency for Palestine Refugees in the Near East regarding the care and maintenance of the refugees in the area. In this connection, Israel was ready to work out with the United Nations a suitable relationship with respect to the Gaza Strip.

The position of the Secretary-General was set out in his report of 24 January 1957:[37]

—In connection with the question of Israeli withdrawal from the Sharm el Sheikh area, attention had been directed to the situation in the Strait of Tiran and the Gulf of Aqaba. This problem was of longer duration and was not directly related to the current crisis. It followed from principles guiding the United Nations that the Israeli military action and its consequences should not be elements influencing the solution of this problem. The Secretary-General concluded that upon the withdrawal of the Israeli forces, UNEF would have to follow them in the same way as it had in other parts of the Sinai, its movements being determined by its duties in respect of the cease-fire and the withdrawal. In accordance with the general legal principles recognized as decisive for the deployment of the Force, UNEF should not be used in such a way as to prejudice the solution of the controversial questions involved.

—Regarding the status of Gaza, the United Nations could not recognize a change of the *de facto* situation created under the Armistice Agreement, by which the administration and security in the Strip were left in the hands of Egypt, unless the change was brought about through settlement between the parties. Nor could it lend its assistance to the maintenance of a *de facto* situation contrary to the one created by the Agreement. These considerations excluded the United Nations from accepting Israeli control over the area even if it were of a non-military character. Deployment of UNEF in Gaza under the resolutions of the General Assembly would have to be on the same basis as its deployment along the Armistice Demarcation Line and in the Sinai peninsula. Any broader function for it in that area, in view of the terms of the Armistice Agreement and a recognized principle of international law, would require the consent of Egypt.

Second withdrawal of Israeli forces: February 1957

On 2 February 1957, the General Assembly, after receiving the Secretary-General's report, adopted two resolutions.

By resolution 1124(XI), it deplored the failure of Israel to complete its withdrawal behind the Armistice Demarcation Line and called upon it to do so without delay. By resolution 1125(XI), the Assembly, recognizing that withdrawal by Israel must be followed by action which would assure progress towards the creation of peaceful conditions, called upon Egypt and Israel scrupulously to observe the provisions of the 1949 General Armistice Agreement and considered that "after full withdrawal of Israel from the Sharm el Sheikh and the Gaza areas, the scrupulous maintenance of the Armistice Agreement requires the placing of the United Nations Emergency Force on the Egyptian-Israel Armistice Demarcation Line and the implementation of other measures as proposed in the Secretary-General's report, with due regard to the considerations set out therein with a view to assist in achieving situations conducive to the maintenance of peaceful conditions in the area". The General Assembly further requested the Secretary-General, in consultation with the parties concerned, to take steps to carry out these measures and to report to it as appropriate.

On 4 February, the Secretary-General met with the representative of Israel to discuss implementation of the Assembly's resolutions. Israel presented to him an aide-mémoire in which it raised two points. First, it requested the Secretary-General to ask the Government of Egypt whether Egypt agreed "to the mutual and full abstention from belligerent acts, by land, air and sea, on withdrawal of Israeli troops". Secondly, Israel sought clarification as to whether "immediately on the withdrawal of Israeli forces from the Sharm el Sheikh area, units of the United Nations Emergency Force will be stationed along the western shore of the Gulf of Aqaba in order to act as a restraint against hostile acts, and will remain so deployed until another effective means is agreed upon between the parties concerned for ensuring permanent freedom of navigation and the absence of belligerent acts in the Strait of Tiran and the Gulf of Aqaba".[38]

During the same meeting, the Secretary-General asked whether, with regard to Gaza, it was understood by the Government of Israel that the withdrawal had to cover elements of civilian administration as well as military troops. Hammarskjöld considered a clarification on this point to be a prerequisite to further consideration of the Israeli aide-mémoire. There was, in his view, an unavoidable connection between Israel's willingness to comply fully with General Assembly resolution 1124(XI) as concerned the Gaza Strip and what might be done towards maintaining quiet in the Sharm el Sheikh area, and it was unrealistic to assume that the latter question could be solved while Israel remained in Gaza.

With regard to the second point raised by Israel, the Secretary-General noted that the debate in the General Assembly and the report on which it was based made it clear that the stationing of the United Nations Emergency Force at Sharm el Sheikh would require Egyptian consent. In the light of this implication of Israel's question, the Secretary-General considered it important, as a basis for his consideration of the aide-mémoire, to learn whether Israel itself consented in principle to the stationing of UNEF units on its territory in implementation of the functions established for the Force by the Assembly's resolutions and, in particular, its resolution 1125(XI) where it was indicated that the Force should be placed on the Egyptian-Israeli Armistice Demarcation Line.

This meeting was followed by an exchange of communications between the Secretary-General and the representative of Israel, and a meeting between them was held on 10 February. But these were all inconclusive, as each side wanted to receive the clarifications it had sought before replying to the questions addressed to it. In this connection, the Secretary-General stated that the fact that Israel had not found it possible to clarify elements decisive for the consideration of its requests had complicated the efforts to achieve implementation of the Assembly's resolutions.

In reporting on this matter to the General Assembly on 11 February,[39] the Secretary-General commented that the relationship between resolution 1124(XI) on withdrawal and resolution 1125(XI) on measures to be carried out after withdrawal afforded the possibility of informal explorations of the whole field covered by these two resolutions, preparatory to negotiations. Later, the results of such explorations might be used in the negotiations through a constructive combination of measures, representing for the two countries parallel progress towards the peaceful conditions sought. However, such explorations could not be permitted to invert the sequence between withdrawal and other measures, nor to disrupt the evolution of negotiations towards their goal. Progress towards peaceful conditions, following the general policy suggested in the last report of the Secretary-General, on which General Assembly resolution 1125(XI) was based, had to be achieved gradually.

Final withdrawal of Israeli forces: March 1957

In concluding his report, the Secretary-General stated that, in the situation now facing the United Nations, the General Assembly, as a matter of priority, might wish to indicate how it wished him to proceed with further steps to carry out its decisions.

The Assembly did not adopt any further resolution on this matter after the Secretary-General's report, but the Israeli Government eventually softened its position on the withdrawal from the Gaza Strip, although it maintained its denunciation of the 1949 General Armistice Agreement with Egypt and continued to oppose the stationing of the United Nations Emergency Force on its side of the Armistice Demarcation Line.

On 1 March, the Foreign Minister of Israel announced in the General Assembly the decision of her Government to act in compliance with the request contained in Assembly resolution 1124(XI) to withdraw behind the Armistice Demarcation Line.

The same day, the Secretary-General instructed the Commander of UNEF as a matter of utmost urgency to arrange for a meeting with the Commander-in-Chief of the Israeli forces in order to agree with him on arrangements for the complete and unconditional withdrawal of Israel in accordance with the Assembly's decision.

On 4 March, the declaration of 1 March was confirmed by the Israeli Government. The same day, General Burns met at Lydda with General Dayan. Technical arrangements were agreed upon for the withdrawal of the Israeli forces and the entry of UNEF troops into the Gaza Strip during the hours of curfew on the night of 6/7 March. Agreement was also reached for a similar takeover of the Sharm el Sheikh area on 8 March.

On 6 March, General Burns reported that UNEF troops were in position in all camps and centres of population in the Gaza Strip. The operation was carried out according to plan and without incident. By 0400 hours GMT, all Israelis had withdrawn from the Strip with the exception of an Israeli troop unit at Rafah Camp. By agreement, that last Israeli element was to be withdrawn at 1600 hours GMT on 8 March and full withdrawal from the Sharm el Sheikh area would be effected at the same time. These withdrawals took place as agreed and thus the Secretary-General was able to report to the General Assembly on 8 March 1957 full compliance with its resolution 1124(XI) of 2 February 1957.

C. UNEF deployment

Deployment along the Armistice Demarcation Line

In its resolution 1125(XI), on measures to be taken after the withdrawal of the Israeli forces from Egyptian territory, the General Assembly called upon the Governments of Egypt and Israel to observe scrupulously the provisions of the 1949 General Armistice Agreement and considered that, after full withdrawal of Israel from the Sharm el Sheikh and Gaza areas, "the scrupulous maintenance of the Armistice Agreement requires the placing of the United Nations Emergency Force on the Egyptian-Israel Armistice Demarcation Line".

On 11 February 1957,[40] the Secretary-General reported to the Assembly that Egypt had reaffirmed its intent to observe fully the provisions of the Armistice Agreement to which it was a party, on the assumption that observance would be reciprocal. The Secretary-General drew attention to the desire expressed by Egypt to see an end to all raids and incursions across the Armistice Line in both directions, with effective assistance from United Nations auxiliary organs to that effect.

Israel maintained its denunciation of the Armistice Agreement. In a letter of 25 January,[41] the representative of Israel had stated that "Israel does not claim that the absence of an armistice agreement means the existence of a state of war with Egypt, even though Egypt insisted on the existence of a state of war even when the Agreement was in existence. Israel is prepared to confirm its position on this by signing immediately with Egypt an agreement of non-belligerency and mutual non-aggression, but the Agreement, violated and broken, is beyond repair''.

The Secretary-General did not accept Israel's denunciation as valid, as there was no provision in the 1949 Agreement for unilateral termination of its application. Consequently, the machinery for the supervision of the Armistice Agreement was maintained by UNTSO *(see chapter II above)*.

In his report of 8 March 1957,[42] the Secretary-General informed the General Assembly that arrangements would be made through which, without any change in the legal structure or status of UNTSO, its functions in the Gaza area would be placed under the operational control of UNEF. Close co-operation between the two United Nations peace-keeping operations was maintained.

Regarding the placing of UNEF along the Armistice Demarcation Line, the Secretary-General interpreted this as requiring the deployment of the Force on both sides of the Line. The Egyptian Government had consented to the deployment of UNEF on its territory along the Line as well as in the Sharm el Sheikh area on the basis of the "good faith agreement" set out in the aide-mémoire of November 1956 *(see above)*. At the beginning of February 1957, the Secretary-General had sought clarification from Israel as to whether, as a question of principle, it agreed to the stationing of UNEF units on its side of the Armistice Demarcation Line. No clarification was obtained and, in a letter dated 6 February to the representative of Israel,[43] the Secretary-General said he assumed that, at least for the present, Israel's reply to this question was essentially negative. In view of the Israeli position, UNEF could be deployed only on the Egyptian side.

As of 8 March 1957, UNEF was deployed along the western side of the Armistice Demarcation Line along the Gaza Strip, the international frontier between the Sinai and Egypt, as well as in the Sharm el Sheikh area.

Phases of deployment and activities

UNEF began operating in Egypt on 12 November 1956, when the Force Commander and a group of military observers detached from UNTSO set up a temporary headquarters in Cairo. It was withdrawn ten-and-a-half years later, on 18 May 1967, at the request of the Egyptian Government. The operation of the Force during this period may be divided into four phases: The first phase, which extended from mid-

November to late December 1956, was centred on the withdrawal of the Anglo-French forces from the Port Said area. The second, from that time to early March 1957, concerned the withdrawal of the Israeli forces from the Sinai peninsula, except the Gaza Strip and the Sharm el Sheikh area. The third, in March, related to those areas. The fourth and last phase, which began with the deployment of UNEF along the borders between Egypt and Israel, covered a period of more than 10 years from March 1957 until May 1967, during which time the Force effectively maintained peace in those sensitive areas.

First phase: Suez Canal area
(November-December 1956)

When UNEF became operational in mid-November 1956, the cease-fire had been achieved and was generally holding. The Anglo-French forces were occupying the Port Said area including Port Fuad in the northern end of the Suez Canal. The Israeli forces were deployed west of the Canal about 10 kilometres from it. The Secretary-General was actively negotiating with the three Governments concerned and pressing for the early withdrawal of their forces from Egyptian soil.

The objectives of UNEF were to supervise the cessation of hostilities and to assist in the withdrawal process once agreement was reached on this matter. Shortly after its arrival in Egypt, UNEF was interposed between the Anglo-French and the Egyptian forces, occupying a buffer zone. All incidents involving the cease-fire were reported to the proper authorities, who were urged to prevent recurrences. No provisions had been made for the establishment of joint machinery whereby incidents could be examined and discussed. UNEF's role was limited to investigating, reporting and, if warranted, protesting to the relevant authorities.

By arrangements with the Anglo-French forces, units of UNEF entered Port Said and Port Fuad and took responsibility for maintaining law and order in certain areas, in co-operation with the local authorities. The Force also undertook guard duty of some vulnerable installations and other points.

In the period of transition, when the Anglo-French forces were preparing to leave and during the withdrawal process, UNEF undertook certain essential administrative functions such as security and the protection of public and private property, with the co-operation of the Governor and the Police Inspector in Port Said. With the sanction of the local authorities, UNEF personnel also performed administrative functions with respect to public services, utilities and arrangements for the provisioning of the local population with foodstuffs, and exercised limited powers of detention. All administrative and policing responsibilities were turned over to the Egyptian authorities the day following the Anglo-French evacuation.

Other tasks of the Force included clearing minefields in the Suez Canal area and arranging for exchanges of prisoners and detainees between the Egyptian Government and the Anglo-French command. In the last stage of the withdrawal of the Anglo-French troops from Port Said and Port Fuad, UNEF units were stationed around the final perimeter of the zone occupied by the withdrawing forces, thus preventing clashes between them and the Egyptian troops.

Second phase: Sinai peninsula
(December 1956–March 1957)

After the withdrawal of the Anglo-French forces, UNEF concentrated its efforts on maintaining the cease-fire between the Egyptian and Israeli forces and on arranging for Israeli withdrawal from Egyptian-controlled territory.

The Israeli forces withdrew from the Sinai peninsula, with the exception of the Gaza and the Sharm el Sheikh areas, in three stages: on 3 December 1956, on 7 and 8 January 1957 and from 15 to 22 January 1957.

On the whole, the functions performed by UNEF in the Sinai were similar to those undertaken in the Canal area. The Force was interposed between the Egyptian and Israeli forces in a temporary buffer zone from 3 December onwards, moving eastbound as the Israeli forces withdrew, and in accordance with pre-arranged procedures.

During the successive stages of the Israeli withdrawal, UNEF temporarily undertook some local civic responsibilities, including security functions in a few inhabited areas, handing over such responsibilities to the Egyptian civilian authorities as soon as they returned to their posts. The Force also arranged and carried out exchanges of prisoners of war between Egypt and Israel and discharged certain investigatory functions. It cleared minefields in the Sinai and repaired portions of damaged roads and tracks crossing the peninsula.

Third phase: Gaza Strip and Sharm el Sheikh
(March 1957)

After 22 January 1957, Israel held on to the last two areas it still occupied. The persistent negotiations to ensure withdrawal are described above. The withdrawal from the Gaza Strip took place on 6 and 7 March 1957 and that from the Sharm el Sheikh area from 8 to 12 March.

In accordance with the arrangements agreed to by the Egyptian Government, a UNEF detachment was stationed in Sharm el Sheikh following the withdrawal of the Israeli forces. This detachment maintained an observation post and kept the Strait of Tiran under constant watch.

In the Gaza Strip, two local conditions were of special concern to UNEF as it moved into the area. It was across the Armistice Demarcation Line along the Strip that the greatest number of infiltrations and raids had occurred during past years and there were in the area a large number of Palestinian Arab refugees, who were being assisted by UNRWA.

UNEF units entered the Gaza Strip on 6 March as the withdrawal of Israeli forces began. As a first step, arrangements were made between the Force Commander and the Israeli authorities for the United Nations to assume its responsibilities in the Strip as the Israeli troops and civil administrators withdrew.

On 7 March, General Burns notified the population of Gaza that UNEF, acting in fulfilment of its functions as determined by the General Assembly and with the consent of the Government of Egypt, was being deployed in the area for the purpose of maintaining quiet during and after the withdrawal of the Israeli forces. He also announced that until further arrangements were made, UNEF had assumed responsibility for civil affairs in the area and that UNRWA would continue to provide food and other services as in the past.

The involvement of UNEF in civil administration was of a purely temporary nature, pending the re-establishment of local civilian authority. In this connection, UNEF co-operated closely with UNRWA in meeting the needs of the local population. The operation of the Force during this initial period was greatly facilitated by the presence in Gaza of an important branch of UNRWA and by the fact that the Egypt-Israel Mixed Armistice Commission had its headquarters in Gaza and made available to the Force its personnel and its communications facilities.

Final phase: deployment along the borders (March 1957–May 1967)

After the completion of the withdrawal of all foreign forces from Egyptian territory, the main objective of UNEF was to supervise the cessation of hostilities between Egypt and Israel. Its basic functions were to act as an informal buffer between the Egyptian and Israeli forces along the Armistice Demarcation Line (ADL) and the international frontier in order to avoid incidents, prevent illegal crossings of the Line by civilians of either side for whatever purposes, and to observe and report on all violations of the Line whether on land, sea or in the air.

To perform these functions, UNEF troops were deployed on the western side of the ADL and the international frontier, covering a distance of 273 kilometres. The Sinai coast from the northern end of the Gulf of Aqaba to the Strait of Tiran, a further distance of 187 kilometres, was kept under observation by UNEF air reconnaissance. As indicated earlier, a UNEF detachment was stationed at Sharm el Sheikh near the Strait of Tiran.

By day, the entire length of the ADL (about 59 kilometres) was kept under observation by some 72 intervisible observation posts. Each post was manned during daylight hours; by night, the sentries were withdrawn and replaced by patrols of five to seven men each. The patrols moved on foot, covering the length of the ADL on an average of three rounds each night and giving particular attention to roads likely to be used by infiltrators. Platoon camps were set up to the rear of the posts, each holding a reserve detachment available to go to the aid of an observation post or patrol should the need arise. Telephone communications by day and a system of flare signals, supplemented by wireless, at night ensured a speedy response to calls for help.

Along the international frontier, rough terrain and scattered minefields restricted the access roads for potential infiltrators, who tended to confine their activities to certain areas. These sensitive areas were covered by a system of patrols. Eight outposts were established along the frontier. Motor patrols from these outposts covered the areas between the outposts and certain tracks. In addition to ground observers, the entire length of the international frontier was also patrolled by air reconnaissance planes on a daily basis, later reduced to three times a week. Any suspicious activity seen from the air could be checked by ground patrols dispatched from the outposts.

To prevent infiltration and incidents, UNEF secured the co-operation of the Egyptian authorities. The inhabitants of Gaza were officially informed that the Government of Egypt, as a matter of policy, was opposed to infiltration across the Armistice Demarcation Line. They were notified that they were forbidden to approach the ADL within 50 to 100 metres by day and 500 metres by night. The police in Gaza were instructed to take effective measures to find persons responsible for laying mines and for other incidents and to prevent recurrences. The local Palestinian police also co-operated with UNEF in preventing infiltrations. UNEF was authorized to apprehend infiltrators and persons approaching the ADL in suspicious circumstances. In practice, this applied to a zone extending up to 500 metres from the line. The persons so apprehended were interrogated by UNEF and then were handed over to the local police.

In the performance of their duties, UNEF soldiers were not authorized to use force except in self-defence. They were never to take the initiative in the use of force, but could respond with fire to an armed attack upon them, even though this might result from a refusal on their part to obey an order from the attacking party not to resist. UNEF maintained close liaison with the two parties, particularly with the Egyptian authorities as representatives of the host Government.

UNEF enjoyed full freedom of movement in the Gaza Strip and between the Sinai posts, UNEF headquarters and the units deployed along the Armistice Demarcation Line. This included freedom of flight over the Sinai peninsula and the Gaza Strip for UNEF aircraft, as well as the manning of the Gaza airport by UNEF.

The deployment of UNEF along the ADL raised a question of the respective responsibilities of the Force and UNTSO. As indicated earlier, Israel denounced the General Armistice Agreement with Egypt in early November 1956, but the United Nations did not accept this unilateral action. Therefore, the Chairman of the Egypt-Israel Mixed Armistice Commission and the UNTSO military observers had remained at their posts throughout the Israeli occupation of the Gaza Strip and afterwards. Upon the withdrawal of the Israeli forces, the Secretary-General, as a practical arrangement and without any change in the legal status of the Mixed Armistice Commission, placed the UNTSO personnel assigned to EIMAC under the operational control of the Commander of UNEF. In view of its position with respect to the General Armistice Agreement, the Government of Israel lodged its complaints of violations of the ADL only with UNEF, but the Force maintained that official investigations of incidents should be carried out through the Armistice Commission. In practice, problems arising between Israel and the United Nations relating to matters covered by the General Armistice Agreement were resolved in a practical way, with UNEF taking over some of the duties previously performed by UNTSO.

The activities carried out by UNEF following its deployment along the Armistice Demarcation Line and the international frontier, and the methods followed in this connection, remained virtually unchanged until the withdrawal of the Force in May 1967. Its area of operations, which had been one of the most disturbed areas in the Middle East, became remarkably quiet. Incidents, such as crossings of the ADL/international frontier, firing across the Line and air violations, naturally continued to occur, but they were relatively infrequent and generally of a minor nature. Virtually uninterrupted peace prevailed in the area, thanks to the presence and activities of UNEF.

UNEF withdrawal, 1967

While quiet prevailed along the Egyptian-Israeli borders after November 1956, there was continued tension in other sectors of the Middle East, particularly on the Israel-Jordan and Israel-Syria fronts. After the creation, in 1964, of the Palestine Liberation Organization and its main group, El Fatah, there appeared to be a new level of organization and training of Palestinian commandos. Palestinian raids against Israel, conducted mainly from Jordanian and Syrian territory, became a regular occurrence, and the Israeli forces reacted with increasingly violent retaliation. There was a marked contrast between the quiet along the Egyptian border and the confrontation situation in other sectors.

In early 1967, tension between Israel and Syria again reached a critical level, mainly because of disputes over cultivation rights in the demilitarized zone near Lake Tiberias. For years, Syria complained that Israelis were illegally seizing lands belonging to Arab Palestinians in the demilitarized zone, and the cultivation of disputed land had led to frequent firing incidents between Israeli and Syrian forces. Efforts within the Mixed Armistice Commission failed. On 7 April 1967, an exchange of fire across disputed farmland led to heavy shelling of Israeli villages by Syrian artillery and intensive air attacks by Israel against Syrian targets—the most serious clash since 1956. The incidents of 7 April were followed by a heightening of tension in the entire region, despite appeals by Secretary-General U Thant for restraint, and the moderating efforts of UNTSO.

In the evening of 16 May, the UNEF Commander received a request from the Egyptian Commander-in-Chief of the armed forces for withdrawal of "all UN troops which installed OP's [observation posts] along our borders".[44] The general who handed the message to the Force Commander told him that UNEF must order immediate withdrawal from El Sabha and Sharm el Sheikh, commanding the Strait of Tiran and therefore access to the Red Sea and southern Israel. The UNEF Commander replied that he did not have authority to do that.

The Secretary-General, on being informed, gave instructions to the Commander to "be firm in maintaining UNEF positions while being as understanding and as diplomatic as possible in your relations with local UAR [United Arab Republic] officials". While the Secretary-General sought clarifications from Cairo, Egyptian troops moved onto UNEF's line, occupying some United Nations posts.

The Secretary-General met with members of the UNEF Advisory Committee and told them of the events in the field, making it known that if a formal request for UNEF's withdrawal came from the Egyptian Government he would have to comply. He pointed out that the Force was on Egyptian territory only with the consent of the Government and could not remain there without it. He also consulted members of the Security Council. The various meetings held by the Secretary-General showed that within the United Nations there was a deep division among the membership of the Advisory Committee and the Security Council on the course of action to be followed. After consulting the Advisory Committee, the Secretary-General informed the representative of Egypt that while he did not question in any sense Egypt's authority to deploy its troops as it saw fit on its own territory, the deployment of Egyptian troops in areas where UNEF troops were stationed might have very serious implications for UNEF and its continued presence in the area.

In the mean time, the Egyptian Foreign Minister in Cairo summoned representatives of nations with troops in UNEF to inform them that UNEF had terminated its tasks in Egypt and the Gaza Strip and must depart forthwith. The Governments of India and Yugoslavia decided that, whatever the decision of the Secretary-General, they would withdraw their contingents from UNEF. The same day, 18 May, Egyptian soldiers prevented UNEF troops from entering their posts.

While these activities were taking place, the Secretary-General raised with the Israeli Government the question of stationing UNEF on the Israeli side of the Line, thus maintaining the buffer, but this was declared entirely unacceptable to Israel. Shortly thereafter, the Permanent Representative of Egypt delivered a message to the Secretary-General stating his Government's decision to terminate UNEF's presence in the territory of Egypt and the Gaza Strip and requesting steps for withdrawal as soon as possible. The Secretary-General informed contributing countries he would report to the General Assembly and the Security Council about the events, stating it was up to Member countries to decide whether the competent organs should or could take up the matter and pursue it accordingly. He then informed Egypt that the request would be complied with, while indicating his serious misgivings. UNEF's Commander was instructed to take the necessary action for withdrawal to begin on 19 May and end in the last days of June.

During two tense days from 16 to 18 May 1967, the Secretary-General did all he could to persuade Egypt not to request the withdrawal of UNEF and to persuade Israel to accept the Force on its side of the border. But neither Government agreed to co-operate. In such circumstances, U Thant could have brought the matter before the Security Council by invoking Article 99 of the Charter, but he chose not to do so because he knew that with the United States and the Soviet Union firmly on opposing sides of the question, no action could be taken by the Council.

The fundamental fact is that United Nations peace-keeping operations are based on the principle of consent. To maintain UNEF in Egypt against the will of the Egyptian Government, even if it had been possible to do so, which was not the case, would have created a dangerous precedent which would have deterred potential host Governments from accepting future United Nations peace-keeping operations on their soil.

In the case of UNEF, its withdrawal would not have, in itself, necessarily led to war in the area. Following an appeal by the Secretary-General, the Government of Israel made it known to U Thant that it would exercise restraint but would consider a resumption of terrorist activities along the borders, or the closure of the Strait of Tiran to Israeli shipping, as *casus belli*. Immediately after the withdrawal of UNEF, U Thant increased the number of UNTSO observers of the Egypt-Israel Mixed Armistice Commission to provide a United Nations presence along the Armistice Demarcation Line, and he arranged to visit Cairo on 22 May to discuss with the Egyptian Government possible security arrangements along the Egyptian-Israeli borders. However, just before he arrived in Cairo, President Nasser announced the closure of the Strait of Tiran. With this decision the die was cast, and, on 5 June, full-fledged war erupted.

Some UNEF units which were awaiting repatriation were caught up in the fighting in Gaza, and 15 United Nations troops were killed. All military personnel had gone by 13 June, except for the Force Commander and a small group of staff officers who left on 17 June.

UNEF is a telling example of the importance of United Nations peace-keeping forces and their limitations. Its establishment in October 1956 put an end to a destructive war and, for more than 10 years, it effectively maintained peace in one of the most sensitive areas of the

Middle East. But in the absence of a complementary peace-making effort, the root cause of the conflict between Egypt and Israel remained unresolved. Moreover, because Israel refused to accept UNEF on its territory, the Force had to be deployed only on the Egyptian side of the border, and thus its functioning was entirely contingent upon the consent of Egypt as the host country. Once that consent was withdrawn, its operation could no longer be maintained.

Chapter IV

Second UN Emergency Force

A. Background

The situation in the Suez Canal sector and on the Golan Heights from June 1967 until October 1973 is described in the chapter on UNTSO, which had set up cease-fire observation operations in those areas *(see chapter II above)*.

On 6 October 1973, in a surprise move, Egyptian forces crossed the Canal and soon advanced beyond the UNTSO observation posts on its eastern bank, while, in a co-ordinated move, Syrian troops simultaneously attacked the Israeli positions on the Golan Heights. By 9 October, following a request by Egypt acceded to by the Security Council, United Nations observation posts on both sides of the Canal were closed and the observers withdrawn.

The Security Council met from 8 to 12 October to consider the conflict and the overall situation, but, because of the opposing positions of the major Powers, could not reach a decision. Meanwhile war raged on. By 21 October, the situation had become critical; an Israeli armoured column had crossed the Canal where it was engaging Egyptian forces, and the Egyptian Third Army on the east bank was about to be cut off. The Soviet Union and the United States jointly requested an urgent meeting of the Security Council. On 22 October, the Council, on a proposal submitted jointly by the two major Powers, adopted resolution 338(1973) which called for a cease-fire and a start to implementing resolution 242(1967). The cease-fire call was confirmed in a further resolution (339(1973)) on 23 October, and the Secretary-General was requested to dispatch United Nations observers immediately.

Fighting continued, however, and President Anwar Sadat of Egypt issued direct appeals to the Soviet Union and the United States, requesting them to send American and Soviet troops to the area to enforce the cease-fire. The United States Government was opposed to the request, but the USSR agreed. The two major Powers, in disagreement after their joint cease-fire initiative, were suddenly on a collision course, each threatening military action. It was probably the most dangerous situation confronting the world since the Cuban missile crisis of October 1962.

At the request of Egypt, the Security Council was convened again on 24 October. The non-aligned members of the Council, in close cooperation with the Secretary-General, worked out a resolution calling for an increase in UNTSO observers in the area and the establishment of a new United Nations peace-keeping force, which became the second United Nations Emergency Force (UNEF II). The establishment and dispatch of the new peace-keeping operation effectively brought the crisis to an end.

Establishment

On 25 October 1973, on a proposal by Guinea, India, Indonesia, Kenya, Panama, Peru, the Sudan and Yugoslavia, the Security Council adopted resolution 340(1973), by which it demanded that immediate and complete cease-fire be observed and that the parties return to the positions occupied by them at 1650 hours GMT on 22 October 1973. The Council also requested the Secretary-General, as an immediate step, to increase the number of United Nations military observers on both sides, and decided to set up immediately under its authority a United Nations Emergency Force to be composed of personnel drawn from United Nations Member States except the permanent members of the Security Council. It requested the Secretary-General to report within 24 hours on the steps taken to that effect.

Immediately after the adoption of the resolution, the Secretary-General addressed a letter to the President of the Security Council,[45] indicating that he would deliver the requested report within the time-limit set by the Council. In the mean time, as an urgent measure and in order that the Emergency Force might reach the area of conflict as soon as possible, he proposed to arrange for units of the Austrian, Finnish and Swedish contingents serving with the United Nations Peace-keeping Force in Cyprus (UNFICYP) to proceed immediately to Egypt. He also proposed to appoint Major-General (later Lieutenant-General) Ensio P.H. Siilasvuo, of Finland, the Chief of Staff of UNTSO, as interim Commander of the new Force and to ask him to set up a provisional headquarters in Cairo with personnel from UNTSO.

The Secretary-General requested the Council President to let him know urgently whether the proposal was acceptable to the members of the Council, adding that the proposed steps would be without prejudice to the more detailed and comprehensive report on the Emergency Force which he would submit to the Council on the next day. The President, after informally consulting the members of the Council, conveyed the Council's agreement to the Secretary-General on the same evening. This procedure would henceforth be used frequently by the Secretary-General to get the Security Council's consent when measures needed to be taken urgently.

Guidelines for UNEF II

The Secretary-General's report requested by the Council set forth proposals regarding the guidelines for the functioning of the Force as well as a plan of action for the initial stages of the operation.[46]

The proposed principles and guidelines for the Emergency Force were as follows:

(a) Three essential conditions must be met for the Force to be effective. Firstly, it must have at all times the full confidence and backing of the Security Council. Secondly, it must operate with the full co-operation of the parties concerned. Thirdly, it must be able to function as an integrated and efficient military unit.

(b) The Force would be under the command of the United Nations, vested in the Secretary-General, under the authority of the Security Council. The command in the field would be exercised by a Force Commander appointed by the Secretary-General with the Council's consent. The Commander would be responsible to the Secretary-General. The Secretary-General would keep the Security Council fully informed of developments relating to the functioning of the Force. All matters which could affect the nature or the continued effective functioning of the Force would be referred to the Council for its decision.

(c) The Force must enjoy the freedom of movement and communication and other facilities necessary for the performance of its tasks. The Force and its personnel should be granted all relevant privileges and immunities provided for by the Convention on the Privileges and Immunities of the United Nations. The Force should operate at all times separately from the armed forces of the parties concerned. Consequently, separate quarters and, wherever desirable and feasible, buffer zones would have to be arranged with the co-operation of the parties. Appropriate agreements on the status of the Force would also have to be concluded with the parties.

(d) The Force would be composed of a number of contingents to be provided by selected countries, upon the request of the Secretary-General. The contingents would be selected in consultation with the

Security Council and with the parties concerned, bearing in mind the accepted principle of equitable geographical representation.

(e) The Force would be provided with weapons of a defensive character only. It would not use force except in self-defence. Self-defence would include resistance to attempts by forceful means to prevent it from discharging its duties under the Security Council's mandate. The Force would proceed on the assumption that the parties to the conflict would take all the necessary steps for compliance with the Council's decisions.

(f) In performing its functions, the Force would act with complete impartiality and would avoid actions which could prejudice the rights, claims or positions of the parties concerned.

(g) The costs of the Force would be considered as expenses of the Organization to be borne by the Members, as apportioned by the General Assembly.

In the same report, the Secretary-General set forth certain urgent steps to be taken. In order that UNEF II might fulfil the responsibilities entrusted to it, it was considered necessary that the Force should have a total strength in the order of 7,000. The Force would initially be stationed in the area for a period of six months, subject to extension.

The Secretary-General engaged in the necessary consultations with a number of Governments, in addition to Austria, Finland and Sweden, regarding provision of contingents of suitable size for the Force at the earliest possible time. In addition to his requests to countries to provide contingents for the Force, the Secretary-General proposed to seek logistic support as necessary from a number of other countries, which might include the permanent members of the Security Council.

Finally, the Secretary-General stated that, while there were many unknown factors, the best possible preliminary estimate of cost, based upon past experience and practice, was approximately $30 million for the Force for a six-month period.

This report was approved by the Security Council on 27 October (resolution 341(1973)). In accordance with the Secretary-General's recommendations, the Council set up the new Force—for an initial period of six months, subject to extension.

Composition and strength of the Force

UNEF II had already begun its operations on the basis of interim arrangements approved by the Security Council. On the morning of 26

October, General Siilasvuo and his group of UNTSO military observers set up temporary headquarters in Cairo using UNTSO's liaison office. During the same afternoon, advance elements of Austrian, Finnish and Swedish troops arrived from Cyprus and were immediately deployed along the front line. They were joined a few days later by an Irish company. The four contingents were quickly reinforced, and their presence and activities effectively defused a highly explosive situation.

Having taken these emergency measures, the Secretary-General had now to secure other contingents and build up the Force to its authorized level of 7,000 all ranks. In accordance with the guidelines approved by the Security Council, the Force was to be composed of contingents from countries selected by the Secretary-General, in consultation with the parties and the Security Council, bearing in mind the principle of equitable geographical representation.

The question of the composition of the Force gave rise to some difficulties during the consultations with the Security Council. In view of the need to set up a working force without delay, the Secretary-General wanted to secure contingents from countries that could provide the required troops at short notice. In particular, he had planned to ask Canada to supply the logistics component, since it was, aside from the major Powers, one of the few countries which could readily do so. But the Soviet Union insisted that a Warsaw Pact country should be included in the new Force if a North Atlantic Treaty Organization member was. After a lengthy debate held in closed session, the Security Council decided that the Secretary-General should consult with Ghana (African regional group), Indonesia and Nepal (Asian regional group), Panama and Peru (Latin American regional group), Poland (Eastern European regional group) and Canada (Western European and other States group)—the two last-mentioned having particular responsibility for logistic support.

In accordance with this decision, the Secretary-General held urgent consultations with the various Governments concerned with a view to obtaining the required personnel and equipment and working out acceptable administrative and financial arrangements. As a result of these contacts, in addition to Austria, Finland, Ireland and Sweden, whose troops had already arrived, Canada, Ghana, Indonesia, Nepal, Panama, Peru, Poland and Senegal were asked to provide contingents.

The Secretary-General had planned to set a ceiling of 600 for each contingent. However, in view of the complexity of the logistical problems and the decision of the Security Council to divide responsibilities in this regard between Canada and Poland, whose respective military establishments were differently organized and had different equipment and weapons, the strength of the logistical support elements had to be considerably increased.

The strength of the Canadian and Polish logistics components and the division of responsibilities between them were the subject of lengthy negotiations between the military representatives of those two countries and experts from the Secretariat. After more than two weeks of such discussions, an understanding was reached.[47] The logistics support system was to be composed of a Polish road transport unit including a maintenance element, and a Canadian service unit consisting of a supply company, a maintenance company, a movement control unit and a postal detachment. In addition, Canada would provide an aviation unit and Poland a medical unit subject to the availability of a suitable building. The Canadian contingent would have a total strength of about 1,000 and the Polish contingent about 800.

While these negotiations were going on, General Siilasvuo was pressing for the early arrival of the logistics units. He indicated that because of the difficulty of getting local supplies, it was important that the logistics facilities be set up before the arrival of additional contingents. In light of this recommendation, it was decided that the Austrian, Finnish, Irish and Swedish units which had arrived in the area at the beginning of the operation should be brought up to battalion strength as soon as possible, and operate with vehicles, stores and equipment borrowed from UNFICYP and from UNTSO.

By mid-November, advance parties of the Canadian and Polish contingents had arrived in the area and they were soon followed by the main bodies of those contingents. By the end of November, the logistics components were well established and the other contingents of UNEF II began to arrive in the area at a steady rate. By 20 February 1974, the strength of UNEF II had reached the authorized level of 7,000 (actually, 6,973). It included contingents from 12 countries: Austria (604), Canada (1,097), Finland (637), Ghana (499), Indonesia (550), Ireland (271), Nepal (571), Panama (406), Peru (497), Poland (822), Senegal (399), Sweden (620).

From February until May 1974, the strength of UNEF II was slightly decreased (to 6,645), mainly because of some reduction of the Finnish, Peruvian and Swedish contingents. In May, the Irish contingent was withdrawn at the request of its Government. Following the adoption of Security Council resolution 350(1974) of 31 May 1974 on the establishment of the United Nations Disengagement Observer Force (UNDOF), and the approval by the Council of interim arrangements proposed by the Secretary-General to give effect to that resolution, the Austrian and Peruvian contingents and elements of the Canadian and Polish logistics contingents (approximately 1,050 troops in all) were transferred from UNEF II to UNDOF in Syria. As a result, the total strength of UNEF II decreased to 5,079 in June 1974. It was brought up to 5,527 at the end of July with the arrival of additional Canadian and Polish personnel.

The Nepalese contingent was withdrawn beginning in August 1974 and the Panamanian contingent in November 1974. The total strength of UNEF II, with contingents from seven countries, was progressively reduced to 3,987 by October 1975.

On 17 October 1975,[48] the Secretary-General reported to the Security Council that, owing to the more extensive responsibilities entrusted to UNEF II under an Agreement between Egypt and Israel signed at Geneva on 4 September 1975 and the large increase in the areas of operation, additional military personnel would be needed to enable the Force to execute its new functions adequately. He proposed accordingly to reinforce each non-logistic contingent by one company (an increase of some 750 all ranks) and the Polish and Canadian logistics contingents by 50 and 36 men, respectively. He also proposed to reinforce the air unit by additional aircraft and helicopters. In accordance with the Secretary-General's request, Finland, Ghana, Indonesia and Sweden each agreed to supply an additional rifle company while Canada and Poland provided additional personnel for logistic support. After consulting the Security Council in May 1976,[49] the Secretary-General accepted the offer of the Government of Australia to supply four helicopters with their crews and supporting personnel (45 men) to UNEF II.

The Senegalese contingent was withdrawn in May and June 1976. In a report of 18 October 1976,[50] the Secretary-General noted that in view of the satisfactory results in operational arrangements in the current circumstances, and in the interest of economy, there was for the time being no intention to provide for the replacement of the Senegalese contingent unless a change in the situation should make it necessary. Upon the withdrawal of the Senegalese contingent, the total strength of UNEF II was reduced to 4,174. It remained more or less at that level during the next three years. At the time of its withdrawal in July 1979, UNEF II had 4,031 personnel, and its various contingents were: Australia (46), Canada (844), Finland (522), Ghana (595), Indonesia (510), Poland (923), Sweden (591). Of this total, 99 all ranks were assigned to UNEF II headquarters. The international civilian supporting staff of that headquarters numbered 160. In addition to the above, UNEF II was assisted by 120 military observers from UNTSO.

Mandate renewals

The mandate of UNEF II which was originally approved for six months, until 24 April 1974, was subsequently renewed eight times. Each time, as the date of expiry of the mandate approached, the Secretary-General submitted a report to the Security Council on the activities of the Force during the period of the mandate. In each of those reports, the Secretary-General expressed the view that the continued presence of UNEF II in the area was essential, and he recommended, after consultations with the parties, that its mandate be extended for a further period. In each case, the Council took note of the Secretary-General's report and decided to extend the mandate of the Force accordingly. Thus the mandate of UNEF II was extended for six months in April 1974 (resolution 346(1974)), for another six months in October (resolution 362(1974)), for three months in April 1975 (resolution 368(1975)), another three months in July (resolution 371(1975)), and for one year in October 1975 (resolution 378(1975)), in October 1976 (resolution 396(1976)) and again in October 1977 (resolution 416(1977)). In October 1978, the mandate of UNEF II was extended a last time for nine months, until 24 July 1979 (resolution 438(1978)).

The discussions and decisions of the Security Council on the extension of the mandate naturally reflected the situation on the ground and the status of the negotiations undertaken for the disengagement of the forces in the area. Following the conclusion of the first disengagement agreement, in January 1974, both sides readily agreed to have the mandate extended for a further period of six months beyond 24 April 1974. But in April and July 1975, when negotiations aimed at the second disengagement of forces were deadlocked, Egypt declined to extend the mandate of the Force for more than three months and, in fact, consented to the extension in July 1975 only after a special appeal by the Security Council. In contrast, when the September 1975 disengagement agreement was finally concluded, both parties wanted the period of extension to be expanded to one year, and the Security Council so agreed. In October 1978, the Soviet Union, which was opposed to the Camp David accords concluded earlier that year, opposed a further extension for one year, and the Security Council finally settled for an extension period of nine months. In July 1979, after the signing of the peace treaty between Egypt and Israel, which had entered into force on 25 April 1979, the Council was unable to extend the mandate of UNEF II and decided to let it lapse.

In this connection, in his report to the Security Council of 19 July 1979,[51] the Secretary-General noted that the original context in which UNEF II had been created and in which it had previously functioned had basically changed during the past nine months. While the Governments of Egypt and Israel had both expressed themselves in favour of an extension of the mandate of UNEF II , the Soviet Union had expressed opposition to such a course. In this regard, the Secretary-General recalled that, according to the guidelines approved by the Security Council in October 1973, all matters which might affect the nature or the continued effective functioning of the Force would be referred to the Council for its decision. The Secretary-General added that whatever decisions the Council might reach, he would be ready to make the necessary arrangements.

The Security Council did not extend the mandate of UNEF II, which lapsed on 24 July 1979.

UNEF command

General Siilasvuo, who had commanded UNEF II on an interim basis during its initial period, was appointed UNEF Commander on 12 November 1973 by the Secretary-General, with the consent of the Security Council. In August 1975, he was assigned to the new post of Chief Co-ordinator of the United Nations Peace-keeping Missions in the Middle East and was replaced as UNEF Commander by Major-General (later Lieutenant-General) Bengt Liljestrand of Sweden, who held the post until 1 December 1976. Major-General Rais Abin of Indonesia, who became Acting Force Commander on that date, was appointed UNEF Commander on 1 January 1977 and held the post until the withdrawal of the Force in 1979.

Status of the Force

In accordance with established practice, the United Nations sought to work out an agreement on the status of the Force with Egypt as the host country and also with Israel as the other party concerned. The Office of Legal Affairs of the Secretariat engaged in negotiations to this end with both countries' Permanent Missions to the United Nations.

While no special agreement could be drawn up, it was agreed that as a practical arrangement the parties would be guided by the provision of the status of the Force agreement for UNEF I as well as by the Convention on the Privileges and Immunities of the United Nations.

With this understanding, the Force functioned smoothly and effectively. There were, of course, a number of organizational, operational and administrative problems. One of the main difficulties concerned the question of freedom of movement. The Israeli Government had opposed the inclusion in UNEF II of contingents from Ghana, Indonesia, Poland and Senegal on the grounds that these countries had no diplomatic relations with Israel, and it refused to extend to the personnel of their contingents freedom of movement in the areas it controlled.

The Secretary-General strongly protested against these restrictions for practical reasons and as a matter of principle. He took the position that UNEF II must function as an integrated and efficient military unit and that no differentiation should be made regarding the United Nations status of the various contingents. But despite his efforts and those of the Force Commander, the Israeli authorities maintained the restrictions, and the contingents affected had to be deployed within the United Nations buffer zones or in the Egyptian-controlled areas. The restrictions on the freedom of movement were also applied to Soviet observers attached to UNEF II.

B. Activities of the Force

The terms of reference of UNEF II were to supervise the implementation of Security Council resolution 340(1973), which demanded that immediate and complete cease-fire be observed and that the parties return to the positions they had occupied at 1630 hours GMT on 22 October 1973. The Force would use its best efforts to prevent a recurrence of the fighting, and in the fulfilment of its tasks it would have the co-operation of the military observers of UNTSO. UNEF II was also to co-operate with the International Committee of the Red Cross in its humanitarian endeavours in the area.

These terms of reference,[52] which were approved by the Security Council on 27 October, remained unchanged during UNEF's entire mandate, but within this general framework the activities of the Force varied considerably over the years in the light of prevailing circumstances and of the agreements reached between the parties.

In the light of changing developments, the activities of UNEF II may be divided into four main phases.

First phase: October 1973–January 1974

Following the establishment of UNEF II, its immediate objective was to stop the fighting and prevent all movement forward of the troops on both sides. Urgent measures also had to be taken to provide Suez city and the Egyptian Third Army trapped on the east bank of the Canal with non-military supplies.

Troops from Austria, Finland, Sweden and, later, Ireland were dispatched to the front line as soon as they arrived. They interposed themselves whenever possible between the forward positions of the opposing forces. Observation posts and check-points were set up and patrols undertaken, with the assistance of UNTSO observers, in sensitive areas. These activities were carried out in close liaison with the parties concerned. With these measures, the situation was stabilized, the cease-fire was generally observed, and there were only a few incidents, which were resolved with the assistance of UNEF II.

A meeting between high-level military representatives of Egypt and Israel took place in the presence of UNEF representatives on 27 October 1973 at kilometre-marker 109 on the Cairo–Suez road to discuss the observance of the cease-fire demanded by the Security Council, as well as various humanitarian questions. At this meeting, preliminary arrangements were also agreed upon for the dispatch of non-military supplies to the town of Suez and the Egyptian Third Army. In accordance with these arrangements, convoys of lorries driven by UNEF II personnel were organized under the supervision of the Force and the International Committee of the Red Cross (ICRC) to bring supplies of a non-military nature through Israeli-held territory to Suez, and then to the Egyptian Third Army across the Canal.

These priority tasks having been met, UNEF II turned to the Security Council's demand for the return of the forces of both parties to the positions they had occupied on 22 October 1973. More meetings were held at kilometre-marker 109 to discuss this matter, together with possible mutual disengagement and the establishment of buffer zones to be manned by UNEF II.

In the mean time, the United States Secretary of State, Henry A. Kissinger, during visits to Egypt and Israel, succeeded in working out a preliminary agreement between the two countries for the implementation of Council resolutions 338 (1973) and 339 (1973). He transmitted it on 9 November[53] to Secretary-General Kurt Waldheim, who immediately instructed General Siilasvuo to take the necessary measures and to make available his good offices, as appropriate, for carrying out the terms of that agreement. On 11 November, at kilometre-marker 101 on the Cairo–Suez road, the new site for meetings, the agreement was signed by Major-General Mohamed El-Gamasy for Egypt and by Major-General Aharon Yaariv for Israel. It was also signed by General Siilasvuo on behalf of the United Nations.

The agreement, which was to enter into force immediately, contained the following six points:

(1) Egypt and Israel agreed to observe scrupulously the cease-fire called for by the Security Council;

(2) both sides agreed that discussions between them would begin immediately to settle the question of the return to the 22 October positions;

(3) the town of Suez would receive daily supplies of food, water and medicine and all wounded civilians in the town would be evacuated;

(4) there would be no impediment to the movement of non-military supplies to the east bank;

(5) the Israeli check-points on the Cairo–Suez road would be replaced by United Nations check-points; and

(6) as soon as the United Nations check-points were established on that road, there would be an exchange of all prisoners of war, including wounded.

Immediately after the signing of this agreement, the parties started discussions under the auspices of General Siilasvuo on the modalities of its implementation. These discussions continued sporadically until January 1974. Except for the provision on the return to the 22 October positions, the agreement was implemented without much difficulty.

On the morning of 15 November, the Israeli personnel at the checkpoints on the Cairo–Suez road were replaced by UNEF II personnel. Convoys of non-military supplies plied smoothly to and from Suez. As these convoys had to be driven by UNEF II personnel, some 100 military drivers were supplied by the Governments of Austria, Finland and Sweden at very short notice at the request of the Secretary-General. The exchange of prisoners of war took place in mid-November with aircraft made available without cost by the Swiss Government to the International Committee of the Red Cross.

But the most important clause, which concerned the return to the 22 October positions and the separation of the opposing forces under United Nations auspices, remained unresolved despite General Siilasvuo's efforts. On 29 November, Egypt broke off the negotiations, a decision which inevitably created a heightening of tension in the area. However, thanks to the presence of UNEF II, the cease-fire continued to hold.

Until mid-November, the operations were carried out by the Austrian, Finnish, Irish and Swedish battalions. After that date, the Canadian and Polish logistics components started to arrive. These were followed by other contingents. By mid-January 1974, 10 contingents were at hand. These contingents were deployed as follows:[54]

— The Swedish battalion had established its headquarters in Ismailia and was deployed in the northern sector, both east and west of the Suez Canal, north of the town. The battalion provided the Force Reserve and drivers for the UNEF II convoys carrying non-military supplies to the Egyptian troops on the east bank of the Canal.

— The Austrian battalion had its headquarters in Ismailia and was deployed south of that town, west of the Canal. The battalion also provided drivers for the UNEF II convoys.

— The Finnish battalion had its headquarters in Suez city, and was deployed south of the Cairo–Suez road, including the Suez city and Adabiya areas. The battalion supervised the UNEF II convoys, as well as the supply convoys for Suez city.

— The Irish battalion, with headquarters in Rabah, was deployed in the northern sector east of the Suez Canal in the Qantara area.

— The Peruvian battalion, with headquarters in Rabah, was carrying out reconnaissance of its future positions, which would be located in the central sector east of the Suez Canal, south of the Irish battalion's area of responsibility.

The Panamanian battalion, also with headquarters in Rabah, was carrying out reconnaissance of its future positions, which would be located in the southern sector east of the Suez Canal, south of the Peruvian battalion's area of responsibility.

— The Indonesian battalion was to be deployed west of the Canal with base camp at Ismailia.

— The Senegalese battalion had not yet arrived except for an advance party which was carrying out reconnaissance for future operational assignment.

— The Canadian logistic support unit, with base camp in Cairo, provided supply, maintenance, communications and postal services throughout the mission area.

— The Polish logistic support unit, with base camp in Cairo, provided drivers for UNEF II transport and was carrying out reconnaissance in preparation for the establishment of the UNEF II field hospital.

The headquarters of UNEF II, with an international staff on which the various contributing countries were represented, remained in Cairo.

Second phase: January 1974—October 1975

While the negotiations at kilometre-marker 101 for the return to the 22 October positions were dragging on, the United States and the Soviet Union initiated a joint effort to promote the implementation of Security Council resolution 338(1973), which called for negotiations to start between the parties concerned under appropriate auspices aimed at establishing a just and durable peace in the Middle East. This effort resulted in the convening of the Peace Conference on the Middle East at Geneva on 21 December 1973 under the auspices of the United Nations and the co-chairmanship of the two Powers. The Secretary-General was asked to serve as the convener of the Conference and to preside at the opening phase which would be held at the Foreign Minister level. The Governments of Egypt, Israel and Jordan accepted to attend, but Syria refused and the Palestine Liberation Organization (PLO) was not invited.

The Conference, which discussed the disengagement of forces in the Egypt-Israel sector, as well as a comprehensive settlement of the Middle East problem, was inconclusive and adjourned on 22 December 1973 after three meetings. Before adjourning, it decided to continue to work through the setting up of a Military Working Group, which would start discussing forthwith the question of disengagement of forces. The Working Group was composed of the military representatives of Egypt and Israel and the Commander of UNEF II as Chairman.

During the first half of January 1974, the United States Secretary of State undertook a new mediation effort. In negotiating separately with the Government of Egypt and Israel, in what was known as his "shuttle diplomacy", he worked out an agreement on the disengagement and separation of their military forces. This agreement was signed on 18 January 1974 by the military representatives of Egypt and Israel, and by General Siilasvuo as witness, within the framework of the Military Working Group of the Geneva Peace Conference at a meeting held at kilometre-marker 101 on the Cairo–Suez road. The agreement provided for the deployment of Egyptian forces on the eastern side of the Canal, west of a line designated on the map annexed to the agreement (the line ran parallel to the Canal, about 10 kilometres west of it), the deployment of Israeli forces east of another line, the establishment of a zone of disengagement manned by UNEF II, and areas of limited forces and armament on both sides of that zone.

In subsequent meetings held at kilometre-marker 101 under the chairmanship of General Siilasvuo, the military representatives of

Egypt and Israel worked out a detailed procedure for the implementation of the agreement.

In accordance with this procedure, the disengagement operation began on 25 January. The operation proceeded by phases. At each phase, Israeli forces withdrew from a designated area after handing it over to UNEF II, and UNEF II held that area for a few hours before turning it over to the Egyptian forces. During the entire disengagement process, UNEF II interposed between the forces of the two sides by establishing temporary buffer zones. UNEF II was also responsible for the survey and marking of the lines of disengagement, which was carried out by UNTSO military observers under UNEF II supervision, with the assistance of Egyptian and Israeli army surveyors for their respective sides. The whole operation was carried out smoothly according to plan and was completed by 4 March 1974.[55]

After the completion of the operation, most non-logistic contingents were deployed in or near the newly established zone of disengagement. By mid-March, UNEF II had a total strength of 6,814 all ranks. The various contingents were deployed as follows:[56]

— The Irish battalion had its base camp at Rabah. It manned eight outposts in the zone of disengagement from the Mediterranean Sea to a line immediately south of Qantara.

— The Peruvian battalion had its base camp at Rabah. It manned 10 outposts in the zone of disengagement, in a sector from the southern limit of the Irish battalion to a line directly east of Ismailia.

— The Swedish battalion had its base camp at Ismailia. It manned 14 outposts in the zone of disengagement, in a sector from the southern limit of the Peruvian battalion to a line east of Déversoir.

— The Indonesian battalion had its base camp at Ismailia. It manned 14 outposts in the zone of disengagement, in a sector from the southern limit of the Swedish battalion to a line east of Kabrit.

— The Senegalese battalion had its base camp at Suez city. It manned 12 outposts in the zone of disengagement, in a sector from the southern limit of the Indonesian battalion to a line east of a point 10 kilometres north of Suez.

— The Finnish battalion had its base camp at Suez city. It manned 15 outposts in the zone of disengagement, in a sector from the southern limit of the Senegalese battalion to the Gulf of Suez.

The headquarters of UNEF II was moved to Ismailia in August 1974.

As a result of this disengagement, the situation in the Egypt-Israel sector became much more stable. The main task of UNEF II was the manning and control of the zone of disengagement and, to do this, it established static check-points and observation posts and conducted mobile patrols. It also carried out, with the assistance of UNTSO observers, weekly and later bi-weekly inspections of the areas of limited forces and armament (30 kilometre zone), as well as inspections of other areas agreed by the parties. The Force Commander continued the practice of separate meetings with the military authorities of Egypt and Israel concerning the implementation of the Force's terms of reference and the inspections carried out by UNEF II, and he continued to lend his assistance and good offices in cases where one of the parties raised questions concerning the observance of the agreed limitations of forces and armament.

In addition, UNEF II continued to co-operate with the International Committee of the Red Cross on humanitarian matters. It played an important part in assisting in exchanges of prisoners of war and the transfer of civilians from one side to the other. UNEF II also undertook an operation, which was completed in July 1974, for the search for the remains of soldiers killed during the October 1973 war.

In view of the quiet that prevailed in the area, it was possible to reduce gradually the strength of UNEF II. The Irish Government decided to withdraw its troops in May 1974. In June, following the establishment of the United Nations Disengagement Observer Force on the Golan Heights, the Security Council decided, upon the recommendation of the Secretary-General, to transfer the Austrian and Peruvian contingents and elements of the Canadian and Polish logistics components to the new UNDOF. The Nepalese contingent, which had been made available to the United Nations for six months only, was repatriated in August and September 1974. Finally, the Panamanian contingent was withdrawn in November 1974. As a result of these and later developments, the total strength of UNEF II decreased to 5,079 in June 1974, 4,029 in April 1975 and 3,987 in October 1975.

Third phase: November 1975–May 1979

In September 1975, the United States Secretary of State, through further indirect negotiations, succeeded in obtaining the agreement of Egypt and Israel for a second disengagement of their forces in the Sinai. The new agreement[57] provided for the redeployment of Israeli forces east of lines designated in a map annexed to the agreement, the redeployment of the Egyptian forces westwards and the establishment of buffer zones controlled by UNEF II. It also provided that there would be no military forces in the southern areas of Ras Sudar and Abu Rudeis. On both sides of the buffer zones, two areas of limited forces and armament were to be set up where the number of military personnel should be limited to 8,000 and the armament to 75 tanks and 72 artillery pieces, including heavy mortars.

Finally, the agreement set up a joint commission, under the aegis of the United Nations Chief Co-ordinator of the United Nations Peace-keeping Missions in the Middle East, to consider any problems arising from the agreement and to assist UNEF II in the execution of its mandate. Attached to the agreement was a United States plan to establish an early warning system in the area of the Giddi and Mitla Passes, consisting of three watch stations set up by the United States and of two surveillance stations, one operated by Egyptian personnel and the other by Israeli personnel.

The Secretary-General submitted reports to the Security Council on this matter in September 1975.[58] He advised the Council that the new agreement between Egypt and Israel had been initialled by the parties on 1 September and would be signed by them in Geneva on 4 September. Following the signing, the representatives of Egypt and Israel were, within five days, to begin preparation of a detailed protocol for the implementation of the basic agreement in the Military Working Group of the Geneva Peace Conference on the Middle East. In accordance with previous practice, the Secretary-General instructed General Siilasvuo, the Chief Co-ordinator, who had presided at the previous meetings of the Military Working Group, to proceed to Geneva so as to be available in the same capacity for the forthcoming meetings of the Working Group.

The Working Group, meeting under the chairmanship of General Siilasvuo, reached agreement on the protocol of the agreement, which was signed on 22 September by the representatives of the two parties and by General Siilasvuo as witness. The protocol set out a detailed procedure for the implementation of the agreement.

The responsibilities entrusted to UNEF II under the agreement of 4 September and its protocol were much more extensive than those it had had previously, and its area of operations was much larger. The Force's first task was to mark on the ground the new lines of disengagement. To carry out this work, a group of surveyors was supplied by Sweden, at the request of the Secretary-General. Work began in October 1975 and was completed in January 1976, in accordance with the timetable set out in the protocol.

In November 1975, UNEF II began its assistance to the parties for the redeployment of their forces. The first phase of the redeployment took place in the southern area and was completed on 1 December 1975.

During that period, UNEF II, through the Chief Co-ordinator, supervised the transfer of the oilfields and installations in the area. The second phase of the redeployment, which took place in the northern area, began on 12 January 1976 and was completed on 22 February. The Force monitored the redeployment of the forces of the two parties by providing buffer times for the transfer of evacuated areas to Egyptian control, occupying temporary buffer zones and manning temporary observation posts. The Force acted as a secure channel of communication and contact between the parties throughout the redeployment process.

After the completion of the redeployment operation, UNEF II carried out the long-term functions specified in the protocol. In the southern area, its task was to assure that no military or paramilitary forces of any kind, military fortifications or military installations were in the area. To perform that task, it established check-points and observation posts in accordance with the protocol and conducted patrols throughout the area, including air patrols. It also ensured the control of buffer zones in the southern area and, to this effect, it maintained permanent check-points along the buffer-zone lines. It also supervised the use of common road sections by the parties in accordance with arrangements agreed to by them and it provided escorts in those sections when necessary.

The functions of UNEF II in the buffer zone in the northern area were carried out by means of a system of check-points, observation posts and patrols by land. In the early-warning-system area, which was located in the buffer zone, UNEF II provided escorts, as required, to and from the United States watch stations and the Egyptian and Israeli surveillance stations. The Force was also entrusted with the task of ensuring the maintenance of the agreed limitations of forces and armament within the areas specified in the agreement and, to this effect, it conducted bi-weekly inspections. Those inspections were carried out by UNTSO military observers under UNEF supervision, accompanied by liaison officers of the respective parties.

The joint commission established by the disengagement agreement met in the buffer zone under the chairmanship of the United Nations Chief Co-ordinator as occasion required. The Force received a number of complaints from both parties alleging violations by the other side. Those complaints were taken up with the party concerned by the Force Commander or the Chief Co-ordinator and, in some instances, were referred to the joint commission.

The Force maintained close contact with representatives of the International Committee of the Red Cross in its humanitarian endeavours and extended its assistance in providing facilities for family reunions and student exchanges, which took place at an agreed site in the buffer zone.

All these tasks were carried out efficiently. There were few incidents and problems and, whenever they occurred, they were resolved without difficulty with the co-operation of the parties concerned.

Fourth phase: May–July 1979

The peace treaty concluded in March 1979 between Egypt and Israel as a result of negotiations conducted under the auspices of the United States, and which entered into force on 25 April, had a direct bearing on the termination of UNEF II and affected its activities during the final period.

The treaty provided that, upon completion of a phased Israeli withdrawal over three years, security arrangements on both sides of the Egyptian-Israeli border would be made with the assistance of United Nations forces and observers. Article VI stipulated that "the parties will request the United Nations to provide forces and observers to supervise the implementation of the security arrangements". The United Nations forces and observers would have been asked to perform a variety of duties, including the operation of check-points, reconnaissance patrols and observation posts along the boundaries of and within the demilitarized zone, and ensuring freedom of navigation through the Strait of Tiran. United Nations forces would also have been stationed in certain areas adjoining the demilitarized zone on the Egyptian side, and United Nations observers would have patrolled a specified area on the Israeli side of the international boundary. In an annex to the treaty, the United States undertook to organize a multinational force of equivalent strength if the United Nations were unable to monitor the forces as envisaged by the treaty.

The intention of the parties was to have UNEF II perform these tasks. However, there was strong opposition to the treaty from the PLO and many Arab States, and opposition by the Soviet Union in the Security Council. As previously stated, the Security Council decided to allow the mandate of the Force to lapse on 24 July 1979.

On 25 May 1979, in pursuance of the relevant provisions of the peace treaty, the Israeli forces withdrew from the northern Sinai to the east of El Arish and the Egyptians took over control of that area. UNEF II was not involved in this move except by permitting access of Egyptian personnel to the buffer zone and the areas of limited forces and armament and by providing escorts to the parties within these areas as the Israeli withdrawal was being carried out. During this process, UNEF II withdrew from the northern part of the buffer zone, which was handed over to the Egyptian authorities. Except in areas of the Sinai controlled by Egyptian forces, UNEF II continued to function as previously. In particular, it continued to provide a physical separation of the areas of limited forces and armament. It also provided escorts to authorized non–United Nations visitors and to personnel of the parties travelling to and from the early-warning-system stations.

After the mandate of UNEF II lapsed in July 1979, the various contingents were rapidly repatriated, except for a Swedish guard unit and limited groups of the Canadian and Polish logistics contingents which remained in the area to assist in the winding up of the Force.

UN Disengagement Observer Force

A. Background and establishment

Background

At the end of the October 1973 war, while tranquillity was restored on the Egyptian front with the deployment of the second United Nations Emergency Force (UNEF II), no new peace-keeping force was established on the Syrian front in the Golan Heights. There, fighting subsided following the cease-fire call contained in Security Council resolution 338(1973) of 22 October 1973. By that time, the Israeli forces had crossed the 1967 cease-fire lines and occupied a salient up to and including the village of Saassa on the Quneitra–Damascus road. United Nations military observers set up temporary observation posts around that salient and, with these changes, the cease-fire observation operation in the Israel-Syria sector was resumed.

However, tension remained high in the area. There was a continuous pattern of incidents in and around the buffer zone supervised by the United Nations military observers. These involved artillery, mortar and automatic-weapon fire, and overflights by Israeli and Syrian aircraft. Frequent complaints of cease-fire violations were submitted by the two parties, although cease-fires proposed from time to time by the United Nations observers resulted in temporary cessation of firing. From early March 1974 until the end of May, the situation in the sector became increasingly unstable, and firing—involving use of artillery, tanks and rockets—intensified. Against this background, the United States Secretary of State undertook a mediation mission, which resulted in the conclusion of an Agreement on Disengagement between Israeli and Syrian Forces in May 1974.

Agreement on disengagement of forces

The Secretary-General, who was kept informed of these developments, reported to the Security Council on 29 May[59] that the signing of the Agreement would take place on 31 May 1974 in the Egyptian-Israeli Military Working Group of the Geneva Peace Conference on the Middle East. He also informed the Council that he had instructed General Ensio P.H. Siilasvuo, the Commander of UNEF, to be available for the signing of the Agreement, under the aegis of the United Nations.

On 30 May, the Secretary-General transmitted to the Security Council the text of the Agreement as well as the Protocol to that Agreement which deals with the establishment of the United Nations Disengagement Observer Force (UNDOF).[60]

Under the terms of the Agreement, Israel and Syria were scrupulously to observe the cease-fire on land, sea and in the air, and refrain from all military actions against each other from the time of the signing of the document, in implementation of Security Council resolution 338(1973). It further provided that the two military forces would be separated in accordance with agreed principles, which called for the establishment of an area of separation and of two equal areas of limitation of armament and forces on both sides of the area. The detailed plan for the disengagement of forces would be worked out by the military representatives of Israel and Syria in the Military Working Group. They were to begin their work 24 hours after the signing of the Agreement and complete it within five days. Disengagement was to begin within 24 hours thereafter and be completed not later than 20 days after it had begun. The provisions of the Agreement concerning the cease-fire and the separation of forces were to be inspected by UNDOF personnel. All wounded prisoners of war were to be repatriated within 24 hours after signature of the Agreement, and all other prisoners upon completion of the work of the Military Working Group. The bodies of all dead soldiers held by either side would be returned for burial within 10 days. The final paragraph of the Agreement stated that it was not a peace agreement, but that it was a step towards a just and durable peace on the basis of Security Council resolution 338(1973).

Protocol on UNDOF

According to the Protocol to the Agreement, Israel and Syria agreed that the function of UNDOF would be to maintain the cease-fire, to see that it was strictly observed, and to supervise the Agreement and Protocol with regard to the areas of separation and limitation. In carrying out its mission, the Force was to comply with generally applicable Syrian laws and regulations and not hamper the functioning of local civil administration. It was to enjoy the freedom of movement and communication necessary for its mission and be provided with personal weapons of a defensive character to be used only in self-defence.

The strength of UNDOF was set at 1,250 men, to be selected by the Secretary-General, in consultation with the parties, from Member States of the United Nations which were not permanent members of the Security Council.

In transmitting the documents, the Secretary-General, noting that the Protocol called for the creation of a United Nations Disengagement Observer Force, indicated that he would take the necessary steps in accordance with the Protocol's provisions, if the Security Council should so decide. He intended that the proposed Force would be drawn, at least initially, from United Nations military personnel already in the area.

Establishment of UNDOF

On 30 May 1974,[61] the representative of the United States requested an urgent meeting of the Security Council to consider the situation in the Middle East, in particular the disengagement of Israeli and Syrian forces. At the meeting, the Secretary-General drew attention to his reports on this matter and said that, were the Council so to decide, he would set up UNDOF on the basis of the same general principles which had governed the establishment of UNEF II.

On 31 May, the Agreement on disengagement and the Protocol were signed at Geneva by the military representatives of Israel and Syria. Later on the same day, the Security Council adopted resolution 350(1974) by which it decided to set up UNDOF immediately, under its authority, and requested the Secretary-General to take the necessary steps.

The Force was established for an initial period of six months, subject to renewal by the Security Council. The Secretary-General was asked to keep the Council fully informed of further developments.

Secretary-General's proposal

After the adoption of the resolution, the Secretary-General presented his proposals for interim arrangements. He suggested that initially UNDOF should comprise the Austrian and Peruvian contingents from UNEF II, supported by logistical elements from Canada and Poland, also to be drawn from UNEF II, and by UNTSO military observers who were already deployed in the area (except those from permanent member countries of the Security Council). The Secretary-General also proposed to appoint, as interim Commander, Brigadier-General Gonzalo Briceño Zevallos of Peru, who was at the time commanding the northern brigade of UNEF II. The interim Commander was to be assisted by staff officers drawn from UNEF and UNTSO. The Security Council agreed to the Secretary-General's proposals.

Military Working Group

The Military Working Group met in Geneva from 31 May 1974 until 5 June under the chairmanship of General Siilasvuo to work out practical arrangements for the disengagement of forces.[62]

Military representatives of the Syrian Arab Republic joined the Group, and the representatives of the Soviet Union and the United States, as co-chairmen of the Geneva Peace Conference, also participated in the meetings.

Full agreement was reached on a disengagement plan, with a timetable for the withdrawal of Israeli forces from the area east of the 1967 cease-fire line, as well as on a map showing different phases of disengagement. The map was signed at the final meeting on 5 June.

Redeployment of Israeli forces

The disengagement plan involved not only the redeployment of Israeli forces from east of the 1967 line but also provided for the withdrawal of the Israeli forces from Quneitra and Rafid and the demilitarization of an area west of Quneitra.

The redeployment of the Israeli forces would take place in four phases. After the completion of each phase, UNDOF would carry out an inspection of the evacuated area and report its findings to the parties. The disengagement process would be completed by 26 June, and thereafter UNDOF would man the area of separation between the two forces. After verifying on that date that the agreed limitation of forces was being observed, UNDOF would carry out regular bi-weekly inspections of the 10-kilometre restricted-forces area.

In the negotiations in the Military Working Group, the two parties also agreed that both sides would repatriate all prisoners of war by 6 June, that they would co-operate with the International Committee of the Red Cross in carrying out its mandate, including the exchange of bodies, which was also to be completed by 6 June. They would make available all information and maps of minefields in their respective areas and the areas to be handed over by them.

UNDOF beginnings

On 3 June 1974, the Secretary-General, having obtained the agreement of the Government of Peru, appointed General Briceño as interim Commander of UNDOF. He arrived in Damascus from Cairo on the same day and immediately established a provisional headquarters in the premises of the Israel-Syrian Mixed Armistice Commission, assuming command over the 90 UNTSO observers detailed to UNDOF.

Later the same day, advance parties of the Austrian and Peruvian contingents arrived in the mission area. They were joined on the following days by the remainder of the two contingents and the Canadian and Polish logistic elements. Some logistic support was given by UNEF.

By 16 June, the strength of UNDOF was brought to 1,218 all ranks, near its authorized level of 1,250.

Extension of the mandate

The initial six-month mandate of UNDOF expired on 30 November 1974. Since then, the mandate has been repeatedly extended by the Security Council upon the recommendation of the Secretary-General and with the agreement of the two parties concerned.

In November 1975, Syria was reluctant to agree to a further extension because no progress had been made in the settlement of the wider Middle East problem. The Secretary-General met with President Hafez Al Assad in Damascus that month and, after extensive discussions, the President gave his agreement for the renewal of the UNDOF mandate for another period of six months, to be combined with a specific provision that the Security Council would convene, in January 1976, to hold a substantive debate on the Middle East problem, including the Palestine question, with the participation of representatives of the Palestine Liberation Organization.[63]

Extending the UNDOF mandate for a further six months, the Security Council, in resolution 381(1975) of 30 November 1975, decided to reconvene on 12 January 1976 to continue the debate on the Middle East problem, taking into account all relevant United Nations resolutions.

In May 1976, the Secretary-General again had to travel to Damascus to secure the agreement of the Syrian Government for a further extension. However, from November 1976 onwards, the two parties readily gave their agreement for further extensions. On each occasion since that date, the Security Council, in renewing UNDOF's mandate for further six-month periods, called on the parties concerned to implement resolution 338(1973) and requested the Secretary-General to submit at the end of the extension period a report on the measures taken to implement that resolution. In connection with the adoption of the resolutions on the renewal of the mandate, the President of the Security Council made complementary statements endorsing the view of the Secretary-General that, despite the prevailing quiet in the Israel-Syria sector, the situation in the Middle East as a whole would remain unstable and potentially dangerous unless real progress could be made towards a just and lasting settlement of the Middle East problem in all its aspects. The latest extension of UNDOF, approved by the Security Council in May 1985, was for a period of six months—until 30 November of the same year.

On 14 December 1981, the Israeli Government decided to apply Israeli law in the occupied Golan Heights. Syria strongly protested against this decision, and both the Security Council and the General Assembly declared that it was null and void. The Israeli decision, however, has not affected the operation of UNDOF in any significant way.

Organization of UNDOF

The organization of UNDOF is similar to that of UNEF II. The Force is under the exclusive command and control of the United Nations at all times. The Force Commander is appointed by the Secretary-General with the consent of the Security Council and is responsible to him. Following General Briceño, who was interim Commander until 15 December 1974, the command of UNDOF was assumed by Colonel (later Major-General) Hannes Philipp of Austria (December 1974–April 1979), Colonel (later Major-General) Guenther G. Greindl, also of Austria (until February 1981), Major-General Erkki R. Kaira of Finland (until June 1982), Major-General Carl-Gustav Stahl of Sweden (until May 1985) and Major-General Gustav Hägglund of Finland (since May 1985).

UNDOF was originally composed of the Austrian and Peruvian contingents and the Canadian and Polish logistic elements transferred from UNEF II. The Peruvian contingent was withdrawn in July 1975 and replaced by an Iranian contingent in August of that year. This contingent was in turn withdrawn in March 1979 and replaced by a Finnish contingent.

UNDOF in October 1985 was composed of contingents from Austria, Canada, Finland and Poland. A number of observers, detailed from UNTSO, who are not nationals of permanent members of the Security Council are included in UNDOF as an integral part of the Force. In addition, UNTSO observers assigned to the Israel-Syria Mixed Armistice Commission may assist UNDOF as occasion requires.

UNDOF strength

Within two weeks of its establishment, the total strength of UNDOF was brought to near its authorized level of about 1,250. From that time until August 1979—except for a brief period from March to August 1979 when the strength of the Force was temporarily below the authorized level as a result of the withdrawal of the Iranian battalion—the strength of UNDOF remained around that figure. In August 1979,[64] the Secretary-General informed the Security Council that, as a result of the withdrawal of UNEF II which had hitherto provided third-line logistic support to UNDOF, it had become necessary to strengthen the existing Canadian and Polish logistic units. The Security Council agreed to the proposed increase. Following consultations with the parties, the strength of UNDOF was gradually brought up to 1,331 in May 1985. As of that date, the strength and composition of UNDOF was as follows: Austria (533); Canada (226); Finland (411); Poland (153). In addition, eight UNTSO observers were assigned to the Force.

B. Activities of UNDOF

Initial deployment

Following the signing of the Agreement on disengagement, all firings ceased in the Israel-Syria sector as of 1109 hours GMT on 31 May 1974. This was confirmed by the United Nations military observers stationed in the sector. These observers, who were later incorporated into UNDOF, continued to man selected observation posts and patrol bases along the cease-fire line while the newly arrived contingents of UNDOF began deployment in the area. The Austrian and Peruvian infantry battalions set up positions between the Israeli and Syrian forces, the former in the Saassa area and the latter from Quneitra south along the cease-fire lines.

Disengagement operation

The disengagement operation began on 14 June and proceeded apace until 27 June. In accordance with the agreed plan, the operation was carried out in four phases.

During the first phase, the Israeli forces handed over to UNDOF an area of some 270 square kilometres (about 28 square kilometres in the Saassa area and about 243 square kilometres east of Lake Tiberias) in the afternoon of 14 June. The next morning, the Syrian forces commenced deploying in that area while UNDOF established a new buffer zone east of the evacuated area.

The same procedure was followed for the second phase, which took place on 18 and 19 June and covered an area of some 374 square kilometres (about 214 square kilometres east of Lake Tiberias and about 160 square kilometres north and north-west of the Saassa area), and for the third phase, which took place on 23 June and involved an area of about 132 square kilometres east and north of Quneitra.

The fourth phase took place on 24 and 25 June. During that phase, the Israeli forces evacuated the area of separation, which was taken over by UNDOF. On 25 June, after UNDOF completed its deployment, Syrian civilian administration was established in the area of separation. On 26 June, UNDOF observers inspected the areas of limited forces and armament (10-kilometre zone) on each side of the area of separation. The next day they proceeded with the inspection of the 20- and 25-kilometre zones, thus completing the implementation of the disengagement operation.

The disengagement process was marred by a serious incident during its last phase. Early on the morning of 25 June, four Austrian soldiers were killed and another wounded when their vehicle ran over a land-mine near Mount Hermon in the area of separation. From 25 to 27 June, at the request of the Syrian Government and on the basis of an agreement reached with the Israeli authorities through UNDOF headquarters, a body of 500 Syrian soldiers equipped with mine-clearing tanks carried out mine-clearing operations at various locations in the area of separation, under the close supervision of UNDOF observers.

Supervision of the Agreement

Following the completion of the disengagement operation, UNDOF undertook the delineation and marking of the lines bounding the area of separation. This task, which was carried out with the co-operation and assistance of the Israeli and Syrian forces on their respective sides, proceeded smoothly and was completed in early July 1974.

After the delineation of the area of separation, UNDOF set up a series of check-points and observation posts within that area. In addition, two base camps were established, one on the east side of the area of separation and the other on the west side. At the same time, UNDOF headquarters, which remained in Damascus, was moved from the office of the Israel-Syrian Mixed Armistice Commission to a building made available by the Syrian Government. The Quneitra communication relay station, which had been set up by UNTSO, was placed under the control of UNDOF. This set-up has remained essentially unchanged.

The Chief of Staff of UNTSO performs liaison functions in Jerusalem for UNDOF as occasion arises, normally through the Israeli senior liaison officer. At the local level, the commanders of the UNDOF contingents maintain liaison with one side or the other through liaison officers designated by the parties.

The Austrian battalion and the Polish logistic unit are currently in a base camp near Wadi Faouar, eight kilometres east of the area of separation, while the Finnish battalion and the Canadian logistic unit share a base camp near the village of Ziouani, west of that area. As of May 1985, the Austrian battalion manned 19 positions and seven outposts; the Finnish battalion, 15 positions and eight outposts—the former in the area north of the Damascus–Quneitra road and the latter south of that road. The UNTSO military observers attached to UNDOF, who operate out of Damascus on the Syrian side and Tiberias on the Israeli side, manned 11 observation posts near the area of separation.

The main function of UNDOF is to supervise the area of separation to make sure that there are no military forces within it. This is carried out by means of static positions and observation posts which are manned 24 hours a day, and by foot and mobile patrols operating along predetermined routes by day and night. Temporary outposts and additional patrols may be set up from time to time as occasion requires.

In accordance with the terms of the Agreement on disengagement, UNDOF conducts fortnightly inspections of the area of limitation of armament and forces. These inspections, which cover the 10-, 20- and 25-kilometre zones on each side of the area of separation, are carried out by United Nations military observers with the assistance of liaison officers from the parties, who accompany the inspection teams on their respective sides.

These inspections have generally proceeded smoothly with the co-operation of the parties concerned, although restrictions have occasionally been placed on the movement of the inspection teams in some localities. The findings of the inspection teams are communicated to the two parties but are not made public. When one party complains about the other party's violation of the agreement on the limitation of armament and forces, the Force Commander will try to resolve the matter through his good offices. So far, no serious problems have arisen in this connection.

Humanitarian activities

In addition to its normal peace-keeping functions, UNDOF has carried out activities of a humanitarian nature as occasion requires. At the request of the parties, UNDOF has from time to time exercised its good offices in arranging for the release and hand-over of prisoners and bodies between Israel and Syria. It has assisted the International Committee of the Red Cross (ICRC) by providing it with facilities for the hand-over of prisoners and bodies, for the exchange of parcels and mail across the area of separation, and for the transit of Druse students from the occupied Golan to attend school in Syria. Of particular note was the assistance extended to ICRC on 28 June 1984 when 297 prisoners of war, 16 civilians and the remains of 77 persons were exchanged between Israel and Syria. In 1976, UNDOF worked out arrangements, with the co-operation of the two parties, for periodic reunions of Druse families living on different sides of the line of separation. Those family reunions took place every fortnight in the village of Madj-el-Shams (Majdel Chams) in the area of separation, under the supervision of UNDOF, until February 1982, when they had to be discontinued because of the controversy arising from Israel's decision in December 1981 to apply Israeli law to the occupied Golan Heights.

Incidents and casualties

During the initial period, there were a number of serious incidents. Besides the four Austrian soldiers killed and another wounded in a mining incident on 25 June 1974, another mine explosion occurred on 20 April 1977 in which an Austrian officer was killed and an Iranian officer was wounded. Despite the mine-clearing operations undertaken by the Syrian forces in 1974, there were still many unexploded mines in and near the area of separation. The engineers of the Polish logistic unit continue to search for and defuse unexploded mines, shells and bombs in and near the area.

On 9 August 1974, a United Nations aircraft, flying from Ismailia to Damascus in the established air corridor, crashed as a result of anti-aircraft fire, north-east of the Syrian village of Ad Dimas. All nine Canadians aboard were killed.

In November 1975, there was a shooting incident in which two Syrian shepherds were killed by an Israeli patrol. There were also alleged crossings of the area of separation, resulting in one case in the death of three Israeli citizens. In November 1977, two members of the Iranian battalion came under fire from the Israeli side and both were wounded.

Whenever such incidents occurred, UNDOF sought to resolve the situation by negotiation and appropriate corrective measures. The incidents have not seriously affected the operations of the Force.

Problems affecting UNDOF

Since November 1977, there have been no major incidents. The main problems in the area arise from the presence of Syrian shepherds grazing their flocks near the line. They often cross the line, either in ignorance or because there are good grazing lands on the other side.

Another problem faced by UNDOF are the restrictions placed upon its troops by one party or the other. Because Poland has no diplomatic relations with Israel, the Israeli forces have severely restricted the movement of the Polish forces on the Israeli side of the line. The Force Commander, fully supported by the Secretary-General, has strongly protested against these restrictions on the grounds that UNDOF is an integrated unit and all its elements must enjoy freedom of movement on an equal basis. As a result of this approach, the Israeli authorities have relaxed restrictions on the Polish unit, but the situation has not been fully resolved.

Some restrictions have also been placed by both sides on the movement of the UNDOF inspection teams, which were not allowed to visit certain localities when inspecting the area of limitation of armament and forces. These restrictions have been routinely protested by the Force Commander, but they are not considered as major issues impeding the functioning of UNDOF in this field.

On the whole, the difficulties encountered by UNDOF are not of a serious nature and have not affected its smooth functioning. In each periodic report on the activities of the Force, the Secretary-General has been able to report that the situation in the Israel-Syria sector has remained quiet and that UNDOF has continued to perform its functions effectively with the co-operation of the parties.

UN Interim Force in Lebanon

A. Background and beginning

Background

Although the Lebanese civil war which had broken out in April 1975 officially ended in October 1976—after the election of President Elias Sarkis, the constitution of a new central Government and the establishment of an Arab Deterrent Force—fighting did not completely stop in southern Lebanon. When Syrian troops of the Deterrent Force deployed towards the south, the Israeli Government threatened to take stern counter-measures if they should advance beyond an imaginary east-west red line, extending south of the Zahrani River. Whether because of this threat or for some other reasons, the Syrian forces stopped short of the red line. The authority of the central Government was not restored in the south. Sporadic fighting continued in that area between the Christian militias, which were assisted by Israel, and the armed elements of the Lebanese National Movement, a loose association of a variety of Moslem and leftist parties, supported by the armed forces of the Palestine Liberation Organization (PLO). The PLO was the dominant force in southern Lebanon at the time and had established many bases in the area, from which it launched commando raids against Israel which were followed by intensive Israeli retaliation.

On 11 March 1978, a commando raid, for which the PLO claimed responsibility, took place in Israel near Tel Aviv and, according to Israeli sources, resulted in 37 deaths and 76 wounded among the Israeli population.[65] In retaliation, the Israeli forces invaded Lebanon on the night of 14/15 March, and in a few days occupied the entire region south of the Litani River except for the city of Tyre and its surrounding area.

Establishment of UNIFIL

On 15 March, the Lebanese Government submitted a strong protest to the Security Council against the Israeli invasion.[66] It stated that it was not responsible for the presence of Palestinian bases in southern

Lebanon and had no connection with the Palestinian commando operation. It said it had exerted tremendous efforts with the Palestinians
and the Arab States in order to keep matters under control, but Israeli
objections regarding the entry of the Arab Deterrent Force to the south
had prevented the accomplishment of Lebanon's desire to bring the
border area under control. The Security Council met on 17 March 1978
and on the following days to consider the Lebanese complaint.

On 19 March, on a proposal by the United States, the Security
Council adopted resolution 425(1978), by which it called for strict
respect for the territorial integrity, sovereignty and political independence of Lebanon within its internationally recognized boundaries. It
called upon Israel immediately to cease its military action against Lebanese territorial integrity and withdraw forthwith its forces from all
Lebanese territory. It also decided, "in the light of the request of the
Government of Lebanon, to establish immediately under its authority
a United Nations interim force for southern Lebanon for the purpose
of confirming the withdrawal of Israeli forces, restoring international
peace and security and assisting the Government of Lebanon in ensuring the return of its effective authority in the area, the force to be
composed of personnel drawn from Member States". The Council requested the Secretary-General to submit a report to the Council within
24 hours on the implementation of the resolution.

Terms of reference and guidelines

On the same afternoon, the Secretary-General submitted a report
to the Security Council in which he set forth the terms of reference
of the new Force, to be called the United Nations Interim Force in Lebanon (UNIFIL), the guidelines for the Force and a plan of action for its
speedy establishment.[67]

The Force was to confirm the withdrawal of Israeli forces, restore
international peace and security, and assist the Government of Lebanon in ensuring the return of its effective authority in the area. It would
establish and maintain itself in an area of operation to be defined in
the light of those tasks, and would use its best efforts to prevent the
recurrence of fighting and to ensure that its area of operation would
not be utilized for hostile activities of any kind. In the fulfilment of
its tasks, the Force would have the co-operation of the military observers of the United Nations Truce Supervision Organization (see chapter
II above), who would continue to function on the Armistice Demarcation Line (ADL) after the termination of UNIFIL's mandate.

In the first stage, the Force would confirm the withdrawal of the

Israeli forces from Lebanese territory to the international border. Once this was achieved, it would establish and maintain an area of operation to be defined in consultation with the parties concerned. It would supervise the cessation of hostilities, ensure the peaceful character of the area of operation, control movement and take all measures deemed necessary to assure the effective restoration of Lebanese sovereignty. The Secretary-General also indicated that, with a view to facilitating UNIFIL's tasks, it might be necessary to work out arrangements with Israel and Lebanon as a preliminary measure for the implementation of the Security Council resolution, and it was assumed that both parties would give their full co-operation to UNIFIL in this regard.

In working out the terms of reference of UNIFIL, the Secretary-General had wanted to define more clearly the area of operation of the Force and its relationship with the PLO. But he could not do so, as the discussions he held with the member States of the Security Council and with other Governments concerned revealed a profound disagreement among them on both subjects. As will be seen later, these two questions weighed heavily on the operations of UNIFIL.

The guidelines proposed by the Secretary-General were essentially the same as those applied to UNEF II and UNDOF *(see chapters IV and V above on both operations)*. Important decisions on the organization of UNIFIL, such as the appointment of the Force Commander or the selection of contingents, would be taken by the Secretary-General, but he would need to consult the Security Council and obtain its consent. All matters which might affect the nature or the continued effective functioning of the Force would be referred to the Council for its decision.

Particular emphasis was placed on the principles of non-use of force and non-intervention in the internal affairs of the host country. UNIFIL would not use force except in self-defence, which would include resistance to attempts by forcible means to prevent it from discharging its duties under the Council's mandate. Like any other United Nations peace-keeping operation, UNIFIL could not and must not take on responsibilities which fell under the Government of the country in which it was operating. Those responsibilities must be exercised by the competent Lebanese authorities, and it was assumed that the Lebanese Government would take the necessary measures to co-operate with UNIFIL in this regard.

In his report, the Secretary-General also proposed certain measures for the speedy establishment of the Force. Lieutenant-General Ensio P.H. Siilasvuo, Chief Co-ordinator of the United Nations Peace-keeping Missions in the Middle East, would be instructed to contact immediately the Governments of Israel and Lebanon and initiate meetings with their representatives for the purpose of reaching agreement on the modalities of the withdrawal of the Israeli forces and the establishment of a United Nations area of operation. Major-General (later Lieutenant-General) E.A. Erskine of Ghana, the Chief of Staff of UNTSO, would be appointed immediately as interim Commander and, pending the arrival of the first contingents of the Force, would perform his tasks with the assistance of a group of UNTSO military observers. At the same time, urgent measures would be taken for the early arrival in the area of contingents of the Force. The Secretary-General proposed that the Force have a total strength of the order of 4,000 and that it be stationed initially in the area for six months. The best possible preliminary cost estimate was approximately $68 million for a Force of 4,000 all ranks for that period. As with UNEF II and UNDOF, the costs of UNIFIL were to be considered as expenses of the Organization to be borne by Member States as apportioned by the General Assembly.

The Secretary-General's report was considered by the Security Council later in the same day. By resolution 426(1978) of 19 March 1978, the Council approved the report and decided that UNIFIL should be established for an initial period of six months, subject to extension.

Beginnings of the Force

While the members of the Security Council, in close consultation with the Secretary-General, were discussing the establishment of UNIFIL, the situation in southern Lebanon remained extremely tense and volatile. Israeli forces had occupied most of southern Lebanon up to the Litani River, but the PLO troops regrouped with much of their equipment in the Tyre pocket and in their strongholds north of the Litani, particularly Nabatiyah and Château de Beaufort. Intense exchanges of fire continued between the opposing forces.

The Secretary-General's two immediate objectives were to set up the new Force and deploy it along the front lines as soon as possible, and to initiate negotiations on the withdrawal of the Israeli forces.

General Erskine, who had been appointed as interim Commander of UNIFIL on 19 March, immediately set up temporary headquarters at Naqoura in southern Lebanon, in the premises of the UNTSO outstation, with the 45 military observers who were already in the area. These were soon reinforced by 19 additional observers transferred from other sectors of UNTSO. In order to make UNIFIL operational without delay, the Secretary-General transferred some military personnel from the two existing peace-keeping forces in the Middle East, after obtaining the concurrence of the Governments concerned. One reinforced company from the Iranian contingent of UNDOF and another from the Swedish contingent of UNEF were temporarily assigned to the new Force, together with a movement control detachment and a signal detachment of the Canadian logistic unit of UNEF.

Meanwhile, urgent action had to be taken to seek and obtain 4,000 troops for the Force. During the Security Council debate, France, Nepal and Norway had offered to provide contingents. On 21 March, after securing the agreement of the Council, the Secretary-General accepted the offers of the three Governments. Later, in response to an appeal by the Secretary-General, Nigeria and Senegal each agreed to provide an infantry battalion.

The first French troops arrived in Beirut on 23 March and were brought to battalion strength within a few days. The Norwegian contingent came a week later and the Nepalese by mid-April. With the Canadian, Iranian and Swedish units already in the area, the strength of UNIFIL reached 1,800 all ranks by 8 April, 2,502 by 17 April and 4,016 by the beginning of May.

Strength of the Force

On 1 May 1978,[68] shortly after the Israeli withdrawal began, the Secretary-General recommended that the total strength of the Force should be brought to 6,000. He also indicated that the Governments of Fiji, Iran and Ireland were prepared to make available a battalion each for service with UNIFIL. By resolution 427(1978) of 3 May 1978, the Security Council approved the Secretary-General's recommendation. The three new battalions arrived in the mission area during the first days of June. The Swedish and Iranian companies that had been temporarily detached from UNEF and UNDOF returned to their parent units.

As of mid-June 1978, the strength of the Force was 6,100. The contingents were: Infantry battalions—Fiji (500), France (703), Iran (514), Ireland (665), Nepal (642), Nigeria (669), Norway (723), Senegal (634); Logistic units—Canada (102), France (541), Norway (207). In addition, 42 military observers of UNTSO assisted UNIFIL in the performance of its tasks.

From June 1978 until June 1981, the strength of UNIFIL oscillated between 5,750 and 6,100, according to the movements of the various contingents. The Canadian logistic detachments were returned to UNEF in October 1978. At the request of their Governments, the Iranian battalion was withdrawn beginning in January 1979 and the French infantry battalion in March 1979. The last was replaced by a Dutch battalion, which arrived in the mission area by early March, and a Ghanaian contingent joined UNIFIL in September 1979.

The strength of UNIFIL was further increased to about 7,000 in early 1982 on the recommendation of the Secretary-General (resolution 501(1982) of 25 February 1982). In response to a request of the Secretary-General, the French Government agreed to provide a new infantry battalion of about 600 all ranks and the Ghanaian and Irish Governments to increase their battalions. These changes brought the strength of UNIFIL to 6,945 at the beginning of June 1982. The composition of the Force at that date was: Infantry battalions—Fiji (628), France (595), Ghana (557), Ireland (671), Nepal (432), Netherlands (810), Nigeria (696), Norway (660), Senegal (561); Headquarters camp command—Ghana (140), Ireland (51); Logistic units—France (775), Italy (34), Norway (191), Sweden (144).

Following the second Israeli invasion of Lebanon, in June 1982, the strength and composition of UNIFIL underwent important changes. In September 1982, at the request of the French Government, 482 officers and men of the French infantry battalion were temporarily released from UNIFIL to their national authorities and were incorporated in the French contingent of the multinational force in Beirut (see section below). The Nepalese battalion was withdrawn by 18 November 1982 and replaced by a Finnish battalion. Two companies of the Nigerian battalion were repatriated without replacement in November 1982 and the remainder in January 1983. In October 1983, the Netherlands decided to reduce its contingent from 810 to 150. In February 1984, the French unit withdrawn in 1982 was returned to UNIFIL. In October 1984, the Senegalese contingent was withdrawn and was replaced by a Nepalese battalion which arrived in the area in January-February 1985. In October 1985, the Netherlands contingent was withdrawn. Thus, by late October 1985 the strength of UNIFIL stood at 5,773, with the following composition: Fiji (628), Finland (502), France (1,396), Ghana (707), Ireland (828), Italy (49), Nepal (665), Norway (849), Sweden (149).

Force Commanders

General Erskine, who acted as interim Commander at the outset of the operation, was appointed Force Commander on 12 April 1978. He remained at this post until 14 February 1981 when he was reappointed Chief of Staff of UNTSO and was succeeded at UNIFIL by Lieutenant-General William Callaghan, from Ireland. During the initial period of UNIFIL, General Siilasvuo, the Chief Co-ordinator of the

United Nations Peace-keeping Missions in the Middle East, played a leading role in the negotiations with the Israeli authorities concerning the withdrawal of the Israeli forces from Lebanon. After the termination of UNEF II, the post of Chief Co-ordinator was discontinued, at the end of 1979, and since then the Chief of Staff of UNTSO has performed general liaison functions in Jerusalem regarding the activities of UNIFIL.

B.   UNIFIL activities: March–April 1978

Negotiating problems

Like all United Nations peace-keeping forces, UNIFIL has no enforcement power and requires the co-operation of the parties concerned to fulfil its tasks. Resolution 425(1978) mentioned only Israel and Lebanon. Immediately after the adoption of the resolution, the Secretary-General sought and obtained an undertaking from both of those countries to co-operate with UNIFIL.

But the same procedure could not be followed with the PLO because the Security Council did not mention it as a party to the conflict. To obtain the co-operation of Yasser Arafat, Chairman of the Executive Committee of that organization, the Secretary-General on 27 March issued an appeal to all the parties concerned, including the PLO, for a general cease-fire.[69] This was followed up with a meeting between Arafat and General Erskine, the Force Commander, during which a pledge was secured from the PLO to co-operate with UNIFIL.

Another complication arose from the presence and activities in southern Lebanon of various Lebanese armed elements not controlled by the central Government. UNIFIL could not officially negotiate with these armed elements, although they were very much a part of the problem, some of them having sided with the PLO and others with Israel. The PLO was allied with the Lebanese National Movement (LNM), a loose association of Lebanese Moslem and leftist parties, and the armed elements of the two groups operated under a joint command. When difficulties arose with the armed elements, UNIFIL generally endeavoured to resolve them in negotiations with the PLO leadership.

On the opposite side, UNIFIL had to contend with the so-called *de facto* forces, which were composed mainly of Christian militias led by Major Saad Haddad, a renegade officer of the Lebanese National Army. When UNIFIL encountered problems with the *de facto* forces, it sought the co-operation and assistance of the Israeli authorities, since these forces were armed and supplied by Israel and, by all evidence, closely controlled by it.

Operations area problems

A second major difficulty encountered by UNIFIL arose from the lack of a clear definition of its area of operation. Security Council resolution 425(1978), which was the result of a compromise, was vague on this point. It indicated only that UNIFIL would operate in southern Lebanon and that one of its tasks was to confirm withdrawal of the Israeli forces to the international border. In his report on the implementation of the resolution,[70] which had to take into account the views of the various members of the Security Council, the Secretary-General was unable to propose a clearer definition and merely stated that UNIFIL would set up an area of operation in consultation with the parties. But the parties had very different perceptions of the tasks of UNIFIL and no agreement could be reached on a definition of its area of operation. This difficulty gravely hampered UNIFIL's work from the very start.

First deployment

On 20 March 1978, General Erskine established temporary headquarters in Naqoura, while urgent action was being taken to bring a sufficient number of ground troops to the area at an early date.

At the same time, General Siilasvuo initiated negotiations with the Israeli authorities in Jerusalem to secure their agreement to withdraw their troops from Lebanon without delay. Pending the withdrawal, plans were made to deploy the UNIFIL troops in a strip of land immediately south of the Litani River and, in particular, to assume control of the Kasmiyah, Akiya and Khardala bridges, which were the three main crossing-points into southern Lebanon.

The Iranian company of UNDOF and the Swedish company of UNEF, which had been temporarily transferred to UNIFIL at the outset of the operation, were instructed to proceed to the Akiya bridge in the central sector and the Khardala bridge in the eastern sector, respectively. Their movement to their destinations was initially delayed by the opposition of the Christian *de facto* forces which were deployed near those areas. However, this opposition was overcome through negotiations with the Israeli authorities, and the proposed deployment took place on 24 March and the following days. The Iranians established a position at the Akiya bridge and expanded their presence around it, while the Swedes were deployed at the Khardala bridge and in the area of Ebel es Saqi farther east. At the end of March, the Norwegian battalion had arrived and was deployed in the eastern sector and the Swedish company redeployed in the central/western sector.

The French battalion, which began to arrive in Beirut on 23 March, was immediately sent to the Tyre region. The initial plan was for the French troops to deploy throughout the Tyre pocket and take control of the Kasmiyah bridge. But this plan was strongly opposed by the PLO, and it became clear that it could not be achieved without heavy fighting and considerable casualties. In New York, the Arab representatives to the United Nations strongly supported the PLO's view that the Tyre pocket should not be included in UNIFIL's area of operation. In these conditions, the Secretary-General decided to delay the proposed deployment, pending negotiations with the PLO.

Meanwhile, the French battalion set up its headquarters in former Lebanese army barracks outside the city of Tyre. It established checkpoints around its headquarters and carried out patrolling activities along the front line, on the coastal road from Zahrani to Tyre and in the city of Tyre itself.

In his first periodic report to the Security Council,[71] the Secretary-General stated that, in the absence of a precise initial definition of the limits of the UNIFIL area of operation, attempts originally had been made to deploy elements of UNIFIL in the vicinity of the Kasmiyah bridge, as well as in the Tyre pocket. When this deployment was challenged on the grounds that the Israel Defence Forces (IDF) had not in fact occupied either the bridge or the city of Tyre during the fighting, UNIFIL deployment in the vicinity of that bridge and the Tyre pocket was not pressed.

The UNTSO observers assigned to UNIFIL played an extremely useful role during this formative phase, since they were already familiar with local conditions. They continued to man the five observation posts established by UNTSO in 1972 along the Armistice Demarcation Line. Selected observers served as staff officers at the Naqoura headquarters. Teams of two observers each were attached to the various contingents for liaison and other purposes. Other observers were providing liaison with the Lebanese authorities, the Israeli forces, the PLO and various other armed groups in southern Lebanon. The office of the Israel-Lebanon Mixed Armistice Commission in Beirut ensured liaison between UNIFIL and the Lebanese central Government.

Cease-fire

The situation in southern Lebanon remained volatile during the first days of UNIFIL. As previously mentioned, on 27 March 1978,[72] the Secretary-General had issued an appeal to all the parties concerned to observe a general cease-fire. On 8 April,[73] General Erskine reported that the area had been generally quiet since then. However, con-

siderable tension with occasional exchanges of fire continued to prevail in the Tyre area and the eastern sector, which was close to the
main base of the Christian *de facto* forces in Marjayoun (Marj Uyun)
and the PLO stronghold of Château de Beaufort north of the Litani
River. UNIFIL troops, which were deployed between the opposing
forces in these two sensitive areas, endeavoured to maintain a precar-
ious cease-fire, while the Secretary-General and General Siilasvuo, the
Co-ordinator for the United Nations Peace-keeping Missions in the
Middle East, continued to press the Israeli authorities to withdraw their
troops from Lebanon without delay.

C. UNIFIL activities: April–June 1978

Initial withdrawal of Israeli forces

On 6 April 1978, the Chief of Staff of the Israel Defence Forces
submitted to General Siilasvuo a plan for an initial withdrawal of the
Israeli forces in two phases.[74] In a first phase, to take place on 11
April, the Israeli forces would withdraw from an area west of Marja-
'youn. The Khardala bridge and a number of villages would be evacuated, but strategic villages such as El Khirba and Deir Mimess (Dayr
Mimas) would remain occupied. A second withdrawal would follow
on 14 April and would cover a zone extending from a point on the
Litani River two kilometres west of the Akiya bridge to a point about
one kilometre west of Deir Mimess. The area to be evacuated during
the two first phases would cover about 110 square kilometres, about
one tenth of the total occupied territory.

The next day,[75] the Secretary-General indicated that the Israeli
plan was not satisfactory since Security Council resolution 425(1978)
called for the withdrawal of Israeli forces without delay from the entire occupied Lebanese territory. The plan, however, was accepted on
the understanding that a further withdrawal would be agreed upon
at an early date. The proposed withdrawal took place as scheduled
without incident. All the positions evacuated by the Israeli forces were
handed over to UNIFIL troops.

Further negotiations between General Siilasvuo and the Israeli
authorities led to a third phase of the Israeli withdrawal, which took
place on 30 April.[76] This withdrawal was more extensive and covered
an area of about 550 square kilometres with an average width of about
18 kilometres. As in the previous withdrawals, the positions evacuated
by the Israeli forces were taken over by UNIFIL troops without incident.

Following the third phase of the Israeli withdrawal, UNIFIL was deployed in two separate zones south of the Litani River within an area of about 650 square kilometres or approximately 45 per cent of the territory occupied by Israel. The western zone had an area of about 600 square kilometres and the eastern zone about 50 square kilometres. Between the two zones, there was a gap some 15 kilometres wide just south of Château de Beaufort. In this gap, UNIFIL was able to maintain only four isolated positions, including one at the Khardala bridge.

Pending further withdrawals of the Israeli forces, UNIFIL acted to consolidate its control of the area in which it was deployed. Its main objectives were to supervise and monitor the cease-fire and to ensure that no unauthorized armed personnel entered its area. To this end, observation posts and check-points were set up at various points of entry in its area of deployment, and frequent patrols were conducted throughout the area. All unauthorized armed and uniformed personnel were turned back at entry points and, if they were discovered within the area, UNIFIL troops would endeavour to disarm them and escort them out of its area.

Problems after the initial Israeli withdrawal

Following the third phase of the Israeli withdrawal, UNIFIL was faced with two major problems. First, the Israeli Government was reluctant to relinquish the remaining area and the United Nations efforts to achieve further withdrawal met with increasing resistance. Secondly, PLO armed elements attempted to enter the area evacuated by the Israeli forces on the grounds that they had a legitimate right to do so under the terms of the Cairo agreement of 3 November 1969, concluded between Lebanon and the PLO, under the auspices of President Nasser of Egypt, which dealt with the presence of Palestinians in Lebanon.

The unco-operative attitude of certain PLO armed elements led to some serious clashes during the first days of May in the Tyre area. On 1 May, a group of armed elements attempted to infiltrate a UNIFIL position manned by French soldiers in the Tyre area. When challenged, they opened fire on the French guards, who returned the fire in self-defence and killed two infiltrators. In the following days, French troops were ambushed at various locations and, during the ensuing exchanges of fire, three UNIFIL soldiers were killed and 14 wounded, including the Commander of the French battalion.[77]

Negotiations in the area

Strenuous negotiations were engaged in by the Secretary-General and his representatives in the field to prevent infiltration attempts by

PLO armed elements and to avoid further incidents. Arafat confirmed that the PLO would co-operate with UNIFIL and that it would not initiate hostile acts against Israel from southern Lebanon, although it would continue its armed struggle from other areas. While the PLO's presence in southern Lebanon was a matter to be settled between itself and the Lebanese Government, the PLO would facilitate UNIFIL's tasks in response to the Secretary-General's appeal. In particular, the PLO would refrain from infiltrating armed elements into the UNIFIL area of operation. In exchange, Chairman Arafat insisted that the Palestinian armed elements who were already in the UNIFIL area of operation should be allowed to remain there. In order to secure the co-operation of the PLO, UNIFIL agreed to this condition, on the clear understanding that the limited number of armed elements allowed to remain in its area of operation would not be used for military purposes. The agreement involved about 140 armed elements belonging to various groups of the PLO, assembled in six positions.

The Secretary-General reported to the Security Council[78] that for humanitarian reasons, and as an *ad hoc* arrangement, UNIFIL had agreed to allow the delivery, under UNIFIL control, of certain non-military supplies—food, water and medicine—to limited Palestinian groups still in its area of operation. Strict instructions were given to the UNIFIL contingents concerned to keep a close watch over the six PLO positions.

Under the pressure of the United Nations, the Israeli Government announced its decision to withdraw its forces from the remaining occupied territory in Lebanon by 13 June 1978. The modalities for the withdrawal were to be determined between the Israeli authorities and Generals Siilasvuo and Erskine.

Following the announcement of this decision, intensive discussions were held between United Nations representatives and the Lebanese Government regarding the deployment of UNIFIL in the area to be evacuated and, in particular, regarding its relationship with the *de facto* forces under the command of Major Haddad. Pending full establishment of its authority in southern Lebanon, the Lebanese Government announced that it provisionally recognized Major Haddad as *de facto* commander of the Lebanese forces in his present area. The Lebanese army command would issue instructions to Major Haddad to faciliate UNIFIL's mission and deployment.[79]

UNIFIL also engaged in discussions with the Israeli authorities to work out practical arrangements for its deployment in the border area following the Israeli withdrawal. However, no common ground could be reached, and the instructions issued by the Lebanese Government to Major Haddad to facilitate UNIFIL's mission were totally ignored.

D. UNIFIL activities: June 1978–July 1981

Last phase of the Israeli withdrawal

On the afternoon of 13 June 1978, General Erskine reported that the Israeli forces had withdrawn from southern Lebanon. This information was transmitted by the Secretary-General to the Security Council.[80] The manner in which the Israeli forces carried out the last phase of withdrawal, however, created major problems for UNIFIL. In contrast to the procedure followed during the previous three withdrawal phases, the IDF on 13 June turned over most of its positions not to UNIFIL but to the *de facto* forces of Major Haddad, on the grounds that the IDF considered him a legitimate representative of the Lebanese Government. UNIFIL units were able to occupy only five positions evacuated by the Israeli forces on that day, because the *de facto* forces, which had been strongly armed by the Israelis, threatened to use force to oppose any attempts by UNIFIL to gain wider deployment.

In a letter dated 13 June,[81] Foreign Minister Moshe Dayan informed the Secretary-General that Israel had fulfilled its part in the implementation of Security Council resolution 425(1978). In his reply,[82] the Secretary-General observed that the difficult task lying ahead for UNIFIL had not been facilitated by the decision of the Israeli Government not to turn over control of the evacuated area to UNIFIL. He added that he was making efforts to deal satisfactorily with the consequences of that development, in co-operation with the Lebanese Government.

Difficulties in deployment

In order to fulfil its mandate, UNIFIL had to be fully deployed in its entire area of operation, including the enclave controlled by the *de facto* forces of Major Haddad. The first objective of the Force after the events of 13 June 1978 was therefore to expand its deployment in the enclave. Pending realization of this objective, UNIFIL would continue to ensure that the area where it actually was deployed would not be used for hostile activities of any kind. It would endeavour to stop and contain infiltrations by the armed elements of the PLO and the Lebanese National Movement, as well as incursions and encroachments by the *de facto* forces or the Israeli forces. It would also endeavour to maintain the cease-fire and prevent a resumption of hostilities in and around its area. At the same time, UNIFIL would exert all possible efforts to assist the Lebanese Government in restoring its authority and promote the return to normalcy in its area of deployment.

In these various fields of activity, UNIFIL encountered serious difficulties. No significant further deployment could be achieved in the enclave and, although hostile actions could be contained in UNIFIL's area of deployment to a large extent, there were frequent and destructive exchanges of fire between the opposing forces over and across its area until 24 July 1981, when cease-fire arrangements were worked out through a joint effort by the United States and the United Nations *(see below)*.

The various objectives pursued by the Interim Force were closely interconnected, and set-backs in one inevitably affected the others.

Efforts towards further deployment in the enclave

Immediately after 13 June, the Secretary-General instructed General Siilasvuo and General Erskine to exert every effort, in close co-operation with the Lebanese Government, to achieve progressively wider deployment of UNIFIL in the enclave until the Force would ultimately be in a position effectively to discharge its mandate in its entire area of operation. He made it clear, however, that it remained his intention to utilize peaceful and diplomatic means to achieve this objective.

As a result of renewed efforts, UNIFIL was able to occupy 14 additional positions in the enclave in June and July and another five positions in September 1978. By that date, UNIFIL held a total of 24 positions in the enclave, in addition to its headquarters at Naqoura and the five posts previously established by UNTSO along the Armistice Demarcation Line. But no further deployment could be achieved.

In his periodic report of 13 September 1978 to the Security Council,[83] and in subsequent periodic reports, the Secretary-General pointed to the efforts made by him and his representatives to secure the full deployment of UNIFIL in its area of operation and the lack of progress in this regard. The Council repeatedly reaffirmed its determination to implement its resolutions on UNIFIL in the totality of the area of operation assigned to the Force, and called upon all the parties to extend the necessary co-operation to UNIFIL. The requests of the Security Council remained unheeded.

This situation prevented UNIFIL from fulfilling an essential part of its mandate and made its other tasks considerably more difficult.

Prevention of infiltration by armed elements

Infiltration attempts resumed and increased soon after 13 June 1978. The inability of UNIFIL to take over the enclave from the pro-Israeli *de facto* forces was undoubtedly a contributing cause of the increase of infiltration attempts.

In order to prevent infiltration, UNIFIL established check-points at points of entry and along the main and secondary road networks in its area of deployment. UNIFIL soldiers, often assisted by Lebanese gendarmes, checked and inspected vehicles and personnel for military equipment and supplies at the check-points. Foot and motorized patrols were conducted day and night along key highways, in villages, as well as in remote wadis (ravines), and random night-time listening posts were established at selected localities to detect unauthorized armed movement.

After July 1979, UNIFIL's troops were redeployed in greater density along the perimeter of the UNIFIL area in order better to control infiltration, and a steady effort was made to improve its surveillance and detection capability. In particular, the number of night-vision binoculars and strong searchlights was markedly increased, while the introduction of sophisticated ground surveillance radar provided the Force with an effective early warning system at medium range. Uniformed and armed personnel stopped at the check-points or caught by patrols were escorted out of the UNIFIL area.

According to the records of UNIFIL, 40 major attempts involving some 140 armed elements were thwarted by the Force during the first six months of 1979. Some 785 infiltration attempts were stopped and turned back during the second half of 1979, 500 during the first half of 1980, 384 during the second half of the same year, and 490 from January to June 1981.

The armed elements stopped at check-points generally surrendered their weapons and left the UNIFIL area peacefully. There were, however, exceptions, when the efforts of UNIFIL to stop infiltrations were resisted and led to violent incidents. In some cases, the armed elements stopped at check-points or by patrols reacted by firing at UNIFIL soldiers, who then had to return fire in self-defence. At other times, the infiltrators, after being turned back, would return with reinforcements to attack the UNIFIL position involved. In the most serious instances, armed elements retaliated by laying in ambush against

UNIFIL personnel, not only at the scene of the original incident but also against UNIFIL positions or patrols elsewhere. As often as possible, UNIFIL tried to resolve all incidents by negotiation.

Given the difficulty of the terrain, the limited size of UNIFIL and its lack of enforcement power, it was virtually impossible to prevent all infiltration attempts. The difficulty in controlling infiltration was compounded by the existence of many arms caches in the UNIFIL area. Over the years, the PLO had set up a network of such caches throughout southern Lebanon. Unifil found and destroyed many of them, but many others remained.

Since UNIFIL did not want to hamper the movement of innocent civilians, persons in civilian clothes could freely enter its area, provided that they had a valid identification card and did not carry weapons. It was relatively easy for PLO personnel and their Lebanese allies to pass through UNIFIL check-points unarmed and, once inside the area, get the weapons from the caches. Armed elements could also infiltrate into the UNIFIL area with their weapons through uncharted trails and dirt tracks which could not be covered by UNIFIL check-points or observation posts. Inside the UNIFIL area, the PLO, and particularly the Lebanese National Movement, still had many sympathizers who voluntarily or under pressure gave the infiltrators shelter or other assistance. Despite its vigilance, UNIFIL could not detect and stop all such infiltrators.

In those conditions, the most effective way of stopping or at least controlling infiltration was to secure the co-operation of the PLO. The PLO leadership did co-operate with UNIFIL to a significant degree. There were no major-scale infiltration attempts and, when incidents involving infiltration occurred, the PLO leadership assisted UNIFIL in resolving them. But in a number of exceptional cases, the PLO was either unwilling or unable to help, and a number of armed elements succeeded in infiltrating into the UNIFIL area and in setting up some additional positions inside it.

By July 1981, the number of Palestinian armed elements inside the UNIFIL area had increased to about 450, according to UNIFIL estimates, and they had established some 30 positions inside that area. There was, in particular, a concentration of armed element positions in the Jwayya area near the Tyre pocket. Unifil tried to have those positions removed by negotiations with the PLO at the highest level, but its efforts were inconclusive.

Nevertheless, UNIFIL did control infiltration by armed elements to an important degree. The number of such elements who succeeded in infiltrating the UNIFIL area was relatively limited, and most of those remained confined to the northern part of the area, well away from the frontier.

Records of UNIFIL indicate that after its establishment in March 1978, there was only one major raid into northern Israel by PLO armed elements coming from its area. This happened on 6/7 April 1980, when five armed elements belonging to the Arab Liberation Front crossed the Armistice Demarcation Line and attacked the kibbutz of Misgav Am. To do this, a group would have had to cross not only UNIFIL areas but also the enclave and the border. All five infiltrators and three Israeli civilians were killed during the incident.[84]

Harassment by de facto forces

The activities of the *de facto* forces under the command of Major Haddad also created serious difficulties for UNIFIL. No precise figures on the strength of those forces are available, but it is generally estimated that they numbered about 1,500 in June 1978. The *de facto* forces were formed around a nucleus of some 700 former Christian soldiers of the Lebanese National Army, to which were added smaller groups of Christian phalangists from the north and locally recruited Christian and Shi'ite villagers. They were financed, armed and uniformed by the Israeli authorities.

The measures devised by UNIFIL to prevent infiltrations by the Palestinians and Lebanese leftist armed elements were also applied to the *de facto* forces, but there were few infiltrators from the enclave, and the main problems the United Nations encountered with these forces concerned the actions taken by them to harass UNIFIL and the local population, and their attempts to encroach upon the UNIFIL area.

While making clear that full deployment in the enclave remained its main objective, UNIFIL concentrated its immediate efforts on preserving the installations it held there and on securing the freedom of movement it required to this effect. With the assistance of the Israeli army, a *modus vivendi* was reached with the *de facto* forces whereby UNIFIL troops would enjoy freedom of movement on the main roads in the enclave five days a week in order to rotate personnel and resupply its installations. UNIFIL helicopters could fly over the enclave when necessary, but each overflight had to be cleared with Major Haddad's command on an *ad hoc* basis. However, even this limited freedom of movement was occasionally denied UNIFIL. When difficulties of one kind or another arose between UNIFL and the *de facto* forces, Major Haddad would retaliate by closing the roads in the enclave to United

Nations personnel and vehicles. This retaliatory measure would be taken either against UNIFIL as a whole or against specific contingents.

During periods of tension, some UNIFIL positions in the enclave, and particularly the five observation posts along the Armistice Demarcation Line, were at times completely isolated, and the United Nations personnel manning them subjected to severe harassment. In some cases, the observation posts were broken into by militiamen, their equipment stolen and the United Nations personnel threatened. On three occasions, the *de facto* forces attacked the UNIFIL headquarters itself with mortar and artillery fire, causing casualties and considerable material damage.

In October 1978, at about the same time as the PLO intensified its attempts to infiltrate the UNIFIL area, the attitude of the *de facto* forces hardened further. These forces began to harass the local population in the UNIFIL area in various ways. A number of Shi'ite villages were subjected to occasional shelling from positions in the enclave, and the villagers were threatened with punitive measures if they continued to co-operate with UNIFIL. In a few instances, the *de facto* forces sent raiding parties into the UNIFIL area to abduct persons suspected of pro-PLO sentiments or to blow up their houses. This sort of pressure on the local population markedly increased after Haddad proclaimed the constitution of the so-called "State of Free Lebanon" in April 1979. UNIFIL strongly protested the harassment with the Israeli authorities. To deter attacks against villages in its area, it established additional positions in their vicinity.

From December 1978 onwards, the *de facto* forces made several attempts to set up positions within the UNIFIL area. These attempts were carried out by strongly armed groups, sometimes supported by tanks. Whenever this occurred, UNIFIL sent reinforcements to surround the raiding parties and, at the same time, tried by negotiation to have their positions removed, usually with the assistance of the Israeli army. In some cases, the raiding parties were persuaded to leave peacefully, but in others the negotiations were unsuccessful. Thus, five encroachment positions were established by the *de facto* forces between July 1979 and July 1980, all of which were located in strategic areas commanding views of important access roads.

To remove these positions, UNIFIL would have had to use force against the *de facto* forces and possibly the Israel Defence Forces, and casualties would have been heavy. In the circumstances, it was decided instead to seek a negotiated solution through the Israeli authorities. The Secretary-General raised this matter with the Israeli Government at the highest level but was told that Israel considered those positions important for its security and would not intercede to have them removed.

While, as a matter of principle and policy, UNIFIL sought to contain the actions of the *de facto* forces by negotiation, its troops were sometimes obliged to resist harassments and to use force in self-defence. Despite the restraint displayed by UNIFIL soldiers, violent incidents occurred in some cases.

On 24 April 1980, following an incident in which the *de facto* forces directed heavy shelling at UNIFIL headquarters, the Security Council adopted resolution 467(1980), by which it deplored all acts of hostilities against UNIFIL in or through its area of operation and condemned the deliberate shelling of the headquarters.

Israeli activities in and near the enclave

After 13 June 1978, the Israeli Government took the position that its forces had withdrawn from Lebanese territory in accordance with Security Council resolution 425(1978) and that henceforth it was no longer responsible for what happened in the enclave.

During the initial months, the presence of the Israel Defence Force in the enclave appeared limited, but from November 1979 onwards, IDF activities increased. Israeli soldiers were frequently observed laying mines, manning check-points, transporting water and supplies and constructing new positions inside Lebanon in the border areas.

In late 1980,[85] UNIFIL reported an increasing number of encroachments by the IDF along the Armistice Demarcation Line. The original border-fence remained intact, but beyond it the IDF established new positions at selected points, laid minefields, fenced in certain strips of land and built dirt tracks and asphalt roads. At the same time, the presence of the IDF inside the enclave was greatly expanded. IDF gun and tank positions were established near Marjayoun, Major Haddad's headquarters, and along the coastal road. IDF personnel were sighted in various locations well inside the enclave. In the course of 1980, the IDF openly conducted military exercises near OP Khiam, a United Nations observation post north of the border.

On a number of occasions, the IDF carried out incursions into the UNIFIL area in search of PLO armed elements. UNIFIL took all possible measures to stop those incursions, and its efforts led at times to confrontations with IDF personnel, which were generally resolved by negotiation.

In addition to its activities in the enclave, the IDF frequently intruded into Lebanese air space and territorial waters. Its aircraft constantly flew over Lebanon for observation purposes and its patrol boats were often observed cruising near the Lebanese coast. The air and sea violations greatly increased after June 1980. During November 1980 alone, UNIFIL observed 312 air violations and 89 sea violations.

E. Hostile actions near the UNIFIL area

Introduction

The UNIFIL area constituted an imperfect buffer between the opposing forces. The area was divided into two parts, with a gap of about 15 kilometres between them. In this gap, where the two opposing sides were separated only by the Litani River, UNIFIL was able to set up four positions, including one at the Khardala bridge, to provide at least a limited United Nations presence. But the gun positions of the PLO in its stronghold of Château de Beaufort north of the river, and those of the de facto forces in and around Marjayoun, reinforced in 1980 by IDF tanks and artillery, were not far apart. From its positions in the Tyre pocket and Château de Beaufort, the PLO's heavy artillery and rockets could easily reach villages and towns in northern Israel, including Nahariyya, Metulla and Kiryat Shemona.

From March 1979 onwards, there were frequent exchanges of fire between the PLO and the de facto forces across the gap and over the UNIFIL area. When fighting intensified, the IDF would come to the support of the de facto forces and, in retaliation, PLO fighters would direct their heavy artillery and rockets at targets in northern Israel, which would in turn provoke violent reprisals by the IDF. Whenever PLO shelling resulted in Israeli casualties, and also after incidents inside Israel or Israeli-occupied territories for which the PLO claimed responsibility, IDF would send its war-planes to launch massive attacks against PLO targets north of the UNIFIL area, sometimes as far as Beirut. In some cases, Israeli commandos were dispatched to destroy PLO installations.

Both the Israeli war-planes and the commandos would, as a rule, avoid the UNIFIL area by flying over the gap or taking the sea route. Since the armed forces engaged in the hostilities were located outside its area, UNIFIL could not take direct action to prevent or stop them. It did, however, endeavour to arrange cease-fires whenever possible, and brought the most serious cases to the attention of the Security Council.

Within one year, there were two series of serious hostilities; one in August 1980 and the other in July 1981.

Hostilities of August 1980

During the evening of 18 August 1980, a heavy exchange of fire broke out between *de facto*/IDF forces and PLO positions north of the Litani and continued with varying intensity for five days. According to UNIFIL observers,[86] the *de facto* forces fired approximately 2,460 rounds of artillery, mortar and tank fire, and the PLO armed elements about 300 rounds. On 19 and 20 August, Israeli war-planes attacked various PLO targets in the Château de Beaufort and Arnun areas.

On 19 August,[87] while the shelling and bombing were in progress, a group of about 200 IDF troops, transported by helicopter, carried out a commando raid to destroy PLO installations in and around the villages of Arnun and Kafr Tibnit. This operation was preceded by a buildup of IDF personnel and equipment throughout the enclave, where about 50 artillery pieces, 70 assorted vehicles and seven heavy helicopters were sighted by UNIFIL. According to Lebanese and Palestinian sources, the attacks resulted in at least 25 killed, including five Lebanese civilians, and 26 wounded, as well as very heavy destruction of houses and other property. The Israeli authorities indicated that the operation was intended to destroy PLO artillery and mortar nests which had shelled Israel's northern settlements and Major Haddad's enclave in southern Lebanon.

Hostilities of July 1981

The fighting which broke out in July 1981 was even more extensive. On 10 July, during an exchange of fire with the *de facto*/IDF positions, PLO forces shelled the town of Kiryat Shemona in northern Israel with rockets, resulting, according to Israeli authorities,[88] in the wounding of six civilians. On the same day,[89] Israeli war-planes attacked PLO targets in Lebanon north of the UNIFIL area. The air attacks were followed by renewed exchanges of fire between the PLO armed elements' and the IDF and *de facto* forces' positions.

On 13 and 14 July, widespread Israeli air attacks continued and PLO armed elements again fired rockets into northern Israel, wounding, according to Israeli sources, two Israeli civilians in the coastal town of Nahariyya. The next day, there was a particularly heavy exchange of fire with a total of about 1,000 rounds of artillery, mortar and rockets fired by the two sides.

On 16 and 17 July, exchanges of fire intensified, with Israeli naval vessels joining in, while Israeli aircraft destroyed bridges on the Zahrani and Litani rivers and launched an intense attack on Beirut itself, causing heavy loss of life and damage to property. Exchanges of fire in all sectors, as well as Israeli air strikes and naval bombardments, continued on 18 and 19 July and, on a gradually declining scale, until 24 July.

During the period of intense violence in July, UNIFIL recorded the firing of some 7,500 rounds of artillery, mortar, tank and naval cannons by the IDF and the *de facto* forces, in addition to Israeli air strikes, and the firing of about 2,500 rounds of artillery, mortar and rockets by PLO armed elements. The total casualties during this period were six dead and 59 wounded on the Israeli side, immeasurably more among the Palestinians and Lebanese.

Security Council action

The Security Council met on 17 July 1981 at the request of the Lebanese Government. On the same day, the Council President issued an urgent appeal to the parties for restraint and an immediate end to all armed attacks.

On 21 July, the Council unanimously adopted resolution 490 (1981), by which it called for an immediate cessation of all armed attacks and reaffirmed its commitment to the sovereignty, territorial integrity and independence of Lebanon within its internationally recognized boundaries.

July cease fire

Following adoption of the resolution, parallel efforts undertaken by the United Nations and the United States Government led to the establishment of a *de facto* cease-fire on 24 July 1981.

On the morning of that day, Ambassador Philip Habib, the personal representative of the President of the United States, issued a statement in Jerusalem to the effect that, as of 1330 hours, 24 July 1981, all hostile military action between Lebanese and Israeli territory in either direction would cease.

The Secretary-General, who had been kept fully informed of the efforts of Ambassador Habib, immediately brought this statement to the attention of the Security Council.[90] He also reported to the Council that the Israeli Government had endorsed the statement, that the Lebanese Government had welcomed it, and that the PLO had assured him that it would observe the cease-fire called for by the Security Council.

The Commander of UNIFIL reported on 24 July that, as of 1320 hours local time, the area was quiet.

F. Efforts to restore the authority of the Lebanese Government in southern Lebanon

Civilian administration

After 13 June 1978, when it became apparent that Israeli control would continue in the enclave for an indefinite period, UNIFIL had to alter its original plan. While the Force would continue its efforts to assume control of the enclave through negotiations, it took action to help the Lebanese to deploy as many administrators and elements of the Lebanese army and the internal security forces as possible in the area controlled by it.

Initially, UNIFIL's attention was focused on getting the Lebanese Government to send civilian administrative and technical personnel and elements of the Lebanese internal security forces (gendarmes) to southern Lebanon. By late July 1978,[91] the Lebanese Government was represented south of the Litani River by a civilian administrator residing at Tyre, and by nearly 100 gendarmes based at Tyre and at three centres in the UNIFIL area. The gendarmes worked in close co-operation with UNIFIL in its area. They assisted UNIFIL soldiers in the inspection of personnel and vehicles at check-points and, in many instances, served as interpreters and liaison officers with the local population. Civil offences reported to UNIFIL were handed over to the gendarmes for investigation.

UNIFIL carried out various humanitarian activities and rehabilitation programmes in close co-operation with the Lebanese authorities and the Co-ordinator of United Nations Assistance for the Reconstruction and Development of Lebanon. It took an active part in the execution of projects involving restoration of water, electricity and health services, distribution of supplementary food supplies and the rebuilding and repair of houses, schools and roads. The UNIFIL hospital and the medical facilities of its contingents were open to the local population, which used those services frequently.

Army deployment, 1978

In the course of July 1978, extensive consultations were held between the Lebanese authorities and UNIFIL regarding the possibility of bringing Lebanese army units to the UNIFIL area of operation. Many obstacles had to be overcome. The de facto forces and the Israeli authorities were opposed to any move of the Lebanese army to the south. For different reasons, the PLO, which controlled the key coastal road from Sidon to Tyre, also opposed such a move.

The Lebanese National Army was still in the process of reconstruction and reorganization. Despite the difficulties involved, the Government of Lebanon decided to dispatch a task force of the Lebanese army to southern Lebanon on 31 July.[92] This task force, consisting of 700 men, and equipment, was to travel to Tibnin through the Bekaa Valley, through Kaoukaba (Kawkaba), a village on the northern edge of the UNIFIL area, and through Marjayoun, the headquarters of the de facto forces. The Secretary-General was informed of this decision on 25 July and an announcement was made by the Lebanese Government on the same day.

Following this announcement, UNIFIL contacted the Israeli authorities at various levels and requested their help to ensure that the de facto forces would not oppose the proposed move. The Israeli authorities refused to intervene on the grounds that it was a Lebanese internal affair.

The task force left the Beirut area in the early morning of 31 July and reached Kaoukaba a few hours later. On arrival, it was subjected to intense artillery and mortar fire by the de facto forces. Confronted with this hostile action, the task force decided to remain in Kaoukaba while the United Nations tried to secure by negotiation the co-operation of the de facto forces for the peaceful transit of the Lebanese army contingent. But the efforts of the Secretary-General and his representatives in the field proved inconclusive in the face of the adamant opposition of Major Haddad and with the Israeli authorities declining to help.

On the following days, the de facto forces continuously harassed the task force and fired more than 300 artillery rounds at it, killing one Lebanese soldier and wounding nine others. In August, the task force withdrew from Kaoukaba.

Army deployment, 1979

Following this attempt, UNIFIL engaged in new consultations with the Lebanese authorities in an effort to find alternative ways of bringing Lebanese army units into southern Lebanon.

On 22 December 1978,[93] joint working group of UNIFIL and Lebnese army officials was set up to work out a plan of action. On the proposal of the group, small teams of Lebanese army personnel were flown to southern Lebanon by UNIFIL helicopters and were assigned to various UNIFIL contingents to represent the Lebanese Government in their respective sectors.

In renewing the mandate of UNIFIL for a further period of five months, the Security Council, by resolution 444(1979) of 19 January 1979, invited the Lebanese Government to draw up, in consultation with the Secretary-General, a phased programme of activities to be carried out over the next three months to promote the restoration of its authority in southern Lebanon. The programme as worked out by the Lebanese Government with the assistance of UNIFIL set for its first phase four main objectives: (1) an increase of the Lebanese civilian administrative presence in the south; (2) the introduction of a battalion of the Lebanese National Army in the UNIFIL area; (3) the consolidation of the cease-fire in the area; and (4) further deployment of UNIFIL in the enclave.[94]

Within this programme, a Lebanese army battalion of 500 men was deployed in the UNIFIL area in April 1979. The *de facto* forces tried to prevent the deployment by subjecting UNIFIL headquarters and some of its positions to intense shelling from 15 to 18 April. These attacks caused casualties and heavy material damage, but UNIFIL stood firm, and the deployment of the Lebanese battalion proceeded as planned and was completed on 17 April. The Lebanese battalion, which was placed under the operational control of the Force Commander, set up its headquarters at Arzun in the Nigerian sector.

Army deployment, 1980–1981

In December 1980, the strength of the Lebanese battalion was increased to 617 men with the addition of some medical and engineering elements. Initially, the Lebanese battalion confined its activities to the immediate vicinity of Arzun, but, from early 1981 on, some of its units were gradually deployed in various UNIFIL sectors.

In June 1981,[95] a second Lebanese battalion was brought to the UNIFIL area, this time without incident, and raised the total strength of the Lebanese army presence in southern Lebanon to 1,350 all ranks. The new battalion included an engineering unit of 130, which assisted in various local projects, and a medical team of 10 assigned to the Tibnin hospital.

Efforts to reactivate the General Armistice Agreement

To promote the restoration of its authority and sovereignty in southern Lebanon, the Lebanese Government sought to reactivate the 1949 General Armistice Agreement between Israel and Lebanon and the Israel-Lebanon Mixed Armistice Commission (ILMAC) established under that Agreement.

In resolution 450(1979) of 14 June 1979, on a further extension of UNIFIL s mandate, the Security Council reaffirmed the validity of the General Armistice Agreement and called upon the parties to take the necessary steps to reactivate ILMAC. A plan of action, which the Secretary-General worked out in consultation with the Lebanese Government in September 1979,[96] set as the main long-term objective of the Force the restoration of the effective authority of the Lebanese Government in southern Lebanon up to the internationally recognized boundary, and the normalization of the area, including the reactivation of ILMAC in accordance with the 1949 Agreement.

In resolution 467(1980) of 24 April 1980, the Security Council requested the Secretary-General to convene a meeting of ILMAC, at an appropriate level, to agree on precise recommendations and further to reactivate the General Armistice Agreement conducive to the restoration of the sovereignty of Lebanon over all its territory up to the internationally recognized boundaries.

The Chief of Staff of UNTSO, General Erskine, who had been asked by the Secretary-General to follow up on that resolution, proposed on 18 November 1980 that a meeting preliminary to the convening of ILMAC be held at Naqoura on 1 December.[97] On 25 November, the Lebanese authorities agreed to the proposed meeting and insisted that it be attended by the Chairman of ILMAC. On 26 November, the Israeli authorities replied, stating that the Mixed Armistice Commission was no longer valid and that, as far as they were concerned, the proposed meeting could not be regarded as a preliminary meeting of ILMAC. They added, however, that this should not stand in the way of a meeting between Israeli and Lebanese representatives at the appropriate level, and they agreed to meet with the Lebanese representatives on the date and at the venue suggested by General Erskine.

The meeting took place at UNIFIL headquarters on 1 December 1980,[98] under the chairmanship of the Chief of Staff of UNTSO. Israel and Lebanon were represented by senior military officers. Although the two sides disagreed on the validity of the General Armistice Agreement, they discussed the situation in southern Lebanon, particularly along the border. The Lebanese representative complained about the establishment of IDF positions in southern Lebanon and incursions by IDF personnel into Lebanese territory, while the Israeli representative asserted that Israel had no designs on Lebanon. Following this meeting, the UNTSO Chief of Staff kept in contact with both sides with a view to arranging another meeting in the near future, but no agreement could be reached.

G. Cease-fire: July 1981–April 1982

The cease-fire arrangements of 24 July 1981 were accepted by all the parties, and on that day all firing stopped *(see section E above)*.

UNIFIL kept close contact with the parties to ensure the maintenance of the cease-fire. Lieutenant-General William Callaghan, Commander of UNIFIL, obtained an undertaking from each of the parties that in the event of a breach of the cease-fire by the opposing side, the other side would exercise maximum restraint and, rather than take retaliatory action, would refer the matter to UNIFIL for resolution.

During the following days, however, the situation remained unstable because a dissident PLO group led by Ahmed Jebril continued to fire sporadically at targets in the enclave. General Callaghan strongly protested those violations of the cease-fire to the PLO command. Chairman Arafat replied that the firings were due to a misunderstanding and that the PLO was determined to observe strictly the cease-fire. On 27 July, following a meeting with Arafat, Jebril announced that his group would respect the cease-fire.

A second problem which threatened the cease-fire during the initial period arose from the continuing overflights of Israeli reconnaissance aircraft in southern Lebanon, which the PLO protested as violations of the cease-fire arrangements. In spite of approaches by the Commander of UNIFIL, Israel refused to stop such overflights on the grounds that they were not covered by the cease-fire arrangements. The Israeli overflights did not, however, provoke retaliatory action by the PLO.

The cease-fire held remarkably well until April 1982. For eight months the situation in southern Lebanon was quiet and there were no firings between the PLO and the *de facto*/IDF forces in the area.

With the restoration of the cease-fire in July 1981, the general situation in southern Lebanon had become much less tense. However, UNIFIL continued to experience serious difficulties with both the armed elements of the PLO and the Lebanese National Movement and with the *de facto* forces of Major Haddad. The armed elements continued their infiltration attempts after July 1981, though at a lower level. UNIFIL soldiers turned back 175 infiltrators in July 1981, 95 in August, 18 in September, 90 in October, 27 in November, 25 in December, 70 in January 1982, 27 in February, 98 in March, 69 in April and 27 in May. In a more serious development, PLO armed elements established additional positions in the UNIFIL area near the Tyre pocket. The Force immediately placed those positions under close surveillance to ensure that they would not be used for tactical or hostile purposes. At the same time, negotiations were engaged in with the PLO leadership to have them removed, but the talks were inconclusive.

Relations with the *de facto* forces also remained tense. Those forces continued to impose restrictions on UNIFIL's freedom of movement in the enclave. In the UNIFIL area of deployment, they not only continued to maintain four positions they had established, but set up a new one near the village of At Tiri, in the Irish sector.[99] The Force Commander sought the assistance of the Israeli authorities in this regard, stressing that the position was clearly provocative and might jeopardize the cease-fire. While the negotiations were in progress, the *de facto* forces harassed the UNIFIL headquarters at Naqoura and some of its positions in the enclave by cutting off their supply lines. The harassments were eventually stopped with the help of the IDF, but the new position remained.

During this period of relative quiet, UNIFIL had to contend with a new problem in its area. In the later months, Amal, a Shi'ite paramilitary organization, became more active in southern Lebanon, and there was mounting animosity between its followers and members of the pro-Palestinian Lebanese National Movement. Serious clashes broke out between the two groups in January and in April 1982 in the Senegalese sector, and UNIFIL had to intervene to help restore law and order.

H. Israeli invasion: 1982–1985

Breakdown of the cease-fire

In early April 1982, tension markedly increased in southern Lebanon, not because of any violations of the cease-fire in the area but as a consequence of events elsewhere.

On 3 April, an Israeli diplomat was assassinated in Paris and the Israeli Government held the PLO responsible, although responsibility was denied by that organization. On 13 April,[100] the Permanent Representative of Israel to the United Nations complained to the Security Council that, on the previous night, two PLO terrorists with large quantities of explosives had attempted to infiltrate into Israel from Jordanian territory. On 21 April, Israel launched massive air attacks against PLO targets in southern Lebanon. The PLO took no retaliatory action.

On the same day, the Secretary-General appealed for an immediate cessation of all hostile acts and urged all parties to exercise maximum restraint so that the cease-fire could be fully restored and maintained. On 22 April, the President of the Security Council issued a statement on behalf of the members of the Council in which he demanded an end to all armed attacks and warned against any recurrence of violations of the cease-fire, in accordance with Security Council resolution 490(1981) of 21 July 1981.

On 9 May 1982, Israeli aircraft again attacked PLO targets in several localities in Lebanon, causing many casualties. Following these attacks, PLO positions in the Tyre pocket fired rockets into northern Israel, for the first time since July 1981. The next day, the Lebanese Government strongly protested the Israeli air attacks as an act of aggression against Lebanon.[101] The Permanent Representative of Israel also addressed a letter to the President of the Council on that day in which he drew attention to recent terrorist attacks against civilians in Israel, for which Israel held the PLO responsible.[102] Intense efforts were made by the United Nations both at its New York Headquarters and in the field to restore the cease-fire. There were no further incidents in the area in May, but the situation remained extremely volatile.

On the night of 3 June, the Israeli Ambassador to the Court of St. James was seriously wounded in London in a terrorist attack. Although the PLO disclaimed any responsibility for this assassination attempt, Israel launched on 4 June massive bombing raids against PLO targets in and around Beirut, causing heavy loss of life and destruction. Shortly after those attacks, intense exchanges of fire broke out between the PLO and the *de facto*/IDF positions in southern Lebanon, over the UNIFIL area. The Israeli towns of Nahariyya, Kiryat Shemona and Metulla came under PLO artillery and rocket fire.

On the same afternoon, the Secretary-General urgently appealed to all concerned to desist from all hostile acts and to make every effort to restore the cease-fire. Later that day, the President of the Security Council made a similar appeal on behalf of the members of the Council. Nevertheless, the exchanges of artillery fire continued unabated on 5 June in the same general areas. There were also intense Israeli air strikes in the vicinity of Beirut and Damur, and shelling by Israeli naval vessels in the Tyre area.

The Secretary-General, who was in continuous touch with the parties concerned, again made an urgent appeal on 5 June for a simultaneous cessation of hostilities at the earliest possible time. Later the same day, the Security Council met and unanimously adopted resolution 508(1982), by which it called upon all the parties to the conflict to cease immediately and simultaneously all military activities within Lebanon and across the Israeli-Lebanese border at no later than 0600 hours local time on Sunday, 6 June.

Immediately after the adoption of that resolution, the Secretary-General instructed the Commander of UNIFIL to utilize every possibility of following up on the Council's resolution.[103] On the same evening, the PLO reaffirmed its commitment to stop all military operations across the Lebanese border, while reserving the right to respond to Israeli attacks. The Permanent Representative of Israel to the United Nations informed the Secretary-General that, while Israeli actions were taken in the exercise of its right of self-defence, the Council's resolution would be brought before the Israeli Cabinet. From 2300 hours local time on 5 June until 0600 hours the next morning, there were intermittent and relatively light exchanges of fire between the opposing sides, but shortly after 0600 hours, which was the cease-fire time set by the Security Council, Israeli forces launched intensive air attacks against various PLO targets in southern Lebanon.

Israeli invasion, June 1982

At 1030 hours local time on the morning of 6 June, General Callaghan met with Lieutenant-General Rafael Eitan, the Chief of Staff of the IDF, at Metulla in northern Israel.[104] General Callaghan's purpose was to discuss the implementation of Security Council resolution 508(1982), but instead he was told by General Eitan that the IDF planned to launch a military operation into Lebanon within half an hour, at 1100 hours local time. General Eitan also intimated that the Israeli forces would pass through or near UNIFIL positions and that he expected that UNIFIL would raise no physical difficulty to the advancing troops. General Callaghan protested in the strongest terms to this totally unacceptable course of action.

Immediately after the meeting, General Callaghan issued instructions to all UNIFIL units, in case of attack by one of the parties, to block advancing forces, take defensive measures and stay in their positions unless their safety was "seriously imperilled".

At 1100 hours local time, about two IDF mechanized divisions, with full air and naval support, crossed the border and entered the UNIFIL area. They advanced along three main axes: in the western sector, along the coastal road; in the central sector, towards Ett Taibe (At Tayyibah) and the Akiya bridge; and in the eastern sector, through the Kafr Shuba–Shab'a (Chouba–Chebaa) area.

In accordance with their general instructions, UNIFIL troops took various measures to stop, or at least delay, the advance of the Israeli forces. On the coastal road leading to Tyre, Dutch soldiers planted obstacles before an advancing Israeli tank column and damaged one tank. During the encounter, Israeli tank barrels were trained on the Dutch soldiers while Israeli troops pushed aside the obstacles.

Other UNIFIL battalions also put up obstacles of various kinds, which were forcibly removed or bulldozed. A small Nepalese position guarding the Khardala bridge stood its ground for two days despite continued harassments and threats. Only after two days, on the morning of 8 June, could the Israeli tanks cross the bridge after partially destroying the Nepalese position.

Despite these efforts, the UNIFIL soldiers with their light defensive weapons could not withstand the massive Israeli invading forces, and the UNIFIL positions in the line of the invasion were bypassed or overrun within 24 hours. One Norwegian soldier was killed by shrapnel on 6 June.

On the morning of 6 June, the Security Council met again and unanimously adopted resolution 509(1982), by which it demanded that Israel withdraw all its military forces forthwith and unconditionally to the internationally recognized boundaries of Lebanon, and that all parties observe strictly the cease-fire.

On the evening of 7 June, Chairman Arafat informed the Secretary-General that the Lebanese-Palestinian joint command had decided to abide by the Security Council's resolution.[105] The Permanent Representative of Israel replied on behalf of his Government that the "Peace for Galilee" operation had been ordered because of the intolerable situation created by the presence in Lebanon of a large number of "terrorists" operating from that country and threatening the lives of the civilians of Galilee, and that any withdrawal of Israeli forces prior to the conclusion of concrete arrangements which would permanently and reliably preclude hostile action against Israel's citizens was inconceivable.[106]

UNIFIL's interim tasks

In commenting on the invasion in his report of 14 June 1982 to the Security Council,[107] the Secretary-General stated that UNIFIL, like all other United Nations peace-keeping operations, was based on certain fundamental principles, foremost of which was the non-use of force, except in self-defence. The Force was not meant to engage in combat to attain its goals; it had a strictly limited strength, armed only with light defensive weapons. It was for these reasons that certain essential conditions had been laid down at the time of the establishment of the Force. Those included, first, that it must function with the full co-operation of the parties concerned and, second, that it must have at all times the full confidence and backing of the Security Council. In this connection, it was a fundamental assumption that the parties would fully abide by the Council's decisions and that, in the event of non-compliance, the Council itself and those Member States in a position to bring their influence to bear would be able to act decisively to ensure respect for those decisions.

In the case of UNIFIL, those conditions were not met. Instead, UNIFIL had been faced with inadequate co-operation throughout its existence, culminating in an overwhelming use of force. Once the Israeli action commenced, it was evident that UNIFIL troops could, at best, maintain their positions and take defensive measures, seeking to impede and protest the advance.

The Israeli invasion of June 1982 radically altered the circumstances in which UNIFIL had been set up and under which it had functioned since March 1978. By 8 June, the UNIFIL area of operation had fallen under Israeli control and the Force had to operate behind the Israeli lines. Under those conditions, UNIFIL could no longer fulfil the tasks entrusted to it by the Security Council. Pending a Council decision on the Force's mandate, which was due to expire on 19 June 1982, the Secretary-General instructed General Callaghan, as an interim measure, to ensure that all UNIFIL troops and the UNTSO military observers attached to it continued to man their positions unless their safety was seriously imperilled, and to provide protection and humanitarian assistance to the local population to the extent possible.[108]

These interim tasks were endorsed by the Security Council on 18 June, when it decided, by resolution 511(1982), to extend the mandate of UNIFIL for an interim period of two months. At the same time, the Council made clear that the Force's original terms of reference remained valid, and reaffirmed its call for the complete withdrawal of the Israeli forces from Lebanese territory. The mandate of UNIFIL was later repeatedly extended with the same reservations for further interim periods varying from two to six months.

In accordance with the instructions of the Secretary-General, UNIFIL remained deployed in its area of operation with only minor adjustments. Some positions considered as non-essential in the changed circumstances were closed down, while others were reinforced. UNTSO observers continued to man the five observation positions along the Armistice Demarcation Line and to maintain three teams outside the UNIFIL area—at Tyre, at Metulla in northern Israel and at Château de Beaufort north of the Litani River.

Much in the same way as they had done before the invasion, UNIFIL troops operated observation posts and check-points and conducted patrols in sensitive areas in order to prevent hostile actions and to ensure the security and safety of the local population. They continued to prevent infiltrations and incursions into the UNIFIL area by non-authorized armed elements, but they could not control the movement and actions of the Israeli forces or of the armed irregulars acting with those forces' direct support. In such cases, UNIFIL could only monitor their activities and report to the Secretary-General. In carrying out their functions, the UNIFIL troops co-operated closely with the local authorities and with the Lebanese gendarmes when they were available.

Much of UNIFIL's efforts was now devoted to humanitarian assistance. In co-operation with the United Nations Children's Fund (UNICEF) and the International Committee of the Red Cross, UNIFIL humanitarian teams distributed to needy local inhabitants food and water and other essential supplies. A UNIFIL hospital maintained by the Swedish medical company and the medical teams of the various national contingents dispensed medical care to the local population, including conducting vaccination campaigns for Lebanese children. UNIFIL also assisted the local authorities with various community projects and with the repair of public buildings such as schools and local dispensaries. A French engineering unit did much to clear the area of mines, shells and explosive devices, which were a constant danger to the population. In many cases, the officers and soldiers of the various contingents and their Governments made voluntary contributions to help villages in their sectors in various ways, for example by giving them water trucks, by helping them to repair school-buildings or by providing the manpower to clean sewage systems.

In the new situation created by the invasion, the capacity of UNIFIL to operate was necessarily contingent upon the degree of co-operation received from the Israeli occupation authorities. Despite the difficulties encountered, UNIFIL was able to carry out its interim tasks in its area of operation most of the time without impediment. However, serious problems were encountered on occasion, particularly during the first days of the invasion, as a result of activities of the Israeli forces and the Lebanese local armed groups they controlled.

Immediately after the invasion, the Israeli forces frequently searched houses in sensitive areas, confiscated weapons they uncovered and arrested local inhabitants suspected of affiliation with the PLO or the Lebanese National Movement. These activities subsided after July 1982, and the presence of the IDF in the UNIFIL area of deployment was reduced to approximately battalion strength. However, the situation deteriorated again after April 1983, when the activities of a Shi'ite resistance movement against the Israeli occupation, which became increasingly active in the northern part of the occupied territory, began to spill over into the UNIFIL area. Although the area remained relatively quiet until February 1985, there were occasional attacks against the Israeli forces by resistance groups, particularly in the form of roadside bombs planted along the IDF-patrolled routes, and countermeasures by the Israeli forces, mainly in the form of cordon-and-search operations in the Shi'ite villages. UNIFIL could not prevent countermeasures by the Israeli forces, but endeavoured, by pressure and suasion, to mitigate violence, and protect the civilian population as much as possible. It also provided medical care and humanitarian assistance to the affected population.

Following the invasion, the *de facto* forces of Major Haddad attempted to extend their activities into the UNIFIL area. Although some of those groups were able to penetrate the UNIFIL area on the tail of the Israeli invading forces, in most cases UNIFIL was able to turn them back.

In April 1984, three months after the death of Major Haddad, Major-General Antoine Lahad, also a former officer of the Lebanese National Army, took over the command of the *de facto* forces, which were renamed the "South Lebanon Army" (SLA). According to available information, the strength of the SLA had been increased to approximately 2,100 as of October 1984. Although Israel gave the SLA an expanded role in the northern part of the occupied territory, it did not make any determined attempt to increase its activities in the UNIFIL area.

More serious problems were encountered by UNIFIL when new local militias, armed and uniformed by Israel, began to appear in its area towards the end of June 1982.[109] These militias were recognized neither by the Lebanese Government nor by the established local authorities. Acting with the assistance of the IDF and under its control, they attempted to set up check-points and conduct patrols in the villages. They were generally ill-disciplined and their actions were deeply resented by the local inhabitants and often led to friction with them. UNIFIL was under standing instructions to disarm the local militias and to contain their activities whenever they were not accompanied and directly protected by the Israeli forces. A number of incidents occurred at UNIFIL check-points when militiamen refused to submit to having their vehicles searched or to surrender their weapons.

Until February 1985, the incidents outlined above were exceptions rather than the rule, and the situation in the UNIFIL area was generally quiet—much quieter than in other parts of Lebanon during those years of turmoil. This was widely recognized by the Lebanese Government and the local population alike. Each time the mandate of UNIFIL neared its expiration, many *mukhtars* (village mayors) would write to the Secretary-General to beseech him not to withdraw the Force, and the Lebanese Government would request its extension in insistent terms.

The Secretary-General repeatedly recommended the extension of UNIFIL's mandate in accordance with the requests of the Lebanese Government. In support of his recommendation, he pointed out that despite the difficulties confronted by it, UNIFIL remained an important element of stability in southern Lebanon. Its presence represented the commitment of the United Nations to support the independence, sovereignty and territorial integrity of Lebanon and to help bring about the withdrawal of the Israeli forces from Lebanese territory, in accordance with Security Council resolutions 425(1978) and 509(1982). A withdrawal of the Force before the Lebanese Government was in a position to assume effective control of the area with its national army and its internal security forces would unquestionably be a serious blow to the prospect of restoring the authority of that Government in southern Lebanon, as well as to the security and welfare of the local population.[110]

I. Aftermath of the invasion

The 1982 invasion set off a train of events which deeply affected Lebanon as well as Israel and the PLO. Although they took place outside the UNIFIL area of operation, these events had an important bearing on the activities and future of the Force.

As the Israeli forces neared west Beirut, to where large numbers of PLO fighters had retreated, the situation in and around the Lebanese capital became increasingly critical, and the need for a peace-keeping operation to prevent further escalation of the conflict was urgently felt. The PLO called for the deployment of UNIFIL in the Beirut area, but this was strongly opposed by Israel. Various proposals for the establishment of a United Nations military observer group in and around Beirut were examined by the Security Council in June and July, but no agreement could be reached.

Security Council actions

On 1 August, upon learning that an IDF unit had entered west Beirut, the Security Council met again and adopted resolution 516(1982), by which it took note of the massive violations of the cease-fire in and around Beirut and expressed alarm at the intensification of military activities there. It demanded an immediate cessation of all military activities within Lebanon and across the Lebanese-Israeli border, and authorized the Secretary-General to deploy immediately, on the request of the Government of Lebanon, United Nations observers to monitor the situation in and around Beirut.

Following the adoption of that resolution, the Lebanese Government immediately submitted a request for the stationing of United Nations observers in Beirut.[111] Although Israel withheld its support for the proposed operation, the Secretary-General decided to proceed with the establishment of an observer mission in Beirut, which was called the Observer Group Beirut (OGB).[112] On 3 August, OGB became operational, but with only the 10 UNTSO observers already stationed in Beirut, because Israel prevented additional observers from reaching the capital *(see chapter II above)*.

On 4 August, the Security Council met again and adopted resolution 517(1982), in which it expressed shock and alarm at the consequences of the Israeli invasion of Beirut. It confirmed its demand for an immediate cease-fire and withdrawal of Israeli forces from Lebanon, censured Israel for its failure to comply with its resolutions, and called for the prompt return of Israeli troops which had moved forward after 1325 hours, New York time, on 1 August. The Council also took note of the PLO's decision to remove the Palestinian armed forces from Beirut and authorized the Secretary-General, as an immediate step, to increase the number of United Nations observers in and around the city.

Meeting again on 12 August, the Security Council adopted resolution 518(1982), by which, expressing most serious concern about continued military activities in Lebanon, it demanded that Israel and all parties to the conflict observe strictly the terms of Council resolutions relevant to the immediate cessation of all military activities within Lebanon and, particularly, in and around Beirut. It further demanded the immediate lifting of all restrictions on the city of Beirut in order to permit the free entry of supplies to meet the urgent needs of the civilian population in the city. The Council also requested the United Nations observers to report on the situation in and around Beirut, and demanded that Israel co-operate fully in the Secretary-General's efforts to secure the effective deployment of the observers.

On the afternoon of the same day, a cease-fire was established according to an agreement worked out by Ambassador Habib of the United States. The agreement provided that, following the establishment of the cease-fire, the Israeli forces would withdraw from west Beirut and the PLO fighters in the area would be evacuated from Lebanon.

Multinational force

On 20 August,[113] Lebanon informed the Secretary-General that it had requested the deployment of a multinational force in Beirut to assist the Lebanese armed forces as they carried out the orderly and safe departure from Lebanon of Palestinian armed personnel in the Beirut area, in a manner which would further the restoration of the sovereignty and authority of the Government of Lebanon over the Beirut area. France, Italy and the United States had entered into agreements with the Government of Lebanon for the deployment of their troops to participate in that multinational force.

The cease-fire that had gone into effect on 12 August was generally effective. The first contingent of the multinational force arrived in Beirut on 21 August and the remainder on 25 and 26 August. The evacuation from the Beirut area of the Palestinian armed elements, together with a Syrian battalion of the Arab Deterrent Force, began on 21 August and was completed on 1 September without incident. In all, some 10,000 PLO fighters and about 3,500 Syrian troops were evacuated. Immediately after their departure, elements of the Lebanese army and the internal security forces moved into west Beirut. A few days later, on 10 September, the multinational force began to withdraw from Beirut, and by 13 September the last soldiers of the force had left the area.[114]

Assassination of the Lebanese President-elect

One day after the completion of the withdrawal of the multinational force, Bashir Gemayel, the President-elect of Lebanon, was assassinated in a bomb explosion. The next morning, Israeli forces moved back in strength into west Beirut.

On 16 September,[115] the Secretary-General issued a statement expressing concern at the developments in Lebanon following the assassination, and, in particular, at the movement of Israeli forces into west Beirut. The same day, the Security Council met at the request of Lebanon and, on 17 September, adopted resolution 520(1982), by which it condemned the recent Israeli incursions into Beirut in violation of the cease-fire agreements and of Council resolutions. It called again for strict respect for Lebanon's sovereignty, territorial integrity, unity and political independence under the sole and exclusive authority of the Lebanese Government through the Lebanese army throughout Lebanon, and it reaffirmed its resolutions 512(1982) and 513(1982) calling for respect for the rights of the civilian population. The Council also expressed its support for the efforts of the Secretary-General to implement resolution 516(1982) concerning the deployment of United Nations observers, and requested all the parties concerned to co-operate fully in the application of the resolution.

Palestinian camps massacre

While the Security Council was meeting in New York, a most tragic event was unfolding in west Beirut. In the afternoon of 17 September, Kataeb (phalange) units were able to enter the Sabra and Shatila Palestinian refugee camps in the southern suburbs of Beirut and soon went on a rampage, killing large numbers of Palestinian refugees, including women, children and old people, in a most brutal manner. The freedom of movement of the 10 United Nations observers of OGB was restricted by the Israeli forces after their re-entry into west Beirut and they were not able to approach the camps before 18 September. Their report, which was received by the Secretary-General on that day, confirmed the massacre which had taken place and the involvement of phalangists.

Upon receiving the first reports of the massacre, the Secretary-General issued, on the morning of 18 September, a statement expressing shock and horror, and calling urgently for an end to the violence. Later the same morning, he submitted a report to the Security Council on the developments mentioned above.[116] After recalling his repeated efforts since 13 June 1982 to increase the number of United Nations observers in Beirut, the Secretary-General indicated that he had instructed General Erskine, the UNTSO Chief of Staff, to make a renewed approach to the Israeli authorities in that regard. At the same time, he expressed the view that, in the situation that prevailed, unarmed military observers, however courageous or numerous, were not enough. He noted in this connection that in the UNIFIL area in the south, conditions had remained quiet and UNIFIL had successfully prevented the harassment of the civilian population by any armed groups.

On the evening of 18 September, the Security Council met to consider the above developments. In the early morning of 19 September, it adopted resolution 521(1982), by which it condemned the criminal massacre of Palestinian civilians in Beirut, and authorized the Secretary-General, as an immediate step, to increase the number of United

Nations observers in and around Beirut from 10 to 50. The Council also requested the Secretary-General to initiate urgent consultations, in particular with the Government of Lebanon, on additional steps which the Council might take, including the possible deployment of United Nations forces, to assist that Government in ensuring full protection for the civilian population in and around Beirut.

Observation in Beirut

On 20 September, the Secretary-General reported to the Security Council[117] that General Erskine was sending 40 additional observers to Beirut. He also indicated that the Commander of UNIFIL, General Callaghan, had said that, if required, he could send to Beirut a group of about 2,000 men drawn from selected contingents of UNIFIL. However, the Government of Lebanon decided to request the return of the multinational force to Beirut.[118]

At the end of September 1982, the situation in Beirut was generally quiet. The French, Italian and United States contingents of the multinational force had started returning to Beirut on 24 September and by 30 September the total strength of the force had reached approximately 4,000. Later they were joined by a small British contingent of 90 men. Following the arrival of the multinational force, the Israeli forces withdrew from the Beirut area to a line near Khalde, south of the Beirut International Airport.[119]

During the following months, the United States launched a peace initiative which led to the signing, on 17 May 1983, of an agreement between Israel and Lebanon. In essence, this agreement provided for the withdrawal of the Israeli and other non-Lebanese forces from Lebanon and for joint security arrangements by the two countries in the border area of southern Lebanon. The agreement, however, never came into effect and was eventually abrogated by the Government of Lebanon.

In early September 1983, the Israeli forces, which had been frequently attacked by Lebanese Moslem guerrilla groups in the Aley and Shouf areas, decided to redeploy south of the Awali River. Withdrawal of the Israeli forces set the stage for fierce fighting between Government forces and Christian phalangists on the one hand, and Shi'ite and Druse militias on the other, in the evacuated areas.

In this new serious situation, the Secretary-General sought to expand the activities of OGB so as to provide a restraining element in the areas evacuated by the Israeli forces. But his efforts were abortive because of the opposition of some of the parties concerned.

As hostilities spread and intensified in these areas, the French and United States contingents of the multinational force became embroiled in the fighting and there were some serious and tragic incidents involving them and certain Moslem groups.

In February 1984, Moslem militias took control of west Beirut and most of the Aley and Shouf areas. The situation of the multinational force which was deployed in and around west Beirut became rapidly untenable.

The four contingents of the multinational force were successively withdrawn from Beirut during the first half of 1984. Before the final withdrawal of the force, the Security Council met at the end of February 1984 at the request of France, and considered a French draft resolution which would have had the Council issue an urgent appeal for an immediate cease-fire throughout Lebanon and decide to constitute a United Nations force to take up positions in the Beirut area as soon as all elements of the multinational force had withdrawn from Lebanese territory.[120] The draft resolution, however, could not be adopted because of the veto of the Soviet Union.

In the mean time, national reconciliation talks were held at Lausanne, Switzerland, among leaders of the major political and religious groups of Lebanon, and, as a result, a National Unity Government headed by Prime Minister Rashid Karami was set up in Beirut in May 1984. This development, however, did not end intersectarian fighting in Beirut and other areas of Lebanon.

J. Withdrawal of the Israeli forces

Secretary-General's views on UNIFIL's mandate

The Secretary-General, in his report of 9 April 1984 to the Security Council,[121] expressed the view that an expanded role for UNIFIL in southern Lebanon might be useful in the future, taking into account the concerns of the various parties involved and the objectives of the Security Council. He suggested that, at the appropriate time, the Council consider making the mandate of UNIFIL more effective in southern Lebanon, in the context of a withdrawal of the Israeli forces, by: the temporary deployment of UNIFIL, with elements of the Lebanese army and internal security forces, in areas vacated by Israeli forces; the immediate deployment of elements of UNIFIL in the Sidon area upon Israeli withdrawal from that area, with a view to assuring the safety and security of the population, including Palestinian refugees in the camps in that area; and the working out of the necessary arrangements to ensure that southern Lebanon became a zone of peace under the sovereignty and authority of the Lebanese Government.

In a further report dated 9 October 1984,[122] the Secretary-General again brought these suggestions to the Council's attention. He indicated that in recent weeks there had been a number of developments which seemed to him to have brought about more positive prospects for the realization of the course of action he had outlined. It was his impression, from recent contacts with the leaders concerned, that there was general agreement on the objective of the withdrawal of Israeli forces from southern Lebanon and on the necessity of working out arrangements which would ensure peace and security in the region and the restoration of Lebanese authority and sovereignty in the wake of the Israeli withdrawal. He also noted that there was general agreement that an expanded mandate for UNIFIL and a widening of its area of operation would be key elements in such future arrangements. The Secretary-General went on to say that if these conclusions were valid, he hoped that it would be possible in the near future to move forward in agreeing upon the necessary practical arrangements which would have to be made. Naturally, the United Nations machinery, and in particular UNIFIL, would be available to the parties to facilitate the reaching of agreements and to provide the auspices for the necessary discussions, if they so desired.

After considering the report of the Secretary-General, the Security Council adopted resolution 555(1984) on 12 October 1984, by which it extended the mandate of UNIFIL for a further interim period of six months, until 19 April 1985. The Council reiterated that UNIFIL should fully implement its mandate as defined by the Council in resolution 425(1978) and all other relevant resolutions, and requested the Secretary-General to continue consultations with the Government of Lebanon and other parties directly concerned, and report to the Council.

Withdrawal discussions, Naqoura
(November 1984–January 1985)

Following the adoption of the Security Council's October 1984 resolution, the Secretary-General approached the Governments of Israel and Lebanon and suggested that they begin negotiations as soon as possible on the withdrawal of Israeli forces from Lebanese territory and related security arrangements in southern Lebanon. After consultations with those Governments, he convoked a conference of military representatives of the two countries at UNIFIL headquarters in Naqoura to discuss those topics. The conference began on 8 November 1984 and met intermittently until 24 January 1985.[123]

From the outset of the conference, the Lebanese representative insisted on the full withdrawal of Israeli forces from Lebanese territory and the subsequent deployment of the Lebanese Army together with UNIFIL down to the international boundary, in accordance with Security Council resolution 425(1978). The Israeli representative took the position that UNIFIL should be deployed in the entire area to be evacuated by the Israeli forces, with the positioning of the main forces of UNIFIL between the Zahrani and the Awali rivers up to the border between Lebanon and Syria. While Israel would accept a limited UNIFIL presence further south, the Israeli representative maintained that local forces should be responsible for security arrangements in the southernmost part of Lebanon. There was little change in these basic positions as the conference progressed.

On 14 January 1985, the Israeli Government announced a plan for the unilateral redeployment of the Israeli forces in three phases. This redeployment plan was formally presented to the Naqoura conference on 22 January. In the first phase, relating to the western sector, the Israel Defence Forces would evacuate the Sidon area and deploy in the Litani–Nabatiyah region. In the second phase, relating to the eastern sector, the IDF would deploy in the Hasbayya area. In the third phase, it would deploy along the Israel-Lebanon international border, while maintaining a security zone in southern Lebanon where local forces (the so-called "South Lebanon Army") would function with IDF backing.

The first phase would be carried out within five weeks of the Government's decision. Notification of the timing would be given to the Lebanese Government and the United Nations Secretariat in order to allow them to make arrangements and deploy forces in the areas to be evacuated by the IDF. The timing of each subsequent phase would be decided by the Government. Israeli officials indicated subsequently that the second and third phases of the redeployment were tentatively scheduled to be completed in the spring and summer of 1985.

On 24 January 1985, the Lebanese representative announced at the conference that the Israeli redeployment plan did not satisfy his Government's demand for a detailed plan and timetable for the complete withdrawal of Israeli forces from Lebanese territory. While reiterating his Government's willingness to co-operate with the United Nations with a view to expediting the withdrawal of those forces, he maintained that the role of the United Nations could not be discussed before the presentation of such a detailed plan and timetable by Israel.

At the end of the fourteenth meeting, on that date, the Naqoura conference was adjourned *sine die.*

Withdrawal of Israeli forces from the Sidon area

On 16 February, the Israeli forces proceeded with the first phase of the redeployment plan and withdrew from the Sidon area. Early that morning, the Commander of UNIFIL was informed of the withdrawal and immediately communicated it to the Lebanese army authorities. Those authorities advised General Callaghan the next day that the Lebanese army had taken over the evacuated area without incident.

From early February onwards, and particularly after the withdrawal from Sidon, there was an intensification of guerrilla attacks against the Israeli forces by Shi'ite resistance groups and of Israeli cordon-and-search operations against Shi'ite villages. An increasing number of these operations occurred in the UNIFIL area. In a statement made on 27 February,[124] the Secretary-General outlined the dilemma faced by UNIFIL. He stated that for obvious reasons the Force had no right to impede Lebanese acts of resistance against the occupying forces, nor did it have the mandate and the means to prevent Israeli countermeasures. In the circumstances, the men of UNIFIL had done their utmost to mitigate violence, protect the civilian population and reduce acts of reprisal to the minimum.

On 25 February, Lebanon requested an urgent meeting of the Security Council to consider "the continuing acts of aggression and abusive practices of Israeli occupying forces in southern Lebanon, the western Bekaa and the Rashaya district".[125] The Security Council held four meetings from 28 February to 12 March on this question. During the debate, Lebanon submitted a draft resolution[126] which would have had the Council: reaffirm the urgent need to implement Security Council resolutions 425(1978), 508(1982) and 509(1982), which demand that Israel withdraw all its military forces forthwith and unconditionally to the internationally recognized boundary of Lebanon; reiterate its call for strict respect for the sovereignty, independence, unity and territorial integrity of Lebanon; affirm that the fourth Geneva Convention of 1949 (on the protection of civilian persons in time of war) applied to the territories occupied by Israel in southern Lebanon, the western Bekaa and the Rashaya district; and demand that Israel desist forthwith from its practices against the civilian population in those territories, and immediately lift all restrictions and obstacles to the restoration of normal conditions in the area under its occupation. On 12 March, the Security Council voted on the draft resolution, which was not adopted owing to the negative vote of the United States.

Before the expiry of UNIFIL's mandate the Permanent Representative of Lebanon, in a letter dated 27 March to the Secretary-General,[127] requested, on behalf of his Government, an extension of UNIFIL for a further six months. In his report of 11 April,[128] the Secretary-General said he considered that the presence of UNIFIL was essential in the present circumstances and recommended an extension of the Force, taking into account the request of the Lebanese Government. As regards the role of UNIFIL, he recalled his efforts to bring together the positions of the Lebanese and Israeli Governments. He felt that the main problem was to reach a situation in Lebanon south of the Litani, after the Israeli withdrawal, in which international peace and security could be assured and normal conditions progressively restored. He believed that the best means of achieving this would be an orderly takeover from Israeli forces, perhaps in the first instance by UNIFIL with elements of the Lebanese army, with the ultimate aim of restoring the complete authority of the Lebanese Government and army. He also believed that to achieve effective and constructive results, some form of consultative mechanism under United Nations auspices would be essential. If the Naqoura talks or the 1949 Israel-Lebanon General Armistice Agreement were not acceptable for one reason or another to one or the other of the parties, the Secretary-General would be prepared to consider convoking a new conference of military representatives of the two Governments for the purpose.

After considering the Secretary-General's report, the Security Council decided, by resolution 561(1985) of 17 April 1985, to extend UNIFIL's mandate for a further interim period of six months, until 19 October 1985. In the same resolution, the Council reiterated its strong support for the territorial integrity, sovereignty and independence of Lebanon within its internationally recognized boundaries and called on all the parties concerned to co-operate with UNIFIL for the full implementation of its mandate.

Further withdrawals of the Israeli forces

Meanwhile, the Israeli forces proceeded with the second phase of redeployment, which was carried out gradually in the course of March and April 1985.[129] They withdrew from the Nabatiyah area on

11 March. The Jezzine area and the north-eastern sector, including the Bekaa Valley and the strategic position of Jebal Baruk, were evacuated on 14 April. On 29 April, the Israeli forces withdrew from the Tyre pocket and from the positions they had established in the western sector of the UNIFIL area. At the end of the second phase, the Israeli forces were redeployed in a strip of land north of the international border extending from the Mediterranean Sea to the Hasbayya area, with a depth varying between about two kilometres at its narrowest point and about 20 kilometres at its widest. In accordance with the Israeli plan, this strip of land, which extended into part of the UNIFIL area, was to be maintained as a "security zone" where the "South Lebanon Army" and other local militias armed and controlled by the Israeli forces were to function with the latter's backing, after the completion of the third and last phase of the Israeli redeployment.

Following the adoption of Security Council resolution 561(1985), the Secretary-General initiated a new effort to work out, in consultation with the Lebanese and Israeli authorities, arrangements which would lead to the full withdrawal of the Israeli forces, the deployment of UNIFIL to the international border and the establishment of international peace and security in the area. Unfortunately, these efforts were inconclusive, and the Israeli forces proceeded with the third phase of the unilateral redeployment plan, without change, in May and the early part of June. During that period, those forces progressively withdrew from positions established in the "security zone", handing them over to elements of the SLA. On 10 June, the Israeli Government announced that the third phase had been completed. It indicated that, while all combat units had been withdrawn from Lebanese territory, some Israeli troops would continue to operate in the "security zone" for an unspecified period of time and act as advisers to the SLA.

In these circumstances, UNIFIL was not able to extend its deployment to the border. Moreover, in that part of its area of deployment which overlapped with the "security zone", it found itself confronted with many positions manned by the Israeli forces and/or elements of the SLA. There were 18 such positions as of October 1985.

The greater part of the UNIFIL area was relatively quiet after its evacuation by the Israeli forces. UNIFIL continued to maintain liaison with the local leaders of Amal and other Lebanese resistance groups, which generally co-operated with the Force in the performance of its tasks.

In contrast, the situation in the "security zone" was very tense. Lebanese resistance groups launched frequent attacks on Israeli troops and the Lebanese irregulars associated with them throughout that zone, both within and outside UNIFIL's area of deployment. In those attacks, small arms, rocket-propelled grenades, rockets and roadside bombs were employed against IDF/SLA positions and personnel. There were also a number of suicide bomb attacks.

On the other hand, the IDF and elements of the SLA carried out a number of cordon-and-search operations against Shi'ite villages, some of them in the UNIFIL area. Elements of the SLA also shelled Shi'ite villages in the UNIFIL area on several occasions. UNIFIL strongly protested to the Israeli authorities the attacks directed at villages in its area and endeavoured, within the limits of its means, to protect the civilian population and reduce acts of violence to the minimum.

Renewal of UNIFIL's mandate, October 1985

Before the expiry of UNIFIL's mandate, the Permanent Representative of Lebanon, in a letter dated 3 October 1985,[130] informed the Secretary-General of his Government's decision to request an extension of UNIFIL's mandate for a further period of six months. He stated that his Government was convinced that despite the present circumstances, UNIFIL continued to be an important factor in providing stability in southern Lebanon.

In his report to the Security Council of 10 October 1985,[131] the Secretary-General stated that the current situation in Lebanon south of the Litani was not only unsatisfactory but also dangerous. UNIFIL found itself once again between opposing forces and was precluded from deploying right up to the international border in accordance with its mandate. The Secretary-General had little doubt that, if the Israeli presence in the "security zone" was to continue for long, violence would inevitably escalate and spread. In such an event, UNIFIL's situation would become even more difficult.

The Secretary-General went on to say that in these circumstances, making a recommendation to the Security Council on UNIFIL posed a dilemma. On the one hand, the conditions still did not exist in which UNIFIL could fully perform its functions or completely fulfil its mandate, and the situation was more likely to deteriorate than to improve. Such a state of affairs was contrary to the Council's intentions and also imposed a severe strain on the UNIFIL contingents and on the Governments which had so loyally supported the operation by making troops available. On the other hand, he was convinced that UNIFIL was an extremely important factor in whatever peace and normality existed in southern Lebanon. He believed that, if for some reason UNIFIL were to disappear, the level of violence would inevitably increase dramatically, with resistance operations giving rise to reprisals in a spiral of violence. Such a situation could well develop into a new and serious international crisis. After much thought, the Secretary-General had concluded that, especially in the light of Lebanon's request, it was his duty to recommend a further extension of the mandate. He believed, however, that such a decision must not be understood to mean that UNIFIL would be allowed to become an open-ended commitment for the troop-contributing countries and for the United Nations if the requisite conditions for the effective operation of the Force continued to be absent. He believed that there was still a good chance of re-establishing international peace and security in southern Lebanon if the correct actions were taken soon by all concerned, but he also believed that further undue delay was likely to produce a new and serious crisis, possibly with widespread ramifications.

After considering the Secretary-General's report, the Security Council decided, by resolution 575(1985) of 17 October 1985, to extend UNIFIL's mandate for six months, until 19 April 1986. In this connection, the Council expressed once again its strong support for the territorial integrity, sovereignty and independence of Lebanon within its internationally recognized boundaries, and called on all parties concerned to co-operate with UNIFIL for the full implementation of its mandate.

K. Financial aspects

UNIFIL and the United Nations Peace-keeping Force in Cyprus (UNFICYP) are the two existing United Nations peace-keeping operations with serious financial problems. The difficulties of UNFICYP stem from the fact that the Force is financed mainly by voluntary contributions, and it was to avert this kind of problem that the Secretary-General insisted that the forces subsequently established by the Security Council should have a more stable source of income. When the Second United Nations Emergency Force was set up in October 1973, the Council decided, upon a proposal of the Secretary-General, that the costs of the new Force should be considered as expenses of the Organization to be borne by the Members as apportioned by the General Assembly. This method was applied again to the United Nations Disengagement Observer Force in May 1974 and to UNIFIL in March 1978.

However, in the case of UNIFIL, a number of Member States have refused, for political reasons, to pay their assessments, and as a result there has been a deficit in the UNIFIL Special Account which has steadily increased with the passing of time. In this situation, the United Nations has been forced to fall behind more and more in reimbursing Governments for the costs they have incurred in contributing troops, equipment and supplies to UNIFIL.

In December 1979, on a proposal of the Secretary-General, the General Assembly established a Suspense Account for UNIFIL—supplementing the Special Account—to be financed by voluntary contributions from Governments, international organizations and private sources. The funds in the Suspense Account were to be used solely for reimbursing Governments which contributed troops to UNIFIL.

The Secretary-General has repeatedly appealed to all Member States to pay their assessments without delay. Since 1979, he has also appealed to the Governments of the developed countries to consider making available, as a practical measure, voluntary contributions to UNIFIL's Suspense Account. However, the deficit in the UNIFIL budget has remained serious.

In his report to the Security Council on UNIFIL dated 10 October 1985,[132] the Secretary-General stated that there was, as of the beginning of that month, an accumulated shortfall in the UNIFIL Special Account of some $224 million and that, as a result, the Organization was falling far behind in reimbursement of the troop-contributing countries, thus placing an increasingly heavy burden on them, particularly on the less wealthy ones. He expressed his extreme concern about this state of affairs, not only for the reasons just mentioned but also because it could jeopardize the functioning of the Force.

Reference notes

Chapter II: UN Truce Supervision Organization

[1]A/648, S/829. [2]S/7930/Add.29. [3]S/7896. [4]A/6701/Add.1. [5]S/8053/Add.1,2. [6]S/9902. [7]S/10611, annex. [8]Ibid. [9]S/11013. [10]S/11017. [11]S/12611. [12]S/13578. [13]S/15334/Add.1. [14]S/16627.

Chapter III: First UN Emergency Force

[15]S/3654. [16]S/3656. [17]S/3710. [18]S/3713/Rev.1. [19]A/3289. [20]A/3302. [21]Ibid. [22]A/3375, annex. [23]A/3375. [24]A/3526. [25]A/3287. [26]Ibid. [27]A/3294 and A/3293. [28]A/3310. [29]A/3306 and A/3307. [30]A/3415. [31]Ibid. [32]A/3384, annex 2. [33]A/3389/Add.1. [34]A/3410. [35]A/3500.

[36]A/3511. [37]A/3512. [38]A/3527, annex I. [39]A/3527. [40]*Ibid.* [41]A/3527, annex V. [42]A/3568. [43]A/3527, annex III. [44]A/6669 and A/6730.

Chapter IV: Second UN Emergency Force

[45]S/11049. [46]S/11052/Rev.1. [47]S/11056/Add.6, annex. [48]S/11849. [49]S/12089. [50]S/12212. [51]S/13460. [52]S/11052/Rev.1. [53]S/11091 and S/11056/Add.3, annex. [54]S/11056/Add.7. [55]S/11056/Add.13. [56]S/11056/Add.14. [57]S/11818/Add.1. [58]S/11818 and Add.1-4.

Chapter V: UN Disengagement Observer Force

[59]S/11302. [60]S/11302/Add.1, annexes I and II. [61]S/11304. [62]S/11302/Add.2. [63]S/11883/Add.1. [64]S/13479.

Chapter VI: UN Interim Force in Lebanon

[65]S/12598. [66]S/12600. [67]S/12611. [68]S/12675. [69]S/12620/Add.1. [70]S/12611. [71]S/12845. [72]S/12620/Add.1. [73]S/12620/Add.2. [74]*Ibid.* [75]*Ibid.* [76]S/12620/Add.4. [77]*Ibid.* [78]S/12620/Add.5. [79]*Ibid.* [80]*Ibid.* [81]S/12736. [82]S/12738. [83]S/12845. [84]S/13888. [85]S/14295. [86]*Ibid.* [87]S/14118. [88]S/14591. [89]S/14789. [90]S/14613/Add.1. [91]S/12845. [92]*Ibid.* [93]S/13026. [94]S/13258. [95]S/14537. [96]S/13691. [97]S/14295. [98]*Ibid.* [99]S/14789. [100]S/14972. [101]S/15064. [102]S/15066. [103]S/15194/Add.1 [104]*Ibid.* [105]S/15178. [106]*Ibid.* [107]S/15194/Add.2. [108]S/15194/Add.1. [109]S/15357. [110]S/16036. [111]S/15333. [112]S/15334/Add.1. [113]S/15451. [114]S/15382/Add.1. [115]S/15451. [116]S/15400. [117]S/15408. [118]S/15451. [119]*Ibid.* [120]S/16351/Rev.2. [121]S/16472. [122]S/16776. [123]S/17093. [124]*Ibid.* [125]S/16983. [126]S/17000. [127]S/17062. [128]S/17093. [129]S/17557. [130]S/17526. [131]S/17557. [132]*Ibid.*

Part Three:
India/Pakistan

The UN Military Observer Group
in India and Pakistan and the
UN India-Pakistan Observation Mission

A. Background

The United Nations Military Observer Group in India and Pakistan (UNMOGIP) had its origin in the conflict between India and Pakistan over the status of the State of Jammu and Kashmir (referred to here as Kashmir). The United Nations India-Pakistan Observation Mission (UNIPOM) was an administrative adjunct, created when conflict occurred in 1965 along the borders of the two countries outside the UNMOGIP area.

In August 1947, India and Pakistan became independent dominions, in accordance with a scheme of partition provided by the Indian Independence Act of 1947. Under that scheme, the State of Jammu and Kashmir was free to accede to India or Pakistan. The accession became a matter of dispute between the two countries and fighting broke out later that year.

The question first came before the Security Council in January 1948,[1] when India complained that tribesmen and others were invading Kashmir and that extensive fighting was taking place. India charged that Pakistan was assisting and participating in the invasion. Pakistan denied India's charges and declared that Kashmir's accession to India following India's independence in 1947 was illegal.

B. United Nations Commission for India and Pakistan

Security Council action

On 20 January, the Council adopted resolution 39(1948) establishing a three-member United Nations Commission for India and Pakistan (UNCIP) "to investigate the facts pursuant to Article 34 of the Charter of the United Nations" and "to exercise . . . any mediatory influence likely to smooth away difficulties . . .".

Although India and Pakistan were consulted on the above resolution, serious disagreement arose between the two Governments regarding its implementation, and the proposed Commission could not be constituted.

On 21 April 1948, the Security Council met again and adopted resolution 47(1948), by which it decided to enlarge the membership of the Commission from three to five (originally it was composed of representatives of Argentina, Czechoslovakia and the United States; Belgium and Canada were now added), and instructed it to proceed at once to the subcontinent and place its good offices at the disposal of the two Governments.to facilitate the taking of the necessary measures with respect to both the restoration of peace and the holding of a plebiscite in the State of Jammu and Kashmir. The Council also authorized the Commission to establish in Jammu and Kashmir such observers as it might require.

Commission action

The United Nations Commission on India and Pakistan arrived in the subcontinent on 7 July 1948 and immediately engaged in consultations with the Indian and Pakistan authorities. On 20 July, the Commission asked the Secretary-General to appoint and send, if possible at once, a high-ranking officer to act as military adviser to the Commission, and further to appoint officers and necessary personnel who would be ready to travel to the Indian subcontinent at a moment's notice in order to supervise the cease-fire if and when it was reached.[2]

UNCIP mission

After undertaking a survey of the situation in the area, UNCIP unanimously adopted a resolution on 13 August,[3] proposing to India and Pakistan that their respective high commands order a cease-fire and refrain from reinforcing the troops under their control in Kashmir. The resolution provided for the appointment by the Commission of military observers who, under the Commission's authority and with the co-operation of both commands, would supervise the observance of the cease-fire order. It also proposed to the Governments that they accept certain principles as a basis for the formulation of a truce agreement, and stated that UNCIP would have observers stationed where it deemed necessary.

C. Supervision of the cease-fire, 1948–1965

Military adviser

On 19 November 1948, the Commission received an urgent communication from the Minister for Foreign Affairs of Pakistan concerning alleged reinforcements of the Indian troops in Kashmir and attacks by those troops against positions held by forces of the Azad (Free) Kashmir movement.[4] There was immediate need for an independent source of information on the military situation in the State, and UNCIP recommended urgently that a military adviser be appointed and proceed forthwith to the subcontinent. It further requested the Secretary-General to provide an adequate number of military observers to assist the adviser. On 11 December 1948,[5] UNCIP submitted to India and Pakistan some new proposals for the holding of a plebiscite in Kashmir upon the signing of a truce agreement, which were accepted by the two Governments.[6] On 1 January 1949, both Governments announced their agreement to order a cease-fire effective one minute before midnight, local time, on that day.[7]

Arrival of observers

The Secretary-General appointed Lieutenant-General Maurice Delvoie of Belgium as Military Adviser to the Commission. General Delvoie arrived in the mission area on 2 January 1949. On 15 January, the Indian and Pakistan high commands conferred in New Delhi and formalized the cease-fire in Kashmir. The UNCIP Military Adviser, who was invited to join the conference, presented to them a plan for the organization and deployment of the military observers in the area.[8] This plan was put into effect on the Pakistan side on 3 February, and on the Indian side on 10 February 1949. A first group of seven United Nations military observers had arrived on 24 January. Their number was increased to 20 in early February. These observers, under the command of the Military Adviser, formed the nucleus of UNMOGIP.

Observers' tasks

In accordance with the Military Adviser's plan, the observers were divided into two groups, one attached to each army. The senior officer of each group established a "control headquarters" under the direct command of the Military Adviser and in close liaison with the commander of the operations theatre on his side. Each group was divided into teams of two observers, attached to the tactical formations in the field and directly responsible to the control headquarters. The control headquarters on the Pakistan side was located at Rawalpindi. The one on the Indian side was first established at Jammu; later, at the end of March, it was transferred to Srinagar.

The tasks of the observers, as defined by the Military Adviser, were to accompany the local authorities in their investigations, gather as much information as possible, and report as completely, accurately and impartially as possible to the observer in charge of the group.

Any direct intervention by the observers between the opposing parties or any interference in the armies' orders were to be avoided.

The local commanders might bring alleged violations of the cease-fire by the other side to the attention of the observers for their action. These arrangements remained in effect until the conclusion of the Karachi Agreement *(see below)*.

The administrative arrangements laid down for the UNMOGIP observers and the general principles under which they function are the same as those for the United Nations Truce Supervision Organization in Palestine *(see Part Two, chapter II)*.

Plebiscite Administrator

With the entering into force of the cease-fire, the situation became quieter. After a brief visit to New York, UNCIP returned to the subcontinent on 4 February 1949 and resumed negotiations with the parties towards the full implementation of Security Council resolution 47 (1948). Earlier in the year, Fleet Admiral Chester W. Nimitz, of the United States, had been appointed by the Secretary-General, in consultation with the two parties and with UNCIP, as United Nations Plebiscite Administrator.

Supervision of the Karachi Agreement

On 18 July 1949, military representatives of the two Governments met at Karachi under the auspices of UNCIP, and on 27 July they signed an Agreement establishing a cease-fire line.[9] The Agreement specifies that UNCIP would station observers where it deemed necessary, and that the cease-fire line would be verified mutually on the ground by local commanders on each side with the assistance of the United Nations military observers. Disagreements were to be referred to the Commission's Military Adviser, whose decision would be final. After verification, the Adviser would issue to each high command a map on which would be marked the definitive cease-fire line. The Agreement further sets forth certain activities which are prohibited on either side of the cease-fire line, such as the strengthening of defences or the increase of forces in certain areas, as well as the introduction of additional military potential into Kashmir.

Listing of cease-fire breaches

Interpretations of the Agreement were agreed upon during the demarcation of the cease-fire line on the ground and during the resulting adjustment of forward positions by both armies. An agreed list of acts to be considered as breaches of the cease-fire was established by the Military Adviser on 16 September 1949.

This list was later revised with the agreement of the parties and, in its final form,[10] encompassed six categories of activity, namely: (1) crossing of the cease-fire line, (2) firing and use of explosives within five miles of the line, (3) new wiring and mining of any positions, (4) reinforcing existing forward defended localities with men or warlike stores, (5) forward movement from outside Kashmir of any warlike stores, equipment and personnel, except for relief and maintenance, and (6) flying of aircraft over the other side's territory.

While the Karachi Agreement established a cease-fire line in Kashmir, it did not include the border between Pakistan and that State, which runs in a general easterly direction from the southern extremity of the cease-fire line at Manawar. In this connection, the Chief Military Observer agreed on 11 February 1950, at the request of both parties, that the UNMOGIP observers would investigate all incidents on the border between Pakistan and Kashmir reported to them by both armies, solely for the purpose of determining whether or not military forces from either side were involved.

UNCIP report to the Security Council

In September 1949, UNCIP decided to return to New York to report to the Security Council. In a press statement issued on 22 September on this subject,[11] the Commission recalled that Security Council resolution 47(1948) of 21 April 1948 envisaged three related but distinct steps: a cease-fire, a truce period during which the withdrawal of forces would take place and, finally, consultations to establish the conditions by means of which the free will of the people of Kashmir would be expressed. The first objective had been achieved but, despite the Commission's efforts, no agreement could be secured on the other two.

Concluding that the possibilities of its mediation had been exhausted, UNCIP decided to return to New York. In so doing, it reaffirmed its belief that a peaceful solution of the problem of Kashmir could be reached, and expressed the hope that its report to the Council would further this purpose.

Termination of UNCIP

Before leaving the subcontinent, the Chairman of the Commission, on 19 September, addressed letters to the two Governments informing them of the above decision. In so doing, he stressed that the Military Adviser and the military observers would remain and pursue their normal activities.[12]

Following the Commission's return to New York, the Security Council decided, on 17 December 1949, to request the Council President, General A.G.L. McNaughton of Canada, to meet informally with the representatives of India and Pakistan and examine with them the possibility of finding a mutually satisfactory basis for dealing with the Kashmir problem. On 14 March 1950, the Security Council, after examining the reports of UNCIP and of General McNaughton, adopted resolution 80(1950), by which it decided to terminate the United Nations Commission for India and Pakistan.

Appointment of a United Nations Representative

At the same time ,the Security Council decided to appoint a United Nations representative who was to exercise all of the powers and responsibilities devolving upon UNCIP. Sir Owen Dixon, of Australia, was appointed by the Council as United Nations Representative for India and Pakistan. A Chief Military Observer (Brigadier H. H. Angle of Canada) was appointed by the Secretary-General as head of UNMOGIP.

Continuance of UNMOGIP

On 30 March 1951, the Security Council, by resolution 91(1951), decided that UNMOGIP should continue to supervise the cease-fire in Kashmir, and requested the two Governments to ensure that their agreement regarding the cease-fire would continue to be faithfully observed. The United Nations Representative (at the time, Frank P. Graham of the United States, who succeeded Sir Owen Dixon) subsequently pointed out, in his report of 15 October 1951,[13] that the debate in the Security Council leading to the adoption of resolution 91(1951) had indicated that it was the Council's intention that the Representative should deal only with the question of the demilitarization of Kashmir. The Representative was therefore not concerned with the existing arrangements for the supervision of the cease-fire, the responsibility for which the Council had placed with UNMOGIP.

Since that time, UNMOGIP has functioned as an autonomous operation, directed by the Chief Military Observer under the authority of the Secretary-General. Its headquarters alternates between Srinagar in summer (mid-May to mid-November) and Rawalpindi in winter. An operational staff office is maintained in one of those two cities when it is not hosting the headquarters. The supervision of the cease-fire in the field is carried out by a number of field observation teams stationed on both sides of the cease-fire line and also along the border between Pakistan and Kashmir.

Between 1949 and 1964, the number of military observers fluctuated between 35 and 67, according to need. Just before the outbreak of the hostilities of 1965, there were 45 observers, provided by 10 countries: Australia, Belgium, Canada, Chile, Denmark, Finland, Italy, New Zealand, Sweden and Uruguay.

Brigadier Angle served as Chief Military Observer until his death in an air crash in July 1950, and he was later replaced by Lieutenant-General Robert H. Nimmo, of Australia. Like the UNCIP Military Adviser, the Chief Military Observer of UNMOGIP, during the initial years, had the status of an observer, and continued to receive his military salary from his Government. In 1959, General Nimmo was given an appointment as an official of the United Nations Secretariat with the rank of Assistant Secretary-General. This administrative arrangement, which had been also applied to the Chief of Staff of UNTSO, was to become the general rule for all heads of United Nations peace-keeping operations.

Role and activities of UNMOGIP

With the conclusion of the Karachi Agreement in 1949, the situation along the cease-fire line became more stable. Incidents took place from time to time, but they were generally minor and were dealt with in accordance with the provisions of the Agreement. This situation continued until 1965.

The role and activities of UNMOGIP were described by the Secretary-General in a report dated 3 September 1965[14] in this manner:

> The United Nations maintains UNMOGIP with its 45 observers along the CFL [cease-fire line] of almost 500 miles, about half of which is in high mountains and is very difficult of access. UNMOGIP exercises the quite limited function of observing and reporting, investigating complaints from either party of violations of the CFL and the cease-fire and submitting the resultant findings on those investigations to each party and to the Secretary-General, and keeping the Secretary-General informed in general on the way in which the cease-fire agreement is being kept. Because the role of UNMOGIP appears frequently to be misunderstood, it bears emphasis that the operation has no authority or function entitling it to enforce or prevent anything, or to try to ensure that the cease-fire is respected. Its very presence in the area, of course, has acted to some extent as a deterrent, but this is not the case at present. The Secretary-General exercises responsibility for the supervision and administrative control of the UNMOGIP operation.

D. The hostilities of 1965 and the establishment of UNIPOM

Background

In early 1965, relations between India and Pakistan were strained again because of their conflicting claims over the Rann of Kutch at the southern end of the international border.

The situation steadily deteriorated during the summer of 1965, and, in August, military hostilities between India and Pakistan erupted on a large scale along the cease-fire line in Kashmir. In his report of 3 September 1965,[15] the Secretary-General stressed that the cease-fire agreement of 27 July 1949 had collapsed and that a return to mutual observance of it by India and Pakistan would afford the most favourable climate in which to seek a resolution of political differences.

Security Council action for a cease-fire

On 4 September 1965, the Security Council, by resolution 209(1965), called for a cease-fire and asked the two Governments to co-operate fully with UNMOGIP in its task of supervising the observance of the cease-fire. Two days later, the Council adopted resolution 210(1965), by which it requested the Secretary-General "to exert every possible effort to give effect to the present resolution and to resolution 209(1965), to take all measures possible to strengthen the United Nations Military Observer Group in India and Pakistan, and to keep the Council promptly and currently informed on the implementation of the resolutions and on the situation in the area".

From 7 to 16 September, the Secretary-General visited the sub-continent in pursuit of the mandate given to him by the Security Council. In his report of 16 September to the Council,[16] he noted that both sides had expressed their desire for a cessation of hostilities, but that each side had posed conditions which made the acceptance of a cease-fire very difficult for the other. In those circumstances, the Secretary-General suggested that the Security Council might take a number of steps: first, it might order the two Governments, pursuant to Article 40 of the United Nations Charter,* to desist from further military action; second, it might consider what assistance it could provide in

---

*In order to prevent an aggravation of a situation, the Security Council, under Article 40 of the Charter, before making recommendations or deciding on measures to be taken, may call upon the parties concerned to comply with provisional measures it deems necessary or desirable, without prejudice to the rights, claims or position of those parties.

ensuring the observance of the cease-fire and the withdrawal of all military personnel by both sides; and, third, it could request the two Heads of Government to meet in a country friendly to both in order to discuss the situation and the problems underlying it, as a first step in resolving the outstanding differences between their two countries.

On 20 September, after the hostilities had spread to the international border between India and West Pakistan, the Council adopted resolution 211(1965), by which it demanded that a cease-fire take effect at 0700 hours GMT on 22 September 1965 and called for a subsequent withdrawal of all armed personnel to the positions held before 5 August. The Council also requested the Secretary-General to provide the necessary assistance to ensure supervision of the cease-fire and the withdrawal of all armed personnel.

Establishment of UNIPOM

In Kashmir, the supervision called for by the Security Council was exercised by the established machinery of UNMOGIP. For this purpose, its observer strength was increased to a total of 102 from the same contributing countries as before.

Since the hostilities extended beyond the Kashmir cease-fire line, the Secretary-General decided to set up an administrative adjunct of UNMOGIP, the United Nations India-Pakistan Observation Mission (UNIPOM), as a temporary measure for the sole purpose of supervising the cease-fire along the India-Pakistan border outside the State of Jammu and Kashmir.[17]

The function of UNIPOM was primarily to observe and report on breaches of the cease-fire called for by the Security Council. In case of breaches, the observers were to do all they could to persuade the local commanders to restore the cease-fire, but they had no authority or power to order a cessation of firing. Ninety observers from 10 countries (Brazil, Burma, Canada, Ceylon (now Sri Lanka), Ethiopia, Ireland, Nepal, the Netherlands, Nigeria and Venezuela) were assigned to UNIPOM.

The Mission was closely co-ordinated both administratively and operationally with UNMOGIP. The Chief Military Observer of UNMOGIP, General Nimmo, was initially also placed in charge of UNIPOM. After the arrival of the newly appointed Chief Officer of UNIPOM, Major-General B.F. Macdonald of Canada, in October 1965, General Nimmo was asked by the Secretary-General to exercise oversight functions with regard to both operations.

Further Security Council action

On 27 September 1965, after learning that the cease-fire was not holding, the Security Council adopted resolution 214(1965), by which it demanded that the parties urgently honour their commitments to the Council to observe the cease-fire, and called upon them to withdraw all armed personnel as necessary steps in the full implementation of resolution 211(1965).

As cease-fire violations continued to occur and there were no prospects of the withdrawal of troops, the Security Council met again in November and adopted resolution 215(1965) of 5 November. By this decision, the Council called upon the Governments of India and Pakistan to instruct their armed personnel to co-operate with the United Nations and cease all military activity.

The Security Council further demanded the prompt and unconditional execution of the proposal already agreed to in principle by India and Pakistan that their representatives meet with a representative of the Secretary-General to formulate an agreed plan and schedule of withdrawals. In this connection, the Secretary-General, after consultation with the parties, appointed Brigadier-General Tulio Marambio, of Chile, as his representative on withdrawals.

On 15 December, the Secretary-General reported[18] that the two parties directly involved, India and Pakistan, had informed him of their desire that the United Nations should continue its observer function after 22 December 1965, which was the end of the first three months of the cease-fire demanded by the Security Council in its resolution 211(1965) of 20 September 1965.

In the circumstances, the Secretary-General indicated his intention to continue the United Nations activities relating to the cease-fire and withdrawal provisions of the resolution by continuing UNIPOM for a second period of three months and maintaining the added strength of the Military Observer Group.

Tashkent agreement

On 10 January 1966, the Prime Minister of India and the President of Pakistan, who had met in Tashkent, USSR, at the invitation of the Chairman of the Council of Ministers of the USSR, announced their agreement that the withdrawal of all armed personnel of both sides to the positions they held prior to 5 August 1965 should be completed by 25 February 1966 and that both sides should observe the cease-fire terms on the cease-fire line.[19]

Withdrawal plan

The principles of a plan and schedule of withdrawals were subsequently agreed upon by military representatives of India and Pakistan, who had held meetings for that purpose since 3 January 1966 at Lahore and Amritsar under the auspices of General Marambio, the Secretary-General's representative on withdrawals. The plan for disengagement and withdrawal was agreed upon by the military commanders of the Indian and Pakistan armies in New Delhi on 22 January.[20]

At a joint meeting on 25 January, under the auspices of the Secretary-General's representative, the parties agreed upon the ground rules for the implementation of the disengagement and withdrawal plan.[21] The plan was to be implemented in two stages and the good offices of UNMOGIP and UNIPOM were to be requested to ensure that the action agreed upon was fully implemented. In the event of disagreement between the parties, the decision of General Marambio would be final and binding on both sides. The good offices of UNMOGIP and UNIPOM were similarly requested for the implementation of the second stage of the agreement, as were the good offices of the Secretary-General's representative on withdrawals.

Termination of UNIPOM

The Secretary-General reported on 23 February 1966[22] that the first stage of the withdrawals had been completed on 20 February and that it was expected that the entire operation would be completed by the target date of 25 February. In that event, the responsibilities of the Secretary-General's representative on withdrawals would come to an end on 28 February and his mission would be terminated on that date. The task of UNIPOM would also have been successfully completed and that phase of the cease-fire operation would be discontinued no later than 22 March 1966. There would also be a gradual reduction of the 59 additional observers appointed in September 1965 to the Military Observer Group.

On 26 February 1966,[23] the Secretary-General reported that the withdrawal of the troops by India and Pakistan had been completed on schedule on 25 February, and that the withdrawal provisions of the Security Council's resolutions had thus been fulfilled by the two parties. As planned, UNIPOM was terminated and the observer strength of UNMOGIP was reduced to 45, drawn from the same 10 contributing countries, by the end of March. From that date until December 1971, UNMOGIP functioned on the basis of the Karachi Agreement in much the same way as it had done before September 1965.

E.   Hostilities of 1971 and their aftermath

Background

At the end of 1971, hostilities broke out again between the Indian and Pakistan forces. They started along the borders of East Pakistan and were related to the movement for independence which had developed in that region and which ultimately led to the creation of Bangladesh.

Secretary-General's actions

When tension was mounting in the summer of 1971, Secretary-General U Thant, invoking his responsibilities under the broad terms of Article 99* of the United Nations Charter, submitted a memorandum to the Security Council on 20 July[24] in which he drew attention to the deteriorating situation in the subcontinent and informed the Council of the action he had taken in the humanitarian field.

On 20 October,[25] the Secretary-General sent identical messages to the heads of the Governments of India and Pakistan expressing increasing anxiety over the situation and offering his good offices with a view to avoiding any development that might lead to disaster. In these messages, he recalled the efforts of the Chief Military Observer of UNMOGIP to ease tension and prevent military escalation along the cease-fire line in Kashmir.

In early December, after the outbreak of hostilities, the Secretary-General submitted a series of reports[26] to the Security Council on the situation along the cease-fire line in Kashmir, based on information received from the Chief Military Observer. The reports showed that from 20 October onwards, both India and Pakistan greatly reinforced their forces along the cease-fire line. Both sides admitted that violations of the Karachi Agreement were being committed by them, but they continued to use the machinery of UNMOGIP to prevent escalation. However, on 3 December, hostilities broke out along the cease-fire line, with exchanges of artillery and small-arms fire and air attacks by both sides. The Secretary-General pointed out that he could not report on military developments in other parts of the subcontinent since the United Nations had no observation machinery outside Kashmir.

---

*Article 99 of the Charter states: "The Secretary-General may bring to the attention of the Security Council any matter which in his opinion may threaten the maintenance of international peace and security."

General Assembly resolution

On 4 December, the Security Council met to consider the situation in the subcontinent. But it could not reach agreement and decided two days later to refer the matter to the General Assembly. On 7 December, the Assembly considered the question referred to it and adopted resolution 2793(XXVI), calling upon India and Pakistan to take forthwith all measures for an immediate cease-fire and withdrawal of their armed forces to their own side of the borders.

Between 7 and 18 December, the Secretary-General submitted another series of reports[27] on the situation along the cease-fire line in Kashmir. Fighting continued, with varying intensity, until 17 December, 1930 hours local time, when a cease-fire announced by the two Governments went into effect. By that time, a number of positions on both sides of the 1949 cease-fire line had changed hands.

Security Council action

The Security Council met again on 12 December, and, on 21 December, adopted resolution 307(1971), by which it demanded that a durable cease-fire in all areas of conflict remain in effect until all armed forces had withdrawn to their respective territories and to positions which fully respected the cease-fire line in Kashmir supervised by UNMOGIP.

Following the adoption of this resolution, the representative of India stated that Kashmir was an integral part of India. In order to avoid bloodshed, he added, his Government had respected the cease-fire line supervised by UNMOGIP, but there was a need to make some adjustments in that line and India intended to discuss and settle this matter directly with Pakistan. The representative of Pakistan insisted that Kashmir was disputed territory whose status should be settled by agreement under the aegis of the Security Council.

Reports on the cease-fire

Subsequent reports of the Secretary-General[28] indicated that following a period of relative quiet, complaints of violations of the cease-fire were received by the Chief Military Observer of UNMOGIP in late January from the military commands of both sides. The Secretary-General observed that, pending the withdrawals of the armed forces, the cease-fire under Security Council resolution 307(1971) must be regarded, for the time being and for practical purposes, as a simple cease-fire requiring the parties to refrain from any firing or forward movement along the lines where the respective armies were in actual control at the time the cease-fire had come into effect on 17 December.

In order to report to the Secretary-General on the observance of the cease-fire, the observers must have the co-operation of the parties and enjoy freedom of movement and access along the lines of control, but these conditions were not met. In this connection, the Secretary-General remarked, discussions aimed at securing the co-operation of the parties had been satisfactorily completed with Pakistan but were still cóntinuing with the Indian military authorities.

Functioning of UNMOGIP

On 12 May 1972, the Secretary-General reported to the Security Council[29] that, while the Pakistan military authorities continued to submit to UNMOGIP complaints of cease-fire violations by the other side, the Indian military authorities had stopped doing so. The situation concerning the functioning of UNMOGIP remained unchanged and, as a result, the Secretary-General could not keep the Council fully informed of developments relating to the observance of the cease-fire. The Secretary-General expressed the hope that, in keeping with the demand of the Security Council, the cease-fire would be strictly observed and that both sides would take effective measures to ensure that there was no recurrence of fighting. He noted in this connection that the UNMOGIP machinery continued to be available to the parties, if desired.

On the same day,[30] India informed the Secretary-General that its efforts to open direct negotiations with Pakistan had made some progress and that it hoped the talks between the two countries would take place at the highest level as early as possible in a positive and constructive spirit, with a view to achieving durable peace in the subcontinent. India also indicated that many incidents had been satisfactorily settled at flag meetings between local commanders. India had refrained from sending to the Secretary-General lists of cease-fire violations by Pakistan in the firm belief that if Pakistan was indeed ready and willing to settle differences and disputes between the two countries in a truly friendly and co-operative spirit, direct negotiations provided the best means.

During May and June, Pakistan brought to the Secretary-General's attention long lists of alleged cease-fire violations by India in Kashmir and other sectors. In a letter dated 5 June,[31] Pakistan stated that there were no flag meetings between Pakistan and Indian military commanders with regard to incidents along the cease-fire line in Kashmir, although such meetings had been held for incidents along the international border. It was clear that incidents along the cease-fire line should be investigated by UNMOGIP observers, and flag meetings held under the auspices of UNMOGIP, since both the 1949 Karachi Agreement and Security Council resolution 307(1971) prescribed UNMOGIP's responsibilities in this regard. It was therefore the view of the Pakistan Government that the activation of the machinery of UNMOGIP on the Indian side of the cease-fire line in Kashmir would serve to prevent incidents.

Present position

In July 1972, the Prime Minister of India and the President of Pakistan signed, at Simla, India, an agreement defining a Line of Control in Kashmir which, with minor deviations, follows the same course as the cease-fire line established in the Karachi Agreement of 1949. This Line of Control was agreed to by both parties in December 1972 and was delineated on the ground by representatives of the two armies.

After conclusion of the Simla Agreement, relations between India and Pakistan progressively reverted to normal and the number of incidents along the line of control in Kashmir greatly decreased. However, the positions of India and Pakistan on the functioning of UNMOGIP have remained unchanged. The position of the Secretary-General has been that, given the disagreement between the two parties concerned, UNMOGIP can be terminated only by a decision of the Security Council. In the absence of such a decision, UNMOGIP has been maintained with the same administrative arrangements. Its headquarters continue to alternate between Srinagar and Rawalpindi.

Pakistan insists that UNMOGIP continue to carry out all the functions prescribed by the Karachi Agreement. The Indian Government, on the other hand, in light of its views on the applicability of that Agreement, restricts the activities of the observers on its side of the Line of Control. Since January 1972, the Indian military authorities have not submitted any complaints on cease-fire violations by the other side nor have they replied to the complaints submitted by Pakistan, which the Chief Military Observer of UNMOGIP continues to transmit to them. However, the Indian authorities have continued to provide UNMOGIP with the same administrative facilities as before, including the headquarters premises in Srinagar and a liaison office in New Delhi.

The number of observers, which stood at 44 at the end of 1971, had been reduced to 39 by October 1985 as a result of a decision by certain contributing countries to withdraw their observers. As of the latter date, the observers were provided by nine contributing countries: Australia, Belgium, Chile, Denmark, Finland, Italy, Norway, Sweden and Uruguay.

Reference notes

[1]S/628. [2]S/1100, annex 25. [3]S/995, section 1. [4]S/1196, annex 1. [5]S/1196, annex 3. [6]S/1196, annexes 4 and 5. [7]S/1196, annex 6. [8]S/1430, annex 47. [9]S/1430, annex 26. [10]S/6888. [11]S/1430, annex 41. [12]S/1430, annex 40. [13]S/2375. [14]S/6651. [15]Ibid. [16]S/6686. [17]S/6699/Add.3. [18]S/6699/Add.11. [19]S/7221. [20]S/6719/Add.5, annex. [21]Ibid. [22]S/6699/Add.12. [23]S/6179/Add.6. [24]S/10410. [25]Ibid. [26]S/10412 and Add.1, 2. [27]S/10432 and Add.1-11. [28]S/10467 and Add.1-3. [29]S/10467/Add.4. [30]S/10648. [31]S/10681.

Part Four:

Other UN observation operations: Lebanon, Yemen, Dominican Republic

Introduction

The United Nations Truce Supervision Organization (UNTSO) and the United Nations Military Observer Group in India and Pakistan (UNMOGIP) are the two oldest and longest-lived United Nations observation operations *(see Parts Two and Three above)*. Established in the early years of the Organization, they have continued to function to this day, since the root problems which had led to their creation have not yet been resolved.

Three other observation operations, which were set up at later dates, have all been terminated after completing their assigned missions. They were the United Nations Observation Group in Lebanon (UNOGIL) in 1958, the United Nations Yemen Observation Mission (UNYOM) in 1962 and the Mission of the Representative of the Secretary-General in the Dominican Republic (DOMREP) in 1965. The establishment and functioning of these operations are set out in the following chapters.

UN Observation Group in Lebanon

Background

In May 1958, armed rebellion broke out in Lebanon when President Camille Chamoun (a Maronite Christian) made known his intention to seek an amendment to the Constitution which would enable him to be re-elected for a second term. The disturbances, which started in the predominantly Moslem city of Tripoli, soon spread to Beirut and the northern and north-eastern areas near the Syrian border, and assumed the proportions of a civil war.

On 22 May,[1] the Lebanese Government requested a meeting of the Security Council to consider its complaint "in respect of a situation arising from the intervention of the United Arab Republic in the internal affairs of Lebanon, the continuance of which is likely to endanger the maintenance of international peace and security". It charged that the United Arab Republic* was encouraging and supporting the rebellion by the supply of large quantities of arms to subversive elements in Lebanon, by the infiltration of armed personnel from Syria into Lebanon, and by conducting a violent press and radio campaign against the Lebanese Government.

On 27 May, the Security Council decided to include the Lebanese complaint on its agenda but, at the request of Iraq, agreed to postpone the debate to permit the League of Arab States to try to find a settlement of the dispute. After the League had met for six days without reaching agreement, the Council took up the case and, on 11 June, adopted resolution 128(1958), by which it decided to dispatch urgently to Lebanon an observation group "so as to ensure that there is no illegal infiltration of personnel or supply of arms or other *matériel* across

---

*From February 1958 until October 1961, Egypt and Syria joined together to form the United Arab Republic.

the Lebanese borders''. The Secretary-General was authorized to take the necessary steps to dispatch the observation group, which was asked to keep the Council informed through him.

This resolution, supported by both Lebanon and the United Arab Republic, formed the basis for the establishment of the United Nations Observation Group in Lebanon (UNOGIL).

Creation of UNOGIL

Following adoption of the Security Council's 11 June resolution, Secretary-General Dag Hammarskjöld told the Council that the necessary preparatory steps had already been taken. The Observation Group proper would be made up of highly qualified and experienced men from various regions of the world. They would be assisted by military observers, some of whom would be drawn from UNTSO and could be in Beirut on the very next day. Hammarskjöld stressed that the Group would not be a police force like the United Nations Emergency Force (UNEF) deployed in Sinai and the Gaza Strip.

Following the adoption of the resolution, the Secretary-General appointed Galo Plaza Lasso of Ecuador, Rajeshwar Dayal of India and Major-General Odd Bull of Norway as members of UNOGIL. Plaza acted as Chairman.

In order to start the operation without delay, 10 observers were immediately detached from UNTSO for assignment with UNOGIL. Five of them arrived in Beirut on 12 June and began active reconnaissance the following morning. The plan was to cover as many areas as possible and to probe further each day in the direction of the Syrian border so as to observe any illegal infiltration of personnel and supply of arms across the border. The number of observers was rapidly increased with new arrivals and reached 100 by 16 June. They were drawn from 21 countries: Afghanistan, Argentina, Burma, Canada, Ceylon (now Sri Lanka), Chile, Denmark, Ecuador, Finland, India, Indonesia, Ireland, Italy, Nepal, the Netherlands, New Zealand, Norway, Peru, Portugal, Sweden and Thailand.

The contributing countries were selected by the Secretary-General in accordance with the same criteria as those he had developed for UNEF in 1956, namely the agreement of the host Government and exclusion of nationals of the permanent members of the Security Council and of ''special interest'' countries. Two helicopters with Norwegian pilots were placed at the disposal of the Group on 23 June and they were supplemented shortly thereafter by four light observation aircraft.

Method of operation

The three members of UNOGIL assembled in Beirut on 19 June under the personal chairmanship of Dag Hammarskjöld, who had arrived in the area the day before. As outlined by the Secretary-General, the role of UNOGIL was strictly limited to observation, to ascertain whether illegal infiltration of personnel or supply of arms or other *matériel* across the Lebanese borders was occurring. It was not UNOGIL's task to mediate, arbitrate or forcefully to prohibit illegal infiltration, although it was hoped that its very presence on the borders would deter any such traffic. The borders meant those between Lebanon and Syria, since the Armistice Demarcation Line between Israel and Lebanon was covered by UNTSO and not involved in the present case.

It was decided that the Group should discharge its duties by the following methods:[2]

(a) The UNOGIL military observers would conduct regular and frequent patrols of all accessible roads from dawn to dusk, primarily in border districts and the areas adjacent to the zones held by the opposition forces. Following the practice already established by UNTSO, the patrolling was to be carried out in white jeeps with United Nations markings, equipped with two-way radio sets.

(b) A system of permanent observation posts was to be established and manned by military observers. These posts were in continuous radio contact with UNOGIL headquarters in Beirut, with each other, and with the patrolling United Nations jeeps. There were initially 10 such stations sited with a view to being as close as possible to the dividing-line between the opposing forces, as near to the frontier as possible or at points commanding supposed infiltration routes or distribution centres. The observers at these stations attempted to check all reported infiltration in their areas and to observe any suspicious development.

(c) An emergency reserve of military observers was to be stationed at headquarters and main observation posts for the purpose of making inquiries at short notice or investigating alleged instances of smuggling.

(d) An evaluation team was to be set up at headquarters to analyse, evaluate and co-ordinate all information received from observers and other sources.

(e) Aerial reconnaissance was to be conducted by light aeroplanes and helicopters, the former being equipped for aerial photography. The aircraft were in radio communication with headquarters and military observers in the field.

(f) The Lebanese Government would provide the Observation Group with all available information about suspected infiltration. Based on this information, instructions would be given to observers for maintenance of special vigilance within the areas in question. The Group would also request the military observers to make specific inquiries into alleged activities as occasion required.

First UNOGIL report to the Security Council

On 1 July 1958, UNOGIL submitted its first report to the Security Council.[3] The report, which dealt with the problems of observation arising from the political, military and geographical circumstances prevailing in Lebanon, indicated that the observers were facing difficulties in gaining access to much of the frontier area held by the opposition forces and could provide no substantiated or conclusive evidence of major infiltration.

The Lebanese Government criticized what it called the report's "inconclusive, misleading or unwarranted" conclusions.[4] It took strong exception to the report and insisted that the United Arab Republic was continuing "massive, illegal and unprovoked intervention in the affairs of Lebanon".

Initially, the military observers encountered serious difficulties in approaching the eastern and northern frontiers, where large areas were in opposition hands. In the early stage, these areas could only be patrolled by aircraft, including photographic and night reconnaissance. But the situation greatly improved by mid-July, when UNOGIL finally obtained full freedom of access to all sections of the Lebanese frontier and received assurances of complete freedom to conduct ground patrols throughout the area north of Tripoli and to establish permanent observation posts anywhere in that area. Arrangements were also made for inspection by military observers of all vehicles and cargoes entering Lebanon across the northern frontier.[5]

Dispatch of United States forces

In the mean time, however, new complications arose outside Lebanon's borders. On 14 July 1958, the Hashemite Kingdom of Iraq was overthrown in a *coup d'état* and replaced with a republican régime. This event had serious repercussions both on Lebanon and Jordan. On the same day, President Chamoun requested United States intervention to protect Lebanon's political independence and territorial integrity.

On 15 July, the Security Council was convened at the request of the representative of the United States, who informed it of his Government's decision to respond positively to the Lebanese request. He stated that United States forces were not in Lebanon to engage in hostilities of any kind but to help the Lebanese Government in its efforts to stabilize the situation, brought on by threats from outside, until such time as the United Nations could take the necessary steps to protect the integrity and independence of Lebanon. He added that his Government was the first to admit that the dispatch of United States forces to Lebanon was not an ideal way to solve the current problems and that these forces would be withdrawn as soon as the United Nations could take over.

Secretary-General's position

During the same meeting, the Secretary-General made a statement reviewing the actions he had taken under the mandate given to him in the Security Council's resolution of 11 June. He stated that he had acted solely with the purpose stated by the Council, "to ensure that there is no illegal infiltration of personnel or supply of arms or other *matériel* across the Lebanese borders". His actions had had no relation to developments that must be considered as the internal affairs of Lebanon, nor had he concerned himself with the wider international aspects of the problem other than those referred to in the resolution. As a matter of course, he had striven to give the observation operation the highest possible efficiency. Hammarskjöld also mentioned his own diplomatic efforts in support of the operation, which now had full freedom of movement in the northern area as well as in the rest of Lebanon.

On 16 July, UNOGIL submitted an interim report[6] stating that on the previous day it had completed the task of obtaining full freedom of access to all sections of the frontier of Lebanon. The next day, in a second interim report,[7] the Group expressed its intention to suggest to the Secretary-General that a force of unarmed non-commissioned personnel and other ranks should be assigned to it. It also indicated that the number of observers would have to be raised to 200, with additional aircraft and crews. With the envisaged increase in the observer force, and the addition of enlisted personnel and supporting equipment, it would be possible to undertake direct and constant patrolling of the actual frontier. In transmitting this report, the Secretary-General stated that he fully endorsed the plan contained in it.

Events in Jordan

On 17 July,[8] the representative of Jordan requested the Security Council to give urgent consideration to a complaint by his Government of interference in its domestic affairs by the United Arab Republic. The Council decided on the same day to consider this complaint concurrently with the Lebanese complaint.

During the ensuing discussions, the representative of the United Kingdom stated that his Government had no doubt that a fresh attempt was being prepared to overthrow the régime in Jordan. In response to an appeal by the Jordanian Government, British forces were being dispatched to Jordan to help its King and Government to preserve the country's political independence and territorial integrity. This action would be brought to an end if arrangements could be made by the Council to protect the lawful Government of Jordan from external threats and so maintain international peace and security.

At the beginning of the Council's debate, the Soviet Union submitted a draft resolution, later revised,[9] by which the Council would call upon the United Kingdom and the United States "to cease armed intervention in the domestic affairs of the Arab States and to remove their troops from the territories of Lebanon and Jordan immediately". The United States proposed a draft resolution[10] which would request the Secretary-General "immediately to consult the Government of Lebanon and other Member States as appropriate with a view to making arrangements for additional measures, including the contribution and use of contingents, as may be necessary to protect the territorial integrity and independence of Lebanon and to ensure that there is no illegal infiltration of personnel or supply of arms or other matériel across the Lebanese borders". A third draft resolution[11] was later submitted by Sweden to have the Council request the Secretary-General to suspend the activities of the observers in Lebanon until further notice.

The Soviet and Swedish draft resolutions were rejected by majorities, while the United States proposal was vetoed by the Soviet Union.

Following those votes, Japan proposed a draft resolution[12] under which the Secretary-General would be requested to make arrangements for such measures, in addition to those envisaged by the Council's resolution of 11 June 1958, as he might consider necessary in the light of the present circumstances, "with a view to enabling the United Nations to fulfil the general purposes established in that resolution, and which will, in accordance with the Charter, serve to ensure the territorial integrity and political independence of Lebanon, so as to make possible the withdrawal of the United States forces from Lebanon". This draft resolution was also rejected, owing to a Soviet negative vote.

Secretary-General's plan

Following the rejection of the Japanese proposal, the Secretary-General stated that, although the Security Council had failed to take additional action in the grave emergency facing it, the United Nations responsibility to make all efforts to live up to the purposes and principles of the Charter remained. He was sure that he would be acting in accordance with the Council's wishes if he used all opportunities offered to him, within the limits set by the Charter, towards developing those efforts, so as to help prevent a further deterioration of the situation in the Middle East and to assist in finding a road away from the dangerous point now reached. The continued operation of UNOGIL being acceptable to all Council members would imply concurrence in the further development of the Group, so as to give it all the significance it could have, consistent with its basic character as determined by the Council in its resolution of 11 June 1958 and the purposes and principles of the Charter. He indicated that, should the members of the Council disapprove of the way these intentions were to be translated by him into practical steps, he would, of course, accept the consequences of its judgement.

The Secretary-General's plan was to increase the strength of UNOGIL as soon as possible to enable it to carry out fully its mission and thus expedite the withdrawal of the United States troops. The number of personnel, which stood at 200 on 17 July 1958, was increased to 287 by 20 September and to 591 in mid-November, including 32 non-commissioned officers in support of ground operations and 90 such officers in the air section. In November, UNOGIL had 18 aircraft, six helicopters and 290 vehicles, and 49 permanently manned posts of all types had been established.

Further UNOGIL report

On 30 July, UNOGIL submitted a periodic report on its activities and observations.[13] It stated that the military observers were operating with skill and devotion, often in conditions of considerable danger and difficulty. Intensive air patrolling had been carried out by day and by night, and air observations had been checked against the results of ground patrolling and observation. The Group reached the conclusion that the infiltration which might be taking place could not be anything more than of limited scale and was largely confined to small arms and ammunition.

With regard to illegal infiltration of personnel, UNOGIL stated that the nature of the frontier, the existence of traditional tribal and other bands on both sides of it and the free movement of produce in both directions were among the factors which must be taken into account in making an evaluation. In no case, however, had the observers, who had been vigilantly patrolling the opposition-held areas and had frequently observed armed bands there, been able to detect the presence of persons who had undoubtedly entered from across the border for the purpose of fighting. From the observations made of the arms and organization in the opposition-held areas, the fighting strength of opposition elements was not such as to be able successfully to cope with hostilities against a well-armed regular military force.

The United States troops, which had landed in Beirut on 15 July, were confined at all times to the beach area and there were no contacts between them and the United Nations military observers. However, UNOGIL indicated in its report that the impact of the landing of those forces in the Beirut area on the inhabitants of opposition-held areas had occasioned difficulties and caused setbacks in carrying out the tasks of the observers.

General Assembly emergency session

During the discussions in the Security Council in July, both the USSR and the United States proposed the convening of an emergency special session of the General Assembly, but the matter was not taken up until 7 August. In the intervening period, the leaders of France, India, the USSR, the United Kingdom and the United States held consultations through exchanges of letters in an effort to find a way out of the impasse. The idea of a "summit" meeting on the Middle East was advanced, but no agreement could be reached. On 7 August, the Security Council met again and decided to call an emergency special session of the Assembly.

That session took place from 8 to 21 August 1958. By the time the Assembly convened, two events which had an important bearing on the developments in the Middle East had occurred. First, General Fuad Chehab, who was acceptable to the Moslem leaders, had been elected President of Lebanon, and this effectively removed from the scene the controversial question of a second term for Chamoun. Second, the new Iraqi revolutionary Government had accepted the obligations of States under the United Nations Charter and had been recognized by the United Kingdom and the United States.

In a report, of 14 August,[14] UNOGIL indicated that just before the election of President Chehab there had been a noticeable reduction of tension throughout the country and a comparable absence of armed clashes between Government and opposition forces. Since 31 July, there had been a virtual nation-wide truce with only occasional reports of sporadic firing in some areas. The report also indicated that by dint of their perseverance and tact in dealing with difficult and often dangerous situations, the observers had won back the ground lost after 15 July. Most of the permanent stations in opposition-held areas envisaged by the Group had been established, and other stations were expected to be set up shortly.

At the end of the emergency special session, the General Assembly unanimously adopted, on 21 August, a proposal submitted by 10 Arab States. This became resolution 1237(ES-III), by which the Assembly requested the Secretary-General to make forthwith, in consultation with the Governments concerned and in accordance with the Charter, such practical arrangements as would adequately help to uphold Charter purposes and principles in relation to Lebanon and Jordan in the present circumstances, and thereby facilitate the early withdrawal of the foreign troops from the two countries.

Secretary-General's Special Representative

In a report dated 29 September to the General Assembly,[15] the Secretary-General commented on the practical arrangements mentioned in the Assembly's August resolution.

He noted that, in the case of Lebanon, the United Nations had already made extensive plans for observing the possible infiltration or smuggling of arms across the border. The work of the Observation Group had had to be re-evaluated within the new practical arrangements to be made. As to Jordan, its Government had indicated that it did not accept the stationing of a United Nations force in Jordan nor the organization of a broader observation group like UNOGIL. But it would accept a special representative of the Secretary-General to assist in the implementation of the resolution. Consequently, the Secretary-General asked Pier P. Spinelli, the Under-Secretary in charge of the United Nations Office at Geneva, to proceed to Amman and to serve as his Special Representative, on a preliminary basis.

With regard to the withdrawal issues, the Secretary-General had been informed that Lebanon and the United States were discussing a schedule for the completion of the withdrawal of the United States forces, and that they hoped this might take place by the end of October. Jordan and the United Kingdom were also discussing the fixing of dates for the withdrawal of the British troops from Jordan, which would begin during October.

In its fourth report to the Security Council, which was circulated on 29 September 1958,[16] UNOGIL stated that, during the period being reviewed, its military observers had not only been able to re-establish confidence in the independent nature of their activities, but had won for themselves the trust and understanding of all sections of the population. Despite the presence of a considerable number of men under arms, there had been no significant clashes between the Lebanese army and organized opposition forces. No cases of infiltration had been detected and, if any infiltration was still taking place, its extent must be regarded as insignificant.

Withdrawal of United Kingdom and United States forces

In a letter dated 1 October,[17] the United Kingdom informed the Secretary-General that it had agreed with the Jordanian Government that the withdrawal of British troops should begin on 20 October. On 8 October,[18] the United States announced that, by agreement with the Lebanese Government, it had been decided to complete the withdrawal of United States forces by the end of October. The withdrawal of United States troops was completed by 25 October, and of the British troops by 2 November. Some of the UNOGIL observers played a role in assisting in the evacuation of the British forces from Jordan.

Termination of UNOGIL

In a letter dated 16 November 1958,[19] the Minister for Foreign Affairs of Lebanon stated that cordial and close relations between Lebanon and the United Arab Republic had resumed their normal course. In order to dispel any misunderstanding which might hamper such relations, the Lebanese Government requested the Security Council to delete the Lebanese complaint from its agenda.

In its final report, dated 17 November 1958,[20] UNOGIL recommended that the operation should be withdrawn since its task might be regarded as completed. On 21 November,[21] the Secretary-General submitted to the Security Council a plan for the withdrawal of the operation, formulated by the Observation Group, which was acceptable to Lebanon.

In accordance with that plan, the closing down of stations and substations preparatory to the withdrawal of UNOGIL began on 26 November and was completed by the end of the month. The observers were withdrawn in three phases, with the key staff, the personnel required for air service and the logistic components leaving last. The withdrawal was completed by 9 December.

Chapter II

UN Yemen Observation Mission

Background

A civil war which broke out in Yemen in September 1962 contained the seeds of a wider conflict with international dimensions because of the involvement of Saudi Arabia and the United Arab Republic. Saudi Arabia shared an extended border with Yemen, much of it still undefined. The United Arab Republic (Egypt) had had a special relationship with Yemen in the past. In March 1958, Yemen joined it to form the United Arab States, but this association was dissolved in December 1961, shortly after Syria seceded from the United Arab Republic.

A further factor in the situation was that Yemen had long claimed that the Aden Protectorate was legally part of its territory. The British-controlled Government of the South Arabian Federation, which included the Aden Protectorate, therefore also closely followed developments in Yemen.

On 19 September 1962, Imam Ahmed bin Yahya died and was succeeded by his son, Imam Mohammed Al-Badr. A week later, a rebellion led by the army overthrew the new Imam and proclaimed the Yemen Arab Republic. The new Government was recognized by the United Arab Republic on 29 September and by the USSR the next day, but other major Powers with interests in the area, including the United Kingdom and the United States, withheld action on the question of recognition.

Following his overthrow, Imam Al-Badr managed to escape from San'a, the capital, and, with other members of the royal family, rallied the tribes in the northern part of the country. With financial and material support from external sources, the royalists fought a fierce guerrilla campaign against the republican forces. The revolutionary Government accused Saudi Arabia of harbouring and encouraging Yemeni royalists, and threatened to carry the war into Saudi Arabian territory. The Imam, on the other hand, claimed that the army rebellion was fostered and aided by Egypt, which denied the charge. At the beginning of October, large numbers of United Arab Republic forces were dispatched to Yemen at the request of the revolutionary Government to assist the republican forces in their fight against the royalists.

On 27 November, the Permanent Mission of Yemen to the United Nations, which was still staffed by the royalists, addressed a letter to the Secretary-General urging the United Nations to establish an inquiry to ascertain whether or not the rebellion was fostered from Cairo. This letter was informally circulated to the United Nations missions. A delegation of Yemeni republicans which had arrived in New York by that time let it be known that they would not object to a United Nations on-the-spot investigation.

The General Assembly, which began its seventeenth session in New York in September 1962, had before it credentials from both the royalist and republican régimes in Yemen. It took up the question of the representation of Yemen on 20 December, the very last day of its session. On that day, the Credentials Committee decided, by a vote of 6 to none, with 3 abstentions, to recommend that the Assembly accept the credentials submitted by the President of the Yemen Arab Republic. Later on the same day, the Assembly approved, by 73 votes to 4, with 23 abstentions, the Committee's report.

King Hussein of Jordan earlier that month had suggested that the presence of United Nations observers might be useful in finding a solution.

Secretary-General's initiative

Secretary-General U Thant undertook a peace initiative, which eventually led to the establishment of the United Nations Yemen Observation Mission (UNYOM).

In a report dated 29 April 1963,[22] the Secretary-General stated that, since the autumn of 1962, he had been consulting regularly with the representatives of the Governments of the Arab Republic of Yemen, Saudi Arabia and the United Arab Republic about ''certain aspects of the situation in Yemen of external origin, with a view to making my office available to the parties for such assistance as might be desired towards ensuring against any developments in that situation which might threaten peace of the area''. He had requested Ralph J. Bunche, Under-Secretary for Special Political Affairs, to undertake a fact-finding mission in the United Arab Republic and Yemen. As a result of the activities carried out by Bunche on his behalf, and by Ellsworth Bunker, who had been sent by the United States Government on a somewhat similar but unconnected mission, he had received from each of the three

Governments concerned formal confirmation of their acceptance of identical terms of disengagement in Yemen.

Under those terms, Saudi Arabia would terminate all support and aid to the royalists of Yemen and would prohibit the use of Saudi Arabian territory by royalist leaders for carrying on the struggle in Yemen. Simultaneously with that suspension of aid, Egypt would undertake to begin withdrawal from Yemen of the troops that had been sent at the request of the new Government, the withdrawal to be phased and to take place as soon as possible. A demilitarized zone would be established to a distance of 20 kilometres on each side of the demarcated Saudi Arabia–Yemen border, and impartial observers would be stationed there to check on the observance of the terms of disengagement. They would also certify the suspension of activities in support of the royalists from Saudi Arabian territory and the outward movement of the Egyptian forces and equipment from the airports and seaports of Yemen.

The Secretary-General asked Lieutenant-General Carl C. von Horn of Sweden, Chief of Staff of UNTSO, to visit the three countries concerned to consult on the terms relating to the functioning of United Nations observers in implementation of the terms of disengagement.

In a second report, dated 27 May,[23] the Secretary-General told the Council that on the basis of information provided by General von Horn, he concluded that United Nations observers in the area were necessary and should be dispatched with the least possible delay. The personnel required would not exceed 200, and it was estimated that the observation function would not be required for more than four months. The military personnel in the Yemen operation would be employed under conditions similar to those applying to other United Nations operations of this nature. The total cost was estimated to be less than $1 million, and he hoped that the two parties principally involved, Saudi Arabia and Egypt, would undertake to bear this cost. He submitted more detailed estimates of the costs of the proposed Mission in a supplemental report on 3 June.[24]

In a further report,[25] submitted on 7 June, the Secretary-General informed the Security Council that Saudi Arabia had agreed to accept a "proportionate share" of the costs of the operation, while Egypt agreed in principle to provide $200,000 in assistance for a period of two months, which would be roughly half the costs of the operation for that period. Thus, there would be no financial implications for the United Nations in getting the Observation Mission established and for its maintenance for an initial two-month period. The Secretary-General announced his intention to proceed with the organization and dispatch of the Mission without delay.

Security Council action establishing UNYOM

The next day, the USSR[26] requested the convening of the Council to consider the Secretary-General's reports on developments relating to Yemen, since the reports contained proposals concerning possible measures by the United Nations to maintain international peace and security, which, under the Charter, should be decided by the Council.

After considering the reports, the Council adopted, on 11 June 1963, resolution 179(1963), requesting the Secretary-General to establish the observation operation as he had defined it, and urging the parties concerned to observe fully the terms of disengagement set out in his 29 April report and to refrain from any action that would increase tension in the area. The Council noted with satisfaction that Saudi Arabia and Egypt had agreed to defray, over a period of two months, the expenses of the observation function called for in the terms of disengagement.

This resolution constituted the basis for the establishment of UNYOM. It did not set a specific time-limit for the Mission, although two months was mentioned in the preamble in connection with its financing. The Secretary-General took the position that he could extend UNYOM without a decision of the Security Council if he considered that its task had not been completed, provided that he could obtain the necessary financial support.

Reports on UNYOM operations

In his first report on the operation, which was submitted to the Security Council on 4 September 1963,[27] the Secretary-General pointed out that the Mission's task would not be completed on the expiration of the two-month period, and for that reason he had sought and received assurances from both parties that they would defray the expenses of the operation for a further two months.

In his second report, dated 28 October,[28] the Secretary-General reported that there had been no decisive change in the situation in Yemen and, because of the limiting and restrictive character of the UNYOM mandate, the Mission would have to be withdrawn by 4 November 1963, since there would be no financial support for it after that date. However, three days later, he informed the Council[29] that Saudi Arabia and Egypt had agreed to participate in the financing of UNYOM for a further two-month period and, accordingly, preparations for the withdrawal of the Mission had been cancelled. He indicated that, although no Security Council meeting was required for the extension of UNYOM, he had consulted Council members to ascertain that there would be no objection to the proposed extension.

On 2 January 1964,[30] before the expiration of the third two-month period, the Secretary-General reported that he considered that the continuing functioning of UNYOM was highly desirable, that the two Governments concerned had agreed to continue their financial support for another two months, and that he had engaged in informal consultations with the members of the Council before announcing his intention to extend the Mission. This process was repeated at the beginning of March, May and July 1964, and UNYOM was extended for successive periods of two months until 4 September 1964.

In late August 1964, Saudi Arabia informed the Secretary-General that it found itself unable to continue the payment of expenses resulting from the disengagement agreement, and Egypt indicated that it had no objection to the termination of UNYOM on 4 September. The Secretary-General therefore advised the Council of his intention to terminate the activities of the Mission on that date.[31]

Organization of UNYOM

Following the adoption of resolution 179(1963), the Secretary-General appointed General von Horn as Commander of UNYOM and took steps to provide the Mission with the required personnel and equipment. The resolution had requested the Secretary-General to establish UNYOM as he had defined it in his report of 29 April 1963, and he selected the various components of the Mission accordingly. In selecting those components and the contributing countries, he informally consulted the parties concerned. Practical considerations were also taken into account, including the proximity of the existing United Nations peace-keeping operations, namely UNTSO and UNEF.

In the initial stage, UNYOM was composed mainly of six military observers, a Yugoslav reconnaissance unit of 114 personnel and a Canadian air unit of 50 officers and men. In addition, 28 international staff members and a small military staff were assigned to UNYOM headquarters. The military observers were detailed from UNTSO and the reconnaissance unit personnel were drawn from the Yugoslav contingent of UNEF, which had experience in United Nations peace-keeping operations in similar terrain. The UNEF air base at El Arish provided support for the Canadian air unit, including six aircraft and a similar number of helicopters.

The strength and composition of UNYOM remained unchanged until November 1963, when a reappraisal of its requirements in terms of personnel and equipment was undertaken. It was felt that in view of the co-operation shown by the parties and the peaceful and friendly attitude of the people in the area covered by the Mission, it was no longer necessary to maintain a military unit in the demilitarized zone; therefore, it was decided to withdraw progressively the Yugoslav reconnaissance unit and to deploy instead up to 25 military observers, while the aircraft of the Mission were reduced to two. The new observers were provided by Denmark, Ghana, India, Italy, the Netherlands, Norway, Pakistan, Sweden and Yugoslavia.

With the arrival of General von Horn and the first group of military personnel, UNYOM began operations on 4 July 1963. In August, General von Horn resigned, and his deputy, Colonel Branko Pavlović of Yugoslavia, took over as acting Commander until September 1963 when Lieutenant-General P. S. Gyani of India, then Commander of UNEF, was temporarily detailed from that Force and appointed Commander of UNYOM.

Secretary-General's Special Representative

At the end of October 1963,[32] when the Secretary-General thought UNYOM had to be withdrawn for lack of financial support, he announced his intention to maintain a civilian presence in Yemen after the withdrawal of the Observation Mission, and he had in mind the appointment of Pier P. Spinelli, head of the United Nations Office at Geneva, as his Special Representative for this purpose. After the withdrawal plan was cancelled, as mentioned earlier, the idea of appointing Spinelli was retained, particularly since General Gyani had to return to his command in UNEF.

In November 1963, upon the departure of General Gyani, Spinelli was appointed Special Representative of the Secretary-General, as well as head of UNYOM. Spinelli assumed this dual responsibility until the end of the Mission.

Functioning of UNYOM

The mandate of UNYOM stemmed from the disengagement agreement entered into by the three Governments concerned, namely, Saudi Arabia, the United Arab Republic and the Arab Republic of Yemen, set out in the report of the Secretary-General of 29 April 1963.[33] The function and authority of UNYOM as defined in the agreement were considerably more limited than in the case of other United Nations observation missions. For example, its establishment was not based on any cease-fire agreement and there was no cease-fire to supervise. The tasks of UNYOM were limited strictly to observing, certifying and reporting in connection with the intention of Saudi Arabia to end activities in support of the royalists in Yemen and the intention of Egypt to withdraw its troops from that country.

To carry out these tasks in the initial stage, detachments of the Yugoslav reconnaissance unit were stationed in Jizan, Najran and Sa'dah in the demilitarized zone and the surrounding areas. They manned check-posts and conducted ground patrolling. In addition, air patrolling was carried out by the Canadian air unit, which had bases at San'a as well as Jizan and Najran, particularly in the mountainous central part of the demilitarized zone where there were few passable roads. The six military observers detailed from UNTSO, who were stationed at San'a, and the two positions at Hodeida (Al Hadaydah) were primarily responsible for observing and certifying the withdrawal of Egyptian troops.

In order to check on the reduction or cessation of assistance from Saudi Arabia to the royalists, a pattern of check-points and air/ground patrolling was established to cover all main roads and tracks leading into Yemen and the demilitarized zone. Air and ground patrols were carried out daily with varied timings and routes, the patrol plan being prepared and co-ordinated every evening.

Experience quickly showed that air and ground patrolling had two main limitations, namely, that traffic could be observed only by day while, for climatic reasons, travel during hours of darkness was customary in the area, and that cargoes could not be checked. These problems were met by periodically positioning United Nations military observers at various communication centres for 40 hours or more, so that traffic could be observed by day or night and cargoes checked as necessary. Arrangements were also made to have Saudi Arabian liaison officers assigned to United Nations check-points and check cargoes when requested by United Nations observers.

Various complaints were received by UNYOM from one or the other of the parties concerned. They fell mainly into two categories: on the one hand, allegations of offensive actions by Egyptian forces against the royalists in Yemen and in Saudi Arabian territory, and, on the other, alleged activities in support of the royalists emanating from Saudi Arabia. UNYOM authorities would transmit these complaints to the parties involved and, whenever possible and appropriate, investigate them.

In accordance with the disengagement agreement, the responsibilities of UNYOM concerned mainly, in addition to the cities of San'a and Hodeida, the demilitarized zone on each side of the demarcated portion of the Saudi Arabia–Yemen border. It did not extend to the undefined portion of that border nor to the border between Yemen and the British-controlled South Arabian Federation.

From the very start, the Secretary-General pointed out that UNYOM, because of its limited size and function, could observe and report only certain indications of the implementation of the disengagement agreement. However, despite its shortcomings, the Mission did have a restraining influence on hostile activities in the area. The Secretary-General repeatedly expressed the view that the responsibility for implementing the agreement lay with Saudi Arabia and Egypt and progress could be best achieved through negotiations between them.

With this in view, he informed the Security Council that UNYOM could, within limits, serve as an intermediary and as an endorser of good faith on behalf of the parties concerned, and that it was his intention to have the Mission perform these roles to the maximum of its capability. When Spinelli was appointed Special Representative of the Secretary-General and head of UNYOM in November 1963, he devoted a great deal of his time and attention to good-offices efforts and held extensive discussions with officials of the three Governments concerned. These discussions were of an exploratory character to try to ascertain whether there were areas of agreement between the parties which might, through bilateral discussions or otherwise, lead to further progress towards disengagement and the achievement of a peaceful situation in Yemen.

Secretary-General's assessment

The assessment of the Secretary-General on the functioning of UNYOM and the implementation of the disengagement agreement, as set out in his successive periodic reports to the Security Council, are outlined below.

In his first report on this subject, which was dated 4 September 1963,[34] the Secretary-General found no encouraging progress towards effective implementation of the agreement, although both parties had expressed a willingness to co-operate in good faith with UNYOM. He noted reluctance by each side to fulfil its undertakings regarding the agreement before the other side did so.

His second report, which was submitted on 28 October 1963,[35] indicated limited progress. He stated that although the developments observed by UNYOM were far short of the disengagement and regularization of the situation which had been hoped for, they were in a limited way encouraging in that the scale of fighting had been reduced and conditions of temporary truce applied in many areas.

On 2 January 1964,[36] he reported that UNYOM observations tended to confirm that, during the period under review, no military aid of significance had been provided to the royalists from Saudi Arabia, and that there had been a substantial net withdrawal of Egyptian troops from Yemen. Ground operations had further decreased in intensity. The Secretary-General reiterated his belief that the solution of the problem lay beyond the potential of UNYOM under its original mandate, and he referred to the extensive discussions his Special Representative had had with members of the three Governments concerned with a view to furthering progress towards disengagement and the achievement of a peaceful situation in Yemen.

A later report, submitted on 3 March 1964,[37] raised a new problem: Yemeni and Egyptian sources asserted that large quantities of supplies were being sent to the royalists from the Beihan area across the frontier with the South Arabian Federation. The Secretary-General pointed out in this connection that since that frontier was not included in the disengagement agreement, United Nations observers did not operate in that area. However, he mentioned that the nature and extent of the military operations carried out by the royalists during January and February would seem to indicate that arms and ammunition in appreciable amounts had been reaching them from that source.

The Secretary-General also reported that the royalists appeared to be well provided with money and to have engaged foreign experts to train and direct their forces, and that they had recently launched attacks against Egyptian troops. From the developments observed by UNYOM, he felt that progress towards the implementation of the disengagement agreement had been very disappointing during the period under review; a state of political and military stalemate existed inside the country, which was unlikely to be changed as long as external intervention in various forms continued from either side. On the other hand, he noted certain encouraging factors, particularly the increasing unity of feeling and purpose within the Arab world arising from a Conference of Arab Heads of State held in Cairo in mid-January 1964 and the resulting improvement in relations between Saudi Arabia and Egypt. The Secretary-General expressed the hope that the meeting to be held between the two parties in Saudi Arabia would result in some progress towards the implementation of the agreement and towards an understanding between the two Governments to co-operate in promoting political progress and stability in Yemen.

In his report dated 3 May 1964,[38] the Secretary-General stated that there was no progress in troop reduction towards the implementation of the disengagement agreement and that no actual end of the fighting appeared to be in sight. He noted, however, that the two parties had reported noticeable progress in discussions of a number of problems at issue between them, and that a meeting between President Nasser of Egypt and Crown Prince Feisal of Saudi Arabia would be held in Cairo in the near future.

On 2 July,[39] the Secretary-General reported that the military situation in Yemen had remained fairly quiet over the past two months, that no military aid by Saudi Arabia to the Yemeni royalists had been observed and that some slight progress in Egyptian troop reduction appeared to have occurred. Once again he appealed to the parties concerned to meet at the highest level with a view to achieving full and rapid implementation of the disengagement agreement.

Termination of UNYOM

In his final report, dated 2 September 1964,[40] the Secretary-General again acknowledged the failure of the parties to implement the disengagement agreement and the difficulties UNYOM faced in observing and reporting on these matters. There had been a substantial reduction in the strength of the Egyptian forces in Yemen but it seemed that the withdrawal was a reflection of the improvement in the situation of the Yemeni republican forces rather than the beginning of a phased withdrawal in the sense of the agreement. There were also indications that the Yemeni royalists had continued to receive military supplies from external sources. Observing that UNYOM had been able to observe only limited progress towards the implementation of the agreement, he reiterated his view that UNYOM's terms of reference were restricted to observation and reporting only, and that the responsibility for implementation lay with the two parties to the agreement. He stated that UNYOM had actually accomplished much more than could have been expected of it in the circumstances, and that during the 14 months of its presence in Yemen, the Mission had exercised an important restraining influence on hostile activities in the area.

On 4 September 1964, the activities of UNYOM ended and its personnel and equipment were withdrawn.

Shortly after the withdrawal of UNYOM, relations between the parties steadily improved and issues were resolved between them. There has been no consideration of the matter in United Nations organs since the termination of that Mission.

Representative of the Secretary-General in the Dominican Republic

Background

Towards the end of April 1965, a political crisis developed in the Dominican Republic, resulting in civil strife that had considerable international repercussions. On 24 April, the three-man junta headed by Donald Reid Cabral was overthrown by a group of young officers and civilians who sought the return to office of former President Juan Bosch, who had been deposed by a military *coup* in September 1963, and the restoration of the 1963 Constitution.

Bosch's supporters were opposed by a group of high-ranking officers of the Dominican armed forces, with the result that two rival governments emerged in the Dominican Republic during the first weeks of the civil war. The pro-Bosch forces organized themselves into what was called the "Constitutional Government", headed by Colonel Francisco Caamaño Deñó. The opposing forces established a civilian-military junta which called itself the "Government of National Reconstruction", headed by General Antonio Imbert Barrera.

The military phase of the Dominican crisis took place mainly in Santo Domingo, capital of the country, where heavy fighting broke out between the two contending factions on 25 April 1965.

On 28 April, the United States announced that its troops had been ordered to land in the Dominican Republic. On the following day, the United States representative informed the Security Council of his Government's action and of its call for a meeting of the Council of the Organization of American States (OAS). His letter[41] asserted that the President of the United States had ordered troops ashore in the Dominican Republic in order to protect United States citizens there and escort them to safety. The President had acted, the letter stated, after being informed by the military authorities in the Dominican Republic that lives of United States citizens were in danger, that their safety could no longer be guaranteed, and that the assistance of United States military personnel was required.

On 29 April,[42] the Secretary-General of the OAS informed the United Nations Secretary-General that the OAS Council had appealed for the suspension of armed hostilities in the Dominican Republic. On 1 May,[43] the Assistant Secretary-General of the OAS informed the Security Council that the Tenth Meeting of Consultation of Ministers for Foreign Affairs of the American Republics had decided on that day to establish a committee, composed of representatives of Argentina, Brazil, Colombia, Guatemala and Panama, and had instructed it to proceed immediately to Santo Domingo to bring about the restoration of peace and normality and to offer its good offices to the contending factions there with a view to achieving a cease-fire and the orderly evacuation of persons.

On 1 May, the USSR requested an urgent meeting of the Security Council to consider the question of the armed intervention by the United States in the internal affairs of the Dominican Republic.[44]

The Security Council considered this question at 29 meetings held between 3 May and 26 July 1965.

Security Council action, May 1965

On 6 May,[45] the Assistant Secretary-General of the OAS transmitted to the Security Council the text of a resolution by which the Tenth Meeting of Consultation had requested OAS members to make available land, air and naval contingents or police forces for the establishment of an inter-American force, to operate under its authority. The purpose of the force would be to help restore normal conditions in the Dominican Republic, maintain the security of its inhabitants and the inviolability of human rights, and create an atmosphere of peace and conciliation that would allow the functioning of democratic institutions.

On 14 May, Jordan, urging action by the Security Council, submitted, together with Malaysia and the Ivory Coast, a draft resolution whereby the Council would call for a strict cease-fire, invite the Secretary-General to send, as an urgent measure, a representative to the Dominican Republic to report on the situation, and call upon all concerned in the Dominican Republic to co-operate with that representative in carrying out his task.

The three-Power text was unanimously adopted by the Council the same day, as resolution 203(1965).

Representative's activities

In a report dated 15 May,[46] the Secretary-General informed the Council that he had appointed José Antonio Mayobre, Executive Secretary of the Economic Commission for Latin America, as his Representative in the Dominican Republic. An advance party, led by Major-General I. J. Rikhye as Military Adviser, had arrived in Santo Domingo earlier that day. The Military Adviser was assisted by two military observers at any one time from three made available from Brazil, Canada and Ecuador.

On 18 May,[47] the Secretary-General informed the Council that his Representative had left for Santo Domingo on 17 May. He had asked Mayobre to notify formally all the parties concerned of the Council's call for a strict cease-fire and to convey to all those involved in the conflict his most earnest appeal to heed that call so that a propitious climate for finding a solution might be brought about.

On 19 May,[48] the Secretary-General reported that, shortly after his arrival, Mayobre had met with Colonel Caamaño, President of the "Constitutional Government", and with General Imbert, President of the "Government of National Reconstruction".

Late in the evening of 18 May, Mayobre had informed the Secretary-General by telephone of heavy fighting in the northern section of the capital and of the numerous casualties caused by it. It had not been possible to persuade General Imbert to agree to a cease-fire, although he had expressed willingness to agree to a suspension of hostilities some time on 19 May to facilitate the work of the Red Cross in searching for the dead and wounded.

Appeal by the Security Council President

At the Council's meeting on 19 May, the Council President made a statement, which was supported by all Council members, requesting the Secretary-General to convey to his Representative the Council's desire that his urgent efforts be devoted to securing an immediate suspension of hostilities so that the Red Cross's work in searching for the dead and wounded might be facilitated.

Communications from the OAS

Also on 19 May,[49] the OAS transmitted the text of a second report submitted by the Special Committee of the Tenth Meeting of Consultation. The Committee said that efforts to arrange for a meeting between Colonel Caamaño and General Imbert to iron out their differences had proved unsuccessful, and that the Committee had issued an appeal to the parties for strict compliance with the cease-fire agreed upon in the Act of Santo Domingo, signed on 5 May, formalizing a cease-fire achieved earlier through the efforts of the Papal Nuncio in Santo Domingo. The report added that the presence of the United Nations in the Dominican Republic had created a factor which had compromised and interfered with the task of the Committee. It recommended that the Meeting of Consultation agree upon the measures necessary to re-establish peace and normality in the Republic, and that the Security Council be requested to suspend all action until regional procedures had been exhausted.

The OAS also transmitted to the Council[50] the text of a resolution adopted by the Meeting of Consultation on 20 May, entrusting the OAS Secretary-General with negotiating a strict cease-fire and with providing his good offices for establishing a climate of peace and reconciliation that would permit democratic institutions to function. The resolution asked him to co-ordinate his action, in so far as relevant, with that of the Representative of the United Nations Secretary-General.

Further reports by the Secretary-General

The Secretary-General informed the Security Council[51] that his Representative, on the morning of 19 May, had met with representatives of the Dominican Red Cross, the International Red Cross and the Pan American Sanitary Bureau, and had suggested that they meet with the leaders of the two factions engaged in the fighting and request a 12-hour suspension of hostilities to remove the dead and wounded from the battle area. On 21 May,[52] the Secretary-General reported on further information from his Representative that, following negotiations with the leaders of the two factions, agreement had been reached for the suspension of hostilities for 24 hours beginning on 21 May, at 1200 hours local time.

Further Security Council action

During a Council meeting of 21 May, the Secretary-General said that his Representative had reported that the cease-fire of 21 May was effective. The Red Cross, which had gone into the battle area early that morning, had been fully engaged in its humanitarian task. In view of the need to evacuate the sick and wounded to less congested hospitals, the Representative was trying to obtain an extension of the truce.

On 22 May, France submitted a draft resolution by which the Council would request that the suspension of hostilities in Santo Domingo be transformed into a permanent cease-fire, and would invite the Secretary-General to report to it on the implementation of the resolution. This was adopted as resolution 205(1965).

On 25 May, the Council President noted that it appeared that a *de facto* cessation of hostilities continued to prevail in Santo Domingo and that the Secretary-General had informed him that it was being observed. He therefore suggested that the Council adjourn, on the understanding that it could reconvene if the situation required it.

Further OAS communications

On 2 June,[53] the OAS advised the Security Council that the Tenth Meeting of Consultation had appointed an *ad hoc* committee—composed of representatives of Brazil, El Salvador and the United States—to assist all parties in the Dominican Republic to achieve a climate of peace and to enable democratic institutions to function. It also informed the Council of the arrival in Santo Domingo of the Chairman of the Inter-American Commission on Human Rights in response to requests made by both of the contending Dominican groups.[54]

Security Council consideration, 3-11 June 1965

The question of the Dominican Republic was again considered by the Council at four meetings held between 3 and 11 June. The Council was convened at the request of the USSR to take up two communications from the "Constitutional Government", asking for the dispatch of the United Nations Commission on Human Rights to the Dominican Republic to investigate atrocities allegedly carried out by General Imbert's forces against the civilian population in Santo Domingo.

The question of the scope of the mandate of the Secretary-General's Representative arose during these meetings from suggestions made by France, Jordan and Uruguay to enlarge Mayobre's staff to enable him to supervise the cease-fire and to investigate complaints of human rights violations. They considered that his mandate was sufficiently wide to cover both tasks. The suggestions were supported by the USSR.

Bolivia, the Ivory Coast, Malaysia, the United Kingdom and the United States, on the other hand, expressed doubt as to the advisability of extending Mayobre's mandate at that stage. The United States observed, in this connection, that the Inter-American Human Rights Commission, which had been sent to Santo Domingo, was actively investigating human rights violations.

Secretary-General's position

The Secretary-General stated that his Representative's current mandate involved observing and reporting, functions which did not include the actual investigation of complaints and charges about specific incidents, other than those connected with cease-fire violations. Investigative functions would require a directive from the Security Council, a substantially larger staff and increased facilities. Moreover, he could give no assurance that such added responsibility would receive from the contending parties the co-operation necessary to secure effective implementation by his Representative.

The Secretary-General remarked that his Representative was keeping a watchful eye on all aspects of the situation and was reporting what he observed. The size of his staff was under constant review, and he would be provided with the necessary assistance as the circumstances demanded.

Security Council consideration, 16-21 June 1965

On 16 June,[55] the Secretary-General reported that an exchange of fire had taken place on the morning of 15 June between Colonel Caamaño's forces and troops of the Inter-American Peace Force (IAPF). There was no evidence, however, as to which side had started the firing. By nightfall his Representative had arranged for a cessation of hostilities.

In a later report,[56] the Secretary-General informed the Council that, on 16 June, fighting between the Caamaño forces and the IAPF had been renewed along the newly established IAPF positions manned by United States troops. Although the firing had stopped on the evening of 16 June, the situation remained very tense.

This situation was discussed by the Security Council from 16 to 21 June. During these meetings, the Council received from the OAS the text of proposals for a political settlement submitted on 18 June[57] by the OAS ad hoc committee to the "National Reconstruction Government" and the "Constitutional Government". The principal points in the OAS proposals were: general elections within six to nine months, under OAS supervision; a general amnesty for all who had participated in the civil strife; surrender of all arms in the hands of civilians to the OAS; establishment of a provisional government which would exercise its authority under an institutional act and would call elections; and the convening of a constitutional assembly within six months following assumption of office by the elected government.

On 21 June, the Secretary-General informed the Security Council that he had just received a report from his Representative which stated that the cease-fire had been effective since 16 June.

Secretary-General's report, 16 July 1965

On 16 July, the Secretary-General submitted a report on the situation in the Dominican Republic covering the period from 19 June to 15 July 1965.[58]

Despite a number of isolated incidents, the cease-fire in Santo Domingo had been maintained. The Secretary-General indicated that, as of 26 June, the IAPF was composed of 1,700 troops from six Latin American countries and 12,400 from the United States, of which 1,400 would be withdrawn shortly. He went on to report that the situation outside Santo Domingo—which had been potentially explosive since May, owing mainly to deteriorating economic conditions, to the ineffectiveness of civilian authority and to military and police repression—had become more acute following an abortive uprising by armed civilians at San Francisco de Macorís on 25 June and an attack against a police post at Ramón Santana on 2 July.

The Secretary-General drew attention to repeated complaints of violations of human rights in Santo Domingo as well as in the provinces, involving alleged executions, arbitrary arrests, and cases of missing persons following arrest. He also drew attention to the worsening economic situation. In his Representative's view, an early political solution accompanied by an emergency programme of external financial and technical assistance was essential.

Security Council meetings, July 1965

The Security Council resumed consideration of the question at four meetings held between 20 and 26 July.

The Council President ultimately summed up the agreed views of the members of the Council:

— Information received by the Council as well as the Secretary-General's reports showed that, in spite of the Council's resolutions of 14 and 22 May 1965, the cease-fire had been repeatedly violated. Acts of repression against the civilian population and other violations of human rights, as well as data on the deterioration of the economic situation in the Dominican Republic, had been brought to the Council's attention.

— Members of the Council had condemned gross violations of human rights in the Republic, expressed the desire that such violations should cease, and indicated again the need for the strict observance of the cease-fire in accordance with the Council's resolutions.

— The Council members considered it necessary that the Council continue to watch the situation closely and that the Secretary-General continue to report on it.

Secretary-General's reports, 22 July 1965–5 January 1966

In a report covering the period between 22 July and 17 August 1965,[59] the Secretary-General informed the Security Council that, except for a few minor incidents, the cease-fire had been maintained. While his Representative continued to receive complaints of alleged cases of arbitrary arrest by forces of the "Government of National Reconstruction", the situation in general had improved. The report referred to negotiations for a political settlement being carried out by the OAS *ad hoc* committee on the basis of new proposals the committee had submitted to the two contending parties on 9 August 1965.[60]

A proposed Act of Dominican Reconciliation[61] provided that the parties would accept a provisional government presided over by Héctor García Godoy as the sole and sovereign government of the Dominican Republic, and that they would accept a proposed Institutional Act[62] as the constitutional instrument under which the provisional government would exercise its authority. The latter Act also provided for: a proclamation of a general amnesty by the provisional government; the disarmament and incorporation of the "Constitutionalist" zone into the security zone; a procedure for the recovery of arms in the hands of civilians; the reintegration of "Constitutionalist" military personnel who had participated in the conflict; and, finally, a procedure to be followed for the withdrawal of the IAPF.

In a report covering the period of 17 August to 2 September 1965,[63] the Secretary-General reported the resignation on 30 August of the members of the "Government of National Reconstruction" headed by General Imbert, and the signing, on 31 August, of an amended text of the Act of Reconciliation by the leaders of the "Constitutional Government". On the same day, the chiefs of the armed forces and the national police had signed a declaration in which they had pledged acceptance of the Act of Reconciliation and the Institutional Act, and support of Dr. García Godoy as provisional President.

On 3 September, García Godoy was installed as President of the Provisional Government.

On 23 October,[64] the Secretary-General reported to the Security Council that since the inauguration of the Provisional Government much progress had been made in efforts to restore normal conditions in the Dominican Republic. Little progress had been made, however, towards the reintegration of "Constitutionalist" military personnel into the regular armed forces, owing mainly to continuing tension between the high command of the Republic's armed forces and "Constitutionalist" officers. The situation had been aggravated by acts of terrorism and violence, and armed clashes between civilians and elements of the police and regular Dominican troops.

In subsequent reports, the Secretary-General informed the Council that the Government had announced that troops of the Dominican armed forces had been ordered to return to their barracks and that law and order in Santo Domingo would be maintained by the national police with the assistance of the IAPF. By 25 November,[65] he reported, the situation had improved and the country was returning to normalcy. The bulk of the IAPF had been withdrawn from the capital and the national police were gradually assuming responsibility for the maintenance of law and order. There had also been some improvement in the relations between the civilian authorities and the armed forces.

In a report issued on 3 December,[66] the Secretary-General informed the Council that the Provisional Government had promulgated a law calling for national elections to be held on 1 June 1966.

Later in December, the Secretary-General reported on new disturbances. The main disturbance took place on 19 December[67] at Santiago, where former "Constitutionalist" forces and Dominican air force units engaged in heavy fighting that resulted in many casualties, including 25 dead. The Santiago incident was followed by a wave of terrorist activities in Santo Domingo which caused the deaths of eight persons and considerable material damage. The reports indicated that mixed patrols of the IAPF, Dominican troops and national police faced a difficult task in maintaining order, as they were continually stoned and shot at by roving civilian groups.

Tension had again subsided by 25 December. On the evening of 3 January 1966, President García Godoy announced that within a few hours an important group of military personnel would leave the country on missions abroad. The Secretary-General concluded his report by stating that, while Santo Domingo had remained calm since 1 January, the situation there was reported to be tense and unstable.[68]

Secretary-General's observations

The Secretary-General, in the introduction to his annual report on the work of the Organization covering the period from 16 June 1964 to 15 June 1965,[69] discussed the problems and character of the United Nations role in the Dominican Republic situation. He described the task of his Representative there as a "new United Nations mission in the peace-keeping category".

The situation, the Secretary-General wrote, was of unusual complexity and had considerable international repercussions, particularly with regard to the unilateral military involvement of the United States in the initial stage and to the later role of the Inter-American Peace Force. While his Representative's mandate had been a limited one, the effect of his role had been significant, since he had played a major part in bringing about a cessation of hostilities on 21 May 1965, and had supplied information as to the situation both in Santo Domingo and in the interior of the country.

His presence had undoubtedly been a moderating factor in a difficult and dangerous situation, the Secretary-General said, adding that this had been the first time a United Nations peace mission had operated in the same area and dealt with the same matters as an operation of a regional organization, in this instance the OAS.

Further, the Secretary-General maintained the view that the developments in the Caribbean should stimulate thought by everyone concerning the character of the regional organizations and the nature of their functions and obligations in relation to the responsibilities of the United Nations under the Charter.

Secretary-General's reports, January-February 1966

In one of eight reports covering developments in the Dominican Republic during January 1966,[70] the Secretary-General informed the Council that, on 6 January 1966, President García Godoy had issued decrees appointing a new Minister of the Armed Forces and new armed services chiefs, and providing for the transfer abroad of several high-ranking military officers, including Commodore Francisco Rivera Caminero, former Minister of the Armed Forces, and Colonel Caamaño Deñó, former "Constitutionalist" leader. The implementation of these decrees had met with some resistance from the Dominican armed forces, which at one point occupied radio and telecommunications buildings in Santo Domingo. However, by the end of January, 11 high-ranking former "Constitutionalist" officers had left the Dominican Republic to take up diplomatic posts abroad.

In six reports issued during February,[71] the Secretary-General reported to the Security Council several serious incidents and acts of terrorism which occurred in and outside Santo Domingo, beginning

7 February. As a result, economic activity in the city and nearby commercial areas had come to an almost complete standstill. Tension remained high from 12 to 15 February as hostile acts directed against IAPF military police and troops took place in Santo Domingo. A general strike was called off one day after a speech by President García Godoy, broadcast on 16 February, in which he announced orders to put into effect decrees concerning changes and transfers in the Dominican armed forces and ordered all public employees to return to work. The new Minister of the Armed Forces was sworn in on the same day and new chiefs of staff of the army, navy and air force were appointed on 26 February. Also, a new chief of the national police had been appointed by the Provisional Government.

Secretary-General's reports, March-May 1966

In 17 reports issued from March to May 1966,[72] the Secretary-General informed the Security Council that, though fewer in number, acts of terrorism and other disturbances continued to occur in Santo Domingo and in the interior of the country. He stated that the electoral campaign had officially opened on 1 March.

In connection with national elections on 1 June 1966, the Central Electoral Board issued on 15 March a proclamation providing for the election of a President and Vice-President of the Republic, 27 Senators and 74 Deputies for a period of four years beginning 1 July 1966, and for the election, for a period of two years, of 70 mayors and 350 aldermen and their alternates. On 11 May, President García Godoy, in a televised speech, expressed concern over certain signs of pressure exerted by minority groups intent upon disturbing the electoral process. He appealed to all sectors of the population to maintain a peaceful and orderly atmosphere for the elections, and indicated that the problem of the presence of the IAPF in the country should be solved before 1 July. On 13 May,[73] the OAS *ad hoc* committee announced that IAPF personnel would be confined to barracks on election day. This was followed by an announcement on 18 May by President García Godoy of his decision to confine all armed forces to barracks from 19 May until election day. On 29 May,[74] the OAS *ad hoc* committee indicated, in a press statement, that 41 observers invited by the OAS would observe elections in 21 provinces of the Republic and in the National District. The observers would submit a report to the Provisional Government.

At midnight on 30 May, the electoral campaign officially ended. On that day, the Provisional President sent a communication to the Tenth Meeting of Consultation of OAS Foreign Ministers informing it that he had instructed the Dominican representative to the OAS to request a meeting of the Tenth Meeting of Consultation to ask for withdrawal of the IAPF from Dominican territory.

Election of 1 June 1966

During June and July 1966, the Secretary-General submitted four reports[75] to the Council dealing mainly with the elections on 1 June and related events. According to those reports, the elections had proceeded on schedule in a calm and orderly manner. On 21 June, the final results of elections were announced by the Central Electoral Board. They showed 769,265 votes for Joaquín Balaguer, 525,230 for Juan Bosch and 39,535 for Rafael F. Bonnelly.

Installation of the Government, July 1966

In a report dated 2 July,[76] the Secretary-General informed the Security Council that on 1 July, Joaquín Balaguer and Francisco Augusto Lora had been sworn in as President and Vice-President, respectively, of the Dominican Republic by the President of the National Assembly. In his inaugural address, President Balaguer stated that the country was returning to a system of law and that no one would be permitted to live outside legal norms. He set forth a policy of austerity to place the Republic's economic, administrative and financial structure on a sounder footing. His Government would support the OAS and would work within it to ensure that national sovereignty would never again be infringed by foreign troops. While his Government intended to act drastically if extremists sought to disturb the peace, it would protect opponents against persecution and would ensure that the symbols of past oppression would disappear for ever from Dominican life.

Phased withdrawal of the IAPF

Early in July, a plan for the withdrawal of the IAPF in four phases was approved by the OAS *ad hoc* committee in agreement with the Dominican Government.

On 24 June,[77] the OAS Secretary-General had transmitted to the Security Council the text of a resolution adopted by the Tenth Meeting of Consultation that day. By this resolution, the Meeting of Consultation—noting that the purposes of the Tenth Meeting had been fully achieved inasmuch as popular elections had been held in the Dominican Republic, the results of which had given that nation a constitutional and democratic Government—directed that the withdrawal of the IAPF should begin before 1 July 1966 and should be completed within 90 days. It further asked the OAS *ad hoc* committee, in agreement with the Dominican Government, to give the IAPF the necessary instructions concerning the dates for and the manner of effecting the withdrawal.

From 3 August to 21 September 1966, the Secretary-General, on the basis of information received from the office of his Representative in Santo Domingo, submitted a series of reports to the Security Council[78] giving a detailed account of the withdrawal of the United States and the Latin American contingents (Brazil, Costa Rica, El Salvador, Honduras, Nicaragua and Paraguay) of the IAPF and of its military equipment. This withdrawal was completed on 21 September 1966.

Withdrawal of the United Nations Mission

In a letter of 13 October addressed to the Secretary-General,[79] the Dominican Republic's Minister for Foreign Affairs expressed the appreciation of his country to the United Nations for its efforts to bring about the restoration of peace and harmony in the Republic, and stated that, in the view of his Government, the objectives of the Security Council's resolution of 14 May 1965 having been achieved, it would be advisable to withdraw the United Nations Mission from the Dominican Republic.

In a report issued on 14 October,[80] the Secretary-General informed the Security Council that in the light of the developments which had recently taken place in the Dominican Republic, including the installation on 1 July 1966 of the newly elected Government and the withdrawal of the IAPF, he had initiated arrangements for the withdrawal of the Mission in the Dominican Republic, which was expected to be completed shortly.

The withdrawal of the United Nations Mission was completed on 22 October 1966.

Reference notes

Chapter I: UN Observation Group in Lebanon

[1]S/4007. [2]S/4040. [3]S/4040 and Add.1. [4]S/4043. [5]S/4051. [6]*Ibid.* [7]S/4052. [8]S/4053. [9]S/4047/Rev.1. [10]S/4050/Rev.1. [11]S/4054. [12]S/4055/Rev.1. [13]S/4069. [14]S/4085. [15]A/3934/Rev.1. [16]S/4100. [17]A/3937. [18]A/3942. [19]S/4113. [20]S/4114. [21]S/4116.

Chapter II: UN Yemen Observation Mission

[22]S/5298. [23]S/5321. [24]S/5323. [25]S/5325. [26]S/5326. [27]S/5412. [28]S/5447. [29]S/5447/Add.1. [30]S/5501. [31]S/5927. [32]S/5447. [33]S/5298. [34]S/5412. [35]S/5447. [36]S/5501. [37]S/5572. [38]S/5681. [39]S/5794. [40]S/5927.

Chapter III: Representative of the Secretary-General
in the Dominican Republic

[41]S/6310. [42]S/6313. [43]S/6364, annex. [44]S/6316. [45]S/6333/Rev.1. [46]S/6358. [47]S/6365. [48]S/6369. [49]S/6370. [50]S/6372/Rev.1. [51]S/6371. [52]S/6371/Add.1. [53]S/6401. [54]S/6404. [55]S/6447. [56]S/6459. [57]S/6457, annex I. [58]S/6530. [59]S/6615. [60]S/6608. [61]S/6608, annex I. [62]S/6608, annex III. [63]S/6649. [64]S/6822. [65]S/6975. [66]S/6991. [67]S/7032. [68]S/7032/Add.4. [69]A/6001/Add.1. [70]S/7232/Add.4-11. [71]S/7032/Add.12-17. [72]S/7032/Add.18-34. [73]S/7032/Add.32. [74]S/7032/Add.34. [75]S/7338/Add.1-3. [76]S/7338/Add.5. [77]S/7379. [78]S/7338/Add.6-15. [79]S/7551. [80]S/7552.

Part Five:
UN operation in the Congo

A.   Introduction

Background

The United Nations Operation in the Congo (Opération des Nations Unies au Congo, or ONUC), which took place in the Republic of the Congo (now Zaire) from July 1960 until June 1964, is by far the largest peace-keeping operation ever established by the United Nations in terms of the responsibilities it had to assume, the size of its area of operation and the manpower involved. It included, in addition to a peace-keeping force which comprised at its peak strength nearly 20,000 officers and men, an important Civilian Operations component. Originally mandated to provide the Congolese Government with the military and technical assistance it required following the collapse of many essential services and the military intervention by Belgian troops, ONUC became embroiled by the force of circumstances in a chaotic internal situation of extreme complexity and had to assume certain responsibilities which went beyond normal peace-keeping duties. The policy followed by Secretary-General Dag Hammarskjöld in the Congo brought him into direct conflict with the Soviet Union and serious disagreement with some other Powers. The Operation cost the life of Hammarskjöld and led to a grave political and financial crisis within the United Nations itself.

With an area of some 2,344,000 square kilometres (about 1 million square miles), approximately the size of Western Europe, the Congo is the second largest country in Africa, after the Sudan. Encompassing the greatest part of the Congo basin in the very heart of Africa, the country has an important strategic position. The Congo is also exceptionally rich in minerals, much of them in the province of Katanga.

At the time of independence, the Congo had a population of about 14 million. The wind of change that had swept across Africa after the Second World War left the Territory largely untouched. The Belgian colonial administration practised a policy of paternalism which gave the indigenous population one of the highest living standards on the continent, but little political and educational advancement. Few Congolese studied beyond the secondary level and, at the time of independence, there among them only 17 university graduates and no doctors, lawyers or engineers.

Little political activity was allowed the Congolese population until 1959. Early that year, the Belgian Government, confronted with increasing disturbances, announced its intention to prepare the Congo for independence, and soon embarked upon a radical decolonization plan. A charter granting freedom of speech, of the press and of association was put into effect in August 1959, and elections to municipal and territorial councils were held in December. In January 1960, at a round-table conference of Congolese leaders convened in Brussels, Belgium agreed to grant independence to the Congo as of 30 June that same year.

From then on it was a race against time to get the Congo ready for independence. Provisional executive councils with the participation of Congolese leaders were established at the central and provincial levels in March 1960. The *"Loi fondamentale"*, which was to serve as the constitution for the Congo, was adopted by the Belgian Parliament and promulgated by King Baudouin of Belgium on 19 March. General and provincial elections leading to the establishment of the Congolese Parliament and the provincial assemblies were held during the same month.

The Parliament convened in the early part of June and, by 23 June, after lengthy wranglings, the newly elected representatives worked out a compromise whereby the two rival dominant Congolese leaders were elected to the two key positions in the new political structure: Joseph Kasa-Vubu as President of the Republic and Patrice Lumumba as Prime Minister. Thus, the apparatus for the independent State was completed barely six days before independence.

On 29 June 1960, a treaty of friendship, assistance and co-operation between Belgium and the Congo was signed by the representatives of the two Governments (but never ratified). Under that treaty, most of the administrative and technical personnel of the colonial administration would remain in the Congo on secondment to the Congolese Government. The treaty also provided that the two military bases at Kamina and Kitona would be ceded to Belgium and that the Belgian Government could, at the request of the Congolese Government, call out the Belgian troops from the bases to assist the latter Government in maintaining law and order. Belgium hoped that with this massive assistance and the guarantees accompanying it, it would be possible to ensure a smooth transition from colonial status to independence. Its main hope lay in the *Force publique*, the 25,000-man security force which had maintained law and order in the country in a forceful and effective way during the colonial times and which would continue to be commanded by Belgium's Lieutenant-General Emile

Janssens, with an all-Belgian officer corps. It was what the Belgians called at the time the *"Pari congolais"*, the Congolese gamble.

Dag Hammarskjöld, who had visited the Belgian Congo in January 1960, was keenly conscious of the serious problems that would confront the Congolese Government after independence. He felt that the Congo would need, in addition to massive assistance from Belgium, extensive United Nations technical aid that had no political strings attached. With this in mind, he asked his Under-Secretary for Special Political Affairs, Ralph J. Bunche, to attend the independence ceremony in Leopoldville (now Kinshasa) as his personal representative and to take the opportunity to discuss with the Congolese authorities the technical assistance which the United Nations could provide. Bunche arrived in Leopoldville on 26 June and stayed on after the independence ceremony to work out an extensive United Nations technical assistance programme for the country.

Shortly after independence, Congolese soldiers of the *Force publique* became restive and petitioned for more promotion opportunity. Their petition was dismissed by General Janssens. He made it clear that so far as the *Force publique* was concerned, independence had changed nothing. On 5 July, a mutiny broke out in the Leopoldville garrison and spread to several other cities during the following days. As some mutineers attacked Belgians and other Europeans, and in some cases committed rape and other atrocities, most Belgian administrators and technicians fled the country, and this led to the collapse of a number of essential services throughout the country.

The Belgian Ambassador to the Congo repeatedly urged Prime Minister Lumumba to request the assistance of Belgian troops, under the friendship treaty, to maintain law and order, but Lumumba adamantly refused. Instead, he attempted to regain control of the *Force publique* by agreeing to the Congolese soldiers' demand for reform. He renamed the *Force publique* the *Armée nationale congolaise* (ANC), dismissed General Janssens and appointed Victor Lundula, a Congolese, as Commander of the Army with the rank of Major-General, and Joseph Mobutu, also a Congolese, as its Chief of Staff with the rank of Colonel. All Congolese soldiers and non-commissioned officers were promoted by one grade pending further measures to Africanize the entire officer corps.

As disorder spread and intensified, Ralph Bunche, who was in Leopoldville at the time, strongly advised the Belgian Ambassador not to call in Belgian troops without the prior agreement of the Congolese Government. At the same time, he was in close touch with the Congolese authorities and the Secretary-General in New York to work out a plan to help the Government control and strengthen the Congolese army through United Nations assistance. Hammarskjöld envisaged sending a large number of United Nations military advisers, experts and technicians for this purpose. He felt that if the Congolese Government were to request such military personnel as technical assistance of a military nature, rather than as military assistance, he could take immediate action on his own authority without referring the matter to the Security Council.

The Congolese Government agreed to this course of action and, on 10 July, submitted a formal request to the Secretary-General for technical assistance of a military nature, including military advisers, experts and technicians, to assist it in developing and strengthening the national army for the twin purposes of national defence and the maintenance of law and order.

Belgian intervention and Security Council action

However, a new situation developed on the next day when the Belgian Government ordered its troops into the Congo without the agreement of the Congolese Government, for the declared purpose of restoring law and order and protecting Belgian nationals. Belgian troops landed at Leopoldville, Matadi, Luluabourg (now Kananga) and Elisabethville (now Lubumbashi), in Katanga. Their intervention, which was followed in some cases by heavy fighting with Congolese soldiers, further increased tension and disorder throughout the country. On 11 July, shortly after the arrival of Belgian troops in Elisabethville, Moïse Tshombé, the provincial president, proclaimed the independence of Katanga, the richest province of the Congo, which provided the country with more than half of its revenues.

On 12 July, President Kasa-Vubu and Prime Minister Lumumba sent a joint telegram[1] to the Secretary-General requesting United Nations military assistance. They said that the essential purpose of the requested military aid was "to protect the national territory of the Congo against the present external aggression which is a threat to international peace". The next day, they cabled a further message[2] to the Secretary-General to make it clear that they were not asking for aid to restore the internal situation but to respond to Belgian aggression.

On 13 July, Hammarskjöld, invoking Article 99 of the United Nations Charter—which empowers the Secretary-General to bring to the attention of the Security Council any matter which in his opinion may threaten international peace and security—requested an urgent meeting of the Council to consider the situation in the Congo.[3] The Council met on the same evening. In an opening statement, Hammarskjöld outlined his ideas about the actions that the Council might take in response to the request of the Congolese Government. In essence, he recommended the establishment of a United Nations peace-keeping force to assist that Government in maintaining law and order until, with technical assistance from the United Nations, the Congolese national security forces were able fully to meet their tasks. He assumed that, were the United Nations to act as proposed, the Belgian Government would withdraw its forces from Congolese territory.

At the same meeting, during the night of 13/14 July, the Security Council adopted resolution 143(1960), by which it called upon the Government of Belgium to withdraw its troops from the territory of the Congo and decided to authorize the Secretary-General to take the necessary steps, in consultation with the Government of the Republic of the Congo, to provide the Government with such military assistance as might be necessary until, through that Government's efforts with United Nations technical assistance, the national security forces might be able, in the opinion of the Government, to meet fully their tasks. It requested the Secretary-General to report to the Security Council as appropriate.

The Council resolution was adopted by 8 votes in favour (including the USSR and the United States) to none against, with 3 abstentions.

Secretary-General's principles governing the United Nations Force

In his first report on the implementation of the resolution[4] the Secretary-General outlined the principles which would govern the organization and activities of the United Nations Force in the Congo, its composition and the action he had taken or envisaged taking to establish it.

The proposals the Secretary-General set out for the Force were as follows:

(a) The Force was to be regarded as a temporary security force to be deployed in the Congo with the consent of the Congolese Government until the national security forces were able, in the opinion of that Government, to meet fully their tasks.

(b) Although dispatched at the request of the Congolese Government and remaining there with its consent, and although it might be considered as serving as an arm of the Congolese Government for the maintenance of law and order and protection of life, the Force was necessarily under the exclusive command of the United Nations, vested in the Secretary-General under the control of the Security Council. The Force was thus not under the orders of the Congolese Government and could not be permitted to become a party to any internal conflict.

(c) The host Government, when exercising its sovereign rights with regard to the presence of the United Nations Force in its territory, should be guided by good faith in the interpretation of the Force's purpose. Similarly, the United Nations should be so guided when it considered the question of the maintenance of the Force in the host country.

(d) The United Nations should have free access to the area of operation and full freedom of movement within that area as well as all the communications and other facilities required to carry out its tasks. A further elaboration of this rule obviously required an agreement with the Government specifying what was to be considered the area of operation.

(e) The authority granted to the United Nations Force could not be exercised within the Congo either in competition with the representatives of its Government or in co-operation with them in any joint operation. This principle applied also *a priori* to representatives and military units of Governments other than the host Government. Thus, the United Nations Operation must be separate and distinct from activities by any national authorities.

(f) The units of the Force must not become parties to internal conflicts. They could not be used to enforce any specific political solution of pending problems or to influence the political balance decisive for such a solution.

(g) The basic rules of the United Nations for international service were applicable to all United Nations personnel employed in the Congo Operation, particularly as regards loyalty to the aims of the Organization.

(h) The United Nations military units were not authorized to use force except in self-defence. They were never to take the initiative in the use of force, but were entitled to respond with force to an attack with arms, including attacks intended to make them withdraw from positions they occupied under orders from the Commander, acting under the authority of the Security Council. The basic element of influence in this principle was clearly the prohibition of any initiative in the use of armed force.

With regard to the composition of the Force, the Secretary-General reiterated the principle that, while the United Nations must preserve its authority to decide on this matter, it should take full account of the views of the host Government. He recalled that in order to limit the scope of possible differences of opinion with host Governments, the United Nations had in recent operations followed two principles: not to include units from any of the permanent members of the Security Council nor units from any country which, because of its geographical position or for other reasons, might be considered as having a special interest in the situation that had called for the operation. He indicated his intention to seek, in the first place, the assistance of African States for the United Nations Force in the Congo. The Force would be built around a core of military units from African States and should also include suitable units from other regions to give it a truly international character. In selecting the contingents, the Secretary-General would necessarily be guided by considerations of availability of troops, language and geographical distribution within the region.

In order to set up the Force speedily, the Secretary-General said, he had accepted offers of troops by Ethiopia, Ghana, Guinea, Morocco and Tunisia. These five countries would provide seven battalions, with a total strength of 4,000 men. Arrangements were being made to airlift the battalions to the Congo as soon as possible. An offer of troops from Mali had also been received and would be activated at a later stage.

With the deployment of the seven battalions, the first phase of the buildup of the Force would be completed. For the second phase, the Secretary-General had requested troops from three European countries and one Asian and one Latin American country. In one of those cases—Sweden—he had asked and secured permission to transfer to the Congo on a temporary basis the Swedish battalion of the United Nations Emergency Force (UNEF) in Gaza, thus bringing the total strength of the Force to eight battalions.

Requests for aircraft, signal and other logistic support, as well as for air transport facilities, had been addressed to a number of non-African nations.

As soon as Security Council resolution 143(1960) was adopted, the Secretary-General appointed Ralph J. Bunche as his Special Representative in the Congo to head the new Operation. He also appointed Lieutenant-General Carl C. von Horn, of Sweden, as Supreme Commander of the United Nations Force in the Congo. General von Horn, who until then had occupied the post of Chief of Staff of the United Nations Truce Supervision Organization (UNTSO), would be assisted in the initial stage by a small personal staff of officers drawn from UNTSO.

On the evening of 15 July 1960, less than 48 hours after the adoption of the Council's resolution, an advance party of the Tunisian contingent, consisting of about 90 officers and men, landed at Leopoldville. They were followed on succeeding days by the remainder of the Tunisian battalion and personnel of the Ethiopian, Ghanaian, Guinean and Moroccan battalions. Bunche, who was appointed temporary Commander of the Force pending the arrival of General von Horn, immediately deployed these units in sensitive localities in Leopoldville, Stanleyville (now Kisangani), Matadi, Thysville and Coquilhatville (now Mbandaka). On 18 July, General von Horn and his staff officers arrived in Leopoldville and immediately set up Force headquarters at the airport.

As the responsibilities of the United Nations in the Congo expanded, the Secretary-General requested and obtained more battalions and support personnel. The Force reached a total of 19,828 at its peak strength by July 1961. From then on, as some of its responsibilities were fulfilled, the strength of the Force was progressively reduced. In addition to the military units, ONUC had a Civilian Operations component which employed some 2,000 experts and technicians to provide the Congolese Government with extensive assistance in the administrative, technical and humanitarian fields.

While its original mandate as outlined in Council resolution 143(1960) remained valid, ONUC was given new responsibilities and new tasks during the four years of its operation. The history of ONUC may be divided into four periods, as follows: restoration of law and order and withdrawal of Belgian forces (July–August 1960); constitutional crisis (September 1960–September 1961); termination of the secession of Katanga (September 1961–February 1963); and consolidation of the Congolese Government (February 1963–June 1964). Each of these periods is dealt with separately below.

B. Restoration of law and order and withdrawal of Belgian forces (July–August 1960)

ONUC objectives

The two main objectives of ONUC during the initial phase were to help the Congolese Government restore law and order and bring about the speedy withdrawal of the Belgian forces. These objectives were closely related.

In a statement made in the Security Council just before the adoption of resolution 143(1960), the representative of Belgium stated that his Government had no political designs in the Congo and that when the United Nations Force had moved into position and was able to ensure the effective maintenance of order and the security of persons in the Congo, his Government would withdraw its forces.

Immediately after the adoption of the resolution, Bunche initiated negotiations with the Belgian Ambassador in Leopoldville in order to work out agreement for the speedy and orderly withdrawal of the Belgian forces in accordance with the resolution and in the light of the undertaking given by the Belgian Government. The United Nations plan was to bring its forces into the Congo as rapidly as possible and deploy them in various parts of the country, first of all in those positions occupied by Belgian troops. Once deployed, United Nations troops would restore law and order and ensure the protection of civilians in co-operation with the Congolese Government and speed up the withdrawal of the Belgian forces from the area.

Withdrawal of Belgian troops outside Katanga

The first troops of the United Nations Force arrived at Leopold ville on the evening of 15 July and were deployed the next morning at the radio station and the power station and along the main thoroughfare of the capital. Their presence had an immediate calming effect in an extremely tense situation. On 16 July, the Belgian Ambassador informed Bunche that, consequent upon the arrival of the United Nations troops, the first contingents of the Belgian armed forces had left Leopoldville and returned to their bases on that same day. On 19 July, Bunche reported to the Secretary-General that the United Nations was now in a position to guarantee that contingents of the United Nations Force drawn from both African and European countries would arrive during the week in sufficient numbers to ensure order and protect the entire population of Leopoldville, African and European. In the light of this assurance, it was decided that the Belgian forces would begin to withdraw completely from the Leopoldville area and return to their bases on 20 July. This withdrawal operation was to be completed by the afternoon of 23 July.

As more United Nations troops were flown into the Congo, they were deployed in other areas such as Thysville, Matadi, Luluabourg, Coquilhatville and Stanleyville. In each of these places, ONUC immediately began its task of maintaining law and order and protecting the local population, and initiated discussions with the Belgian representative to bring about the withdrawal of Belgian troops at an early date.

Although this speed could be achieved only through strenuous efforts, the Congolese Government did not consider it fast enough. On 17 July 1960, Lumumba and Kasa-Vubu addressed an ultimatum to the Secretary-General, warning that if the Belgian forces were not completely withdrawn within 48 hours, they would request troops from the Soviet Union. The Secretary-General brought the matter before the Security Council, which—by resolution 145(1960) of 22 July 1960, adopted unanimously—commended the action taken by the Secretary-General and called upon Belgium to speed up the withdrawal of its troops.

The original plan was therefore continued without change. As soon as new United Nations contingents arrived, they were deployed in the positions occupied by Belgian troops. They brought about the complete withdrawal of the Belgian troops from Leopoldville and the surrounding area on 23 July 1960, and from the whole of the Congo, except Katanga and the two bases, by the beginning of August 1960.

Withdrawal from Katanga

The next step was the entry of United Nations troops into the province of Katanga. On this question, the Secretary-General ran into a grave conflict with Prime Minister Lumumba, who wanted ONUC to help his Government put down the secession of Katanga by force. The Secretary-General refused to do this, taking the position that under its mandate ONUC could not use force except in self-defence, and could not be a party to, or in any way intervene in or be used to influence the outcome of, any internal conflict in the Congo. He also encountered serious difficulties with the Katangese secessionist authorities and the Belgian Government. The Katangese authorities strongly opposed the entry of United Nations troops and, citing this opposition, the Belgian Government was reluctant to withdraw its forces from Katanga.

On 4 August 1960, the Secretary-General, who had arrived in Leopoldville a few days earlier, sent Bunche to Elisabethville to make arrangements with the Belgian representative there for the entry of United Nations troops into Katanga, which, if no difficulties arose, would take place on 6 August. But in the face of unqualified and unyielding opposition by the Katangese secessionist authorities, Bunche concluded that the entry of United Nations troops could not be achieved without bloodshed. The Secretary-General therefore decided to postpone the original plan and brought the matter before the Security Council.

By resolution 146(1960) of 9 August 1960, the Security Council confirmed the authority conferred upon the Secretary-General by its previous resolutions and called upon Belgium immediately to withdraw its troops from Katanga, under speedy modalities determined by the Secretary-General. At the same time, while declaring that the entry of the United Nations Force into Katanga was necessary, the Council reaffirmed that the Force should not in any way intervene in any internal conflict in the Congo or be used to influence the outcome of any such conflict, constitutional or otherwise. The resolution was adopted by 9 votes to none, with 2 abstentions (France and Italy).

After the adoption of the resolution, the Secretary-General returned to the Congo and, on 12 August, personally led the first United Nations unit into Katanga. But Prime Minister Lumumba strongly criticized the manner in which the Secretary-General had implemented the Council's resolutions and refused henceforth to co-operate with him. In view of the Prime Minister's reaction, the Secretary-General once again referred the matter to the Security Council.

The Council met on 21 August 1960, but did not vote on any resolution. During the discussion, the Secretary-General indicated that, in the absence of any new directive, he would consider his interpretation of the ONUC mandate as upheld. He also made known his intention to appoint an Advisory Committee, composed of Member States which had contributed troops to the United Nations Force, to advise him on future policy on the Congo.

The entry of United Nations troops into Katanga on 12 August 1960 set off a process of withdrawal of Belgian troops from the province, which was completed by the beginning of September. At that time, Belgian troops were also withdrawn from the military bases of Kamina and Kitona, which were taken over by ONUC.

Thus, despite difficult circumstances, ONUC brought about the withdrawal of Belgian troops from the whole of the Congo within six weeks. However, the secession of Katanga remained unresolved.

Maintenance of law and order

The maintenance of law and order was the heaviest of all the tasks falling upon ONUC. In order to carry out that task, the Secretary-General set up a United Nations Force which at its peak strength numbered nearly 20,000. But even at its peak strength, the Force was hardly sufficient and was severely strained, inasmuch as its responsibilities had to encompass such a vast land as the Congo.

On their arrival in the Congo, United Nations soldiers were officially instructed that they were members of a peace force, not a fighting force, that they had been asked to come in response to an appeal from the Congolese Government, that their task was to help in restoring order and calm in a troubled country and that they should give protection against acts of violence to all the people, Africans and Europeans alike. They were also told that although they carried arms, they were to use them only in self-defence; they were in the Congo to help everyone and to harm no one.

What ONUC sought to do was to assist the Congolese authorities to perform their normal duties, for instance by undertaking joint patrols with the local police for the maintenance of law and order in a given area. When, however, this was not possible on account of the breakdown of the security forces, the United Nations Force had to perform the normal security duties in the place of Congolese authorities. But in so doing it sought the consent and co-operation of the Congolese Government. Such was the case in Leopoldville during the operation's first stage, when United Nations soldiers performed police duties along the city's main arteries to ensure the protection of its essential services.

Following these procedures, the Force restored law and order, protected life and property, and ensured the continued operation of essential services wherever it was deployed. In many areas it brought under control unruly ANC elements, many of whom laid down their arms voluntarily or at the request of their Government. Thus the Force carried out its task of maintaining law and order with success in the initial phase of the Operation.

However, the internal situation in August began to worsen rapidly. Tribal rivalries, which had plagued the country before independence, flared up that month with added intensity in Kasai between Baluba and Lulua tribesmen. The Baluba of the Luluabourg area fled *en masse* to their tribal lands in the Bakwanga region, where their leader, Albert Kalonji, proclaimed the secession of South Kasai.

In Equateur and Leopoldville provinces, there was increasing opposition to the Government. To put down opposition and secessionist movements, Prime Minister Lumumba arrested some opposition leaders, and anti-Government newspapers were suspended. At the end of August, ANC troops were sent to South Kasai, and many civilians were killed, including women and children. Other ANC troops were being massed near the northern border of Katanga in preparation for an invasion of the province. During those days, elements of the ANC, which the Government was using to achieve its political objectives but which it was not always able to control, were a constant danger to the civilian population.

Without the co-operation of the Congolese Government which it had come to assist, ONUC faced a frustrating situation. Its activities were further hampered when the Government itself resorted to actions which tended to endanger law and order, or restrict human rights. Whenever this happened, ONUC endeavoured to induce and persuade Congolese authorities to change their course of action, and, to the extent possible, took measures to ensure the protection of the threatened persons. But it refused to use force to subdue Congolese authorities, or the ANC under their orders. Even when its own personnel were attacked, ONUC intervened only to prevent further excesses and to urge the Congolese Government to take disciplinary action against the culprits.

C. Constitutional crisis (September 1960–September 1961)

Introduction

On 5 September 1960, a constitutional crisis developed, when President Kasa-Vubu, invoking the authority conferred upon him by the *Loi fondamentale*, decided to dismiss Prime Minister Lumumba.[5] The crisis lasted 11 months, during which time there was no legal government and the country was divided into four opposing camps, each with its own armed forces. ONUC therefore could only deal with *de facto* authority and do whatever it could to avert civil war and protect the civilian population. It attempted to prevent the leaders who wielded power from subduing opponents by force and at the same time encouraged those leaders to seek a solution through negotiation and conciliation.

Dismissal of Lumumba

In the days following Kasa-Vubu's dismissal of Lumumba, utter confusion prevailed in Leopoldville. Lumumba refused to recognize Kasa-Vubu's decision and, in turn, dismissed Kasa-Vubu as Chief of State. Parliament supported Lumumba, although it refused to endorse his decision to dismiss the Chief of State, but Parliament itself was soon suspended by Kasa-Vubu. Each contending party sought the support of the army and, whenever it could, ordered the arrest of its opponents. On 14 September 1960,[6] Colonel Joseph Mobutu imposed by a *coup* an army-backed régime run by a Council of Commissioners (*Collège des Commissaires*) and supporting Kasa-Vubu. But the *coup* was not fully effective in that Lumumba and his supporters resisted the Commissioners' authority.

Emergency measures

At the outset of the crisis, ONUC took emergency measures to avoid violence and bloodshed.[7] It decided on the night of 5/6 September 1960 to close the Leopoldville airport to prevent the arrival of rival troops. The following day, in view of the likely dangerous effect of inflammatory speeches on an already disturbed populace and after a number of violent demonstrations had taken place in the city, it temporarily closed down the Leopoldville radio station. These measures were lifted by 13 September 1960, as soon as the tension had subsided to below the explosive level.

In response to appeals from political and other leaders of all sides in Leopoldville, ONUC agreed to protect the threatened leaders, and in so doing it endeavoured to show absolute impartiality. ONUC guards were stationed around the residences of both Kasa-Vubu and Lumumba. Protection was also given to the other leaders, though not to the same extent.

Containment of hostilities

In the following months, ONUC endeavoured to prevent or control hostilities between the various Congolese factions.

In South Kasai, ONUC helped in arranging a cease-fire between ANC troops and Kalonji's secessionist army and in establishing a neutral zone under ONUC control. It also persuaded the ANC command to withdraw its troops from the northern border of Katanga.

In northern Katanga, where violent fighting broke out between pro-Tshombé gendarmes and the anti-Tshombé Baluba population, ONUC put an end to the fighting by setting up, in agreement with both parties, neutral zones under its protection.

Protected areas were set up at various times and places, to where threatened persons, Africans and Europeans alike, could repair for safety. Neutral zones were established to stop tribal warfare. During this period of unrest, Europeans, many of whom were settlers in scattered, remote areas, were often threatened by hostile local authorities or populations. Whenever possible, ONUC took measures to rescue and protect them and, if they so desired, to evacuate them to safer areas.

The contending parties turned to ONUC for recognition and support. ONUC continued its policy of avoiding intervening or taking sides in the internal conflicts. While it recognized the unimpaired status of Kasa-Vubu as Chief of State, it refused to help him achieve political aims by force and, in particular, to recognize the Council of Commissioners supported by him.

Security Council and General Assembly consideration

The crisis was examined by the Security Council from 14 to 17 September 1960 and, when the Council failed to take a decision, by an emergency special session of the General Assembly from 17 to 20 September.

By resolution 1474(ES-IV) of 20 September 1960, the Assembly requested the Secretary-General to continue to take vigorous action in line with the Security Council's resolutions. In an effort to resolve the constitutional crisis, it appealed to all Congolese to seek a speedy solution, by peaceful means, of all their internal conflicts, and requested the Advisory Committee on the Congo to appoint a conciliation commission to assist them in that endeavour.

The Conciliation Commission was composed of Ethiopia, the Federation of Malaya, Ghana, Guinea, India, Indonesia, Liberia, Mali, Morocco, Nigeria, Pakistan, Senegal, the Sudan, Tunisia and the United Arab Republic. Subsequently Guinea, Indonesia, Mali and the United Arab Republic withdrew from the Commission.

During the meeting of the Security Council, two Congolese delegations, one appointed by Kasa-Vubu and the other by Lumumba, were sent to New York, but neither could win recognition. Two months later, during the fifteenth regular session of the General Assembly in December, Kasa-Vubu himself came to New York as the head of his delegation, which was seated by the Assembly after a long and heated debate. The Assembly's decision considerably enhanced Kasa-Vubu's personal prestige, but did not bring an immediate solution to the crisis.

Four rival groups

In the mean time, the internal situation rapidly worsened in the Congo. While the Council of Commissioners consolidated its position in Leopoldville, Antoine Gizenga, acting on behalf of Lumumba, succeeded in establishing a "government" in Stanleyville which was formally recognized as the legitimate government of the Republic by a number of Member States. With the support of the local ANC troops, led by General Victor Lundula, Gizenga extended his authority beyond Orientale province to Kivu and the northern part of Katanga.

At the same time, the secessionist authorities headed by Moïse Tshombé and Albert Kalonji consolidated their hold, respectively, over southern Katanga and South Kasai, with the active assistance of certain foreign Powers. Thus the Congo came to be divided into four rival camps, each relying more on armed force than on popular support.

ONUC casualties

In carrying out its mission of peace, the United Nations Force suffered many casualties. On 8 November 1960, a patrol of 11 Irish soldiers was ambushed by tribesmen in northern Katanga and eight of them were killed. Another incident occurred on 24 November when ANC troops attacked the Ghanaian Embassy in Leopoldville. The Tunisian unit which guarded the Embassy incurred several casualties, including one fatality.

Here again, when the authorities in power indulged in actions which endangered peace and order, or violated human rights, ONUC could not always prevent those actions, but sought to redress the situation by the use of persuasion or good offices. Thus ONUC could not prevent a number of political arrests made by the various local régimes. At the time, those régimes endeavoured to strengthen their armed forces by importing arms and military equipment from abroad. While ONUC did its best to stop such imports, its forces were insufficient to control all points of entry, and therefore it could not prevent quantities of arms and equipment from being smuggled into different parts of the country.

Lumumba's death

From the beginning of the constitutional crisis, ONUC troops vigilantly guarded Lumumba's residence and, so long as he remained there, he was in safety. However, it was not possible to protect him when he voluntarily left his residence, as he did on the night of 27/28 November 1960, in an apparent attempt to get to Stanleyville, his political stronghold.[8] Before he could get there, he was arrested by ANC soldiers controlled by Mobutu near Port-Francqui (now Ilebo) and brought back to Leopoldville. Once Lumumba was arrested by the *de facto* authorities of Leopoldville, ONUC was not in a position to take forcible action to liberate him from his captors, but it exerted all possible pressure to secure lawful, humane treatment for him. Upon learning of the arrest, the Secretary-General sent a succession of messages to President Kasa-Vubu,[9] expressing his concern over the event and stressing the importance of giving the prisoner all the guarantees provided by law. Similarly repeated representations were later made to the President by Rajeshwar Dayal of India, at the time Special

Representative of the Secretary-General in the Congo. Onuc could not do more without exceeding the mandate given it by the Security Council and without using force.

Lumumba remained detained in Thysville until 17 January, when he and two other political prisoners, Joseph Okito and Maurice Mpolo, were transferred to Elisabethville in Katanga. This move brought strong protests from both the Secretary-General and the United Nations Conciliation Commission for the Congo, which was then in the territory. In particular, the Secretary-General took immediate action to urge the authorities concerned to return Lumumba to Leopoldville province and to apply the normal legal rules. But no remedial action was taken, and, four weeks later, the news came from Katanga that the three prisoners had been murdered. The circumstances of their death were later investigated by a United Nations commission, which accepted as substantially true evidence indicating that the prisoners had been killed on 17 January 1961 and probably in the presence of high officials of the Katanga provincial government.[10]

Following Lumumba's death, there were a series of reprisals and counter-reprisals by pro-Lumumba and anti-Lumumba factions, including summary executions of political leaders. The civil war, already under way in northern Katanga, threatened to spread to other regions.

Several troop-contributing countries withdrew their national contingents from onuc,[11] reducing its strength from 20,000 to less than 15,000. At United Nations Headquarters, the Soviet Union called for Hammarskjöld's dismissal and announced that it would not, henceforth, recognize him as Secretary-General.

Authorization to use force

The Security Council met again on 15 February 1961, and after long debate adopted, on 21 February, resolution 161(1961), by which it authorized onuc to use force, as a last resort, to prevent civil war in the Congo. It urged that the various Congolese armed units be reorganized and brought under discipline and control, and urged the immediate evacuation of all Belgian and other foreign military and paramilitary personnel and political advisers not under United Nations command, as well as mercenaries. It also urged the convening of Parliament and the taking of the necessary protective measures in that connection.

Provisional government

After January 1961, a number of steps were taken by various Congolese leaders attempting to resolve the crisis. On 25 January, a preliminary round-table was sponsored by Kasa-Vubu in Leopoldville. It was boycotted by pro-Lumumba and pro-Tshombé leaders, which considerably limited its usefulness. However, at the end of the conference, Kasa-Vubu decided to replace the Council of Commissioners by a provisional government headed by Joseph Iléo, a decision which was considered by the United Nations Conciliation Commission as a step in the right direction.

Situation in the Congo: February-April 1961

The period immediately following the adoption of the Security Council's resolution of 21 February 1961 was a critical one for the United Nations Operation in the Congo. Thinly deployed throughout the country, the United Nations Force had great difficulty in coping with its overwhelming tasks, and this difficulty increased with its reduction in strength.

The difficulties were compounded by the hostile attitude of the *de facto* authorities of Leopoldville and Elisabethville. These authorities interpreted the Council's new resolution as an attempt to subdue them by force and, in retaliation, ordered a number of harassing measures against ONUC and its personnel. The most serious of these was an attack by ANC troops on the United Nations garrison in Matadi on 4 March 1961, which forced the garrison to withdraw from the port city. [12]

In order to cope with these difficulties and to implement the resolution, the Secretary-General took urgent action to increase the strength of the United Nations Force. New contributions of personnel were obtained from several Governments, bringing the total of the United Nations troops to more than 18,000 in April 1961.

In April, the situation began to improve, first because of the increased strength of the Force, and secondly because after patient negotiations, ONUC reached an agreement with President Kasa-Vubu on 17 April 1961[13] for the implementation of the Security Council's February resolution.

The limited use of force, as authorized by the Council, was resorted to by ONUC at the beginning of April 1961 to stop the civil war, which was spreading dangerously in northern Katanga. Since mid-March 1961, Katangese gendarmerie led by foreign mercenaries had launched an offensive against the anti-Tshombé forces in northern Katanga in a determined effort to crush all opposition there. On 27 March,[14] the United Nations Force Commander warned Tshombé to stop the offensive, but the warning was unheeded and his gendarmes entered Manono three days later and prepared to attack Kabalo. It was at this point that United Nations troops intervened, stopped the gendarmes and established control of the area between Kabalo and Albertville (now Kalemie).

Further casualties

At the end of April, a tragic incident occurred when a Ghanaian detachment of ONUC in Port-Francqui was suddenly attacked and overpowered by ANC troops, and 44 of its members ruthlessly massacred. It was generally agreed that this brutal assault was mainly an act by undisciplined and unpredictable armed troops. Thereafter, the ONUC command made it a rule not to station small units in isolated areas.

Another series of incidents was related to the ANC campaign, late in 1961, to occupy northern Katanga. In connection with this military campaign, which is described in the section below on the problem of Katanga, a number of grave incidents were caused by undisciplined ANC elements. At the beginning of November 1961, ANC soldiers of the Leopoldville group assaulted several Belgian women in Luluabourg. On 11 November, ANC soldiers of the Stanleyville group massacred 13 ONUC aircrew members of Italian nationality in Kindu. Two days later, ANC soldiers of the same group, who had just entered Albertville, began looting houses and threatening civilians there. On 1 January 1961, 22 European missionaries and an undetermined number of Africans were killed in Kongolo by ANC soldiers, also from Stanleyville, in an incident reminiscent of the Kindu massacre.

Conciliation efforts

During the first days of the constitutional crisis, ONUC endeavoured to prevent the leaders holding the reins of power from using force to subdue their opponents within or outside the zones they controlled and, at the same time, it encouraged all leaders to seek a solution of their differences through negotiation and conciliation.

Conciliation efforts were also made by the United Nations Conciliation Commission, established under the Assembly's resolution of 20 September 1960 *(see above)*. This Commission, which was composed of representatives of African and Asian countries which contributed troops to the United Nations Force, visited the Congo at the beginning of 1961. After spending seven weeks in that country, the Commission concluded that, while there was among most leaders a general feeling of weariness and a sincere desire to achieve a peaceful solution to the crisis, a small number of other leaders, among the very persons holding the reins of power, appeared to prefer a military rather than a political and constitutional solution. Because of those leaders' unco-operative and intransigent attitude, the Commission's attempts to reconcile the opposing groups had not led to positive results. The Commission also came to the conclusion that the crisis could be solved only if Parliament was reconvened and a national unity government was approved by it, and that one of the main obstacles to a speedy solution was foreign intervention in the internal affairs of the Congo.

Tananarive Conference

In the mean time, at the beginning of March 1961, a conference was held in Tananarive (now Antananarivo), Madagascar, on the proposal of Moïse Tshombé. It was attended by a number of top Congolese leaders, but Antoine Gizenga, who had at first agreed to come, did not show up. The Tananarive Conference proposed that the Congo be turned into a confederation of sovereign States. Under the proposed arrangement, the central Government would be abolished, and legislative and executive powers would be vested in the individual States. The Conference proposals also provided for the establishment of new States, but did not determine the criteria to be followed in that connection. This decision led some Congolese leaders, through personal ambition and tribal animosities, to lay claim for the creation of a score of new States. But the influence of the Tananarive Conference was short-lived. Soon afterwards, Kasa-Vubu and other leaders revised their positions and made it clear that the decisions of Tananarive were mere statements of intention and, unless approved by Parliament, had no force of law.

Coquilhatville meeting

The following month, on 24 April 1961, a more important conference was convened in Coquilhatville, on the proposal of Kasa-Vubu. Gizenga again refused to attend. Tshombé came and sought to have the Conference endorse the Tananarive proposals. When his attempt was opposed by the overwhelming majority of the representatives, he decided to boycott the Conference. As he prepared to fly back to Elisabethville, he was arrested by the Leopoldville authorities, although he was released about a month later. The Conference continued nevertheless, and at the conclusion of its work, it recommended a reorganization of the governmental structure of the Congo on a federal basis. From the outset, it had been made clear that Conference decisions would have to be endorsed by Parliament, and during the Conference, on 12 May, President Kasa-Vubu announced that Parliament would be reopened in the near future and requested United Nations assistance and protection for this purpose.

While carefully avoiding interference in the discussions between the Congolese leaders, ONUC assisted them whenever it was requested to do so. Thus it placed a guard at the site of the preliminary round-table conference in Leopoldville. It agreed to facilitate Gizenga's trip to Tananarive when he first accepted to go there. Before the Coquilhatville Conference, a Congolese leader, Cléophas Kamitatu, went to Stanleyville on an ONUC aeroplane in an effort to bring about a *rapprochement* between Gizenga and Kasa-Vubu. ONUC also made representations for Tshombé's release.

Reopening of Parliament

After Kasa-Vubu announced his intention to reconvene Parliament, ONUC spared no effort to help achieve this purpose. An essential condition for reconvening Parliament was a *rapprochement* between leaders of the Leopoldville and Stanleyville groups. To these two groups belonged the great majority of parliamentarians, and if one of them refused to attend meetings of Parliament, there would be no quorum. But the memory of Patrice Lumumba's death and its aftermath was still vivid, and leaders of the two groups were divided by deep suspicion and distrust. Through good offices and persuasion, ONUC officials did everything possible to dissipate their mutual suspicion and lay the groundwork for negotiations between them.

After Kasa-Vubu called the parliamentary session in Leopoldville, Gizenga condemned his action as illegal and ordered Parliament to meet in Kamina. Thanks to ONUC's good offices, Gizenga softened his stand and agreed not to insist on Kamina, provided that full protection was given to parliamentarians by ONUC. Later, a meeting between Leopoldville and Stanleyville representatives was arranged at Leopoldville, under ONUC auspices, to consider the modalities of the reopening of Parliament.[15] The Stanleyville representatives were brought to Leopoldville in an ONUC aircraft and the meeting took place at ONUC headquarters. After long discussions, an agreement was reached by the representatives of the two groups. At their joint request, ONUC accepted the responsibility for making arrangements for the session of Parliament and ensuring full protection to the parliamentarians.

In accordance with a request made by both delegations, ONUC also sought to persuade Congolese leaders of South Kasai and southern Katanga to subscribe to the agreement on the reconvening of Par-

liament. Both Kalonji and Tshombé, who was released from confine-
ment by the Leopoldville authorities on 22 June 1961, promised to co-
operate. Tshombé signed a protocol calling for the reconvening
of Parliament,[16] but he changed his position after he returned to
Elisabethville.

Parliament reopened on 22 July with more than 200—out of a total
of 221—members attending. Most of them were brought to Leopoldville with the assistance of ONUC.

Government of national unity

On 2 August 1961, Prime Minister Cyrille Adoula, at the request
of President Kasa-Vubu, constituted a Government of national unity,
which was unanimously approved by both Chambers.[17]

With the act of approval of the national unity Government, the
constitutional crisis was ended. In response to a letter from Prime
Minister Adoula, the Secretary-General confirmed[18] that the United
Nations would deal with his Government as the Central Government
of the Republic and would render to it whatever aid and support the
United Nations was in a position to give to the Congo.

Adoula endeavoured to secure Gizenga's co-operation, with the
active assistance of other Stanleyville leaders and ONUC. His efforts
seemed successful at first. On 7 August 1961, Gizenga recognized the
Adoula Government as the sole legal Government of the Republic.
Four weeks later, he came back to Leopoldville to assume the post of
Deputy Prime Minister and accompanied Adoula in that capacity to
a conference of non-aligned nations in Belgrade, Yugoslavia. However,
Gizenga left again for Stanleyville at the beginning of October, osten-
sibly to collect some personal effects, and refused to return to Leopoldville despite the many appeals from Adoula. While he was in Stanleyville, he attempted to form a new party, the Parti national lumum-
biste (PANALU), and made several statements strongly hostile to the
Government.

On 8 January 1962, the Chamber of Representatives adopted a
resolution[19] ordering Gizenga to return to Leopoldville without delay
to answer charges of secessionism. Gizenga refused, and his defiant
attitude led to fighting, on 13 January 1962, between gendarmes supporting him and ANC troops loyal to the Government, which was
easily won by the latter. Thereafter, Gizenga was dismissed from the
post of Deputy Prime Minister following a motion of censure by the
Chamber of Representatives.[20]

D. Termination of the secession of Katanga (September 1961–February 1963)

United Nations resolutions

Along with the breakdown of law and order and foreign armed intervention, the secession of Katanga was one of the main problems which confronted the Congo when it appealed to the United Nations for help. However, the Security Council's resolution of 14 July 1960 contained no mention of this point. In a second resolution, of 22 July, the Council requested all States to refrain from any action which might undermine the territorial integrity and political independence of the Congo. In August, the Council called for the immediate withdrawal of Belgian troops from Katanga; however, it emphasized that the United Nations was not to take sides in Congolese internal conflicts, constitutional or otherwise, nor was the Organization to be used to influence the outcome of any such conflict.

Secretary-General's position

The Secretary-General's position was that, while ONUC originated from a request by the Congolese Government, the purpose of United Nations intervention as determined by the Security Council was not to achieve the domestic aims of the Government but to preserve international peace and security. The United Nations Force therefore could not, under the Council's decision, be used on behalf of the Central Government to subdue or to force the provincial government into a specific line of action in regard to an internal political controversy. At the same time, the problem of Katanga clearly had an international dimension.

What the United Nations sought to do was to encourage efforts at reconciliation and to eliminate foreign interference, which had been instrumental in bringing about the secession of Katanga and which had helped it to endure. The withdrawal of Belgian troops from Katanga, which occurred in August 1960, did not end the secession of the province, and Tshombé's secessionist régime was able to consolidate its hold over southern Katanga, with active foreign assistance. While Belgian officers, supplemented by an increasing number of foreign mercenaries, continued to strengthen the gendarmerie, Tshombé imported large quantities of arms and war *matériel*, including aircraft, from abroad. With his improved armed forces, he launched a merciless extermination campaign against the Baluba and other political and tribal enemies. Helping to maintain law and order in Katanga and protecting large parts of the Katangese population against the brutal law-lessness of the gendarmerie accordingly became one of the principal aspects of the ONUC effort, along with the removal of the foreign political advisers, military and paramilitary personnel and mercenaries.

Union Minière du Haut-Katanga

In carrying out its functions in Katanga, ONUC continually found itself opposed by certain foreign financial interests which, in effect, controlled the economy of the province. These interests centred about the vast industrial and mining complex of the Union Minière du Haut-Katanga—with headquarters in Brussels, Belgium—which had apparently committed itself to Tshombé's secessionist policies.

The Union Minière supported Tshombé in four principal ways. Firstly, it paid nearly all of its taxes not to the Central Government, to which they were due, but to the Katangese provincial authorities. Secondly, it shipped its production not by way of the traditional "national" route, but by way of Portuguese Angola; this enabled it to credit hard-currency export duties to the account of the provincial government. Thirdly, the Congo's part of Union Minière stock was withheld from the Central Government and kept in Brussels. Fourthly, the firm allowed its industrial facilities at Elisabethville and other places to be used by the mercenary-led gendarmerie for military purposes, including the making of some implements of war.

Non-recognition of Katanga

Despite Tshombé's efforts and the powerful financial and political support he enjoyed, his separatist movement never gained official international recognition, either in Belgium or elsewhere. Moreover, neither Belgium nor any other Government publicly espoused the cause of Katangese secession. In fact, after the establishment of the coalition Government in Brussels in the spring of 1961, its Minister for Foreign Affairs, Paul-Henri Spaak, announced publicly his Government's opposition to the secession of Katanga.

Mercenaries

The problem of foreign elements who sought to influence the Congo's destiny in their own interests came to light soon after the country's accession to independence.

In the beginning, the bulk of these persons were Belgian professional military and civilian officials placed at the disposal of the Central Government of the Congo under the treaty of friendship with Belgium, which was signed in June 1960 but never ratified. After the severance of diplomatic relations between the Congo and Belgium, many of these men gathered in Katanga, where they gained prominent positions in the provincial administration and the gendarmerie. From these vantage points they vigorously promoted secession. In effect, they waged war on the Congolese Government at whose disposal they had been placed by their Government. Later these Belgians were joined by other nationalities.

On 21 February 1961, the Security Council urged "the immediate withdrawal and evacuation from the Congo of all Belgian and other foreign military and paramilitary personnel and political advisers not under the United Nations Command, and mercenaries". Implicit in this language was the finding that while the Congo was admittedly and direly in need of assistance from outside, and especially of personnel to carry out technical and professional tasks which the Congolese had not hitherto been trained to perform, there were other types of foreign personnel whose actions were incompatible with genuine Congolese independence and unity. In certain parts of the Congo, and especially in Katanga, such personnel had come to play an increasingly questionable role, obstructing the application of United Nations resolutions and, in effect, working in their own interest and in the interest of certain financial concerns, to break up the country into a balkanized congeries of politically and economically unviable states.

Secretary-General's efforts, 1961

Immediately after the adoption of the resolution of 21 February, the Secretary-General undertook intensive diplomatic efforts to bring about the withdrawal of the foreign military and political personnel.

The Belgian Government took the position that there must be no discrimination against Belgians in engaging non-Congolese technical personnel; as for military personnel and mercenaries, the Belgian Government divided them into several categories. Of these, it undertook to recall those whom it considered it had the legal right to request to return. But it would take no such action in respect of mercenaries or of Belgian personnel directly engaged by the Congolese Government, arguing that it was up to the Secretary-General to agree with the Congolese authorities on how to deal with them. The Secretary-General expressed the view that the measures indicated by the Belgian Government fell far short of full compliance with the Security Council's resolution.

The exchanges with Belgium continued, fairly inconclusively, until the change of government in the first half of 1961, when some progress was made. A new Belgian Government notified 23 of its nationals serving in Katanga as political advisers to return to Belgium. It also acted to prevent the recruitment of mercenaries proper. But the effectiveness of these efforts soon became open to doubt. On 30 October 1961, the Government at Brussels acknowledged that this was the case and took more vigorous steps—including the withdrawal of passports from recalcitrant Belgians.

Tshombé, however, would not co-operate with ONUC. He continued to recruit foreign personnel, whose influence in the councils of the provincial government in fact tended to rise sharply. The complexion of the group also changed noticeably as mercenaries replaced Belgian professional officials. Thus the traditional colonial administrative and military elements were being supplemented through an influx of non-Belgian adventurers and soldiers of fortune, including outlawed elements previously involved in extremist, repressive and separatist policies. They drew political sustenance from the substantial non-Congolese community to which Katanga's extractive and processing industries had given rise.

Repatriation and expulsion of some foreign elements, 1961

Only after the United Nations had strengthened its position in April 1961 did the Katanga secessionist authorities, acting while Tshombé was under detention in the west, officially accept resolution 161(1961) of 21 February.

Those authorities drew up lists of persons whom they considered as falling within the terms of the resolution. By the end of June 1961, 44 Belgian nationals were thus selected for repatriation, and the cases of 22 others were under consideration. It was noted, however, that persons clearly not coming under the resolution had been included for political reasons, while others notorious for their activities had been omitted. ONUC representatives continued to press for revision of the lists, and brought home to the provincial authorities their determination to take drastic action, if need be, to comply with the United Nations mandate.

In April 1961,[21] 30 members of a mercenary unit known as the "Compagnie internationale" were apprehended by ONUC personnel and evacuated from the Congo. By mid-June an estimated 60 more mercenaries had withdrawn from Katanga, and on 24 June the Compagnie was formally dissolved by the provincial government.

On 7 June 1961, following discussions with the Katangese authorities, the United Nations Force Commander dispatched a military mission to Katanga to help the authorities there to remove non-Congolese elements falling under the resolution. The mission reported that there were 510 foreign and non-commissioned officers active in the Katangese gendarmerie, as against 142 Congolese "cadres". Of the non-Congolese, 208 were the remaining Belgian professional military men; 302 were mercenaries.

But despite the unrelenting efforts of ONUC, the provincial authorities refused to take effective action to remove the foreign elements, without whom the secessionist movement might have collapsed. For its part, the Belgian Government said it was prepared to help in the removal of its professional and non-commissioned officers who had been serving the Congo and were currently in command of the gendarmerie, but it professed itself unable to do anything about "volunteers" and mercenaries. Persuasion by the Secretary-General, who discussed the matter with Foreign Minister Spaak at Geneva on 12 July 1961, was unavailing in this regard.

Gradually, the United Nations was compelled to shift to more vigorous and direct measures to achieve compliance with the Security Council's resolution. Tshombé's chief military adviser was compelled to leave in June 1961, and a prominent political adviser was apprehended, taken to Leopoldville, and evacuated in July. ONUC warned the Katangese authorities that it was prepared to compel the evacuation of other advisers and officers. Five French officers in politically sensitive gendarmerie posts were dismissed and repatriated, and a joint commission was established to list foreign political advisers, both those in official posts and others acting unofficially, who were to be repatriated.

Formation of the Adoula Government

The formation of the Adoula Government, enjoying unquestionable and internationally recognized authority, was of crucial importance in enabling the United Nations to proceed with the elimination of foreign elements.

Before the formation of a legal government, United Nations efforts had been restricted by the requirement of avoiding political interference or support of one Congolese faction against another. Now the United Nations was able to do more effectively what the 11-month constitutional crisis had impeded—that is, help the Government remove the foreign elements that had provided the teeth of the attempt to sever, in their own interests, the Congo's richest province from the rest of the country.

Government ordinance on expulsions

Soon after the reopening of Parliament, Tshombé somewhat softened his stand and allowed the parliamentarians of his party in Katanga to participate in the work of Parliament. However, he himself remained in Elisabethville and showed no intention of relinquishing the powers he held in Katanga. For weeks, ONUC representatives urged Tshombé to co-operate in removing the remaining foreign elements, but to little avail.

When all attempts at negotiations failed, in order to remove what it believed to be the main obstacle to a peaceful solution to the Katanga question, Prime Minister Adoula's Government formally requested the expulsion of the mercenaries serving in Katanga and requested ONUC to assist it in carrying out the decision. An ordinance was issued on 24 August calling for expulsion of all foreign officers and mercenaries standing behind the secessionist policy.[22]

Round-up of mercenaries

On 28 August 1961, ONUC proceeded to round up the mercenaries for deportation. In the face of inflammatory rumours about an invasion by the ANC which had been disseminated by Godefroid Munongo, the provincial Minister of the Interior, certain security precautions were taken by ONUC in Elisabethville, including surveillance over Radio Katanga, gendarmerie headquarters and some other key points. Inflammatory broadcasts were thus prevented, and appeals for calm were put on the air.

Tshombé, who had been fully informed of the objectives of ONUC's action, expressed his readiness to co-operate. He broadcast a statement to the effect that the Katangese authorities accepted the decisions of the United Nations, and that the services of foreign military personnel were being terminated by his government.[23]

At that point, ONUC representatives met with the Elisabethville consular corps, which offered to assume the responsibility, together with two senior Belgian officers formerly in the gendarmerie, for the orderly repatriation of the foreign personnel, most of whom were Belgians. In the interest of avoiding violence, ONUC accepted this arrangement, and suspended its own rounding-up operation.

However, the foreign military men being selected for repatriation were in the main personnel whose withdrawal had earlier been agreed to by the Belgian Government. By 9 September 1961, 273 had been evacuated and 65 were awaiting repatriation. But, while some of the volunteers and mercenaries had left, many others—about 104 of whom were known to be in Katanga—were "missing". They were reinfiltrating into the gendarmerie, distributing arms to groups of soldiers over whom they could assert control, and getting ready for violent resistance.

At the same time, the political police *(Sûreté)*, under Munongo and largely directed by foreign officers, launched a campaign of assaults and persecution against anti-Tshombé Baluba tribesmen in Elisabethville. An effort was made to convince the world that ONUC's actions were causing disorder. The terrorized Baluba streamed out of the city and sought safety by camping in primitive conditions near ONUC troop quarters. ONUC arranged protection for the encampment, into which 35,000 Baluba had crowded by 9 September, creating a serious food and health problem, as well as a continuing danger of tribal violence.

Attack on ONUC

When ONUC realized that the Katangese authorities had no intention of fulfilling their promises, it pressed its demand for the evacuation of foreign personnel of the Katangese security police and of the remaining mercenaries. The Katangese, however, led by Tshombé, had manifestly fallen back under the domination of the foreign elements, and had let themselves be persuaded to launch violent action against ONUC. ONUC's plans for a solution of the difficulties in Elisabethville were rejected, and when on 13 September 1961 it applied security precautions similar to those of 28 August, the United Nations troops were violently attacked by gendarmes led by non-Congolese personnel.

In the morning of 13 September, Tshombé requested a cease-fire, but the attacks on United Nations troops continued.[24] From the building housing the Belgian Consulate in Elisabethville, where a number of Belgian officers were known to be staying, sustained firing was directed at United Nations troops. The United Nations base at Kamina was attacked, as were the United Nations garrison and installations at Albertville. Reluctantly, United Nations troops had to return the fire. All over Elisabethville, and elsewhere in Katanga, the foreign officers who had gone into hiding reappeared to lead operations against ONUC personnel.

Efforts to reinforce the troops were frustrated by the depredations of a Katangese jet fighter, piloted by a mercenary, which quickly managed to immobilize ONUC's unarmed air transport craft. The jet also played havoc with the ground movements of ONUC, which had deliberately refrained from securing offensive weapons such as fighter-planes or tanks as incompatible with its mission as a peace force.

Dag Hammarskjöld's death

In the mean time, the Secretary-General had arrived in Leopoldville at Prime Minister Adoula's invitation to discuss future prospects
of the United Nations Operation in what was hoped would be a new
setting created by the completion of the principal tasks assigned by
the Security Council and General Assembly. He intended also to bring
about a reconciliation between Leopoldville and Elisabethville. Confronted instead with a situation of confused fighting in Elisabethville,
Hammarskjöld devoted himself to the task of securing a cessation of
hostilities and achieving reconciliation among Congolese factions. In
quest of a cease-fire, he flew to Ndola, in what was then Northern
Rhodesia, to meet Tshombé. On this flight, on the night of 17 September 1961, his aeroplane crashed and he was killed, together with
seven other United Nations staff members and the Swedish crew.[25]

Cease-fire, September 1961

The Secretary-General's mission was immediately taken up by
the authorities of ONUC in Leopoldville. Mahmoud Khiari, the Chief
of ONUC Civilian Operations, flew to Ndola and, on behalf of the United Nations forces, signed a military cease-fire agreement on 20 September.[26] It was understood as an express condition that the agreement would not affect the application of the Security Council and
General Assembly resolutions. A protocol for carrying out the provisions of the cease-fire was signed on 13 October 1961 at Elisabethville.[27] While the protocol allowed firing back in case of attack, it prohibited Katangese and ONUC troop movements. In approving this protocol, the United Nations stressed its military nature, re-emphasized
its support of the unity, integrity and independence of the Congo, and
insisted on continued enforcement of the Security Council resolution
which called for the removal of mercenaries.

Katangese violations of the cease-fire

Although prisoners were exchanged and certain positions held
by ONUC in Elisabethville during the fighting were duly released, in
accordance with the protocol, Tshombé's régime was soon flouting the
provisions of the cease-fire agreement. In Leopoldville, his emissaries
made it clear that nothing less than independence along the lines of
the Tananarive decisions would be acceptable to the Elisabethville
authorities. Meanwhile, the remaining Katangese mercenaries were
leading the gendarmerie in a long series of violations of the cease-fire
agreement, going so far as to launch offensive air action along the Kasai-

Katanga frontier. This was strongly protested by the United Nations. While strictly abiding by the cease-fire in Katanga, ONUC took steps to prevent the recurrence of the September situation when it had found itself powerless to stop the attacks of Katanga's jet fighters. Three Member States—Ethiopia, India and Sweden—provided jet fighter squadrons to the United Nations Force to strengthen its defensive capacity.

At the same time, however, the Force's ground strength was being whittled away. The Tunisian contingent had been withdrawn in August 1961 because of events in Tunisia; the Ghanaian contingent subsequently withdrew, and certain other ONUC units were reduced. Not unaware of these developments, Tshombé and the foreign elements supporting him were determined to turn secession into an accomplished fact. ONUC-sponsored talks between the Central Government and Katanga were subjected to stalling tactics. At least 237 persons, chiefly mercenaries falling under the provisions of the Security Council's resolution, remained in Katanga, many of whom donned civilian garb.

ANC offensives

Despairing of a peaceful solution, the Central Government attempted to deal with Katanga's secession independently, by the use of force, in late October 1961. The strength of the national army was built up on the border of northern Katanga in preparation for entry into that region. At the beginning of November, a detachment of the ANC entered northern Katanga in the Kamina area, but was immediately repelled by Katangese gendarmes. Later, ANC units from Stanleyville succeeded in reaching Albertville, Nyunzu, Kongolo and other towns of northern Katanga. To facilitate this move, the Government had requested ONUC assistance for the transport of its troops. The request was turned down because, as had been the case from the outset, it remained against ONUC principles to become a party to an internal conflict.

Security Council authorizes ONUC to remove mercenaries

In the latter part of November 1961, the Security Council was convened once again to examine the situation in the Congo. By resolution 169(1961) of 24 November 1961, the Council strongly deprecated the secessionist activities in Katanga and authorized the Secretary-General to use force to complete the removal of mercenaries.

After the adoption of the resolution, Tshombé launched an in-

flammatory propaganda campaign against ONUC which soon degener-
ated into incitement to violence. The results were not long in coming.
On 28 November 1961, two senior United Nations officials in Elisabethville were abducted and badly beaten; later an Indian soldier was murdered and an Indian major abducted. Several members of the United
Nations Force were detained, and others were killed or wounded.
Road-blocks were established by the gendarmerie, impeding ONUC's
freedom of movement and endangering its lifelines. It subsequently
became known that this was part of a deliberate plan to cut off the
United Nations troops in Elisabethville, and either force them to surrender or otherwise destroy them. For one week, United Nations officials sought to settle the crisis by peaceful negotiations. But when it
became evident that, in the face of the bad faith displayed by Katangese authorities, no commitments could be relied upon, and that, while
pretending to negotiate, those authorities were preparing for more assaults, ONUC finally decided to take action to regain and assure its freedom of movement.

Fighting of December 1961

ONUC had few troops in Elisabethville when fighting broke out
on 5 December 1961. Until 14 December, ONUC forces endeavoured to
hold their positions and to maintain communications between units
while reinforcements were hurriedly flown in from other parts of the
Congo. On 15 December, having received enough reinforcements,
ONUC troops moved to seize control of those positions in Elisabethville
necessary to ensure their freedom of movement. In so doing, they
worked their way around the perimeter of the city, in order to keep
destruction and civilian casualties to the strict minimum. This objective was achieved within three days.[28]

From the outset of the hostilities, United Nations military and
civilian officers did their best, in co-operation with the International
Committee of the Red Cross, to relieve the distress caused to innocent
civilians. Persons caught in areas where firing had been initiated by
the gendarmerie were escorted to safety, at the risk of ONUC personnel's lives; food supplies were provided where needed; special arrangements for the evacuation of women and children were made by ONUC.
Notwithstanding the shortage of troops, ONUC employed a whole battalion to guard the Baluba refugee camp, where more than 40,000 anti-
Tshombé Baluba lived under United Nations protection.[29] ONUC
troops, on the one hand, prevented them from raiding Elisabethville
and, on the other, protected them from the gendarmes who launched
several attacks on the camp.

Kitona Declaration

On 19 December 1961, having ensured the positions necessary for its security, ONUC ordered its troops to hold fire unless fired upon.[30] The same day, Tshombé left Elisabethville to confer with Prime Minister Adoula at Kitona, the United Nations military base in Leopoldville province. After that, major fighting between ONUC and Katangese forces ceased. ONUC immediately turned its efforts to the re-establishment of normal conditions in Elisabethville. It co-operated closely with the local police to stop looting, to rid private houses of squatters and, in general, to restore and maintain law and order.

The Kitona meeting was arranged with the assistance of ONUC and the United States Ambassador in the Congo following a request by Tshombé on 14 December 1961, when the fighting in Elisabethville was in full swing. After meeting Prime Minister Adoula all day long on 20 December, Tshombé signed early in the morning of 21 December an eight-point Declaration.[31] In this Declaration, he accepted the application of the *Loi fondamentale,* recognized the authority of the Central Government in Leopoldville over all parts of the Congo and agreed to a number of steps aimed at ending the secession of Katanga. He also pledged himself to ensure respect for the resolutions of the Security Council and the General Assembly and to facilitate their implementation.

In accordance with the provisions of the Kitona Declaration, Tshombé sent 14 parliamentarians from Katanga to Leopoldville to participate in the session of Parliament. Three Katangese officials were also dispatched to the capital to participate in discussions for the modification of the constitutional structure of the Congo. In both cases, ONUC ensured the safety of the representatives during their journey to and from Leopoldville and their stay there.

While making the concessions contained in the Declaration, Tshombé stated that he had no authority to decide on the future of Katanga, and he summoned the provincial Assembly to meet in Elisabethville to discuss the Declaration. On 15 February, that Assembly decided to accept the "draft declaration" of Kitona only as a basis for discussions with the Central Government.

Following this action, Prime Minister Adoula invited Tshombé to meet with him in Leopoldville to discuss the procedure for carrying out the provisions of the Declaration,[32] but attempts at peaceful resolution through the talks failed; the agreement was not implemented owing to the procrastination and intransigence of the Katangese leader. The talks were suspended in June 1962 without agreement.[33]

Secretary-General's Plan of National Reconciliation

Given the failure of the negotiations, after consultation with various Member States, Secretary-General U Thant, in August 1962, proposed a "Plan of National Reconciliation",[34] which was ultimately accepted by both Adoula and Tshombé. It provided for: a federal system of government; division of revenues and foreign-exchange earnings between the Central and provincial governments; unification of currency; integration and unification of all military, paramilitary and gendarme units into the structure of a national army; general amnesty; reconstitution of the Central Government giving representation to all political and provincial groups; withdrawal of representatives abroad not serving the Central Government; and freedom of movement for United Nations personnel throughout the Congo.

End of the secession of Katanga

After acceptance of the Plan of National Reconciliation, a draft federal constitution was prepared by United Nations experts,[35] and amnesty was proclaimed by the Central Government in late November 1962. On the Katanga side, however, no substantial steps were taken to implement the Plan. In this situation, U Thant requested Member States, on 11 December,[36] to bring economic pressure on the Katangese authorities, particularly by stopping the export of copper and cobalt. But before that action became effective, the Katangese, unprovokedly, fired on United Nations positions. Although the firing continued for six days, ONUC did not fire back but tried to resolve the situation by negotiation.

Immediately after the breakdown of the negotiations, ONUC began action to restore the security of its troops and their freedom of movement, the first phase being the clearing of the road-blocks from which Katangese troops had been directing fire at ONUC personnel. Ethiopian, Indian and Irish troops took part in the operations.

Wherever ONUC troops appeared, the gendarmerie offered little or no resistance. By 30 December 1962, all the Katangese road-blocks around Elisabethville had been cleared and ONUC forces were in effective control of an area extending approximately 20 kilometres around the city. Meanwhile, around Kamina, Ghanaian and Swedish troops, advancing in a two-pronged attack, had succeeded in occupying that town on the morning of 30 December. Thus, the first phase of the operations was completed.[37]

The second phase started on 31 December,[38] when Indian troops of the United Nations Force began to move towards Jadotville (now

Likasi). The next day, ONUC advance elements reached the Lufira River, which they crossed by nightfall, although both bridges had been destroyed. On 2 January 1963, after having met some gendarmerie resistance on the other side of that river, ONUC troops resumed their advance and reached Jadotville on 3 January, where they were greeted by the cheers of the population. At the same time, ONUC troops also reached the town of Kipushi, south of Elisabethville.

By 4 January, ONUC troops had secured themselves in the Elisabethville, Kipushi, Kamina and Jadotville areas. In all these areas, measures were taken to restore essential services and protect the local population.

In the mean time, Tshombé, who had left Elisabethville on 28 December 1962, had proceeded through Northern Rhodesia to Kolwezi, his last stronghold. To avoid useless bloodshed and destruction of industrial installations, the United Nations ordered its troops to slow their advance towards Kolwezi while the Secretary-General continued his efforts to persuade Tshombé to cease all resistance.

On 14 January 1963, the Secretary-General received, through Belgian Government channels, a message from Tshombé and his ministers meeting at Kolwezi.[39] They announced their readiness to end the secession of Katanga, to grant ONUC troops complete freedom of movement and to arrange for the implementation of the Plan of National Reconciliation. They asked that the Central Government immediately put into effect the amnesty called for in the Plan in order to guarantee the freedom and safety of the Katangese government and of all who worked under its authority.

The Secretary-General welcomed Tshombé's message and informed him on 15 January[40] that the United Nations would do its utmost to assist in the fulfilment of the promise implicit in Tshombé's statement. On 15 January,[41] President Kasa-Vubu and Prime Minister Adoula separately confirmed that the amnesty proclamation of November 1962 remained valid. It was also announced, on 16 January, that Joseph Iléo had been appointed Minister of State Resident at Elisabethville, for the purpose of faciliating the process of reintegration.

On 16 January, Tshombé informed the Secretary-General that he was prepared to discuss at Elisabethville arrangements for ONUC's entry into Kolwezi. The next day, after four hours of discussions at ONUC headquarters, the Acting Representative of the United Nations at Elisabethville, the general officer commanding ONUC troops in the Katanga area and Tshombé signed a document in which Tshombé undertook to facilitate the peaceful entry of ONUC into Kolwezi, to be completed by 21 January.[42] It was understood that pending arrangements for the integration of the gendarmerie, the security of its members would be fully ensured by ONUC. They would not be treated as prisoners of war and would be able to continue to wear their uniforms in Kolwezi.

As agreed, Indian troops of ONUC entered Kolwezi in the afternoon of 21 January. Meanwhile, the situation became increasingly volatile in northern Katanga because of sizeable groups of disorganized but heavily armed gendarmes. Consequently, in the morning of 20 January, Indonesian troops disembarked at Baudouinville (now Moba) and shortly thereafter secured the town and its airport. On the same day, a Nigerian unit starting from Kongolo and a Malayan unit coming from Bukavu cleared the Kongolo pocket where there had remained a considerable gendarme force.

By 21 January, the United Nations Force had under its control all important centres hitherto held by the Katangese, and quickly restored law and order there. The Katangese gendarmerie ceased to exist as an organized fighting force. Thanks to the skill and restraint displayed by ONUC troops, the casualties incurred during the fighting were relatively light. In the 24 days of activity, ONUC casualties were 10 killed and 77 wounded. Katangese casualties also appeared to have been low.

At the beginning of January 1963, 22 officials and officers representing the Central Government arrived at Elisabethville to make up an administrative commission to prepare the way for the integration of the provincial administration into the Central Government. Iléo and his party arrived on 23 January to assume their duties. Shortly before that, Prime Minister Adoula had requested ONUC to give Iléo all the assistance and co-operation he might require. It had been agreed between the Central Government and ONUC that all the military forces in Katanga would be placed under the single command of ONUC. At ONUC's suggestion, Adoula declared that gendarmes who rejoined the Congolese National Army by a certain date would retain their ranks.

Progress was also achieved with regard to the economic reintegration of Katanga. On 15 January, an agreement on foreign exchange was signed at Leopoldville by the representatives of the Central Government and a representative of the Union Minière, who had come from Belgium, in the presence of the Director of the Bank of Katanga. In brief, that agreement provided that the Union Minière would remit all its export proceeds to the Congolese Monetary Council, which would in turn allocate to the Union Minière the foreign exchange it needed to carry out its operations. The allocation of foreign exchange by the Central Government to the provincial authorities was to be discussed separately by that Government and the provincial authorities of southern Katanga.

Under a decree of 9 January 1963, the Monetary Council assumed control of the "National Bank of Katanga" and ensured the resumption of the Bank's operations, with ONUC's assistance.

Thus, the secession of Katanga had been brought to an end, and with this an important phase of ONUC had been completed.

E.   Consolidation of the Congolese Government (February 1963–June 1964)

Introduction

While the period from the end of the Katangese secession until ONUC's withdrawal in June 1964 is the main subject of this section, with the Congolese Central Government authority now extended to the whole country, it is convenient first to consider ONUC's early efforts to assist that Government in regard to civilian operations and the retraining of the Congolese army and security forces.

Civilian Operations

A main objective of ONUC was to provide the Congolese Government with technical assistance for the smooth operation of all essential services and the continued development of the national economy. The situation faced by ONUC at the beginning immediately assumed unprecedented proportions. In the absence of functioning governmental and economic machinery which could receive and use expert advice and training services, the Secretary-General at once mobilized the resources of the United Nations family of organizations under the authority of a Chief of Civilian Operations. A consultative group of experts was set up, consisting of senior officials of the United Nations and the specialized agencies concerned.

The first task was to restore or maintain minimum essential public services. Engineers, air traffic controllers, meteorologists, radio operators, postal experts, physicians, teachers and other specialists were rushed into the country. An emergency project was carried out to halt the silting of the port of Matadi and to restore navigation. In response to the Central Government's appeal, the United Nations agreed, in

August 1960, to provide $5 million to finance essential governmental services as well as essential imports.

In the economic and financial fields, ONUC helped in setting up and managing monetary, foreign exchange and foreign trade controls, without which the country's slender resources might have been drained away and all semblance of a monetary system might have collapsed.

In all these fields, as well as in agriculture, labour and public administration, ONUC's efforts were designed chiefly to improve the ability of the Congolese authorities to discharge their responsibilities towards the population despite the precipitate departure of non-Congolese technicians and administrators. As it soon became obvious that the needs would continue for some time, the Secretary-General proposed and the General Assembly, by resolution 1474(ES-IV) of 20 September 1960, approved the establishment of a United Nations Fund for the Congo, financed by voluntary contributions. Its purpose was to restore the economic life of the country and to carry on its public services as well as possible.

The Assembly's action coincided with the outbreak of the constitutional crisis of September 1960. As a result of that crisis, ONUC could not deal with any authorities, except for President Joseph Kasa-Vubu, on the nation-wide plane, and could not furnish advice at the ministerial level. As the emergency conditions continued, however, the ONUC effort did not flag, and was carried on in co-operation with those Congolese authorities exercising *de facto* control in the provinces or localities where United Nations Civilian Operations were being undertaken.

Famine conditions in some areas, and widespread unemployment, led the Secretary-General to institute refugee relief and relief-work programmes. The worst conditions developed in South Kasai in the second half of 1960, where it was reported that some 200 persons were dying daily from starvation as a result of disruptions caused by tribal warfare. For six months, the United Nations shipped and distributed food and medical supplies in the area. While several thousand persons died before the United Nations effort began, the number of lives saved approximated a quarter of a million.

In the mean time, foreign exchange reserves were running low, owing to the political and economic situation. Accordingly, in June 1961, an agreement was arrived at between President Kasa-Vubu and the Secretary-General, by which the United Nations put funds at the disposal of the Republic for financing a programme of essential imports. It was agreed that such assistance must benefit the population of the country as a whole.

Despite the constitutional crisis, United Nations training services continued as a long-range operation. They were regarded as an investment in the development of human resources so as to fill the huge void caused by the shortage of indigenous operational and executive personnel. Training courses were organized for air traffic controllers, agricultural assistants, farm mechanics, foresters, medical assistants, labour officials, police commissioners, etc. To train Congolese operators and instructors, a telecommunications training centre was set up; to train primary and secondary school teachers and inspectors, a national pedagogical institute was established. Undergraduate medical studies were fostered. A national school of law and administration was opened to produce competent civil servants; a technical college was set up to train junior engineers, public works foremen and the like. Fellowships for study abroad were awarded to school directors, medical students, police officers, social workers and others in need of training, for whom adequate facilities were not available in the Congo. Furthermore, a programme was prepared for the reorganization and retraining of the Congolese National Army *(see section below).*

In 1960 and 1961, ONUC Civilian Operations were able to provide about 600 experts and technicians to do the jobs of departing Belgian personnel. These experts and technicians, drawn from some 48 nationalities, were made available to the Congo by the United Nations and its specialized agencies for work in a variety of fields, such as finance and economics, health, transport, public administration, agriculture, civil aviation, public works, mining and natural resources, postal services, meteorology, telecommunications, judicature, labour, education, social welfare, youth training and community development. In addition, a large number of secondary school teachers were recruited with the assistance of the United Nations Educational, Scientific and Cultural Organization. These assistance programmes continued at about the same level until 1964, despite financial and other difficulties.

The end of the Katangese secession in January 1963 brought with it new responsibilities for the United Nations Civilian Operations programme, since experts became urgently needed to help the Central Government in the reintegration of services previously under Katangese rule, such as postal services, customs and excise, immigration, civil aviation, telecommunications and banking. An expert mission was required to survey the 40 rail and road bridges destroyed or damaged.

As a result of the various training programmes set up by ONUC, it became possible in 1963 to replace some international personnel by qualified Congolese, particularly in the postal, meteorological, telecommunications and civil aviation services. In 1963, 55 of the 130 medical assistants sent abroad for training in 1960-1961 under World Health Organization auspices returned to the Congo and were assigned to various parts of the country.

Reorganization of the Congolese armed forces, 1960-1963

Nearly all the grave incidents mentioned in earlier sections were caused by military elements of Congolese armed forces, whether they were part of the Congolese National Army, the Katangese gendarmerie or the Kalonji forces in South Kasai. From the outset, it was considered an essential task of ONUC to assist the Congolese Government in establishing discipline in the armed forces. These forces were to be brought under a unified command, the rebellious elements eliminated and the remaining ones reorganized and retrained. ONUC offered the Congolese Government full support and co-operation to achieve these objectives.

The United Nations Operation in the Congo took its first step towards the reorganization of the Congolese National Army when the Deputy Commander of the United Nations Force was appointed adviser to the ANC at the end of July 1960, at the request of Prime Minister Lumumba. Shortly thereafter, the ANC began to re-form in new units and to engage in the training of its officers and men. This programme was interrupted at the end of August because of the Government's plan to invade Kasai and Katanga, and later ONUC was compelled to abandon it altogether because of the political struggle which began in September 1960.

After the Adoula Government was set up, in August 1961, ONUC's efforts were resumed and the new Deputy Force Commander prepared a reorganization programme to be carried out in full co-operation with the Government.

Nevertheless, difficulties were later encountered in regard to ONUC assistance in this area. After December 1962, it became clear that Prime Minister Adoula wanted the Secretary-General to request six countries—Belgium, Canada, Israel, Italy, Norway and the United States—to provide personnel and *matériel* for reorganizing and training the various armed services.[43]

The Secretary-General had doubts—which were shared by the Advisory Committee composed of ONUC troop-contributors—about the advisability of the United Nations assuming sponsorship of what was, essentially, bilateral military assistance by a particular group of

States. He therefore concluded that it was not feasible to grant Adoula's specific request, although he continued to hope that a way would be found to make it possible for the ANC to receive the necessary training assistance through ONUC. That hope was not realized, however, and eventually the programme for the training of the ANC was carried out outside the United Nations.

F.   Winding up of ONUC

Situation in February 1963

On 4 February 1963,[44] the Secretary-General reported to the Security Council on the extent to which the mandates given to ONUC by the Council's resolutions had been fulfilled and on the tasks still to be completed.

Regarding the maintenance of the territorial integrity and political independence of the Congo, the secession of Katanga was ended and there was no direct threat to Congo's independence from external sources. That part of the mandate was largely fulfilled.

The mandate to prevent civil war, given in February 1961, was also substantially fulfilled as was, for all practical purposes, the removal of foreign military and paramilitary personnel and mercenaries.

Assistance in maintaining law and order was continuing and, with the vast improvements in that regard, a substantial reduction of ONUC forces was being made.

In view of these accomplishments, the phase of active involvement of United Nations troops was concluded, and a new phase was beginning, which would give greater emphasis to civilian operations and technical assistance.

General Assembly resolution of 18 October 1963

No specific termination date for the United Nations Force in the Congo had been set by any Security Council resolution. However, the General Assembly had, on 27 June 1963 at its fourth special session, adopted resolution 1876(S-IV) appropriating funds for the Force, which, in the absence of any subsequent action, would in effect have established 31 December 1963 as the terminal date for ONUC's military phase.

In a report to the Security Council dated 17 September 1963,[45] the Secretary-General stated that, in the light of the Assembly's resolution, he was proceeding with a phasing-out schedule for the complete withdrawal of the Force by the end of 1963. He drew attention, however, to a letter dated 22 August 1963 from Prime Minister Adoula who, while agreeing with the substantial reduction of the Force that had already been carried out, saw a need for the continued presence of a small United Nations force of about 3,000 officers and men through the first half of 1964.

In this connection, the Secretary-General expressed the opinion that cogent reasons existed in support of prolonging the stay of the Force. There could be no doubt that the presence of a United Nations Force in the Congo would continue to be helpful through the first half of 1964, or longer. But the time must come soon when the Government of the Congo would have to assume full responsibility for security and for law and order in the country.

Acting upon the Congolese Government's request for reduced military assistance up to 30 June 1964, the General Assembly decided, on 18 October 1963, by resolution 1885(XVIII), to continue the *ad hoc* account for the United Nations Operation in the Congo until 30 June 1964, and authorized an expenditure of up to $18.2 million to that effect.

In accordance with the Assembly's resolution, the United Nations Force in the Congo was maintained beyond 1963, but its strength was gradually brought down from 6,535 in December 1963 to 3,297 in June 1964.

Secretary-General's report, 29 June 1964

The Secretary-General, in a report of 29 June 1964,[46] affirmed his earlier conclusions that most of ONUC's objectives had been fulfilled. He indicated his intention to continue technical assistance, within available financial resources, after ONUC's withdrawal.

As to maintenance of law and order, he noted considerable deterioration in a number of localities, especially in Kwilu, Kivu and northern Katanga. He observed, however, that maintenance of law and order, which was one of the main attributes of sovereignty, was principally the responsibility of the Congolese Government, and that ONUC's role had been limited to assisting the Government, to the extent of its means, when it was requested to do so.

The Secretary-General recalled the difficulties ONUC had encountered in attempting to assist the Government in training and reorganizing the Congolese security forces. He said the ANC was now an integrated body of 29,000 soldiers with a unified command, but was still insufficiently trained and officered to cope with a major crisis.

In view of the uncertainties affecting the Congo, the Secretary-General observed, the question was often asked why the stay of ONUC had not been extended beyond the end of June 1964. First, he said, the Congolese Government had not requested an extension. Secondly, a special session of the General Assembly would be required to extend any mandate.

In any case, the Secretary-General concluded, a further extension would provide no solution to the Congo's severe difficulties. The time had come when the Congolese Government would have to assume full responsibility for its own security, law and order, and territorial integrity. He believed this was the position of the Congolese Government, since it had not requested a further extension of ONUC.

Withdrawal of the Force

On 30 June 1964, the United Nations Force in the Congo withdrew from that country according to plan. With the completion of the military phase of ONUC, the Civilian Operations programme was formally discontinued. However, the overall programme of technical assistance which had been supplied by the United Nations family of organizations continued under the responsibility of the Office of the Resident Representative of the United Nations Development Programme.

Reference notes

[1]S/4382. [2]Ibid. [3]S/4381. [4]S/4389. [5]S/4531. [6]S/4557. [7]S/4531. [8]S/4571. [9]S/4571, annexes I and II. [10]S/4976. [11]S/4640. [12]S/4761. [13]S/4807, annex I. [14]S/4791. [15]S/4841. [16]S/4841/Add.2. [17]S/4913. [18]S/4923. [19]S/5053/Add.1, annex I. [20]S/5053/Add.1, annex VI. [21]S/4790. [22]S/4940, annex I. [23]S/4940. [24]S/4940/Add.2. [25]S/4940/Add.5,9. [26]S/4940/Add.7. [27]S/4940/Add.11, annex I. [28]S/4940/Add.18. [29]Ibid. [30]S/4940/Add.19. [31]S/5038. [32]S/5053/Add.8. [33]S/5053/Add.10, annex 46. [34]S/5053/Add.13, annex I. [35]S/5053/Add.13, annex XI. [36]S/5053/Add.14, annexes XIII-XV. [37]S/5053/Add.14. [38]Ibid. [39]S/5053/Add.15, annex V. [40]S/5053/Add.15, annex VI. [41]S/5053/Add.15, annexes VII and VIII. [42]S/5053/Add.15, annex IX. [43]S/5240/Add.2. [44]S/5240. [45]S/5428. [46]S/5784.

Part Six:
UN operation in Cyprus

A. Background

The Constitution

The Republic of Cyprus became an independent State on 16 August 1960, and a Member of the United Nations one month later. The Constitution of the Republic, which came into effect on the day of independence, had its roots in agreements reached between the Heads of Government of Greece and Turkey at Zurich on 11 February 1959. These were incorporated in agreements reached between those Governments and the United Kingdom in London on 19 February. On the same day, the representatives of the Greek Cypriot and Turkish Cypriot communities accepted the documents concerned, and accompanying declarations by the three Governments, as "the agreed foundation for the final settlement of the problem of Cyprus". The agreements were embodied in treaties—the Treaty of Establishment and the Treaty of Guarantee, signed by Cyprus, Greece, Turkey and the United Kingdom, and the Treaty of Alliance, signed by Cyprus, Greece and Turkey—and the Constitution signed in Nicosia on 16 August 1960.

The settlement of 1959 envisaged Cyprus becoming a republic with a régime specially adapted both to the ethnic composition of its population (approximately 80 per cent Greek Cypriot and 18 per cent Turkish Cypriot) and to what were recognized as special relationships between the Republic and the three other States concerned in the agreements. Thus, the agreements recognized a distinction between the two communities and sought to maintain a certain balance between their respective rights and interests. Greece, Turkey and the United Kingdom provided a multilateral guarantee of the basic articles of the Constitution. In the event of a breach of the Treaty of Guarantee, the three Powers undertook to consult on concerted action, and if this proved impossible, each of them reserved the right to take action "with the sole aim of re-establishing the state of affairs" set out in the Treaty. Both the union of Cyprus with any other State and the partitioning of the island were expressly forbidden. The settlement also permitted the United Kingdom to retain sovereignty over two areas to be maintained as military bases, these areas being in fact excluded from the territory of the Republic of Cyprus.

The Constitution assured the participation of each community in the exercise of the functions of the Government, while seeking in a number of matters to avoid supremacy on the part of the larger community and assuring also partial administrative autonomy to each community. Under the Constitution, the President, a Greek Cypriot, and the Vice-President, a Turkish Cypriot, were elected by their respective communities, and they designated separately the members of the Council of Ministers, comprising seven Greek Cypriots and three Turkish Cypriots. The agreement of the President and Vice-President was required for certain decisions and appointments, and they had veto rights, separately or jointly, in respect of certain types of legislation, including foreign affairs. Human rights and fundamental freedoms, as well as the supremacy of the Constitution, were guaranteed.

The application of the provisions of the Constitution encountered difficulties almost from the birth of the Republic and led to a succession of constitutional crises and to accumulating tension between the leaders of the two communities.

On 30 November 1963, the President of the Republic, Archbishop Makarios, publicly set forth 13 points on which he considered that the Constitution should be amended. He did so on the stated grounds that the existing Constitution created many difficulties in the smooth functioning of the State and the development and progress of the country, that its many *sui generis* provisions conflicted with internationally accepted democratic principles and created sources of friction between Greek and Turkish Cypriots, and that its effects were causing the two communities to draw further apart rather than closer together.

The President's proposals would have, among other things, abolished the veto power of the President and the Vice-President, while having the latter deputize for the President in his absence. The Greek Cypriot President of the House of Representatives and the Turkish Cypriot Vice-President would have been elected by the House as a whole and not, as under the Constitution, separately by its Greek and Turkish members. The constitutional provisions regarding separate majorities for enactment of certain laws by the House of Representatives would have been abolished, unified municipalities established, and the administration of justice and the security forces unified. The proportion of Turkish Cypriots in the public service and the military forces would have been reduced, and the Greek Cypriot Communal Chamber abolished, though the Turkish community would have been able to retain its Chamber.

No immediate response was forthcoming from the Vice-President to this proposed programme, but the Turkish Government, to which the President's proposals had been communicated ''for information purposes", rejected them promptly and categorically. Subsequently, the Turkish Cypriot Communal Chamber described the President's claim that the Constitution had proved an obstacle to the smooth functioning of the Republic as "false propaganda" and contended that the Greek Cypriots had never attempted to implement the Constitution in good faith. The Turkish Cypriots maintained that the structure of the Republic rested on the existence of two communities and not of a majority and a minority. They refused to consider the amendments proposed by the other side, which were in their opinion designed to weaken those parts which recognized the existence of the Turkish Cypriot community as such.

Whatever possibility might have existed at the time for calm and rational discussion of the President's proposals between the two communities disappeared indefinitely with the outbreak of violent disturbances between them a few days later, on 21 December 1963.

In the afternoon of 24 December 1963, the Turkish national contingent, stationed in Cyprus under the Treaty of Alliance and numbering 650 officers and other ranks, left its camp and took up positions at the northern outskirts of Nicosia in the area where disturbances were taking place. On 25 December, the Cyprus Government charged that Turkish war-planes had flown at tree-level over Cyprus, and during the next several days there were persistent reports of military concentrations along the southern coast of Turkey and of Turkish naval movements off that coast.

Mission of the personal representative

In the face of the outbreak of intercommunal strife, the Governments of the United Kingdom, Greece and Turkey, on 24 December 1963, offered their joint good offices to the Government of Cyprus, and on 25 December they informed that Government, "including both the Greek and Turkish elements", of their readiness to assist, if invited to do so, in restoring peace and order by means of a joint peace-making force under British command, composed of forces of the three Governments already stationed in Cyprus under the Treaties of Alliance and Establishment. This offer having been accepted by the Cyprus Government, the joint force was established on 26 December, a cease-fire was arranged on 29 December, and on 30 December it was agreed to create a neutral zone along the cease-fire line ("green line") between the areas occupied by the two communities in Nicosia. That zone was to be patrolled by the joint peace-making force, but in practice the task was carried out almost exclusively by its British contingent. It was further agreed that a conference of representatives of the Governments of the

United Kingdom, Greece and Turkey and of the two communities of Cyprus would be convened in London in January 1964. These arrangements were reported to the Security Council in a letter dated 8 January from the Permanent Representative of the United Kingdom to the United Nations.[1]

Meanwhile, on 26 December 1963,[2] the Permanent Representative of Cyprus requested an urgent meeting of the Security Council to consider his Government's complaint against Turkey. The meeting was held on 27 December. The Secretary-General met with the Permanent Representative of Cyprus to explore the best way in which the United Nations could assist in restoring quiet in the country. The representative of Cyprus, as well as the representatives of Greece, Turkey and the United Kingdom, requested the Secretary-General to appoint a personal representative to observe the peace-making operation in Cyprus.

After consultations, during which agreement was reached with all concerned regarding the functions of the representative, the Secretary-General, on 17 January 1964, appointed Lieutenant-General P.S. Gyani, of India, as his personal representative, and observer, to go to Cyprus initially until the end of February. The Secretary-General stated that his function would be to observe the progress of the peace-making operation. General Gyani was to report to the Secretary-General on how the United Nations observer could function and be most effective in fulfilling the task as outlined in the request made by the Government of Cyprus and agreed to by the Governments of Greece, Turkey and the United Kingdom. Gyani's mandate was later extended until the end of March.

B. Establishment of the UN operation

Creation of the Force

The London Conference, which met on 15 January 1964, failed to reach agreement, and proposals to strengthen the international peace-making force were rejected by the Government of Cyprus, which insisted that any such force be placed under the United Nations. From Nicosia, General Gyani reported a rapid and grave deterioration of the situation, involving scattered intercommunal fighting with heavy casualties, kidnappings and the taking of hostages (many of whom were killed), unbridled activities by irregular forces, separation of the members of the two communities, and disintegration of the machinery of government, as well as fears of military intervention by Turkey or

Greece. The British peace-making force was encountering increasing difficulties. While Gyani's presence had been helpful in a number of instances, attention was turning increasingly to the possibility of establishing a United Nations peace-keeping operation.

On 15 February, the representatives of the United Kingdom and of Cyprus requested urgent action by the Security Council.[3] On the same day, the Secretary-General appealed to all concerned for restraint.[4] He was already engaged in intensive consultations with all the parties about the functions and organization of a United Nations force, and, on 4 March, the Security Council unanimously adopted resolution 186(1964), by which it noted that the situation in Cyprus was likely to threaten international peace and security, and recommended the creation of a United Nations Peace-keeping Force in Cyprus (UNFICYP), with the consent of the Government of Cyprus.

The Council also called on all Member States to refrain from any action or threat of action likely to worsen the situation in the sovereign Republic of Cyprus or to endanger international peace, asked the Government of Cyprus, which had the responsibility for the maintenance and restoration of law and order, to take all additional measures necessary to stop violence and bloodshed in Cyprus, and called upon the communities in Cyprus and their leaders to act with the utmost restraint.

As for the Force, the Council said its composition and size were to be established by the Secretary-General, in consultation with the Governments of Cyprus, Greece, Turkey and the United Kingdom. The Commander of the Force was to be appointed by the Secretary-General and report to him. The Secretary-General, who was to keep the Governments providing the Force fully informed, was to report periodically to the Security Council on its operation. The Force's function should be, in the interest of preserving international peace and security, to use its best efforts to prevent a recurrence of fighting and, as necessary, to contribute to the maintenance and restoration of law and order and a return to normal conditions. The Council recommended that the stationing of the Force should be for a period of three months, all costs pertaining to it being met, in a manner to be agreed upon by them, by the Governments providing the contingents and by the Government of Cyprus. The Secretary-General was also authorized to accept voluntary contributions for that purpose. By the resolution, the Council also recommended the designation of a Mediator to promote a peaceful solution and an agreed settlement of the Cyprus problem.

The Minister for Foreign Affairs of Cyprus promptly informed the

Secretary-General that his Government consented to the establishment of the Force.[5]

Operational establishment of UNFICYP

On 6 March,[6] the Secretary-General reported the appointment of General Gyani as Commander of UNFICYP, and referred to his approaches to several Governments about the provision of contingents. Negotiations with prospective troop-contributing Governments encountered certain delays, relating to political as well as financial aspects of the operation.

Meanwhile, as the situation in Cyprus deteriorated further, the Secretary-General on 9 March addressed messages to the President of Cyprus and to the Foreign Ministers of Greece and Turkey, appealing for restraint and a cessation of violence. The Government of Turkey sent messages to President Makarios on 12 March, and to the Secretary-General on 13 March, stating that unless assaults on the Turkish Cypriots ceased, Turkey would act unilaterally under the Treaty of Guarantee to send a Turkish force to Cyprus until the United Nations Force, which should include Turkish units, effectively performed its functions.[7] The Secretary-General replied immediately that measures to establish the United Nations Force were under way and making progress, and he appealed to Turkey to refrain from action that would worsen the situation.[8]

At the request of the representative of Cyprus,[9] the Security Council held an emergency meeting on 13 March and adopted resolution 187(1964). The resolution noted the Secretary-General's assurances that the Force was about to be established, called on Member States to refrain from action or threats likely to worsen the situation in Cyprus or endanger international peace, and requested the Secretary-General to press on with his efforts to implement resolution 186(1964).

Upon the arrival of troops of the Canadian contingent on 13 March, the Secretary-General reported that the Force was in being.[10] However, it did not become established operationally until 27 March, when sufficient troops were available to it in Cyprus to enable it to discharge its functions effectively. The three-month duration of the mandate, as defined in resolution 186(1964), began as of that date. This development marked a new phase in the Cyprus situation. The Secretary-General noted[11] that UNFICYP was a United Nations Force, operating exclusively under the mandate given to it by the Security Council and, within that mandate, under instructions given by the Secretary-General. It was an impartial, objective body which had no responsibility for political solutions and would not try to influence them one way or another.

By 17 March, sizeable elements of the Canadian contingent had arrived in Cyprus, and arrangements for incorporating within UNFICYP the British peace-making forces already in Cyprus were being negotiated with the British Government. As of the date of its establishment operationally on 27 March 1964, the Force consisted of the Canadian and British contingents, and advance parties of Swedish, Irish and Finnish contingents. The main bodies of the last-mentioned three contingents arrived in April. A Danish contingent of approximately 1,000 as well as an Austrian field hospital arrived in May, along with additional Swedish troops transferred from the United Nations Operation in the Congo.

UNFICYP was thus established in 1964, with military contingents from Austria, Canada, Denmark, Finland, Ireland, Sweden and the United Kingdom, and civilian police units from Australia, Austria, Denmark, New Zealand and Sweden. This national composition has remained virtually unchanged except for the reduction of the Irish and Finnish contingents to token units in 1973 and 1977 respectively, and the withdrawal of the New Zealand, Danish and Austrian police units in 1967, 1975 and 1977 respectively.

From a total of 6,369 on 30 April 1964, the strength of the Force increased to 6,411 on 8 June. As units of the new contingents arrived, certain units of the British contingent, which had formed part of the old peace-making force and had been taken into UNFICYP, were repatriated. This accounts for the reduction of the British contingent from 2,719 in April 1964 to 1,792 in June and 1,034 in August. The total strength of the Force on 14 August 1964 was 6,211.

Under the terms of the 1960 Treaty of Alliance, Greece was given the right to maintain an army contingent of 950 officers and men in the island, and Turkey a contingent of 650. When intercommunal strife broke out in December 1963, the Turkish national contingent left its camp and was deployed in tactical positions in the villages of Orta Keuy and Geunyeli, astride the Kyrenia road north of Nicosia, where it remained until 1974. The Government of Cyprus, contending that the Turkish move was a breach of the Treaty, unilaterally abrogated it on 4 April 1964. However, both contingents remained on the island.

During the early stages of the functioning of UNFICYP, the Secretary-General proposed that the Turkish Government should either order its contingent to retire to its barracks, or accept his offer to put both the Greek and Turkish national contingents under United

Nations command, though not as contingents of UNFICYP. Greece accepted the latter suggestion. Turkey put forward the condition that the Force Commander, before issuing orders to the Turkish contingent for any task or movement requiring a change in its present position, must have the prior consent of the Turkish Government. As the Secretary-General considered this condition unacceptable, the two national contingents were not placed under United Nations command.

Deployment and organization

When UNFICYP was established in 1964, the contingents were deployed throughout the island and an effort was made as far as possible to match their areas of responsibility (zones or districts) with the island's administrative district boundaries. This was meant to facilitate a close working relationship with Cyprus Government District Officers, and with the local Turkish Cypriot leaders.

All districts were covered according to the intensity of the armed confrontation. The capital, Nicosia, initially was manned by two UNFICYP contingents (Canadian and Finnish), organized in a single Nicosia zone under Canadian command. The districts of Kyrenia and Lefka were manned by one contingent each. The remaining two contingents covered the districts of Larnaca, Limassol and Paphos.

Over the years, there have been numerous redeployments of UNFICYP contingents to secure better use of available troops in relation to the requirements of the mandate and to cover any new areas of tension.

In Nicosia, UNFICYP troops were positioned for an observation role along the length of the "green line". In two other districts, Kyrenia and Lefka, United Nations posts were deployed between the two defence lines; observation and patrolling took place from those posts. On the rest of the island, UNFICYP troops were generally deployed in areas where confrontation situations were likely to arise, and they were so positioned as to enable them to interpose themselves between the opposing sides in areas of tension and wherever incidents might cause a recurrence of fighting. Observation squads, backed by mobile patrols, were regularly deployed into areas that were likely to be potential areas of trouble.

Force Commanders

Following the retirement of General Gyani in June 1964, General K.S. Thimayya, of India, was appointed Force Commander and remained in that post until his death in December 1965. Brigadier A.J.

Wilson, of the United Kingdom, served as Acting Commander until May 1966 when Lieutenant-General I.A.E. Martola, of Finland, was appointed Commander. He was succeeded by Lieutenant-General Dewan Prem Chand, of India, in December 1969, Major-General J.J. Quinn, of Ireland, in December 1976 and Major-General Guenther G. Greindl, of Austria, in March 1981.

Special Representatives

In his report of 29 April 1964,[12] the Secretary-General referred to the necessity of appointing a high-level political officer, and on 11 May he announced the appointment of Galo Plaza Lasso, of Ecuador, as his Special Representative in Cyprus. Plaza served until his appointment as Mediator in September.

The following have subsequently served as Special Representatives of the Secretary-General: Carlos A. Bernardes (1964-1967), P.P. Spinelli (Acting) (1967), Bibiano F. Osorio-Tafall (1967-1974), Luis Weckmann-Muñoz (1974-1975), Javier Pérez de Cuéllar (1975-1977), Rémy Gorgé (Acting) (1977-1978), Reynaldo Galindo-Pohl (1978-1980), Hugo J. Gobbi (1980-1984) and James Holger (Acting) since 1984.

Guiding principles for UNFICYP

On the basis of the experience gained during the first six months of operation of the Force, guiding principles, which remain in effect to this day, were summarized by the Secretary-General in his report of 10 September 1964,[13] as follows:

> The Force is under the exclusive control and command of the United Nations at all times. The Commander of the Force is appointed by and responsible exclusively to the Secretary-General. The contingents comprising the Force are integral parts of it and take their orders exclusively from the Force Commander.
>
> The Force undertakes no functions which are not consistent with the provisions of the Security Council's resolution of 4 March 1964. The troops of the Force carry arms which, however, are to be employed only for self-defence, should this become necessary in the discharge of its function, in the interest of preserving international peace and security, of seeking to prevent a recurrence of fighting, and contributing to the maintenance and restoration of law and order and a return to normal conditions. The personnel of the Force must act with restraint and with complete impartiality towards the members of the Greek and Turkish Cypriot communities.
>
> As regards the principle of self-defence, it is explained that the expression "self defence" includes the defence of United Nations

posts, premises and vehicles under armed attack, as well as the support of other personnel of UNFICYP under armed attack. When acting in self-defence, the principle of minimum force shall always be applied and armed force will be used only when all peaceful means of persuasion have failed. The decision as to when force may be used in these circumstances rests with the Commander on the spot. Examples in which troops may be authorized to use force include attempts by force to compel them to withdraw from a position which they occupy under orders from their commanders, attempts by force to disarm them, and attempts by force to prevent them from carrying out their responsibilities as ordered by their commanders.

In connection with the performance of its function and responsibilities, UNFICYP has maintained close contact with the appropriate officials in the Government of Cyprus, which has the responsibility for the maintenance and restoration of law and order and which had been asked by the Security Council in its resolution of 4 March to take all additional measures necessary to stop violence and bloodshed in Cyprus.

Deployed in sensitive areas throughout the country, the Force attempted to interpose itself between the Greek and Turkish Cypriot military positions, or if that was not possible, to set up its own posts near by so that its mere presence constituted an effective deterrent to a recurrence of fighting. If, despite its precautionary measures, shooting incidents occurred, the Force was to intervene immediately and endeavour to end the fighting by persuasion and negotiation. In each case it also carried out a thorough investigation of the incident. Frequent patrolling was organized whenever necessary to ensure safety on roads and in towns and villages in sensitive areas.

With further reference to the question of the use of force, the Secretary-General had reported to the Security Council on 29 April 1964[14] that the Force Commander was seeking to achieve the objectives of UNFICYP by peaceful means and without resorting to armed force, the arms of the Force being carried only for self-defence. Despite these efforts and the Secretary-General's appeals, fighting continued. The Secretary-General emphasized that ''the United Nations Force was dispatched to Cyprus to try to save lives by preventing a recurrence of fighting. It would be incongruous, even a little insane, for that Force to set about killing Cypriots, whether Greek or Turkish, to prevent them from killing each other''. Yet this was the dilemma facing UNFICYP, which could not stand idly by and see an undeclared war deliberately pursued or innocent civilians struck down.

When the UNFICYP Civilian Police (UNCIVPOL) became operational on 14 April 1964, the Secretary-General outlined the following duties for it:[15] establishing liaison with the Cypriot police; accompanying

Cypriot police patrols which were to check vehicles on the roads for various traffic and other offences; manning United Nations police posts in certain sensitive areas, namely, areas where tension existed and might be alleviated by the presence of UNFICYP police elements; observing searches of vehicles by local police at road-blocks; and investigating incidents where Greek or Turkish Cypriots were involved with the opposite community, including searches for persons reported as missing.

C. Developments from 1964 to 1966

Extension of the mandate

On 15 June 1964,[16] the Secretary-General reported to the Security Council that it was clearly advisable, in the light of the demonstrated usefulness of the Force, to extend it for another three-month period as from 27 June 1964, and on 20 June 1964 the Security Council did so, unanimously.

Following the outbreak of fighting in the Tylliria area during the first week of August 1964 and the intervention of Turkish aircraft, the Security Council met again on the Cyprus question. On 9 August, it authorized its President to make an urgent appeal to the Government of Turkey to cease instantly the bombardment of and use of military force of any kind against Cyprus, and to the Government of Cyprus to order the armed forces under its control to cease firing immediately. The Council then adopted resolution 193(1964), which reaffirmed its preceding resolutions on Cyprus as well as the President's appeal, called for an immediate cease-fire, called upon all concerned to cooperate with UNFICYP in the restoration of peace and security and called upon all States to refrain from any action that might exacerbate the situation or contribute to the broadening of hostilities.

The Secretary-General informed the Council on 10 August 1964[17] that in view of positive replies of the President of Cyprus and the Prime Minister of Turkey, he would be making every effort towards constructive peace-keeping arrangements and had instructed the Force Commander to take every initiative towards that end. On 11 August, the Council approved a statement by the President as representing the consensus of its members, noting with satisfaction that the cease-fire was being observed throughout Cyprus and requesting the Force Commander to supervise the cease-fire and to reinforce its units in the zones which were the sphere of the recent military operations so as to ensure the safety of the inhabitants.

Further extensions, September 1964 onwards

In his report of 10 September 1964,[18] covering the period 8 June to 8 September 1964, the Secretary-General observed that the United Nations Force was in an unhappy position, since a civil war was the worst possible situation in which a United Nations peace-keeping force could find itself. Strong reasons, other than financial, could be adduced against maintaining UNFICYP. But it was the position of those directly concerned and many others that to withdraw UNFICYP at this time could lead to danger and disaster. The four Governments mentioned in resolution 186(1964) all wished the Force to be continued. Turkey had made certain observations about the shortcomings of the Force and its inability, under its existing authority, to carry out the mandates given to it by the Security Council as interpreted by the Government of Turkey.

On 25 September 1964, the Security Council adopted resolution 194(1964), extending the stationing of UNFICYP for another three-month period ending 26 December of that year. Further three-month extensions followed, and later the Council began extending the mandate by six-month periods, with the Council in 1967 adopting the practice of expressing the hope that by the end of the period of extension, sufficient progress towards a solution would have been achieved so as to render possible a withdrawal or substantial reduction of the Force.

Liaison arrangements

In view of the exceptionally comprehensive functions of UNFICYP as laid down by the Security Council in resolution 186(1964), the United Nations operation in Cyprus became involved, from its inception, in carrying out a vast array of activities that affected almost every conceivable aspect of life in Cyprus, often in extraordinarily difficult conditions. All of UNFICYP's functions were of necessity carried out in contact and consultation with the Government of Cyprus and the Turkish Cypriot authorities, and also, on many occasions, with the Governments of Greece and Turkey, and depended for their success on the co-operation of all concerned.

The legal framework of relations with the host Government was provided on 31 March 1964, when the Secretary-General and the Foreign Minister of Cyprus concluded an exchange of letters constituting an agreement on the status of UNFICYP.[19]

From the outset, UNFICYP made arrangements for close and continuous liaison with the Government of Cyprus and with the Turkish Cypriot leadership. Liaison was likewise maintained at various levels of the administrative and military establishments of both sides, including field military units in the areas of confrontation.

In situations of military confrontation, UNFICYP, not being empowered to impose its views on either party, of necessity negotiated with both, since the consent of both was and is required if peaceful solutions are to be found and violence averted. Time and again, communications, messages and appeals were sent to civilian leaders and military commanders of both sides in Cyprus, calling upon them to exercise restraint, refrain from provocative actions, observe the cease-fire, co-operate with the Force and contribute to a return to normal conditions. This was done either with regard to specific problems or, as in the case of aide-mémoire of October and November 1964, in an effort to generate an across-the-board programme of action in pursuance of the mandate.

Freedom of movement of UNFICYP

Article 32 of the agreement on the status of UNFICYP mentioned above provides for the freedom of movement of the Force throughout Cyprus, subject to a minor qualification relating to large troop movements. Article 33 entitles UNFICYP to use roads, bridges, airfields, etc. Freedom of movement has been regarded from the outset as an essential condition for the proper functioning of the Force; indeed, the function of preventing a recurrence of fighting depends entirely for its implementation on the freedom of movement of the military and police elements of UNFICYP. The Force has encountered many difficulties in this regard. On 6 August 1964,[20] the President of Cyprus granted full freedom of movement for UNFICYP throughout the island, with the sole exception of certain localities connected with the defence of the State. However, the Government took the position that UNFICYP had no valid interest in its activities designed to meet a threat of attack from the outside. UNFICYP patrols were frequently hindered or stopped by the Cyprus National Guard or police. On some occasions, Turkish Cypriots also obstructed UNFICYP patrols.

On 10 November 1964, the Force Commander reached an agreement with the Commander of the National Guard, declaring the whole island open to UNFICYP except for certain stipulated areas (covering about 1.65 per cent of the country) that were accessible only to the Force Commander or to senior officers of UNFICYP. Arrangements were also negotiated for UNFICYP access to Limassol docks, which were used by the Cyprus Government for the importation of military stores. Also in November 1964, it was agreed that the Cyprus security forces would henceforth refrain from searching UNFICYP personnel and vehicles.

During 1965, the Force Commander carried out a thorough review of UNFICYP's reconnaissance procedures, with a view to reducing friction to a minimum. Nevertheless, incidents of obstruction and harassment of UNFICYP continued. In certain cases, these involved even firing at UNFICYP soldiers, manhandling of senior UNFICYP officers and other unacceptable practices. Both the National Guard and Turkish Cypriot fighters were involved in incidents of this kind, especially during periods of tension.

UNFICYP programme of action

In view of the complexity of the situation in Cyprus in relation to the functions of the Force as laid down in resolution 186(1964), it was found necessary to formulate a programme on which to focus the efforts of UNFICYP. That programme, which would require the full co-operation of all those involved, could serve as a yardstick to assess the progress achieved towards the objectives outlined by the Security Council.

The Secretary-General reported on 15 June 1964 on the progress made in implementing the programme.[21] The presence of the Force had clearly prevented a recurrence of open fighting, but hopes of achieving full freedom of movement on the roads or disarming of civilians had diminished after recent serious incidents, and the two communities were far from achieving peaceful coexistence. There had been no progress in having Turkish Cypriot officials or policemen return to their government posts. Suggestions for joint patrols had not received favourable consideration. In short, the Secretary-General felt that while UNFICYP had been able to move forward in certain aspects of its mandate, it was rapidly reaching the point where further progress could only be made if the two sides showed more political flexibility.

At the same time, the efforts of UNFICYP to carry out its mandate were impeded by the parties' conflicting interpretations of the duties of the Force under that mandate. To the Cyprus Government, UNFICYP's task was to assist it in ending the rebellion of the Turkish Cypriots and extending its authority over the entire territory of the Republic. To the Turkish Cypriots, a "return to normal conditions" meant having UNFICYP restore, by force if necessary, the status of the Turkish Cypriot community under the 1960 Constitution, while the Cyprus Government and its acts should not be taken as legal. The Secretary-General in his reports rejected both these interpretations, which if followed would have caused UNFICYP to affect basically the final settlement of the Cyprus problem. This he considered to be in the province of the Mediator, not of UNFICYP.

Supervision of the cease-fire

UNFICYP's operating procedures to prevent a recurrence of fighting and to supervise the cease-fire were worked out pragmatically in the light of the fundamental impasse described above. The Force instituted a system of fixed posts and frequent patrols, intervention on the spot and interposition to prevent incidents from snowballing into serious fighting, demarcation of cease-fire lines where appropriate, and the submission of proposals or plans for remedying situations of military tension or conflict. Thus, UNFICYP endeavoured to secure the withdrawal or elimination of fortifications erected by the two sides, and submitted numerous proposals to that end, designed to reduce the armed confrontation in the island without prejudice to the security requirements of both sides. Wherever violent incidents broke out, UNFICYP made every effort, by persuasion, negotiation and interposition, to stop the fighting; it assisted civilians, evacuated the wounded and endeavoured to resolve the underlying security and other problems.

Despite the efforts of UNFICYP, sporadic violence continued in the island after the Force became operational, punctuated by outbreaks of severe fighting in which United Nations troops would find themselves at times fired upon by both sides, and forced to return the fire. Serious incidents occurred in the Tylliria area on 4 April 1964, at Ayios Theodhoros on 22 April, and in the area north of Nicosia from 25 to 29 April. A number of UNFICYP soldiers were killed as they sought to carry out their duties during continued scattered fighting in May. A major outbreak of fighting occurred from 5 to 8 August in the Tylliria area, reducing the Turkish Cypriot bridgehead there to the village of Kokkina. This was followed by aerial attacks on Government forces by Turkish fighter aircraft, and led to the 8 and 9 August meetings of the Security Council, which adopted resolution 193(1964) as well as the consensus of 11 August. The Governments of Cyprus and Turkey accepted the cease-fire without conditions.[22]

In August and September 1964, the Secretary-General engaged in intensive negotiations with the parties on the explosive issue of the periodic partial rotation of the Turkish national contingent stationed in Cyprus under the Treaty of Alliance (which the Cyprus Government had abrogated, but which Turkey considered to continue to be valid). This was linked to the question of the reopening of the Nicosia–Kyrenia road, which the Turkish Cypriots had closed to Greek Cypriot traffic. On 25 September, U Thant announced in the Security Council that agreement had been reached for the reopening of the road under the exclusive control of UNFICYP, and for the unimpeded rotation of the Turkish national contingent.

The road was reopened on 26 October 1964, and UNFICYP continued until 1974 to supervise the movement of Greek Cypriot civilians on it and to ensure that no armed personnel except those of UNFICYP were allowed to use it. The first rotation of the Turkish national contingent under this agreement was carried out on the same day, with UNFICYP assistance and under UNFICYP observation. UNFICYP also performed observation functions in connection with checking the incoming Turkish troops and their stores by Cyprus Government officials at Famagusta harbour. These functions, too, continued to be carried out, twice a year, until 1974. It should be noted that the UNFICYP functions relating to the Turkish national contingent concerned relations between the Governments of Cyprus and Turkey and therefore did not fall strictly within the terms of UNFICYP's mandate; they were assumed at the request of all concerned, in the interest of maintaining the peace, reducing tension in the island, and creating favourable conditions for carrying out other aspects of UNFICYP's mandate.

As a result of this arrangement, the situation in the island improved somewhat, and in his report of December 1964,[23] the Secretary-General reported that fighting had virtually ceased. However, the underlying tensions continued, and UNFICYP had little or no success in inducing the parties to scale down their military confrontation or dismantle their fortifications, which were the cause of recurrent incidents.

From the beginning of the Cyprus operation, the Secretary-General reported that the influx of arms and military equipment was a cause of concern for UNFICYP with regard to the discharge of its mandate. UNFICYP kept a careful watch on all imports of such arms and equipment, but the question whether it could take any additional action in this regard under resolution 186(1964) remained a controversial one. An agreement was concluded on 10 September 1964 to have UNFICYP present at the unloading of military equipment at Famagusta and Limassol, but additional material was being imported at Boghaz, unobserved by UNFICYP.

The issue came to a head when it became known in December 1966 that the Cyprus Government had imported a quantity of arms for distribution to the Cyprus police. On 12 January 1967, the Cyprus Government indicated to the Secretary-General that the imported arms would not be distributed for the time being, that the Secretary-General would be advised in due time if their distribution should become necessary, and that, in the mean time, the Force Commander could make periodic inspections. This function was carried out thereafter on a regular basis until 1974.

Return to normal conditions

UNFICYP normalization efforts evolved on an *ad hoc* basis and employed persuasion and negotiation exclusively. The principal objective was to restore conditions that would enable the people of the island, Greek Cypriot and Turkish Cypriot alike, to go about their daily business without fear for their lives and without being victimized, and in this connection to restore governmental services and economic activities disrupted by the intercommunal strife. A significant aspect of UNFICYP's procedures under this heading concerned humanitarian and relief assistance. All of UNFICYP's efforts were so framed as to avoid prejudicing the positions and claims of the parties in respect of a final political settlement. However, its task was made difficult by the reluctance of the two communities to modify their positions in the absence of such a settlement.

From the beginning of the United Nations operation, UNFICYP undertook *ad hoc* measures designed to save lives, minimize suffering and, to the extent possible, restore essential civilian activities. These measures included:

(a) Escorts for essential civilian movements, including persons, food and essential merchandise, on the roads of Cyprus, especially for members of the Turkish Cypriot community who feared abduction.

(b) Harvest arrangements, including escorts and patrols, to enable farmers to till their lands in the vicinity of positions held by members of the other community; agricultural arrangements, including grain deliveries by the Turkish Cypriots to the Cyprus Grain Commission; maintenance of abandoned citrus orchards, etc.

(c) Arrangements for government property in Turkish Cypriot-controlled areas; water and electricity supplies to the Turkish Cypriot sectors; postal services; payment of social insurance benefits; efforts to normalize the public services, including arrangements to re-employ Turkish Cypriot civil servants, etc.;

(d) Co-operation with the Red Cross and the Cyprus Joint Relief Commission in providing relief assistance for refugees (mainly Turkish Cypriots). UNFICYP also made intensive efforts to alleviate hardships resulting from the economic restrictions that had been imposed on the Turkish Cypriot community.

In October and November 1964, UNFICYP initiated a major effort to persuade the Government and the Turkish Cypriot leadership to drop most economic and security restrictions directed at members of the other community, to restore free movement and contacts for all, and to consider the return of displaced persons, with UNFICYP assistance. This comprehensive approach resulted in some improvement of the situation, but the basic political problem continued to limit the effectiveness of UNFICYP's normalization efforts.

On 21 April 1965, President Makarios informed the Special Representative of the Secretary-General and the Force Commander that the Government planned a normalization programme in three districts—Larnaca, Limassol and Ktima. This move came in response to UNFICYP's suggestions for a withdrawal of troops from fortified posts, elimination of road-blocks and the lifting of economic restrictions. However, the Turkish Cypriots, noting the limited geographical scope of the programme and the continuation of economic restrictions, declined to remove their defences.

Mediation function

The Security Council, by resolution 186(1964), recommended that the Secretary-General, in agreement with the Government of Cyprus and the Governments of Greece, Turkey and the United Kingdom, designate a mediator for the purpose of promoting a peaceful solution and agreed settlement of the Cyprus problem. On 25 March 1964, the Secretary-General appointed Sakari S. Tuomioja, a Finnish diplomat, as Mediator. Tuomioja died on 9 September. One week later, the Secretary-General appointed Galo Plaza Lasso, of Ecuador, to succeed him. After several rounds of consultations with all concerned, the Mediator in March 1965 submitted a report to the Secretary-General[24] in which he analysed the situation in the island, the positions of the parties and the considerations that would have to be taken into account in devising a settlement. On that basis, the Mediator offered observations under three headings: independence, self-determination and international peace; the structure of the State; and the protection of individual and minority rights. The Mediator recommended that the parties concerned, and in the first instance the representatives of the two communities, should meet together for discussions on the basis of his observations.

The report was commented upon favourably by the Governments of Cyprus and Greece. Turkey, however, rejected the report in its entirety and considered that Plaza's functions as a Mediator had come to an end upon its publication. Plaza resigned in December 1965, and the Secretary-General's efforts to bring about a resumption of the mediation function did not meet with success.

In these circumstances, the Secretary-General, on 4 March 1966, instructed his Special Representative in Cyprus, Carlos A. Bernardes, to employ his good offices with the parties in and outside Cyprus with a view to discussions, at any level, of problems of a local or a broader nature. However, Bernardes's efforts did not succeed in bringing about serious talks between the parties concerning a political settlement.

D. Developments from 1967 to 1974

Incidents at Ayios Theodhoros and Kophinou

In January 1967, General George Grivas, the Greek Commander of the Cyprus National Guard, deployed a battalion of troops in the Kophinou area. These remained in place despite an understanding reached by UNFICYP with the local Turkish Cypriot fighter commander to avoid incidents. As the National Guard unit was reinforced on 28 February, Turkish Cypriot fighters moved forward at nearby Ayios Theodhoros, where they also manhandled senior UNFICYP officers. There was severe friction between UNFICYP and Turkish Cypriot fighters in Kophinou, and the situation also deteriorated in the Paphos and Lefka districts.

In September 1967,[25] the Government announced a normalization programme that included the unmanning of armed posts and fortifications and complete freedom of movement, initially in the Paphos and Limassol districts. The Turkish Cypriot side assured UNFICYP that it would not seek to occupy the vacated positions.

In November 1967,[26] the Cyprus police sought to resume the practice of patrolling Ayios Theodhoros, passing through the Turkish Cypriot quarter, and informed UNFICYP that the National Guard would if necessary escort the policemen. On 15 November, heavy fighting broke out, and the National Guard overran most of that village and part of Kophinou. The Turkish Government protested to the Secretary-General, who requested the Cyprus and Greek Governments to bring about a withdrawal of the National Guard from the areas it had occupied. The withdrawal was carried out on 16 November. On 18 and 19 November, there were several Turkish overflights of Cyprus, and armed clashes spread to the Kokkina and Kyrenia areas.

Non-Cypriot forces

These events set off a severe political crisis. The Secretary-General appealed to the President of Cyprus and to the Prime Ministers of Greece and Turkey, on 22 and 24 November 1967,[27] to avoid an outbreak of hostilities, and he sent a personal representative to the three capitals. In the second appeal, the Secretary-General urged the three parties to agree upon a staged reduction and ultimate withdrawal of non-Cypriot armed forces, other than those of the United Nations, and he offered the assistance of UNFICYP in working out a programme of phased withdrawals and helping to maintain quiet.

The Security Council met on 24 November and, after consultations with the representatives of the parties, unanimously approved a consensus statement noting with satisfaction the efforts of the Secretary-General and calling upon all the parties to assist and co-operate in keeping the peace.

On 3 December 1967,[28] the Secretary-General addressed a third appeal to the President of Cyprus and to the Prime Ministers of Greece and Turkey, in which he called for Greece and Turkey to carry out an expeditious withdrawal of their forces in excess of their contingents in Cyprus. He added:

> "With regard to any further role that it might be considered desirable for UNFICYP to undertake, I gather that this could involve, subject to the necessary action by the Security Council, enlarging the mandate of the Force so as to give it broader functions in regard to the realization of quiet and peace in Cyprus, including supervision of disarmament and the devising of practical arrangements to safeguard internal security, embracing the safety of all the people of Cyprus. My good offices in connection with such matters would, of course, be available to the parties on request."

All three Governments welcomed the Secretary-General's appeal,[29] and Turkey supported the enlargement of the UNFICYP mandate to include supervision of the disarmament in Cyprus of forces constituted after 1963. The Security Council, at a meeting on 22 December 1967, adopted resolution 244(1967), by which, among other things, it noted the Secretary-General's three appeals and the replies of the three Governments.

In response to the Secretary-General's appeals, Greece and Turkey reached an agreement under which Greek national troops were withdrawn from Cyprus between 8 December 1967 and 16 January 1968. However, as no agreement was reached by Greece and Turkey on the issue of reciprocity, UNFICYP did not take on the task of checking that no Greek or Turkish forces in excess of their respective contingents remained in Cyprus.

At the same time, a formula was devised for informal meetings between Glafcos Clerides and Rauf R. Denktash, representating the Greek Cypriot and Turkish Cypriot communities, respectively. After an initial meeting in Beirut, Lebanon, on 2 June, they held meetings in Nicosia.

The intercommunal security situation in Cyprus improved during 1968, and in January 1969, President Makarios confirmed that he intended to extend normalization measures, including freedom of movement for the Turkish Cypriots, throughout the island. The Secretary-General suggested that the Turkish Cypriot leadership should respond by allowing the free movement of Greek Cypriots through Turkish Cypriot areas, but this was not accepted.

Arms importation

In March 1970, increasing tension within the Greek Cypriot community culminated in an attempt on the life of President Makarios and the subsequent killing of a former Minister of the Interior, Polycarpos Georghadjis.

Clandestine activity by pro-*enosis* (union with Greece) elements continued in 1971, and in view of that, the Government of Cyprus in January 1972 imported a large quantity of arms and ammunition. To minimize the resultant increase in tension, UNFICYP negotiated a provisional agreement on 10 March, whereby the Cyprus Government undertook to keep the imported arms in safe-keeping and open to inspection by the Force Commander. On 21 April,[30] the Secretary-General reported that an improved arrangement had been agreed upon, under which the weapons and munitions, except for the high explosives, would be stored in a fenced area within the perimeter of an UNFICYP camp. The fenced area would be in the charge of unarmed Cyprus police personnel, but control of the camp perimeter and access to it would be the responsibility of UNFICYP. The high-explosive munitions were stored at Cyprus police headquarters, but the fuses were removed and stored at the UNFICYP camp. A system of double locks and keys was devised for both storage areas.

UNFICYP continued to carry out its functions under these agreements until 1974. The weapons and arms are still stored in the UNFICYP camp, but the responsibility for their security now rests with UNFICYP alone. The Cyprus police have no involvement with them other than periodic verification carried out jointly with UNFICYP.

It should be noted that General Grivas, whom the Greek Government had summoned to Athens on 19 November 1967, returned to Cyprus secretly in January 1972. His actions were publicly criticized by President Makarios, who stressed the independence of Cyprus.

UNFICYP reductions

The consolidation of the security situation that was achieved by the beginning of 1965, however limited and tenuous, made possible a gradual reduction of the strength of UNFICYP. From a total (military personnel and police) of 6,275 in December 1964, the Force was reduced one year later to 5,764, and to 4,610 by the end of 1966. The strength of the Force in December 1967 was 4,737.

The general lessening of tension throughout the island in 1968, in addition to creating a favourable atmosphere for the Clerides/ Denktash intercommunal talks, also led to a further significant reduction in the strength of the Force. Steps were taken, in co-operation with the Government of Cyprus and the Turkish Cypriot leadership, to ensure that the effectiveness of the Force would not be adversely affected. Between April and December 1968, its strength was brought down to 3,708.

Further reductions took place gradually over the next two years; thereafter, the strength of UNFICYP from 1970 to 1972 remained stable at approximately 3,150. The strength of the Irish battalion was reduced from 420 to 150 during this period. In this connection, Austria, at the request of the Secretary-General, agreed in 1972 to augment its contingent, which had consisted of the UNFICYP field hospital and an UNCIVPOL unit, by providing also a battalion of 276 ground troops.

In October and November 1973, personnel of the Austrian, Finnish, Irish and Swedish contingents of UNFICYP were transferred to the Middle East to form the advance elements of the United Nations Emergency Force. Replacements for the Austrian, Finnish and Swedish personnel were promptly sent to Cyprus by the Governments concerned; however, at the request of the Secretary-General, Ireland agreed to dispatch additional troops only to the Middle East, and the Irish contingent in Cyprus was reduced to a token detachment at UNFICYP headquarters.

A further reduction of 381 troops was made in the spring of 1974. However, this was soon overtaken by the events of July 1974 which resulted in increasing the strength of UNFICYP to some 4,335.

Intercommunal talks

The intercommunal contacts between Clerides and Denktash that had begun in 1968 made little progress. After conversations between Greece and Turkey in June 1971, the Secretary-General suggested in October that his Special Representative, Bibiano F. Osorio-Tafall, of

Mexico, should henceforth take part in the talks in the exercise of the Secretary-General's good offices, and that constitutional experts from Greece and Turkey should attend as advisers. This arrangement was accepted in May 1972. The Secretary-General made it clear that the reactivated talks would be based on the equal status of the representatives of the communities, be exploratory in nature and be limited to internal constitutional matters of an independent Cyprus.

President Makarios was re-elected in February 1973. At the same time, Rauf Denktash succeeded Dr. Fazil Kuchuk as Vice-President and leader of the Turkish Cypriot community. After a series of bombings and raids on police stations by pro-*enosis* Greek Cypriots, the Government set up an auxiliary police force in an attempt to improve security conditions. In view of the continued violence within the Greek Cypriot community, Clerides offered to resign as Greek Cypriot interlocutor in the intercommunal talks, but was dissuaded by Secretary-General Kurt Waldheim.

Early in 1974, it appeared that the parties at the talks had reached a measure of agreement on a "package deal" concerning the structure of the State and the degree of authority to be granted to the Turkish Cypriot community in exchange for its renunciation of certain provisions of the 1960 Constitution. However, political developments, including the reactions of Athens and Ankara, set back the prospects of agreement. On 2 April the intercommunal talks were suspended.

The intercommunal situation was generally quiet during May, June and early July 1974. However, tension within the Greek Cypriot community, and between President Makarios and the Government of Greece, increased during June and early July.

E. *Coup d'état* and Turkish intervention of 1974

Events from the coup d'état of 15 July to 30 July

On 15 July 1974, the National Guard, under the direction of Greek officers, staged a *coup d'état* against the Cyprus Government headed by President Makarios. In view of the seriousness of the matter in relation to international peace and security and in view of the United Nations involvement in Cyprus, the Secretary-General requested the President of the Security Council on 16 July to convene a meeting of the Council.[31] The Permanent Representative of Cyprus also requested a meeting.[32] The Council met on 16 and 19 July.

On 20 July, the Turkish Government, invoking the Treaty of Guarantee of 1960, launched an extensive military operation on the north coast of Cyprus which resulted eventually in the occupation of the main Turkish Cypriot enclave north of Nicosia and areas to the north, east and west of the enclave, including Kyrenia. The Council met on the same day and adopted resolution 353(1974), by which it called upon all parties to cease firing and demanded an immediate end to foreign military intervention, requested the withdrawal of foreign military personnel present otherwise than under the authority of international agreements, and called on Greece, Turkey and the United Kingdom to enter into negotiations without delay for the restoration of peace in the area and constitutional government in Cyprus. The Council also called on all parties to co-operate fully with UNFICYP to enable it to carry out its mandate—thus indicating that UNFICYP was expected to continue to function despite the radically changed circumstances. The cease-fire called for by the Council was announced for 1600 hours, local time, on 22 July.

The fighting resumed on 23 July, especially in the vicinity of Nicosia International Airport, which, with the agreement of the local military commanders of both sides, was declared a United Nations-protected area and was occupied by UNFICYP troops. The Secretary-General reported to the Council on the breakdown of the cease-fire, and sent messages[33] to the Prime Ministers of Greece and Turkey and to the Acting President of Cyprus, expressing his great anxiety and requesting measures to ensure observance of the cease-fire. The Council on 23 July adopted resolution 354(1974), reaffirming the provisions of resolution 353(1974) and demanding that the parties comply immediately with paragraph 2 of that resolution, which called on them to stop firing and refrain from action which might aggravate the situation.

UNFICYP activities

As a consequence of these events, UNFICYP was faced with a situation that had not been foreseen in its mandate. As laid down by the Security Council in resolution 186(1964), the functions of UNFICYP were conceived in relation to the intercommunal conflict in Cyprus, not to large-scale hostilities arising from action by the armed forces of one of the guarantor Powers.

On 15 July, as soon as the *coup d'état* was reported, UNFICYP was brought to a high state of readiness. Additional liaison officers were deployed at all levels, and increased observation was maintained throughout the island in all areas of likely intercommunal confrontation. Special measures were taken to ensure the security of the Turkish Cypriot community. A few cases of firing into the Turkish enclave north of Nicosia were reported; the firing was stopped through liaison with the National Guard.

On 20 July, the day of the Turkish landings, UNFICYP was placed on full alert. An increased level of observation was maintained throughout the entire island, and additional precautions were taken to safeguard isolated Turkish Cypriot villages. The National Guard reacted to the Turkish operations by strong simultaneous attacks in other parts of the island against most of the Turkish Cypriot quarters and villages. The best UNFICYP could achieve under the circumstances was to arrange local cease-fires to prevent further loss of life and damage to property, as the Turkish Cypriot fighters, who were mainly deployed to protect isolated villages and town sectors, were heavily outnumbered. When the war situation made it necessary on 21 July to evacuate foreign missions to the British Sovereign Base Area at Dhekelia, UNFICYP played a major part in the organization and execution of that humanitarian operation. In all areas, including the Kyrenia sector, intensified United Nations patrolling was carried out, a close watch was maintained over the battle zone and all possible efforts were made to promote the safety of civilians.

The Secretary-General reported to the Security Council his understanding that UNFICYP should, and indeed must, use its best efforts to ensure, as far as its capabilities permitted, that the cease-fire called for by the Council was maintained. Obviously, a United Nations peacekeeping force, in a deeply serious situation such as the one prevailing in Cyprus, could not be expected to stand by and not make the maximum effort to ensure that a resolution of the Security Council was put into effect. For this reason, the Special Representative, the Force Commander and all the personnel of UNFICYP made every effort to restore the cease-fire, to ensure that it was observed and to prevent any incidents from escalating into a full recurrence of fighting. In this connection, UNFICYP assisted in delineating the positions of the parties as at 1600 hours on 22 July. Additional United Nations observation posts were established in the confrontation areas, and extensive patrolling was carried out in order to maintain a United Nations presence throughout the island.

In addition, the Secretary-General requested reinforcements from the contributing countries; they arrived between 24 July and 14 August, increasing the total strength of the Force by 2,078 all ranks to a total of 4,444. UNFICYP was redeployed to meet the new situation, two new operational districts were established on both sides of the Turkish bridgehead, and the general level of surveillance throughout the island was increased accordingly. Because of the suffering caused by the hostilities, UNFICYP undertook an increasing number of humanitarian tasks to assist the afflicted population of both communities.

Tripartite Conference and the Geneva Declaration

As called for in Security Council resolution 353(1974), the Foreign Ministers of Turkey, Greece and the United Kingdom began discussions in Geneva on 25 July, and on 30 July they agreed on the text of a declaration concerning the situation in Cyprus, which was immediately transmitted to the Secretary-General.[34] By the Geneva Declaration, the Foreign Ministers agreed on certain measures that involved action by UNFICYP. Thus:

(a) A security zone of a size to be determined by representatives of Greece, Turkey and the United Kingdom, in consultation with UNFICYP, was to be established at the limit of the areas occupied by the Turkish armed forces. This zone was to be entered by no forces other than those of UNFICYP, which was to supervise the prohibition of entry. Pending the determination of the size and character of the security zone, the existing area between the two forces was not to be entered by any forces.

(b) All the Turkish enclaves occupied by Greek or Greek Cypriot forces were to be immediately evacuated and would continue to be protected by UNFICYP. Other Turkish enclaves outside the area controlled by the Turkish armed forces would continue to be protected by an UNFICYP security zone and could, as before, maintain their own police and security forces.

(c) In mixed villages, the functions of security and police were to be carried out by UNFICYP.

(d) Military personnel and civilians detained as a result of the recent hostilities were to be either exchanged or released under the supervision of the International Committee of the Red Cross (ICRC) within the shortest time possible.

At the meeting of the Security Council held on 31 July, the Secretary-General made a statement referring to the above functions envisaged for UNFICYP. The Council, on 1 August, adopted resolution 355(1974), taking note of the Secretary-General's statement and requesting him ''to take appropriate action in the light of his statement and to present a full report to the Council, taking into account that the cease-fire will be the first step in the full implementation of Security Council resolution 353(1974)''.

Immediately after the adoption of resolution 355(1974), the Secretary-General instructed his Special Representative in Cyprus and the Commander of UNFICYP to proceed, in co-operation with the parties, with the full implementation of the role of UNFICYP as provided for in that resolution. UNFICYP promptly informed the parties that it stood ready to carry out all the functions devolving upon it under the resolution and it repeatedly appealed for observance of the cease-fire.

The Secretary-General's interim report of 10 August 1974[35] pursuant to resolution 355(1974) gave an account of the action taken to carry out the various provisions of the Geneva Declaration. The military representatives of Greece, Turkey and the United Kingdom had been meeting since 2 August together with a representative of UNFICYP, but they had not as yet determined the size of the security zone. Accordingly, UNFICYP action regarding that zone had been limited to participation in the deliberations.

Concerning the Turkish enclaves occupied by Greek or Greek Cypriot forces, UNFICYP stood ready to assume its protective functions as soon as they had been evacuated by those forces. In the mean time, UNFICYP's protective functions in respect of Turkish enclaves had continued, including regular patrols, assistance to the population, escorts and convoys for relief supplies (food, medicaments, etc.), and visits to detainees, together with the ICRC, to ensure that their treatment was satisfactory. These protective functions were also being carried out in the Turkish enclaves outside the area controlled by the Turkish forces mentioned in the Declaration, as well as in mixed villages.

On 12 August,[36] the Secretary-General reported that the National Guard had evacuated a number of Turkish Cypriot villages, and UNFICYP had assumed the responsibility for the protection of those areas.

The second round of fighting

Following the breakdown of the Geneva Conference on 14 August, fighting resumed in Cyprus. In the circumstances, UNFICYP resorted to *ad hoc* emergency operating procedures. Armoured reconnaissance units of UNFICYP maintained observation over the battle zone wherever possible. During the night of 14/15 August, and again on 15/16 August, UNFICYP achieved a partial cease-fire in Nicosia to allow all the non-combatants to be evacuated. It made major efforts throughout the country to put an end to the fighting, but was unable to do so in certain combat areas, where UNFICYP posts had to be withdrawn. In a few such areas, killing of civilians took place.

The resumption of heavy fighting on 14 August had placed UNFICYP units in an extremely difficult and dangerous position, resulting in severe casualties. The Security Council noted that development with concern in its resolution 359(1974) of 15 August; it recalled that UNFICYP was stationed in Cyprus with the full consent of the Governments of Cyprus, Turkey and Greece; it demanded that all parties concerned fully respect the international status of the United Nations Force and refrain from any action which might endanger the lives and safety of its members; it further demanded that all parties co-operate with the Force in carrying out its tasks, including humanitarian functions, in all areas of Cyprus and in regard to all sections of the population. After negotiations, the Turkish forces declared a cease-fire at 1800 hours, local time, on 16 August.

On the same day, the Council adopted resolution 360(1974), by which it recorded its "formal disapproval of the unilateral military actions undertaken against the Republic of Cyprus" and urged the parties to comply with its previous resolutions and to resume without delay the negotiations called for in resolution 353(1974).

Humanitarian functions

During the events of July and August 1974, UNFICYP assumed important humanitarian functions, and the Security Council, in its resolution 359(1974), took notice of these tasks. On 22 July, a special humanitarian and economics branch had been set up at UNFICYP headquarters. Every effort was made to protect the civilian population caught up in the hostilities—including both Cypriots and foreigners. In co-operation with the ICRC, a wide range of relief assistance was organized for Greek and Turkish Cypriots. However, it soon became evident that a more systematic and larger scale of operation was needed, since approximately one third of the population of the island had become homeless or was otherwise in need. Accordingly, on 20 August, the Secretary-General designated the United Nations High Commissioner for Refugees as Co-ordinator of United Nations Humanitarian Assistance for Cyprus.[37] In resolution 361(1974) of 30 August, the Security Council, noting that a large number of people in Cyprus were in dire need, and "mindful of the fact that it is one of the foremost purposes of the United Nations to lend humanitarian assistance in situations such as the one currently prevailing in Cyprus", requested the Secretary-General to continue to provide emergency humanitarian assistance to all parts of the island's population in need of such assistance. UNFICYP assisted the Co-ordinator in carrying out his functions.

F. UNFICYP since 1974

Since its establishment in 1964, the main objective of the United Nations operation in Cyprus, as of all other United Nations peace-keeping operations, has been to foster peaceful conditions in which the search for an agreed, just and lasting settlement of the problem could best be pursued. The main instrumentality for maintaining calm and preventing strife in the island has been and remains the United Nations Peace-keeping Force, which continues effectively to carry out its task of conflict control. Accordingly, the Secretary-General has reported to the Security Council, at the end of every six-month mandate period, that in the light of the situation on the ground and of political developments, the continued presence of UNFICYP remains indispensable, both in helping to maintain calm in the island and in creating the best conditions for his good offices efforts. For its part, the Security Council has regularly extended the mandate of the Force for six-month periods.

Until June 1983, the parties concerned consistently informed the Secretary-General of their concurrence in the proposed extension of the stationing of the Force in the island. Following the Turkish Cypriot action of 15 November 1983, the Government of Cyprus as well as the Governments of Greece and the United Kingdom have continued to indicate their concurrence, but Turkey and the Turkish Cypriot community have indicated that they were not in a position to accept the resolutions extending the mandate. Despite their divergent positions, all the parties have continued to maintain excellent co-operation with UNFICYP, both on the military and the civilian sides.

The function of the United Nations Peace-keeping Force in Cyprus was originally defined by the Security Council in its resolution 186(1964) of 4 March 1964 in the following terms ''. . . in the interest of preserving international peace and security, to use its best efforts to prevent a recurrence of fighting and, as necessary, to contribute to the maintenance and restoration of law and order and a return to normal conditions''.

That mandate, which was conceived in the context of the confrontation between the Greek Cypriot and Turkish Cypriot communities and between the Cyprus National Guard and the Turkish Cypriot fighters, has been periodically extended by the Council. As a result of the events that have occurred since 15 July 1974, the Council adopted a number of resolutions which have affected the functioning of UNFICYP and have required UNFICYP to perform certain additional or modified functions. Accordingly, UNFICYP continues to supervise the cease-fire lines of the National Guard and of the Turkish and Turkish Cypriot forces, which since August 1974 extend across the island from Kato Pyrgos in the west to Dherinia in the east, to a length of some 180 kilometres. The area between the lines, which is under exclusive UNFICYP control, varies in width from 20 metres to seven kilometres. Following the transfer of Turkish Cypriots to the north in 1975, UNFICYP, which had been stationed in sensitive areas throughout the island, was redeployed along the cease-fire lines. UNFICYP uses its best efforts to preserve the military *status quo* and to prevent the recurrence of fighting.

UNFICYP surveillance of the area between the cease-fire lines is carried out through a network of observation posts. Additional mobile and standing patrols to provide increased presence in sensitive areas are deployed as necessary.

Disputes have continued in a few areas concerning the delineation of the cease-fire lines. However, the UNFICYP policy that the forces of neither side should enter these areas has remained effective.

In addition to its military tasks, UNFICYP, under its mandate, performs a number of humanitarian and economic tasks in the area between the lines, as well as north and south of it, in its efforts to help bring about a return to normal conditions. Many of these tasks devolve on UNFICYP because personnel of the Cyprus Government and of the Turkish Cypriot community are not in a position to exercise their normal functions in some areas. Accordingly, UNFICYP soldiers provide security coverage for agricultural and other civilian activities within the buffer zone, assist in the maintenance and improvement of water and power lines and sewage services that cross the area between the cease-fire line, are engaged as necessary in fire-fighting and in the eradication of contagious diseases, provide transport and medical facilities across the lines, evacuate by road transport or by helicopter civilian patients in need of medical care, make security arrangements for the performance of religious services in militarily sensitive areas and provide humanitarian assistance to Greek Cypriots and Maronites in the north and Turkish Cypriots in the south. Another important continuing task of UNFICYP involves the support of the relief operations coordinated by the United Nations High Commissioner for Refugees. His programme for 1984 provided $7.5 million to finance 22 projects.[38]

The financial situation regarding UNFICYP has continued to worsen, with a deficit, by December 1984, of $123.1 million, out of a total cost of some $470.5 million since 1964. Nevertheless, this adverse financial situation has not prevented the Force from fulfilling its functions, mainly because troop-contributing countries have continued to carry a disproportionate burden in keeping UNFICYP in operation.

G. Search for a negotiated solution

Secretary-General's mission of good offices

During September 1974, the Special Representative of the Secretary-General, Luis Weckmann Muñoz, of Mexico, arranged for weekly meetings under his auspices between Clerides and Denktash to take up, in the first instance, humanitarian problems. These included the exchange and release of prisoners with the assistance of the International Committee of the Red Cross.[39]

On 1 November, the General Assembly, by its resolution 3212(XXIX), unanimously called on all States to respect the sovereignty, territorial integrity, independence and non-alignment of Cyprus. It urged the speedy withdrawal of all foreign armed forces from Cyprus, a halt to foreign interference, and the safe return of all refugees to their homes. The Assembly considered that the constitutional issues were up to the Greek Cypriot and Turkish Cypriot communities to resolve by negotiations, with the help of the Secretary-General. On 13 December, the Security Council endorsed the Assembly's resolution and urged the parties concerned to implement it as soon as possible (resolution 365(1974)).

During December 1974 and January 1975, Clerides and Denktash met several times with the Special Representative and agreed to begin discussion on 14 January of the powers and functions of the central government in a federal State of Cyprus. On 10 February, Clerides submitted constitutional proposals[40] for a "bicommunal multiregional federal State", the total areas under the administration of the respective communities to correspond approximately to the population ratio. Denktash also submitted proposals, along with a statement[41] indicating that it had been concluded that it was not possible for the two communities to live together. The "autonomous Turkish Cypriot administration" would be restructured on the basis of a federated State.

After an announcement on 13 February 1975 of the establishment of the "Turkish Federated State of Cyprus", the Security Council conducted lengthy consultations and on 12 March adopted resolution 367(1975), by which it expressed regret regarding that unilateral move and affirmed that that decision did not prejudge the final political settlement. It called for new efforts to assist the resumption of negotiations, asking the Secretary-General to undertake a new mission of good offices and to convene the representatives of the two communities under his auspices and with his direction as appropriate.

Vienna rounds of intercommunal talks

The talks called for by the Security Council began on 28 April in Vienna under the personal auspices of Secretary-General Waldheim. Before ending the first round on 3 May, the negotiators decided to meet again in Vienna from 5 to 9 June. During the first two rounds, agreement was reached in principle on reopening Nicosia International Airport and on its repair by the United Nations.[42] The repairs were carried out, but the Airport was not reopened as there were differences concerning implementation of the agreement.

At the third round of talks, held in Vienna from 31 July to 2 August 1975,[43] it was agreed that the Turkish Cypriots in the south of the island would be allowed to proceed north with the assistance of UNFICYP and that a number of Greek Cypriots would be transferred to the north in order to be reunited with their families. Greek Cypriots in the north would be free to go south or to stay, and they would be helped to lead a normal life, including freedom of movement in the north. UNFICYP would have free and normal access to Greek Cypriot villages in that area. The Secretary-General subsequently informed the Council[44] that the transfer of 8,033 Turkish Cypriots to the north had been completed by 7 September 1975. However, other provisions of the 2 August 1975 agreement were implemented to a limited degree only. In particular, only 346 Greek Cypriots had been permitted to move to the north.

After a fourth round of talks in New York, the General Assembly, on 20 November 1975, demanded the withdrawal without further delay of all foreign armed forces from Cyprus and the cessation of all foreign interference in its affairs. A further round of negotiations was held in February 1976, but wide differences persisted.

First high-level meeting

After a preliminary meeting held under the auspices of the Special Representative, Javier Pérez de Cuéllar, of Peru, on 27 January 1977, the leaders of the two communities, Archbishop Makarios and Rauf Denktash, met on 12 February in Nicosia under the personal auspices of the Secretary-General and agreed on guidelines[45] for the representatives of their communities in the intercommunal talks. Those guidelines included agreement to seek an independent, non-aligned, federal and bicommunal Republic of Cyprus, and agreement that the territory under the administration of each community should be discussed in the light of economic viability or productivity and land ownership. Questions of principle such as freedom of movement and settlement and the right of property would be open for discussion, taking into consideration certain practical difficulties that might arise for the Turkish Cypriot community. The powers and functions of the central government should safeguard the unity of the country, having regard to its bicommunal character.

Suspension of the talks

On that basis, a new round of intercommunal talks was held in Vienna from 31 March to 7 April 1977[46] under the auspices of the Secretary-General and his Special Representative. The talks were resumed in Nicosia on 20 May but were not continued after 3 June 1977. President Makarios died on 3 August 1977 and was succeeded by Spyros Kyprianou. On 9 November, the General Assembly, by resolution 32/15, called for the urgent resumption of intercommunal negotiations.

The Secretary-General visited Turkey, Cyprus and Greece in January 1978 to determine the prospects for resuming the intercommunal talks in Vienna. On 13 April, he received in Vienna proposals[47] from the Turkish Cypriot side on the territorial and constitutional aspects. He went to Nicosia to present the proposals to President Kyprianou, who informed him that they were not acceptable as a basis for the resumption of the intercommunal talks.

Suggestions concerning Varosha

In his report to the Security Council of 31 May 1978,[48] the Secretary-General stated that the continued presence of UNFICYP remained indispensable for keeping the dangerous situation under control, supervising the cease-fire, maintaining the *status quo* in the area between the cease-fire lines and helping to resolve incidents and other problems arising between the parties. He gave an account of his good offices efforts and of the difficulties encountered, suggesting steps to deal with important aspects of the current stalemate on the ground so as to improve the situation in the island and create favourable conditions for resuming effective negotiations on the broader issues. In particular, he suggested that certain steps be taken with UNFICYP's assistance concerning Varosha, a section of Famagusta that had been vacated by its Greek Cypriot inhabitants in 1974, as well as the Nicosia International Airport, which had remained closed to traffic.

On 20 July 1978,[49] Denktash issued a proposal for the resettlement of Varosha by its Greek Cypriot inhabitants; he noted that about 35,000 could be accommodated. He also suggested that discussions be undertaken for setting up an interim administration for Varosha, under United Nations auspices and with United Nations technical assistance, to supervise essential municipal and police functions. This offer was contingent on agreement by the Greek Cypriots to reopen intercommunal talks.

This proposal was promptly and publicly rejected by President Kyprianou on the grounds that it was territorially inadequate and would prejudice moves towards a comprehensive settlement. On 25 July,[50] the Cyprus Government issued its plan for the withdrawal of all Turkish troops from Famagusta and the return of all its inhabitants to the city, which would be placed for a period of time under United Nations police and security control.

Second high-level meeting

A high-level meeting between President Kyprianou and Rauf Denktash was held in Nicosia under the auspices of the Secretary-General on 18 and 19 May 1979. The parties issued a communiqué on 19 May[51] agreeing to the resumption of intercommunal talks on the basis of the 12 February 1977 guidelines and the United Nations resolutions relevant to the Cyprus question. The talks would cover all territorial and constitutional aspects. Priority would be given to reaching agreement on the resettlement of Varosha under United Nations auspices, together with the resumption of intercommunal talks to discuss a comprehensive settlement. It was further agreed to abstain from any action which might jeopardize the outcome of the talks; special importance would be given to initial practical measures to promote goodwill, confidence and normalization. The demilitarization of the Republic of Cyprus was envisaged.

The intercommunal talks called for in the high-level agreement resumed on 15 June 1979, but were recessed on 22 June without achieving progress.[52]

After a visit to Nicosia, Ankara and Athens by Pérez de Cuéllar in June 1980, agreement was reached by the parties to resume the talks formally in Nicosia on 9 August, at which time Hugo J. Gobbi, the new Special Representative, delivered an opening statement outlining the Secretary-General's understanding of the common ground that had been worked out.[53] The intercommunal talks thereafter continued on a regular basis. While the atmosphere was constructive, progress was slow. At the same time, the Secretary-General and Gobbi explored with the parties the possible outlines of a partial interim agreement ("mini-package") to be negotiated by the interlocutors, involving the resettlement of Varosha and the reopening of Nicosia International Airport, both under United Nations interim administration.

After further consultations in April and May 1981, it was decided instead to move towards a comprehensive settlement of the conflict, and on 5 August the Turkish Cypriot interlocutor submitted comprehensive proposals, including for the first time maps showing the territorial arrangement favoured by his side.

The intercommunal talks continued for some two years without making any decisive progress. In December 1982, Pérez de Cuéllar, who had become Secretary-General the previous January, warned in his report to the Security Council[54] that a major effort of synthesis was needed, since time appeared to be eroding the "window of opportunity" for the solution of the Cyprus problem. On 13 May 1983, the General Assembly adopted resolution 37/253, which was rejected by Turkey and the Turkish Cypriots. As a result, the Turkish Cypriot side decided not to attend the intercommunal talks on the grounds that the resolution tended to undermine the basis for the negotiations.[55]

On 8 and 9 August 1983,[56] the Secretary-General conveyed to both sides informal soundings designed to narrow the gap between their positions. Denktash suggested that the Secretary-General convene a high-level meeting in order to clarify intentions concerning a federal solution and pave the way for a resumption of the intercommunal talks. In response, President Kyprianou signified his willingness to attend such a meeting if it was well prepared and both sides co-operated in ensuring its success. The Secretary-General thereupon dispatched Gobbi to Cyprus for consultations about the agenda for a high-level meeting.

Turkish Cypriot action of 15 November 1983

When the Special Representative called on Denktash on 15 November 1983, the latter handed him a letter[57] informing the Secretary-General of the proclamation by the Turkish Cypriot community of an independent "Turkish Republic of Northern Cyprus". At the same time, he expressed his readiness to resume negotiations at any time.

At the request of the United Kingdom, Cyprus and Greece, the Security Council met on 17 and 18 November 1983. The Secretary-General stated that the Turkish Cypriot move was contrary to the Council's resolutions and at variance with the high-level agreements of 1977 and 1979, but he voiced his determination to continue his efforts. On 18 November, the Council adopted resolution 541(1983), by which it deplored the Turkish Cypriot declaration of the purported secession of part of the Republic of Cyprus, considered that declaration as legally invalid and called for its withdrawal, requested the Secretary-General to pursue his mission of good offices, and called upon all States not to recognize any Cypriot State other than the Republic of Cyprus.

Scenario of 16 March 1984

After meetings in January 1984 in Casablanca with Rauf Denktash and with President Kenan Evren of Turkey, and in February in New York with President Kyprianou, the Secretary-General, on 16 March, handed to Denktash a "scenario"[58] designed to open the door to a high-level meeting. This provided that there would be no further step to internationalize the Cyprus problem, no follow-up to the Turkish Cypriot declaration of 15 November 1983 and no increase of military forces in the island. The Turkish Cypriots would transfer Varosha, as delineated by them in 1981, to the Secretary-General as part of the UNFICYP–controlled buffer zone. The area would remain under United Nations administration pending an agreement on the settlement of the Cyprus problem, and no armed personnel other than UNFICYP would have access to it. The parties would accept a call by the Secretary-General for holding a high-level meeting and reopening the intercommunal dialogue.

Denktash thereupon announced his intention to proceed to a constitutional referendum and elections and arranged for the submission of "credentials" for the establishment of diplomatic relations with Turkey. The Secretary-General publicly expressed regret over these developments, which jeopardized his current efforts. On 18 April,[59] Denktash handed to Gobbi his side's response to the scenario. The impasse persisted.

On 11 May, the Security Council adopted resolution 550(1984), by which it condemned secessionist actions and declared them illegal and invalid, and asked the Secretary-General to undertake new efforts towards an overall solution in conformity with the United Nations Charter and the pertinent United Nations resolutions.

Proximity talks and high-level meeting

In a new initiative, the Secretary-General met separately with Andreas Mavrommatis and Necati Ertekun, representing the Greek and Turkish Cypriot sides, in Vienna on 6 and 7 August 1984,[60] and outlined to them a number of working points with a view to ascertaining whether these might provide a basis for high-level proximity talks. On 31 August, both sides responded favourably.[61] The Secretary-General then invited the leaders of the two communities to meet with him separately in New York.

Following three rounds of proximity talks with President Kyprianou and Rauf Denktash in September, October and November/December, the Secretary-General announced that he had reached the assessment that the documentation for a draft agreement was ready for submission to a joint high-level meeting, at which an agreement could be concluded containing the overall framework for a comprehensive solution aimed at establishing a Federal Republic of Cyprus.[62]

The joint high-level meeting, convened under the auspices of the Secretary-General and attended by President Kyprianou and Rauf Denktash, was held in New York from 17 to 20 January 1985.[63] It did not prove possible at the meeting to overcome the difficulties that had arisen. The Secretary-General, on 20 January, issued a statement[64] in which he noted that the Turkish Cypriot side fully accepted the draft agreement and that the Greek Cypriot side had accepted the documentation as a basis for negotiations in accordance with the integrated-whole approach. The Secretary-General commented that the gap in the search for a solution had never been so narrow, and appealed to both sides to ensure that the advances that had been made were preserved, and that nothing should be done, in the island or elsewhere, to make the search for a solution more difficult.

Following contacts with the two sides, the Secretary-General decided to concentrate his efforts on overcoming the obstacles which had stood in the way of the acceptance of the documentation by the Greek Cypriot side, while preserving its substance. Towards this end, he incorporated the components of the documentation into a single consolidated draft agreement. He also devised possible procedural arrangements for the follow-up action after agreement was reached by the two sides on the framework for an overall solution to the Cyprus question.[65]

Following contacts with the Greek Cypriot side, including a meeting with President Kyprianou on 11 March 1985, the Secretary-General received an affirmative reply from the Greek Cypriot side in early April. He then informed the Turkish Cypriot side of the status of his efforts and sought its views. After receiving the views of the Turkish Cypriot side in August and after meeting with Rauf Denktash on 12 and 13 September, the Secretary-General concluded that it was now for him to assess the situation and to decide on the next step to be taken, which he would communicate to the both sides in the near future.

On 20 September, the Secretary-General informed the members of the Council on the current state of his efforts. In the light of that information, the President of the Security Council, on behalf of its members, issued a statement[66] expressing the strong support of the members of the Council for the Secretary-General's efforts and called upon all parties to make a special effort in co-operation with the Secretary-General to reach an early agreement.

H. Missing persons

At the high-level meeting of 12 February 1977, agreement in principle was reached to set up an investigatory body for the tracing of and accounting for missing persons of both communities. However, despite intensive consultations over the next months, it did not prove possible to reach agreement on the terms of reference of that body, particularly on the role and identity of its third member.

On 16 December 1977, the General Assembly adopted without a vote resolution 32/128, requesting the Secretary-General to provide his good offices, through his Special Representative, to support the establishment of the investigatory body with the participation of the ICRC. Both sides publicly reiterated their support for such a joint body with ICRC participation, but the differences between them persisted.

On 22 April 1981, the Special Representative of the Secretary-General, Gobbi, announced that agreement had been reached by the two sides on the terms of reference for a Committee on Missing Persons to consist of three members: one person from each of the communities and the third member selected by the ICRC with the agreement of both sides, and appointed by the Secretary-General.[67] Claude Pilloud was appointed as the third member. However, not until 14 March 1984[68] did the Committee reach agreement on its procedural rules. In May it began its practical work, including investigation of cases submitted by the parties. Progress has been slow. Pilloud died in November 1984. His successor, Paul Würth, was appointed by the Secretary-General in April 1985.

I. Financial aspects

The arrangements for the financing of UNFICYP were laid down by the Security Council in paragraph 6 of resolution 186(1964), by which the Council:

"Recommends that the stationing of the Force shall be for a period of three months, all costs pertaining to it being met, in a manner to be agreed upon by them, by the Governments providing the contingents and by the Government of Cyprus; the Secretary-General may also accept voluntary contributions for that purpose".

In accordance with Council resolutions, the Secretary-General has issued regular and special appeals to all Member States or members of specialized agencies to make voluntary contributions to defray the costs of the Force. As of 15 December 1984, pledges of such contributions from 69 Member States and one non-member State, in addition to miscellaneous receipts, totalled $347.4 million. The costs to be borne by the United Nations for the operation of UNFICYP since 1964 were estimated at $470.5 million. Accordingly, the UNFICYP deficit stood at $123.1 million.

In order to provide contingents for UNFICYP, the troop-contributing Governments divert from national duty troops and other resources at an ongoing cost to them currently estimated by them at $36.2 million for each six-month period. This figure includes (a) the troops' regular pay and allowances and normal *matériel* expenses for which, under existing arrangements, the United Nations is not required by the troop contributors to reimburse them; these therefore constitute costs of maintaining the Force which are being financed directly by the troop-contributing Governments, and (b) certain extra and extraordinary costs that troop contributors incur in respect of UNFICYP for which, under existing arrangements, they would be entitled to claim reimbursement from the United Nations, but which they have agreed to finance at their own expense as a further contribution to the United Nations operation in Cyprus.

In view of the nature of the financial arrangements, payments to troop-contributing Governments for costs for which they seek United Nations reimbursement can only be made as and when voluntary contributions or other income are received, and after the operational costs incurred directly by the United Nations have been met.

As a result of this situation, the United Nations has fallen more and more behind in meeting its obligations in respect of the reimbursement claims of the troop contributors. The last disbursement under this heading, made in January 1984, enabled the Organization to meet those Governments' claims through June 1978. This means that the troop-contributing countries not only absorb at their own expense considerable costs incurred in maintaining their contingents but are, in effect, financing the deficit. Since the troop-contributing countries are also, in many cases, substantial voluntary contributors to the UNFICYP

Special Account, it will be realized that those Governments carry a disproportionate burden in keeping UNFICYP in operation.

The Secretary-General has repeatedly voiced his profound concern about the worsening financial situation confronting UNFICYP. The troop-contributing countries have likewise expressed their growing concern. However, despite the Secretary-General's repeated appeals, the deficit of the UNFICYP account continues to worsen.

Reference notes

[1]S/5508. [2]S/5488. [3]S/5543, S/5545. [4]S/5554. [5]S/5578. [6]S/5579. [7]S/5596. [8]S/5600. [9]S/5598. [10]S/5593/Add.2. [11]S/5593/Add.3. [12]S/5671. [13]S/5950. [14]S/5671. [15]S/5679. [16]S/5764. [17]S/5879. [18]S/5950. [19]S/5634, annexes I and II. [20]S/5855. [21]S/5764. [22]S/5879. [23]S/6102. [24]S/6253. [25]S/8141. [26]S/8248. [27]S/8248/Add.3,5. [28]S/8248/Add.6. [29]S/8248/Add.7,8. [30]S/10564/Add.1. [31]S/11334. [32]S/11335. [33]S/11368. [34]S/11398. [35]S/11433. [36]S/11353/Add.20. [37]S/11488. [38]S/16858. [39]S/11468/Add.1. [40]S/11624, annex I. [41]S/11624, annexes II and III. [42]S/11717. [43]S/11789, annex. [44]S/11789/Add.2. [45]S/12323. [46]Ibid. [47]S/12723, annex. [48]S/12723. [49]S/12782. [50]S/12789. [51]S/13369. [52]S/13672. [53]S/14100, annex. [54]S/15002. [55]S/15812. [56]S/16192. [57]Ibid. [58]S/16519. [59]S/16519, annex IV. [60]S/16858. [61]Ibid. [62]Ibid. [63]S/16858/Add.2. [64]S/16858/Add.2, annex B. [65]S/17227/Add.1. [66]S/17486. [67]S/14490. [68]S/16596.

Part Seven:

The UN Temporary Executive Authority and the UN Security Force in West New Guinea (West Irian)

Background

The territory of West New Guinea (West Irian) had been in the possession of the Netherlands since 1828. When the Netherlands formally recognized the sovereign independence of Indonesia in 1949, the status of West Irian remained unresolved. It was agreed in the Charter of Transfer of Sovereignty—concluded between the Netherlands and Indonesia at The Hague, Netherlands, in November 1949—that the issue would be postponed for a year, and that "the *status quo* of the presidency of New Guinea" would be "maintained under the Government of the Netherlands" in the mean time. The ambiguity of the language, however, led the Netherlands to consider itself the sovereign Power in West New Guinea, since this would be a continuation of the *"status quo"*. Indonesia, on the other hand, interpreted the Dutch role there to be strictly administrative, with the implication that West Irian would be incorporated into Indonesia after a year.

The status of the territory was still being disputed when Indonesia brought the matter before the United Nations in 1954.[1] Indonesia claimed that the territory rightfully belonged to it and should be freed from Dutch colonial rule. The Netherlands maintained that the Papuans of West New Guinea were not Indonesians and therefore should be allowed to decide their own future when they were ready to do so.

The future of the territory was discussed at the General Assembly's regular sessions from 1954 to 1957 and at the 1961 session, but no resolutions on it were adopted.

In December 1961, when increasing rancour between the Indonesian and Dutch Governments made the prospect of a negotiated settlement even more elusive, U Thant, who had been appointed Acting Secretary-General following the death of Dag Hammarskjöld, undertook to resolve the dispute through his good offices. Consulting with the Indonesian and Dutch Permanent Representatives to the United Nations, U Thant suggested that informal talks take place between the parties in the presence of former United States Ambassador Ellsworth Bunker, who would act as U Thant's representative. The parties agreed, and talks were begun in early 1962.

A sharpening of tension between the two Governments occurred shortly thereafter, however, when Indonesia landed paratroops in West New Guinea. The Netherlands charged that the landings constituted an act of aggression, but Indonesia refuted this on the grounds that "Indonesians who have entered and who in future will continue to enter West Irian are Indonesian nationals who move into Indonesia's own territory now dominated by the Dutch by force".[2] U Thant urged restraint by both parties but declined a Dutch request to send United Nations observers to the scene, noting that such action could only be considered if both Governments made the request.[3]

Further incidents were reported by the Netherlands during the first months of 1962, and there were intermittent lulls in the progress of Ambassador Bunker's talks. A number of communications from the Netherlands and from Indonesia were circulated as documents of the Security Council in connection with this question.

In one such letter,[4] dated 16 May, the Prime Minister of the Netherlands, stating that Indonesia had landed more parachutists on West New Guinea and had continued its aggressive acts, requested that the Acting Secretary-General make an appeal to Indonesia to remind it of its primary obligations under the United Nations Charter and to refrain from all aggressive acts against the territory and people of West New Guinea. He added that the Netherlands' presence in New Guinea was of a temporary nature and that his Government was prepared to give its fullest co-operation to the Secretary-General's efforts to find an honest and just solution for the territory on the basis of Article 73 of the Charter—concerning responsibilities of administering Powers towards non-self-governing territories—and General Assembly resolutions on the question of colonialism.

In a reply dated 22 May,[5] U Thant stated that, while he was concerned about developments in the area and had appealed already to the parties to exercise the utmost restraint, he could not accept the suggestion to approach Indonesia with an appeal which would imply that he was taking sides in the controversy. He did, however, keep a close eye on the situation, frequently consulting with the representatives of both countries and appealing to them to resume formal negotiations on the basis of Ambassador Bunker's proposals.

The Acting Secretary-General was at last able to announce, on 31 July 1962, that a preliminary agreement had been reached, and that official negotiations were to take place under his auspices. The final negotiations were held at United Nations Headquarters under the chairmanship of U Thant, with Ambassador Bunker continuing to act as mediator. An agreement was signed at New York by Indonesia and the Netherlands on 15 August 1962. Ratification instruments[6] were exchanged between the two countries on 20 September 1962 and, the next day, the General Assembly took note of the agreement in resolution 1752(XVII) of the same date, authorizing the Secretary-General to carry out the tasks entrusted to him therein.

The agreement provided for the administration of West New Guinea (West Irian) to be transferred by the Netherlands to a United Nations Temporary Executive Authority (UNTEA), to be headed by a United Nations Administrator who would be acceptable to both parties and who would be appointed by the Secretary-General. Under the Secretary-General's jurisdiction, UNTEA would have full authority after 1 October 1962 to administer the territory, to maintain law and order, to protect the rights of the inhabitants and to ensure uninterrupted, normal services until 1 May 1963, when the administration of the territory was to be transferred to Indonesia.

The agreement also stipulated that the Secretary-General would provide a United Nations Security Force (UNSF) to assist UNTEA with as many troops as the United Nations Administrator deemed necessary. In "related understandings" to the main agreement, it was established that United Nations personnel would observe the implementation of the cease-fire that was to become effective before UNTEA assumed authority. The United Nations was therefore entrusted with a dual peace-keeping role in addition to its administrative responsibilities as the executive authority.

Arranging a cease-fire

To pave the way for the arrival in West Irian of UNTEA and UNSF, a cease fire between Indonesian and Netherlands forces had to be enforced. The memorandum of understanding concerning the cease-fire—presented on 15 August 1962 in a note to the Acting Secretary-General from the representatives of Indonesia and the Netherlands[7]—requested that U Thant undertake immediately some of the functions outlined in the main agreement, so as to effect a cessation of hostilities as soon as possible. Such action would constitute an "extraordinary measure", because the General Assembly would not be voting on the establishment of UNTEA and UNSF until it convened in late September.

U Thant responded promptly, stating that he was prepared to undertake the responsibilities mentioned in the note. The memorandum on the cessation of hostilities specified that the Secretary-General would assign United Nations personnel to perform certain tasks, including: observing the cease-fire; protecting the security of Dutch and Indonesian forces; restoring the situation in the event of breaches of the cease-fire; assisting in informing Indonesian troops in the jungle of the existence of the cease-fire; and providing a non-military supply line to Indonesian troops.

Although there was no explicit reference to military observers in the memorandum, U Thant selected them to perform these tasks. Furthermore, he agreed to dispatch them without the prior authorization of the General Assembly or the Security Council, a step never before taken by a Secretary-General. Finally, reference was made in the memorandum to UNSF and its law-and-order maintenance role, with the implication that the Secretary-General should address this responsibility with all possible speed.

U Thant appointed Brigadier-General (later Major-General) Indar Jit Rikhye, his Military Adviser, to head the military observer team that was to supervise all arrangements for the cease-fire. Six Member States (Brazil, Ceylon (now Sri Lanka), India, Ireland, Nigeria and Sweden) agreed to provide 21 observers for this purpose. They were drawn from troops of these nations then serving either in the United Nations Emergency Force or the United Nations Operation in the Congo.

The observer force was assembled in West Irian within days of the signing of the agreement at United Nations Headquarters. The observers were informed at that time that the Netherlands military command had proclaimed a cease-fire as of 0001 GMT on 18 August 1962, and had ordered its ground forces to concentrate in the main garrison towns, although air and naval forces continued to patrol the territory. After a visit to Djakarta by General Rikhye, contacts were established with the Indonesian troops in the jungle. In this connection, frequent radio broadcasts on both the Netherlands-owned and Indonesian stations told the troops that hostilities had ceased. Printed pamphlets carrying the cease-fire message were dropped from aeroplanes over the jungle.

Besides supervising the cease-fire, the United Nations observers helped resupply the Indonesian troops with food and medicines and helped them regroup in selected places. The effort was successful owing to the full co-operation of the Indonesian and Netherlands authorities. Aerial support was given by the Thirteenth United States Task Force for the Far East and the Royal Canadian Air Force. Most of the emergency supplies were provided by the Netherlands military command, which also treated any Indonesian troops who were seriously ill. United Nations aircraft landed supplies in four staging areas: Sorong, Fakfak, Kaimana and Merauke.

By 21 September 1962, General Rikhye was able to report that all Indonesian forces in West Irian had been located and concentrated, that resupply had been assured and that over 500 Indonesian political detainees had been repatriated in accordance with the memorandum.

The observers' mandate had thus been fulfilled and all actions concerning the cessation of hostilities had been completed without incident.

Establishment of UNSF and UNTEA

With the cessation of hostilities, the next step was to ensure the maintenance of law and order in the territory. In addition to supervising the observer team, General Rikhye had been charged with making preliminary arrangements for the arrival of UNSF.

Article VIII of the Indonesian-Netherlands agreement stipulated the role and purpose of such a force:

> The Secretary-General will provide the UNTEA with such security forces as the United Nations Administrator deems necessary; such forces will primarily supplement existing Papuan (West Irianese) police in the task of maintaining law and order. The Papuan Volunteer Corps, which on the arrival of the United Nations Administrator will cease being part of the Netherlands armed forces, and the Indonesian armed forces in the territory, will be under the authority of, and at the disposal of, the Secretary-General for the same purpose. The United Nations Administrator will, to the extent feasible, use the Papuan (West Irianese) police as a United Nations security force to maintain law and order and, at his discretion, use Indonesian armed forces. The Netherlands armed forces will be repatriated as rapidly as possible and while still in the territory will be under the authority of the UNTEA.[8]

UNSF was thus essentially an internal law and security force—the "police arm" of UNTEA—whose responsibilities would range from ensuring the smooth implementation of UNTEA's administrative mandate to supervising the buildup of a viable, local police force.

In the memorandum of understanding on the cessation of hostilities, it was provided that UNSF would commence its duties as soon as possible after the General Assembly adopted an enabling resolution, but no later than 1 October 1962. In fact, the UNSF Commander arrived in West Irian weeks before the Assembly resolution was passed.

Major-General Said Uddin Khan of Pakistan, appointed by U Thant as Commander of UNSF, arrived in Hollandia on 4 September for preliminary discussions with Netherlands authorities and for a survey of future requirements. Similar efforts had already been exerted to some extent by General Rikhye, who had been charged earlier with making preliminary arrangements for the arrival of UNSF. The two men co-operated closely before and after the establishment of UNSF in West Irian.

UNSF activities prior to UNTEA

UNSF comprised 1,500 Pakistan troops, made available at the request of the Secretary-General, as were the support units of Canadian and United States aircraft and crews.

By 3 October, an advance party of 340 men of UNSF had arrived in the territory. On 5 October, the balance of the Pakistan contingent took up its positions. Also included in UNSF were some 16 officers and men of the Royal Canadian Air Force, with two aircraft, and a detachment of approximately 60 United States Air Force personnel with an average of three aircraft. These provided troop transport and communications. The Administrator also had under his authority the Papuan Volunteer Corps, the civil police, the Netherlands forces until their repatriation, and Indonesian troops, totalling approximately 1,500.

Establishment of UNTEA

UNSF was created to uphold the authority of UNTEA. Whereas groundwork for the arrival of UNSF troops had been laid in West Irian prior to the General Assembly's recognition of the agreement, it was not until Assembly resolution 1752(XVII) was adopted that personnel associated with UNTEA were dispatched. This resolution, which would make the United Nations directly responsible for the administration of the western half of New Guinea, was approved by a vote of 89 to none, with 14 abstentions.

In the resolution, the Assembly took note of the agreement between Indonesia and the Netherlands concerning West New Guinea (West Irian), acknowledged the role conferred by it upon the Secretary-General, and authorized him to carry out the tasks entrusted to him in the agreement.

Upon adoption of the resolution, U Thant noted that for the first time in its history the United Nations would have temporary executive authority established by and under the jurisdiction of the Secretary-General over a vast territory. He dispatched his Deputy Chef de Cabinet, José Rolz-Bennett, as his Representative in West New Guinea (West Irian), where he would make preliminary arrangements for the transfer of administration to UNTEA. Rolz-Bennett arrived in the territory on 21 September 1962, the date the enabling resolution was passed.

Transfer of administration to UNTEA

Under the agreement, neither Dutch nor Indonesian officials were to hold any of the top administrative positions during the seven-month transition period. In addition, three quarters of the Dutch civil servants of lesser rank had decided to leave the territory before 1 October, thereby creating a vacuum that would have to be filled to prevent a disruption of essential functions and services. In some instances, this was accomplished by promoting Papuan officials to the vacant posts. There was, however, a great shortage of adequately trained Papuans.

Rolz-Bennett immediately set about assembling an emergency task force to be deployed in key areas of the administration, recruiting international as well as Dutch and Indonesian personnel. The Netherlands Governor of the territory and his senior officials assisted in this effort; measures were also taken by the Netherlands Government to encourage Dutch officials to remain and serve the Temporary Executive Authority. In addition, the Indonesian Government was requested to provide urgently a group of civil servants to fill certain high-priority posts. This request was made with a view to the gradual phasing-in of Indonesian officials, whose presence thus facilitated the subsequent transfer of administrative responsibilities to Indonesia. In all, 32 nationalities were represented in UNTEA, among them both Dutch and Indonesian personnel.

The transfer of the administration from the Netherlands to UNTEA took place on 1 October 1962 and, in conformity with article VI of the agreement and its related aide-mémoire, the United Nations flag was raised and flown side by side with the Netherlands flag.

Before his departure from the territory on 28 September, the Netherlands Governor, Peter Johannis Plateel, appealed to the population to give its support to the United Nations administration. In messages from the Secretary-General and from Rolz-Bennett (who was designated as Temporary Administrator for approximately six weeks), the population was informed that UNTEA would endeavour to ensure the welfare of the inhabitants. The Temporary Administrator signed an order effective 15 October granting amnesty to all political prisoners sentenced prior to 1 October 1962.

On 1 October, Indonesia and the Netherlands established liaison missions to UNTEA in Hollandia/Kotabaru. An Australian liaison mission replaced one which had formerly served in Hollandia/Kotabaru as an administrative liaison between the authorities of the territory of Papua/New Guinea and West New Guinea, and now provided effective liaison with UNTEA on matters of mutual interest.

The United Nations Administrator, Djalal Abdoh of Iran, was appointed by the Secretary-General on 22 October 1962, under article IV of the agreement. On 15 November, he arrived in the territory to take up his assignment and Rolz-Bennett returned to Headquarters the following day.

Activities after the creation of UNTEA

The agreement between the Netherlands and Indonesia entrusted to UNTEA a number of broad powers: to "administer the territory" (article V); to appoint government officials and members of representative councils (articles IX and XXIII); to legislate for the territory, subject to certain qualifications (article XI); and to guarantee civil liberties and property rights (article XXII).

Once the international team that comprised UNTEA was assembled in the capital of the territory, they immediately began to address the vast economic and social problems facing them.

The very nature of the country presented major difficulties. Roads were practically non-existent, with a total length estimated at 900 kilometres. There was no other means of land transportation, which made air transport of all supplies from ports to the hinterland essential. Coupled with the difficulties of physical movement were problems of communication. Telephone systems existed only inside the major towns. UNSF was, however, able to tackle adequately the problems which faced it.

The transfer of authority implied a need to adapt existing institutions from the Dutch pattern to an Indonesian pattern. The first problem was to rebuild the officer and inspection cadres which had almost completely disappeared with the exodus of Dutch officers, and to reinstate a sense of loyalty and discipline in the rank and file, at the same time keeping the police service serving the public. The second problem was to reorient the entire service, substituting the Indonesian language and procedures for those of the Dutch so that there would be no upheaval when UNTEA handed over the reins of government to the Republic of Indonesia.

In accordance with the terms of article VII of the Indonesia-Netherlands agreement, the Papuan Volunteer Corps ceased to be part of the Netherlands armed forces upon the transfer of administration to UNTEA. The Corps, consisting of some 350 officers and men, was concentrated at Manokwari and was not assigned any duties in connection with the maintenance of law and order. As Dutch officers and non-commissioned officers left the area, they were replaced by Indonesian officers. This process was completed on 21 January 1963, when the command of the Corps was formally transferred to an Indonesian officer and the last Dutch officers left the territory.

During the period of UNTEA administration, the Papuan police were generally responsible for the maintenance of law and order in the territory. Before the transfer of administration to UNTEA, all the officers of the police corps were Dutch, there being no qualified Papuans. By the time UNTEA had assumed responsibility for the territory, almost all officers of Dutch nationality had left, having been temporarily replaced by officers from the Philippines who, in turn, were later replaced by Indonesians. By the end of March 1963, the entire corps was officered by Indonesians. However, in accordance with the provisions of article IX of the agreement, the chief of police continued to be an international recruit.

On 1 October 1962, when authority was transferred to UNTEA, the Indonesian troops in the territory consisted of those who had been brought in by parachute during the Dutch-Indonesian conflict and those who had infiltrated the territory. Agreement was reached with the Indonesian authorities to replace a large number of these troops with fresh territorial troops from Indonesia. It was also agreed that the number of Indonesian troops in the territory would not exceed the strength of the Pakistan contingent of UNSF, except with the prior consent of the UNTEA administration.

The withdrawal of the Netherlands naval and land forces from the territory was effected in stages in accordance with a timetable agreed upon by the Temporary Administrator, the Commander of UNSF and the Commander-in-Chief of the Netherlands forces in the territory. By 15 November 1962, this process had been completed without incident.

The situation was generally calm throughout the period of UNTEA. On 15 December 1962, however, two incidents involving the police and a small group of Indonesian troops occurred in Sorong and Doom. One police constable was killed and four wounded. Order was immediately restored by UNSF units while the civil administration continued to perform its normal functions. The area remained quiet for the rest of the temporary administration. In general, the inhabitants of the territory were law-abiding and the task of maintaining peace and security presented no problems. The United Nations Administrator had no occasion to call on the Indonesian armed forces in that connection but only for the purpose of occasional joint patrols with elements of the Pakistan contingent.

With regard to UNTEA's responsibility to uphold the rights of the territory's inhabitants (as outlined in article XXII of the agreement), the Administration ensured the free exercise of those rights by the population, and UNTEA courts acted as their guarantor. One of UNTEA's first concerns was, in fact, the reactivation of the entire judiciary since, with the departure of Netherlands personnel from various judiciary organs, the administration of justice practically came to a standstill. Once UNTEA was established, all the vacant positions in the judicial offices were filled through recruitment of qualified judicial officers from Indonesia.

UNTEA was also responsible for opening and closing the New Guinea Council and for appointing new representatives to the Council, in consultation with the Council's members. On 4 December 1962, the Council members met in the presence of the Administrator and took their new oath of office. The Council's Chairman and all members pledged to support loyally the provisions of the agreement and swore allegiance to UNTEA. As it seemed desirable that members should return to their constituencies in order to explain personally to their constituents the new political situation of the territory, the session was closed on 5 December, after consultation with the Chairman.

During the period of UNTEA's administration, a number of vacancies in the membership of the New Guinea Council occurred because of resignation, departure or absence of members. At the request of the Council's Chairman to fill some of these vacancies, the United Nations Administrator, in conformity with article XXIII, signed appropriate decrees appointing two new members. However, no consultation could take place with representative councils since none existed in the districts from which the two members were appointed.

In addition to the New Guinea Council, there were 11 representative councils, known as regional councils, in the various districts. On 14 February 1963, the Administrator opened the new regional council at Ransiki, Manokwari, elections to which had been held in December 1962.

The United Nations Administrator also toured the territory extensively in conjunction with article X of the agreement, which required that UNTEA widely publicize and explain the terms of the agreement. He took part in all public functions in order to explain personally those parts of the agreement which related to the United Nations presence in the territory and the changes that would take place on 1 May 1963. These efforts supplemented a United Nations information campaign which, with the help of special features, texts, posters and discussion groups, helped prepare the population for the transfer of administration to Indonesia, and informed them regarding the provisions of the agreement on the question of self-determination.

Articles XVII through XXI addressed the issue of self-determination. The relevant clauses of the agreement required that Indonesia make arrangements, with the assistance and participation of the United Nations Representative and his staff, to give the people of the territory the opportunity to exercise freedom of choice. The inhabitants were to make the decision to "remain with Indonesia" or to "sever their ties with Indonesia", under the auspices of a plebiscite to be held no later than 1969.

Day-to-day problems of the territory were addressed and handled smoothly by the civilian administration under UNTEA. In the sphere of public health, UNTEA had to deal with an epidemic of cholera which had begun to spread on the south-west coast of the island shortly after its administration was established. In this, it received valuable assistance from the World Health Organization, which provided a health team and the necessary medical supplies. The administration was able not only to contain the epidemic within a short period but also to declare the whole territory free of cholera. The administration also vigorously pursued plans for establishing hospitals and clinics in various parts of the territory.

In the economic sphere, the administration was mainly concerned with maintaining stability and dealing with a serious unemployment problem. Only 32 of a total of 317 Netherlands officials engaged in public works had been willing to stay on after UNTEA's takeover. Contractors stopped work, and gradually maintenance and repair services came to a halt. Over 3,500 men were idle. In a land where only 300,000 people (a third of the population) were in regular contact with the administration and where skilled labour was at a premium, this was a significant figure. With the co-operation of the Indonesian liaison mission, UNTEA was able to reactivate work on existing projects and draw up plans for similar projects which would be useful for the development of the territory. Forty-five projects were completed by the end of UNTEA, and 32 others were under construction. UNTEA was also able to keep in check the general price level of commodities, most of which had to be imported, and ensure adequate supplies for the population.

All costs incurred by UNTEA during its administration were borne equally by the Netherlands and Indonesia in compliance with article XXIV of the agreement. Consultations between the Secretariat and the representatives of the two Governments regarding the preparation of the UNTEA budget had taken place shortly after the agreement was signed. Later, at Hollandia/Kotabaru, a committee composed of the representatives of the two sides met under the chairmanship of the Deputy Controller of the United Nations and agreed on an UNTEA budget for the period 1 October 1962 to 30 April 1963, which was subsequently approved by the Secretary-General. As the budget committee doubted that UNTEA would be able to collect any revenue, no estimates of income were prepared. The Department of Finance was, however, able to collect a total of 15 million New Guinea florins by the end of the UNTEA period through taxes and customs duties. This was credited to the final budget figure.

On 31 December 1962, the Netherlands flag was replaced by the Indonesian flag, which was raised side by side with the United Nations flag, as contemplated in an aide-mémoire attached to the agreement.

In the last months of 1962 and the beginning of 1963, a number of communications from Papuan leaders and various groups in the territory were addressed to the Secretary-General and the United Nations Administrator requesting that the period of UNTEA administration in West Irian be shortened. On 21 November 1962, a joint declaration by the representatives of the New Guinea Council was transmitted to the Secretary-General asking for the early transfer of the administration to Indonesia. A demonstration to the same effect took place on 15 January 1963, when a petition was presented to the Administrator by 18 political leaders from the area of Hollandia/Kotabaru.

These requests were brought to the attention of the Secretary-General in January 1963 by Sudjarwo Tjondronegoro, head of the Indonesian Liaison Mission to UNTEA. After consultation with the representative of the Netherlands, the Secretary-General decided that any shortening of UNTEA would not be feasible. However, he sent his Chef de Cabinet, C. V. Narasimhan, in February 1963, to consult with the United Nations Administrator and the Government of Indonesia, with a view to facilitating the entry of Indonesian officials into the administration of West Irian in order to ensure the continuity and expansion of all essential services. Following these consultations, the Chef de Cabinet announced in Djakarta that the transfer of administration would take place as scheduled on 1 May 1963, and that the replacement of Netherlands officials by Indonesian officials would be accelerated. By the end of March 1963, Indonesian nationals occupied the second highest post in every administrative department in all six divisions in the territory.

The gathering momentum of the phasing-in operation was accompanied by an encouraging development in a different sphere. The resumption of diplomatic relations between Indonesia and the Netherlands was announced on 13 March 1963. Thus began a new era in the relationship between the two countries, one which notably helped UNTEA's work as the time approached for the transfer of authority.

In April, the Indonesian Government announced that a Papuan member of the New Guinea Council, E. J. Bonay, would be installed on 1 May as the first Governor of Irian Barat (the Indonesian name for West Irian). He would be assisted by an Indonesian deputy, and the territory would be administered as a province of the Republic of Indonesia.

The number of Indonesian officials in the Administration towards the end of April reached 1,564, while Papuans and other indigenous people of West Irian occupied 7,625 civil service posts. Only 11 Netherlands officials remained; they were to leave upon the transfer of authority to Indonesia. Stores of goods were procured to ensure adequate supplies for a period after the transfer. Direct negotiations between the Netherlands and Indonesia for the purchase of a number of Dutch interests proceeded smoothly. The economy had been largely stabilized, health and education services were in good order, and all the provisions of the agreement leading up to the transfer of administration fully implemented.

During the last days of April, some 30 Indonesian warships arrived in Biak and Hollandia for the ceremony, as had service squadrons of aircraft of the Indonesian air force. The Pakistan units of UNSF began their withdrawal to Biak, ready for embarkation; the various UNSF garrisons were replaced by incoming Indonesian troops.

Transfer of administration to Indonesia

In accordance with article XII of the agreement, the UNTEA Administrator transferred full administrative control to the representative of the Indonesian Government, Tjondronegoro, on 1 May 1963. The ceremony was performed in the presence of the Chef de Cabinet as the Secretary-General's personal representative for the occasion, and the Indonesian Foreign Minister. At that time, the United Nations flag was taken down.

Secretary-General's observations

On the completion of UNTEA, the Secretary-General declared[9] that it had been a unique experience, which had once again proved the capacity of the United Nations to undertake a variety of functions, provided that it received adequate support from its Member States. He also announced that, in consultation with Indonesia, he had decided in principle to designate a few United Nations experts, serving at Headquarters and elsewhere, to perform the functions envisaged in article XVII of the agreement, in so far as the article required that the Secretary-

General advise, assist and participate in arrangements which were the responsibility of Indonesia for the act of free choice. Those experts would visit West Irian as often as necessary and spend as much time as would enable them to report fully to him, until he appointed a United Nations representative to preside over them as a staff.

Looking to the future, the Secretary-General stated that he was confident that Indonesia would scrupulously observe the terms of the 1962 agreement, and would ensure the exercise by the territory's population of their right to express their wishes as to their future.

In accordance with the Indonesia-Netherlands agreement, the Secretary-General on 1 April 1968 appointed a representative, Fernando Ortiz-Sanz, to advise, assist and participate in arrangements which were the responsibility of Indonesia for the act of free choice, on retaining or severing ties with Indonesia.

In a report[10] submitted to the Secretary-General, the Government of Indonesia stated that between 14 July and 2 August 1969, the enlarged representative councils (consultative assemblies) of West New Guinea (West Irian), which included 1,026 members, were asked to pronounce themselves, on behalf of the people of the territory, as to whether they wished to remain with Indonesia or sever their ties with it. All those councils chose the first alternative without dissent.

The representative of the Secretary-General reported[11] that within "the limitations imposed by the geographical characteristics of the territory and the general political situation in the area, an act of free choice has taken place in West Irian in accordance with Indonesian practice, in which the representatives of the population have expressed their wish to remain with Indonesia".

Those reports were transmitted by the Secretary-General to the General Assembly, which, by resolution 2504(XXIV) of 19 November 1969, acknowledged with appreciation the fulfilment by the Secretary-General and his representatives of the task entrusted to them under the 1962 agreement.

Reference notes

[1]A/2694. [2]S/5128. [3]S/5124. [4]S/5123. [5]S/5124. [6]A/5170, annex C. [7]A/5170, annex B. [8]A/5170, annex A. [9]A/5501, chapter II.15. [10]A/7723, annex II. [11]A/7723, annex I.

Appendices

Composition and organization

Composition

A United Nations peace-keeping operation is considered a subsidiary organ of the United Nations, established pursuant to a resolution of the Security Council or, exceptionally, of the General Assembly.

Military component. A United Nations Force consists of a Commander and a number of contingents provided by selected Member States of the United Nations upon the request of the Secretary-General. In all peace-keeping forces established since October 1973, the contingents are selected in consultations with the Security Council and with the parties concerned, bearing in mind the principle of equitable geographical representation. The members of the Force, although remaining in their national service, are, during the period of their assignment to the Force, international personnel under the authority of the United Nations and subject to the instructions of the Commander, through the chain of command. The functions of the Force are exclusively international, and members of the Force are expected to discharge those functions and regulate their conduct with the interest of the United Nations only in view.

Civilian component. A civilian administrative staff of the Force is provided, as a rule, by the Secretary-General from among existing United Nations staff. These personnel are to follow the rules and regulations of the United Nations Secretariat. Additionally, the Commander may recruit such local personnel as the Force requires. The terms and conditions of employment for locally recruited personnel are prescribed by the Commander and generally, to the extent possible, follow the practice prevailing in the locality.

Chain of command

United Nations peace-keeping operations are normally established by the Security Council and fall under its authority. The Secretary-General is responsible to the Council for the organization, conduct and direction of the Force, and he alone reports to the Council about it. The Secretary-General keeps the Security Council fully informed of developments relating to the functioning of the Force. Under the guidance of the forces established since October 1973, all matters which may affect the nature or the continued effective functioning of the Force are to be referred to the Council for its decision.

The Secretary-General is assisted in the performance of his duties, in this regard, by the Office of the Under-Secretaries-General for Special Political Affairs.

Command in the field. Command within the Force is exercised in the field by a Force Commander appointed by the Secretary-General with the consent of the Security Council. The Commander is responsible to the Secretary-General. The Force Commander exercises full command authority of the Force except for disciplinary questions. The Commander has full authority with respect to all assignments of members of his headquarters staff and, through the chain of command, of all members of the Force, including the deployment and movements of all contingents in the Force and units assigned to the Force. The contingents comprising the Force are integral parts of it and take their orders exclusively from the Force Commander. The Force has its own headquarters, whose personnel are international in character and representative of the contingents comprising the Force. The Commander designates the chain of command for the Force, making use of the officers of his headquarters staff and the commanders of the national contingents made available by troop-contributing Governments. He may delegate his authority through the chain of command. The Force undertakes no functions which are not consistent with the definition of the mandate of the Force set forth in the Security Council resolution establishing the Force. Any doubt about a proposed action of the Force being consistent with such definition must be submitted to the Secretary-General for decision.

Discipline. The Commander has general responsibility for the good order and discipline of the Force. He may make investigations, conduct inquiries and require information, reports and consultations for the purpose of discharging this responsibility. Responsibility for disciplinary action in national contingents provided for the Force, however, rests with the commanders of the national contingents. Reports concerning disciplinary action are communicated to the Force Commander who may consult with the commander of the national contingent and, if necessary, through the Secretary-General with the authorities of the troop-contributing Government concerned.

Administration. The Office of Field Operational and External Support Activities, in general terms, is responsible for organizing the civilian administrative staff to support the Force and, in close collaboration with the Office of the Under-Secretaries-General for Special Political Affairs and the Office of Financial Services, makes arrangements for airlift of the contingents of the Force, prepares the final budgetary proposals for the Force and presents those proposals to the General Assembly's Advisory Committee on Administrative and Budgetary Questions and the Assembly's Fifth (Administrative and Budgetary) Committee. Additionally, it arranges for the procurement of the necessary stores for the maintenance of the Force and directs the operations of the civilian administrative staff in the field.

The Commander with his civilian Chief Administrative Officer, in accordance with procedures prescribed by him within the limits of the budgetary provisions for the Force and financial rules and regulations of the United Nations, arranges for: the billeting and provision of food for the military component of the Force; the establishment, maintenance and operation of service institutes providing amenities for members of the Force and other United Nations personnel as authorized by the Commander; the transportation of personnel and equipment; the procurement, storage and issuance of supplies and equipment required by the Force which are not directly provided by the participating Governments; maintenance and other services required for the operation of the Force; the establishment, operation and maintenance of telecommunication and postal services for the Force; and the provision of medical, dental and sanitary services for personnel in the Force. The foregoing is achieved through the co-ordinated effort of the military logistic staff of the Force and the civilian staff. Formulation of provision systems and review of requirements are the responsibility of the military Chief Logistics Officer and his staff, and the responsibility for procurement and timely delivery of provisions rests with the civilian Chief Procurement Officer.

Privileges and immunities. The Force, as a subsidiary organ of the United Nations, enjoys the status, privileges and immunities of the Organization provided in Article 105 of the Charter of the United Nations and the Convention on the Privileges and Immunities of the United Nations. Additionally, the Secretary-General endeavours to conclude a status of the Force agreement with the host Government concerning the work of the Force. This agreement covers matters such as the status of the Force and its members, responsibility for criminal and civil jurisdiction of the members of the Force, premises of the Force, taxation, customs and fiscal regulation pertaining to the members of the Force, freedom of movement, use of roads, water-ways, port facilities and airfields, water, electricity and other public utilities, locally recruited personnel, settlement of disputes or claims, liaisons, etc.

The following charts indicate the chain of command of United Nations peace-keeping operations and the organizational structure of current operations.

THE CHAIN OF COMMAND OF UN PEACE-KEEPING FORCES

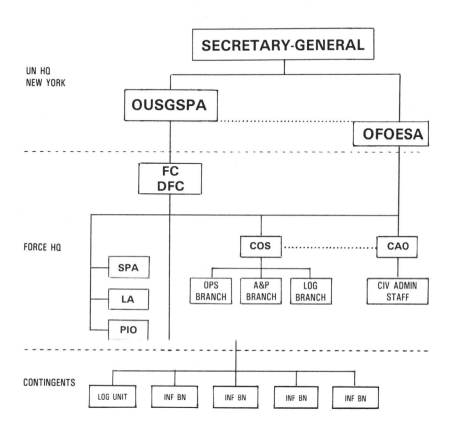

UN HQ
NEW YORK

SECRETARY-GENERAL

OUSGSPA

OFOESA

FC
DFC

FORCE HQ

SPA

LA

PIO

COS

OPS
BRANCH

A&P
BRANCH

LOG
BRANCH

CAO

CIV ADMIN
STAFF

CONTINGENTS

LOG UNIT

INF BN

INF BN

INF BN

INF BN

ABBREVIATIONS

A & P	Administration and Personnel	LA	Legal Adviser
ADMIN	Administrative	LOG	Logistic
CAO	Chief Administrative Officer	OFOESA	Office of Field Operational
CIV	Civilian		and External Support Activities
COS	Chief of Staff	OPS	Operations
DFC	Deputy Force Commander	OUSGSPA	Office of the Under-Secretaries-General
FC	Force Commander		for Special Political Affairs
HQ	Headquarters	PIO	Press Information Officer
INF BN	Infantry Battalion	SPA	Senior Political Adviser

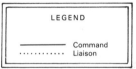

LEGEND

————— Command
·············· Liaison

UNTSO ORGANIZATION CHART

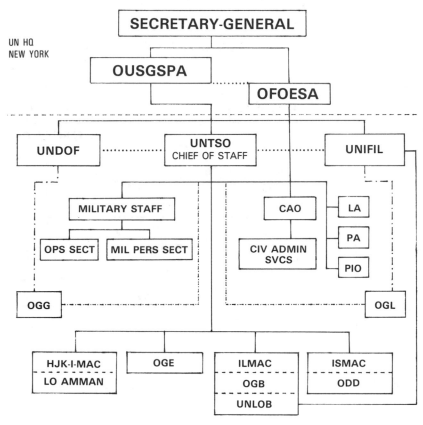

ABBREVIATIONS

ADMIN	Administrative	**OUSGSPA**	Office of the Under-Secretaries-General
CAO	Chief Administrative Officer		for Special Political Affairs
CIV	Civilian	**PA**	Political Adviser
HJK-I-MAC	Hashemite Kingdom of Jordan-	**PERS**	Personnel
	Israel Mixed Armistice Commission	**PIO**	Press Information Officer
ILMAC	Israel-Lebanon Mixed	**SECT**	Section
	Armistice Commission	**SVCS**	Services
ISMAC	Israel-Syria Mixed	**UNDOF**	United Nations Disengagement Observer Force
	Armistice Commission	**UNIFIL**	United Nations Interim Force in Lebanon
LA	Legal Adviser	**UNLOB**	United Nations Liaison Office Beirut
MIL	Military	**UNTSO**	United Nations Truce
LO	Liaison Officer		Supervision Organization
ODD	Observer Detachment		
	Damascus		
OFOESA	Office of Field Operational		
	and External Support Activities		
OGB	Observer Group Beirut		
OGE	Observer Group Egypt		
OGG	Observer Group Golan		
OGL	Observer Group Lebanon		
OPS	Operations		

LEGEND

——————	Command
···············	Liaison
—·—·—·—	Under administrative control
—··—··—··—	Under operational command

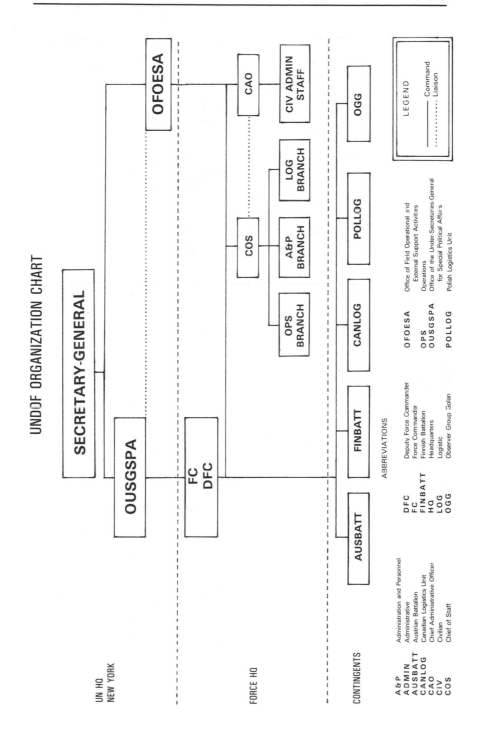

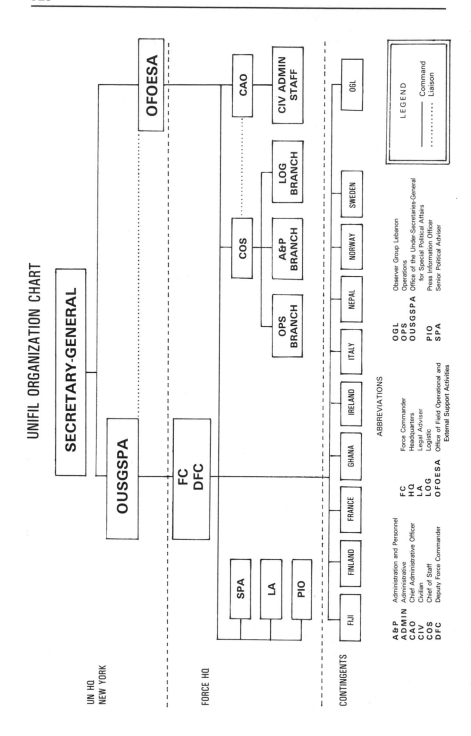

UNIFIL ORGANIZATION CHART

UN HQ
NEW YORK

FORCE HQ

CONTINGENTS

SECRETARY-GENERAL

OUSGSPA

OFOESA

FC
DFC

SPA
LA
PIO

CAO

COS

OPS BRANCH

A&P BRANCH

LOG BRANCH

CIV ADMIN STAFF

FIJI   FINLAND   FRANCE   GHANA   IRELAND   ITALY   NEPAL   NORWAY   SWEDEN   OGL

ABBREVIATIONS

A&P   Administration and Personnel
ADMIN Administrative
CAO   Chief Administrative Officer
CIV   Civilian
COS   Chief of Staff
DFC   Deputy Force Commander

FC   Force Commander
HQ   Headquarters
LA   Legal Adviser
LOG   Logistic
OFOESA Office of Field Operational and
       External Support Activities

OGL   Observer Group Lebanon
OPS   Operations
OUSGSPA Office of the Under-Secretaries-General
         for Special Political Affairs
PIO   Press Information Officer
SPA   Senior Political Adviser

LEGEND

———— Command
.... Liaison

UNMOGIP ORGANIZATION CHART

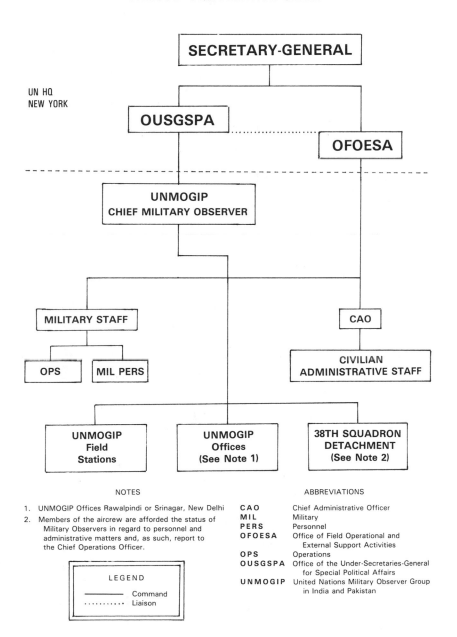

UN HQ
NEW YORK

NOTES

1. UNMOGIP Offices Rawalpindi or Srinagar, New Delhi
2. Members of the aircrew are afforded the status of Military Observers in regard to personnel and administrative matters and, as such, report to the Chief Operations Officer.

LEGEND

———— Command
··········· Liaison

ABBREVIATIONS

CAO	Chief Administrative Officer
MIL	Military
PERS	Personnel
OFOESA	Office of Field Operational and External Support Activities
OPS	Operations
OUSGSPA	Office of the Under-Secretaries-General for Special Political Affairs
UNMOGIP	United Nations Military Observer Group in India and Pakistan

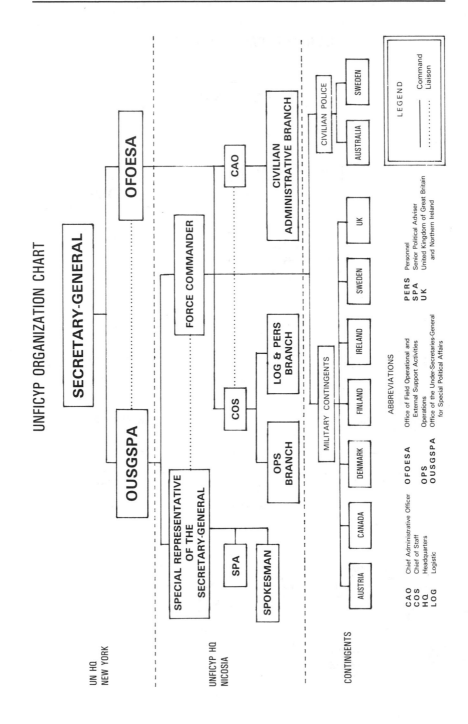

UNFICYP ORGANIZATION CHART

SECRETARY-GENERAL

OUSGSPA

OFOESA

UN HQ
NEW YORK

SPECIAL REPRESENTATIVE OF THE SECRETARY-GENERAL

SPA

SPOKESMAN

FORCE COMMANDER

CAO

UNFICYP HQ
NICOSIA

COS

OPS BRANCH

LOG & PERS BRANCH

CIVILIAN ADMINISTRATIVE BRANCH

MILITARY CONTINGENTS

AUSTRIA

CANADA

DENMARK

FINLAND

IRELAND

SWEDEN

UK

CIVILIAN POLICE

AUSTRALIA

SWEDEN

CONTINGENTS

ABBREVIATIONS

CAO — Chief Administrative Officer
COS — Chief of Staff
HQ — Headquarters
LOG — Logistic

OFOESA — Office of Field Operational and External Support Activities
OPS — Operations
OUSGSPA — Office of the Under-Secretaries-General for Special Political Affairs

PERS — Personnel
SPA — Senior Political Adviser
UK — United Kingdom of Great Britain and Northern Ireland

LEGEND
——— Command
·········· Liaison

Facts and figures

United Nations Truce Supervision Organization (UNTSO)

Authorization:	Security Council resolutions:	50(1948) of 29 May 1948
		54(1948) of 15 July 1948
		73(1948) of 11 August 1949
		101(1953) of 24 November 1953 (to strengthen UNTSO)
		114(1956) of 4 June 1956
		236(1967) of 11 June 1967
	Consensus of 9/10 July 1967 (S/8047) (Suez Canal)	
	Consensus of 19 April 1972 (S/10611) (Southern Lebanon)	
	Security Council resolution 339(1973) of 23 October 1973 (Sinai)	

Function:	Established in June 1948 to assist the Mediator and the Truce Commission in supervising the observance of the truce in Palestine called for by the Security Council. Since then, UNTSO has performed various tasks entrusted to it by the Security Council, including the supervision of the General Armistice Agreements of 1949 and the observation of the cease-fire in the Suez Canal area and the Golan Heights following the Arab-Israeli war of June 1967. At present, UNTSO assists and co-operates with UNDOF and UNIFIL in the performance of their tasks; observer groups are stationed in Beirut and in Sinai
Headquarters:	Government House, Jerusalem
Duration:	11 June 1948 to date
Maximum strength:	572 (1948)
Current strength:	298 military observers (October 1985)
Fatalities:	21 (killed in action/accidents)
	3 (other causes)
	24 (October 1985)
Expenditures:	From inception of mission to October 1985: $224,307,066
Method of financing:	Appropriations through the United Nations regular budget
Mediators:	Count Folke Bernadotte (Sweden) May–Sep. 1948
	Ralph J. Bunche (United States) (Acting) Sep. 1948–Aug. 1949

Chiefs of Staff:	Lieutenant-General Count Thord Bonde (Sweden)	Jun.–Jul. 1948
	Major-General Aage Lundström (Sweden)	Jul.–Sep. 1948
	Lieutenant-General William E. Riley (United States)	Sep. 1948–Jun. 1953
	Major-General Vagn Bennike (Denmark)	Jun. 1953–Aug. 1954
	Lieutenant-General E.L.M. Burns (Canada)	Aug. 1954–Nov. 1956
	Colonel Byron V. Leary (United States) (Acting)	Nov. 1956–Mar. 1958
	Major-General Carl C. von Horn (Sweden)	Mar. 1958–Jul. 1960
	Colonel R. W. Rickert (United States) (Acting)	Jul.–Dec. 1960
	Lieutenant-General Carl C. von Horn (Sweden)	Jan. 1961–May 1963
	Lieutenant-General Odd Bull (Norway)	Jun. 1963–Jul. 1970
	Major-General Ensio Siilasvuo (Finland)	Aug. 1970–Oct. 1973
	Colonel Richard W. Bunworth (Ireland) (Acting)	Nov. 1973–Mar. 1974
	Major-General Bengt Liljestrand (Sweden)	Apr. 1974–Aug. 1975
	Colonel K. D. Howard (Australia) (Acting)	Aug.–Dec. 1975
	Major-General Emmanuel A. Erskine (Ghana)	Jan. 1976–Apr. 1978
	Colonel William Callaghan (Ireland) (Acting)	Apr. 1978–Jun. 1979
	Colonel O. Forsgren (Sweden) (Acting)	Jun. 1979–Jan. 1980
	Major-General Erkki R. Kaira (Finland)	Feb. 1980–Feb. 1981
	Lieutenant-General Emmanuel A. Erskine (Ghana)	Feb. 1981 to date

Contributors of military observers:

	Duration
Argentina	1967 to date
Australia	1956 to date
Austria	1967 to date
Belgium	Jun. 1948 to date
Burma	1967–1969
Canada	1954 to date
Chile	1967 to date
Denmark	1954 to date
Finland	1967 to date
France	Jun. 1948 to date
Ireland	1958 to date
Italy	1958 to date
Netherlands	1956 to date
New Zealand	1954 to date
Norway	1956 to date
Sweden	Jun. 1948 to date
USSR	1973 to date
United States	Jun. 1948 to date

Other contributions (without cost to UN):

United States	1949–Jun. 1967	Aircraft
Netherlands	Jun.–Nov. 1967	Aircraft
Switzerland	Nov. 1967 to date	Chartered commercial aircraft and crew

United Nations Emergency Force (UNEF I)

Authorization:	General Assembly resolutions:	998(ES-I) of 4 November 1956
		1000(ES-I) of 5 November 1956
		1001(ES-I) of 7 November 1956
		1125(XI) of 2 February 1957

Function: To secure and to supervise the cessation of hostilities, including the withdrawal of the armed forces of France, Israel and the United Kingdom from Egyptian territory, and after the withdrawal to serve as a buffer between the Egyptian and Israeli forces

Location: First the Suez Canal sector and the Sinai peninsula. Later along the Armistice Demarcation Line in the Gaza area and the international frontier in the Sinai peninsula (on the Egyptian side)

Headquarters: Gaza

Duration: November 1956—June 1967

Maximum strength: 6,073 (February 1957)

Strength at withdrawal: 3,378 (June 1967)

Fatalities:
64 (killed in action/accidents)
26 (other causes)
90

Expenditures: From inception to end of mission: $220,124,012
(The financial cost was considerably reduced by
the absorption by the countries providing contingents
of varying amounts of the expenses involved)

Method of financing: Assessments in respect of a Special Account

Commanders:

Lieutenant-General E.L.M. Burns (Canada)	Nov. 1956—Dec. 1959
Lieutenant-General P. S. Gyani (India)	Dec. 1959—Jan. 1964
Major-General Carlos F. Paiva Chaves (Brazil)	Jan. 1964— Aug. 1964
Colonel Lazar Musicki (Yugoslavia) (Acting)	Aug. 1964—Jan. 1965
Major-General Syseno Sarmento (Brazil)	Jan. 1965— Jan. 1966
Major-General Indar J. Rikhye (India)	Jan. 1966— Jun. 1967

Contributors:

	Duration	*Contribution*
Brazil	20 Jan. 1957—13 Jun. 1967	Infantry
Canada	24 Nov. 1956—28 Feb. 1959	Medical unit
	24 Nov. 1956—31 May 1967	Signal, engineer, air transport, maintenance and movement control units
Colombia	16 Nov. 1956—28 Oct. 1958	Infantry
Denmark	15 Nov. 1956— 9 Jun. 1967	Infantry
Finland	11 Dec. 1956— 5 Dec. 1957	Infantry
India	20 Nov. 1956—13 Jun. 1967	Infantry, and supply, transport and signal units
Indonesia	5 Jan. 1957—12 Sep. 1957	Infantry
Norway	15 Nov. 1956— 9 Jun. 1967	Infantry
	1 Mar. 1959— 9 Jun. 1967	Medical unit

Contributors: (cont.)		Duration	Contribution
	Sweden	21 Nov. 1956– 9 Jun. 1967	Infantry
	Yugoslavia	17 Nov. 1956–11 Jun. 1967	Infantry

Other contributions (without cost to UN):			
	Canada	Nov. 1956	Airlift
	Italy	Nov. 1956	Airlift, logistic support
	Switzerland	Nov. 1956	Airlift
	United States	Nov. 1956	Airlift

United Nations Emergency Force (UNEF II)

Authorization:	Security Council resolutions: 340(1973) of 25 October 1973 371(1975) of 24 July 1975 341(1973) of 27 October 1973 378(1975) of 23 October 1975 346(1974) of 8 April 1974 396(1976) of 22 October 1976 362(1974) of 23 October 1974 416(1977) of 21 October 1977 368(1975) of 17 April 1975 438(1978) of 23 October 1978
Function:	To supervise the cease-fire between Egyptian and Israeli forces and, following the conclusion of the agreements of 18 January 1974 and 4 September 1975, to supervise the redeployment of Egyptian and Israeli forces and to man and control the buffer zones established under those agreements
Location:	Suez Canal sector and later the Sinai peninsula
Headquarters:	Ismailia
Duration:	25 October 1973–24 July 1979
Maximum strength	6,973 (February 1974)
Strength at withdrawal:	4,031 (July 1979)
Fatalities:	30 (accidents) 13 (other causes) 9 (killed in a UNEF aircraft crash in Syria, as a result of anti-aircraft fire, during a flight in support of UNDOF on 9 August 1974) $\overline{52}$
Expenditures:	From inception to end of mission: $446,487,000
Method of financing:	Assessments in respect of a Special Account

Commanders:	Lieutenant-General Ensio P. H. Siilasvuo (Finland)
	  Interim Commander: 25 Oct. 1973–11 Nov. 1973
	  Commander: 12 Nov. 1973–19 Aug. 1975
	Lieutenant-General Bengt Liljestrand (Sweden) 20 Aug. 1975–30 Nov. 1976
	Major-General Rais Abin (Indonesia) 1 Dec. 1976– 6 Sep. 1979

Contributors:

	Duration	Contribution
Australia	Jul. 1976–Oct. 1979	Air unit (helicopters and personnel)
Austria	26 Oct. 1973– 3 Jun. 1974	Infantry
Canada	10 Nov. 1973–30 Oct. 1979	Logistics: signals, air and service units
Finland	26 Oct. 1973–Aug. 1979	Infantry
Ghana	22 Jan. 1974–Sep. 1979	Infantry
Indonesia	21 Dec. 1973–Sep. 1979	Infantry
Ireland	30 Oct. 1973–22 May 1974	Infantry
Nepal	3 Feb. 1974– 4 Sep. 1974	Infantry
Panama	11 Dec. 1973–25 Nov.1974	Infantry
Peru	25 Nov. 1973– 3 Jun. 1974	Infantry

Contributors: (cont.)		*Duration*	*Contribution*
	Poland	15 Nov. 1973–20 Jan. 1980	Logistics: engineering, medical and transport units
	Senegal	18 Jan. 1974–Jun. 1976	Infantry
	Sweden	26 Oct. 1973–30 Apr. 1980	Infantry

Other contributions (without cost to UN)			
	Australia	Feb. 1974	Airlift: Nepalese troops, Calcutta–Cairo
	Canada	Nov. 1973	Airlift: Canadian troops
	Germany, Federal Republic of	Jan. 1974	Airlift: Ghanaian and Senegalese troops
	Japan	Feb. 1974	Cash contribution for airlift of Nepalese troops Kathmandu–Calcutta, and transport of its equipment to UNEF
	Norway	Oct. 1973	Airlift: Swedish troops, Sweden–UNEF
	Poland	Nov. 1973	Airlift: Polish troops
	Sweden	Oct. 1973	Airlift: Swedish troops
	Switzerland		Aircraft placed at disposal of UNTSO was available to UNEF as required
	United Kingdom	Oct. 1973	Airlift: Austrian, Finnish, Irish and Swedish troops and vehicles, Cyprus–UNEF
	USSR	Nov. 1973	Airlift: Austrian troops, Austria–UNEF, Finnish troops and heavy equipment Finland–UNEF
	United States	Nov. 1973	Airlift: Irish troops, Ireland-UNEF
		Nov. 1973	Finnish troops, Finland–UNEF
		Nov. 1973	Peruvian troops, Peru–UNEF
		Dec. 1973	Austrian troops, Austria–UNEF
		Dec. 1973	Indonesian troops, Indonesia–UNEF
		Dec. 1973	Panamanian troops, Panama–UNEF
		Oct. 1976	$10 million in goods and services

United Nations Disengagement Observer Force (UNDOF)

Authorization: Security Council resolutions:

350(1974) of 31 May 1974	429(1978) of 31 May 1978	506(1982) of 26 May 1982
363(1974) of 29 November 1974	441(1978) of 30 November 1978	524(1982) of 29 November 1982
369(1975) of 28 May 1975	449(1979) of 30 May 1979	531(1983) of 26 May 1983
381(1975) of 30 November 1975	456(1979) of 30 November 1979	543(1983) of 29 November 1983
390(1976) of 28 May 1976	470(1980) of 30 May 1980	551(1984) of 30 May 1984
398(1976) of 30 November 1976	481(1980) of 26 November 1980	557(1984) of 28 November 1984
408(1977) of 26 May 1977	485(1981) of 22 May 1981	563(1985) of 21 May 1985
420(1977) of 30 November 1977	493(1981) of 23 Novemer 1981	

Function: To supervise the cease–fire between Israel and Syria; to supervise the redeployment of Syrian and Israeli forces; and to establish a buffer zone, as provided in the Agreement on Disengagement between Israeli and Syrian Forces of 31 May 1974

Location: Syrian Golan Heights

Headquarters: Damascus

Duration: 3 June 1974 to date

Authorized strength: 1,450

Current strength: 1,316 (October 1985)

Fatalities:
14 (accidents)
 6 (other causes)
20 (October 1985)

Amount apportioned: From inception of mission to 30 November 1984: $702,700,000

Method of financing: Assessments in respect of a Special Account

Commanders:

Brigadier-General Gonzalo Briceño Zevallos (Peru), Interim Commander	3 Jun.–14 Dec. 1974
Colonel Hannes Philipp (Austria), Officer-in-Charge	15 Dec. 1974–7 Jul. 1975
Major-General Hannes Philipp (Austria)	8 Jul. 1975–21 Apr. 1979
Colonel Guenther G. Greindl (Austria), Officer-in-Charge	22 Apr.–30 Nov. 1979
Major-General Guenther G. Griendl (Austria),	1 Dec. 1979–25 Feb. 1981
Major-General Erkki R. Kaira (Finland)	26 Feb. 1981–31 May 1982
Major Carl-Gustav Stahl (Sweden)	1 Jun. 1982–31 May 1985
Major-General Gustav Hägglund (Finland)	1 Jun. 1985 to date

Contributors:

Austria	3 Jun. 1974 to date	Infantry
Canada	5 Jun. 1974 to date	Logistics: signals, supply and transport units
Finland	16 Mar. 1979 to date	Infantry
Iran	26 Aug. 1975–15 Mar. 1979	Infantry
Peru	3 Jun. 1974–10 Jul. 1975	Infantry
Poland	5 Jun. 1974 to date	Logistics: engineers and some transport service

United Nations Interim Force in Lebanon (UNIFIL)

Authorization:	Security Council resolutions:	
	425(1978) of 19 March 1978	498(1981) of 18 December 1981
	426(1978) of 19 March 1978	519(1982) of 17 August 1982
	434(1978) of 18 September 1978	523(1982) of 18 October 1982
	444(1979) of 19 January 1979	529(1983) of 18 January 1983
	450(1979) of 14 June 1979	536(1983) of 18 July 1983
	459(1979) of 19 December 1979	549(1984) of 19 April 1984
	474(1980) of 17 June 1980	555(1984) of 12 October 1984
	483(1980) of 17 December 1980	561(1985) of 17 April 1985
	488(1981) of 19 June 1981	575(1985) of 17 October 1985

Function: To confirm the withdrawal of Israeli forces from southern Lebanon, to restore international peace and security and to assist the Government of Lebanon in ensuring the return of its effective authority in the area

Location: Southern Lebanon

Headquarters: Naqoura

Duration: 19 March 1978 to date

Authorized strength: 7,000

Current strength: 5,773 (October 1985)

Fatalities:
    97 (killed in action/accidents)
    14 (other causes)
   111 (1 October 1985)

Amount apportioned: From inception of mission to 18 October 1984: $945,300,000

Method of financing: Assessments in respect of a Special Account

Commanders:
Lieutenant-General Emmanuel A. Erskine (Ghana)   19 Mar. 1978–14 Feb. 1981
Lieutenant-General William Callaghan (Ireland)   15 Feb. 1981 to date

Contributors:		*Duration*	*Contribution*
	Canada	22 Mar.–7 Oct. 1978	Signals and movement control units
	Fiji	20 May 1978 to date	Infantry battalion
	Finland	4 Nov. 1982 to date	Infantry battalion
	France	23 Mar. 1978–15 Mar. 1979	Infantry battalion
		23 Mar. 1978 to date	Logistics: engineering, supply, transport and maintenance units
	Ghana	7 Sep. 1979 to date	Infantry battalion (advance party from UNEF)
		25 Sep. 1979 to date	Integrated headquarters camp command (defence platoon and engineering platoon)

Contributors: (cont.)		Duration	Contribution
	Iran	22 Mar. 1978–Mar. 1979	Infantry battalion
	Ireland	24 May 1978 to date	Infantry battalion
		16 Oct. 1978–24 Sep. 1979	Headquarters camp command (defence platoon and adm. personnel)
		16 Oct. 1978 to date	Integrated headquarters camp command (administrative personnel)
	Italy	10 Jul. 1979 to date	Air unit: helicopters, ground and air crews
	Nepal	11 Apr. 1978–20 May 1980	Infantry battalion
		1 Jun. 1981–18 Nov. 1982	Infantry battalion
		18 Jan. 1985 to date	Infantry battalion
	Netherlands	27 Feb. 1979–19 Oct. 1985	Infantry battalion
	Nigeria	4 May 1978–23 Feb. 1983	Infantry battalion
	Norway	26 Mar. 1978 to date	Infantry battalion
		26 Mar. 1978–Jul. 1979	Logistics: air unit
		26 Mar. 1978–Aug. 1980	medical unit
		26 Mar. 1978 to date	maintenance company
		26 Mar. 1978 to date	movement control unit
	Senegal	11 Apr. 1978–1 Nov. 1984	Infantry battalion
	Sweden	23 Mar–17 May 1978	Infantry company
		21 Aug. 1980 to date	Logistics: medical unit

Other contributions (without cost to UN):	Australia	Jun. 1978	Arms and ammunition for Fijian contingent
	Germany, Federal Republic of	Mar. 1978	Airlift: Norwegian troops
		Apr. 1978	Provided substantial part of vehicles and equipment for Nepalese contingent
	United Kingdom	Jun. 1978	Airlift: Fijian troops
	United States	Mar.–Jun. 1978	Airlift: Norwegian, Nepalese, Senegalese and Irish troops Airlift: equipment for Fijian troops

United Nations Military Observer Group in India and Pakistan (UNMOGIP)

Authorization:	Security Council resolutions:	47(1948) of 21 April 1948
		91(1951) of 30 March 1951
		201(1965) of 6 September 1965
		(to strengthen UNMOGIP)

Function: To supervise, in the State of Jammu and Kashmir, the cease-fire between India and Pakistan

Location: The State of Jammu and Kashmir and the border between that State and Pakistan

Headquarters: Rawalpindi (November-April)
Srinagar (May-November)

Duration: 24 January 1949 to date

Maximum strength: 102 (October 1965)

Current strength: 39 military observers (October 1985)

Fatalities: 4 (killed in action/accidents)
<u>1</u> (other causes)
5 (1 October 1985)

Expenditures: From inception of mission to 1985: $53,445,005

Method of financing: Appropriations through the United Nations regular budget

Chief Military Observers:

Brigadier H. H. Angle (Canada)	1 Nov. 1949–Jul. 1950
Colonel Siegfried Pl. Coblentz (United States) (Acting)	Jul.– 27 Oct. 1950
Lieutenant-General R. H. Nimmo (Australia)	28 Oct. 1950–3 Jan. 1966
Colonel J. H. J. Gauthier (Canada) (Acting)	4 Jan.–7 Jul. 1966
Lieutenant-General Luis Tassara-Gonzalez (Chile)	8 Jul. 1966–18 Jun. 1977
Lieutenant-Colonel P. Bergevin (Canada) (Acting)	19 Jun. 1977–8 Apr. 1978
Colonel Pospisil (Canada) (Acting)	9 Apr.–3 Jun. 1978
Brigadier-General Stig Waldenstrom (Sweden)	4 Jun. 1978–7 Jun. 1982
Brigadier-General Thor Johnsen (Norway)	8 Jun. 1982 to date

Contributors of military observers:

	Duration
Australia	1952 to date
Belgium	Jan. 1949 to date
Canada	Jan. 1949–Jan. 1979
Chile	1950 to date
Denmark	1950 to date
Ecuador	1952
Finland	1963 to date
Italy	1961 to date
Mexico	1949
New Zealand	1952 to date

Contributors of *military observers: (cont.)*		*Duration*	
	Norway	Jan. 1949–1952	
		1957 to date	
	Sweden	1950 to date	
	Uruguay	1952 to date	
	United States	Jan. 1949 to date	

Other contributions *(without cost to UN):*	Australia	1 Apr. 1975–31 Dec. 1978	Aircraft
	Canada	15 Jun. 1974–31 Mar. 1975	Aircraft
	Italy	1957–1963	Aircraft
	United States	1949–1954	Aircraft

United Nations India-Pakistan Observation Mission (UNIPOM)

Authorization:	Security Council resolution 211(1965) of 20 September 1965	
Function:	To supervise the cease-fire along the India/Pakistan border except the State of Jammu and Kashmir where UNMOGIP operated, and the withdrawal of all armed personnel to the positions held by them before 5 August 1965	
Location:	Along the India/Pakistan border between Kashmir and the Arabian Sea	
Headquarters:	Lahore (Pakistan)/Amritsar (India)	
Duration:	23 September 1965–22 March 1966	
Maximum strength:	96 military observers (October 1965)	
Strength at withdrawal:	78 military observers	
Fatalities:	None	
Expenditures:	From inception to end of Mission:	$1,713,280
Method of financing:	Appropriations through the United Nations regular budget	
Chief Officer:	Major-General B. F. Macdonald (Canada)	Sep. 1965–Mar. 1966
Contributors:	*In its initial stage (from UNTSO and UNMOGIP)*	*28 Sep. 1965–22 Mar. 1966*
	Australia Belgium Canada Chile Denmark Finland Ireland Italy Netherlands New Zealand Norway Sweden	Brazil Burma Canada (also air unit, Oct. 1965–Mar. 1966) Ceylon (now Sri Lanka) Ethiopia Ireland Nepal Netherlands Nigeria Venezuela

United Nations Observation Group in Lebanon (UNOGIL)

Authorization:	Security Council resolution 128(1958) of 11 June 1958
Function:	To ensure that there was no illegal infiltration of personnel or supply of arms or other *matériel* across the Lebanese borders
Location:	Lebanese-Syrian border areas and vicinity of zones held by opposing forces
Headquarters:	Beirut
Duration:	12 June–9 December 1958
Maximum strength:	591 military observers (November 1958)
Strength at withdrawal:	375 military observers
Fatalities:	None
Expenditures:	From inception to end of mission: $3,697,742
Method of financing:	Appropriations through the United Nations regular budget

Members of Observation Group:		
	Galo Plaza Lasso (Ecuador):	Chairman
	Rajeshwar Dayal (India):	Member
	Major-General Odd Bull (Norway):	Executive member in charge of military observers

Contributors of military observers:

Afghanistan	Indonesia
Argentina	Ireland
Burma	Italy
Canada	Nepal
Ceylon (now Sri Lanka)	Netherlands
Chile	New Zealand
Denmark	Norway
Ecuador	Peru
Finland	Portugal
India	Thailand

United Nations Yemen Observation Mission (UNYOM)

Authorization:	Security Council resolution 179(1963) of 11 June 1963
Function:	To observe and certify the implementation of the disengagement agreement between Saudi Arabia and the United Arab Republic
Location:	Yemen
Headquarters:	San'a
Duration:	4 July 1963–4 September 1964

Maximum strength:	25 military observers
	114 officers and other ranks of reconnaissance
	     unit (Yugoslavia)
	  50 officers and other ranks of air unit (Canada)
	189

Strength at withdrawal:	25 military observers and supporting air unit (Canada)
Fatalities:	None
Expenditures:	From inception to end of mission: $1,840,450
Method of financing:	Contributions from Saudi Arabia and Egypt in equal parts

Commanders:		
	Lieutenant-General Carl C. von Horn (Sweden)	4 Jul.– 25 Aug. 1963
	Colonel Branko Pavlović (Yugoslavia) (Acting)	26 Aug.–11 Sep. 1963
	Lieutenant-General P. S. Gyani (India)	12 Sep.– 7 Nov. 1963

Special Representative of Secretary-General and Head of Mission:	P. P. Spinelli (Italy)	4 Nov. 1963–4 Sep.1964
Chiefs-of-Staff:	Colonel Branko Pavlović (Yugoslavia)	8–25 Nov. 1963
	Colonel S. C. Sabharwal (India)	26 Nov. 1963–4 Sep. 1964

Troop contributors:	*Duration*	*Contribution*
Australia	Jul. 1963–Nov. 1963	Military observers
Canada	Jul. 1963–Sep. 1964	Air unit (aircraft and helicopters)
Denmark	Jul. 1963–Sep. 1964	Military observers
Ghana	Jul. 1963–Sep. 1964	Military observers
India	Jan. 1964–Sep. 1964	Military observers
Italy	Jan. 1964–Sep. 1964	Military observers
Netherlands	Jan. 1964–Sep. 1964	Military observers
Norway	Jul. 1963–Sep. 1964	Military observers
Pakistan	Jan. 1964–Sep. 1964	Military observers
Sweden	Jul. 1963–Sep. 1964	Military observers
Yugoslavia	Jul. 1963–Nov. 1963	Reconnaissance unit
	Jul. 1963–Sep. 1964	Military observers

Mission of the Representative of the Secretary-General in the Dominican Republic (DOMREP)

Authorization:	Security Council resolution 203(1965) of 14 May 1965
Function:	To observe the situation and to report on breaches of the cease-fire between the two *de facto* authorities
Location:	Dominican Republic
Headquarters:	Santo Domingo
Duration:	15 May 1965–22 October 1966
Strength:	2 military observers
Fatalities:	None
Expenditures:	From inception to end of mission: $275,831
Method of financing:	Appropriations through the United Nations regular budget
Representative of the Secretary-General:	José Antonio Mayobre (Venezuela)
Military Adviser:	Major-General Indar J. Rikhye (India) (The Military Adviser was provided with a staff of 2 military observers at any one time. These observers were provided, one each, by Brazil, Canada and Ecuador)

United Nations Operation in the Congo (ONUC)

Authorization:	Security Council resolutions: 143(1960) of 14 July 1960 145(1960) of 22 July 1960 146(1960) of 9 August 1960 161(1961) of 21 February 1961 169(1961) of 24 November 1961

Function:	Initially, to ensure withdrawal of Belgian forces, to assist the Government in maintaining law and order and to provide technical assistance. The function of ONUC was subsequently modified to include maintaining the territorial integrity and the political independence of the Congo, preventing the occurrence of civil war, and securing the removal from the Congo of all foreign military, paramilitary and advisory personnel not under the United Nations Command, and all mercenaries

Location:	Republic of the Congo (now Zaire)

Headquarters:	Leopoldville (now Kinshasa)

Duration:	15 July 1960–30 June 1964

Maximum strength:	19,828 (July 1961)

Strength at withdrawal:	5,871 (30 December 1963)

Fatalities:	195 (killed in action/accidents) 39 (other causes) 234

Expenditures:	From inception to end of mission:	$400,130,793

Method of financing:	Assessments in respect of a Special Account

Special Representatives:	Ralph J. Bunche (United States)	Jul. –Aug. 1960
	Andrew W. Cordier (United States)	Aug.–Sep. 1960
	Rajeshwar Dayal (India)	Sep. 1960–May 1961
	Mekki Abbas (Sudan) (Acting)	Mar.–May 1961

Officers-in-Charge:	Sture Linner (Sweden)	May 1961–Jan. 1962
	Robert K.A. Gardiner (Ghana)	Feb. 1962–May 1963
	Max H. Dorsinville (Haiti)	May 1963–Apr. 1964
	Bibiano F. Osorio-Tafall (Mexico)	Apr.–Jun.1964

Commanders:	Lieutenant-General Carl C. von Horn (Sweden)	18 Jul.–Dec. 1960
	Lieutenant-General Sean MacEoin (Ireland)	Jan. 1961–Mar. 1962
	Lieutenant-General Kebbede Guebre (Ethiopia)	Apr. 1962–Jul. 1963
	Major-General Christian Kaldager (Norway)	Aug.–Dec. 1963
	Major-General Aguiyu Ironsi (Nigeria)	Jan.–Jun. 1964

Contributors:	Duration	Contribution
Argentina	Jul. 1960–Feb. 1963	Aircraft personnel (air and ground)
Austria	14 Dec. 1960–Aug. 1963	Aircraft personnel (air and ground), field hospital and personnel, staff personnel
Brazil	Jul. 1960–Jun. 1964	Aircraft personnel (air and ground) staff personnel
Burma	Aug. 1960–Jun. 1964	Staff personnel
Canada	Jul. 1960–Jun. 1964	Aircraft personnel (air and ground), staff personnel, signals
Ceylon (now Sri Lanka)	Aug. 1960–Apr. 1962	Staff personnel
Denmark	Aug. 1960–Jun. 1964	Aircraft personnel (air and ground), staff personnel, workshop control, transport company
Ethiopia	15 Jul. 1960–16 Jun. 1964	Infantry, aircraft personnel (air and ground), staff personnel
Ghana	15 Jul. 1960–25 Sep. 1963	Infantry, 2 medical units, staff personnel, police companies
Guinea	25 Jul. 1960–Jan. 1961	Infantry
India	Jul. 1960–Jun. 1964	Infantry, aircraft personnel (air and ground), field hospital and personnel, staff personnel, supply unit, signal company, air dispatch team, postal unit
Indonesia	4 Oct. 1960–Apr. 1964	Infantry
Iran	Dec. 1962–Jul. 1963	Aircraft and air and ground personnel
Ireland	28 Jul. 1960–11 May 1964	Infantry, staff personnel
Italy	Oct. 1960–Jun. 1964	Aircraft personnel (air and ground), field hospital, staff personnel
Liberia	25 Jul. 1960–May 1963	Infantry, movement control, staff personnel
Malaya	30 Oct. 1960–Apr. 1963	Infantry, staff personnel
Federation of Mali (now Mali and Senegal)	1 Aug. 1960–Nov. 1960	Infantry
Morocco	15 Jul. 1960–31 Jan. 1961	Infantry, parachute company
Netherlands	Aug. 1960–Oct. 1963	Hygiene teams, staff personnel
Nigeria	10 Nov. 1960–30 Jun. 1964	Infantry, police unit, staff personnel
Norway	Jul. 1960–Mar. 1964	Aircraft personnel (air and ground), staff personnel, workshop control
Pakistan	31 Aug. 1960–May 1964	Ordnance and transport units, staff personnel
Philippines	Feb. 1963–Jun. 1963	Aircraft personnel (air and ground), staff personnel
Sierra Leone	Jan. 1962–Mar. 1963	Infantry
Sudan	Aug. 1960–Apr.–Dec. 1961	Infantry
Sweden	20 Jul. 1960–15 May 1964	Infantry, aircraft personnel (air and ground), movement control, engineering personnel, workshop unit, signal detachment, staff personnel
Tunisia	15 Jul. 1960–May 1963	Infantry
United Arab Republic	20 Aug. 1960–1 Feb. 1961	Infantry, parachute battalion
Yugoslavia	Jul. 1960–Dec. 1960	Aircraft personnel (air and ground)

From February 1963 to the end of the United Nations Operation in the Congo, a battalion of the Congolese National Army was incorporated in ONUC

Other contributions
(without cost to UN):

Canada	Beginning of operation	Airlift of food
Switzerland	Beginning of operation	Airlift of food and other supplies
USSR	Beginning of operation	Airlift of food
United Kingdom	Beginning of operation	Airlift of food and Ghanaian troops
United States	Beginning of operation	Airlift of food supplies and equipment
		Aircraft
		Airlift of Ghanaian, Guinean, Moroccan, Swedish and Tunisian troops
		Sealift of Malayan troops

United Nations Peace-keeping Force in Cyprus (UNFICYP)

Authorization: Security Council resolutions:

186(1964) of 4 March 1964	343(1973) of 14 December 1973
187(1964) of 13 March 1964	349(1974) of 29 May 1974
192(1964) of 20 June 1964	364(1974) of 13 December 1974
Consensus of 11 August 1964	370(1975) of 13 June 1975
194(1964) of 25 September1964	383(1975) of 13 December 1975
198(1964) of 18 December 1964	391(1976) of 15 June 1976
201(1965) of 19 March 1965	401(1976) of 14 December 1976
206(1965) of 16 June 1965	410(1977) of 15 June 1977
219(1965) of 17 December 1965	422(1977) of 15 December 1977
220(1966) of 16 March 1966	430(1978) of 16 June 1978
222(1966) of 16 June 1966	443(1978) of 14 December 1978
231(1966) of 15 December 1966	451(1979) of 15 June 1979
238(1967) of 19 June 1967	458(1979) of 14 December 1979
244(1967) of 22 December 1967	472(1980) of 13 June 1980
247(1968) of 18 March 1968	482(1980) of 11 December 1980
254(1968) of 18 June 1968	486(1981) of 4 June 1981
261(1968) of 10 December 1968	495(1981) of 14 December 1981
266(1969) of 10 June 1969	510(1982) of 15 June 1982
274(1969) of 11 December 1969	526(1982) of 14 December 1982
281(1970) of 9 June 1970	534(1983) of 15 June 1983
291(1970) of 10 December 1970	541(1983) of 18 November 1983
293(1971) of 26 May 1971	544(1983) of 15 December 1983
305(1971) of 13 December 1971	553(1984) of 15 June 1984
315(1972) of 15 June 1972	559(1984) of 14 December 1984
324(1972) of 12 December 1972	565(1985) of 14 June 1985
334(1973) of 5 June 1973	

Function: In the interest of international peace and security, to use its best efforts to prevent the recurrence of fighting and, as necessary, to contribute to the maintenance and restoration of law and order and a return to normal conditions. Since the hostilities of 1974, this has included supervising the cease-fire and maintaining a buffer zone between the lines of the Cyprus National Guard and of the Turkish and Turkish Cypriot forces.

Location: Cyprus

Headquarters: Nicosia

Duration: 27 March 1964 to date

Maximum strength: 6,411 (June 1964)

Current strength: 2,345 (October 1985)

Fatalities: 83 (killed in action/accidents)
55 (other causes)
138 (1 October 1985)

Estimated cost: From inception of mission to 15 December 1984: $470,500,000

Method of financing: Voluntary contributions

| *Mediators:* | Sakari S. Tuomioja (Finland) | Mar.–Sep. 1964 |
| | Galo Plaza Lasso (Ecuador) | Sep. 1964–Dec. 1965 |

Special Representative:	Galo Plaza Lasso (Ecuador)	May–Sep. 1964
	Carlos A. Bernardes (Brazil)	Sep. 1964–Jan. 1967
	P.P. Spinelli (Italy) (Acting)	Jan.–Feb. 1967
	Bibiano F. Osorio-Tafall (Mexico)	Feb. 1967–June 1974
	Luis Weckmann-Muñoz (Mexico)	Jul. 1974–Oct. 1975
	Javier Pérez de Cuéllar (Peru)	Oct. 1975–Dec. 1977
	Rémy Gorgé (Switzerland) (Acting)	Dec. 1977–Apr. 1978
	Reynaldo Galindo-Pohl (El Salvador)	May 1978–Apr. 1980
	Hugo Juan Gobbi (Argentina)	May 1980–31 Dec. 1984
	James Holger (Chile) (Acting)	Jan. 1985 to date

Commanders:	Lieutenant-General P.S. Gyani (India)	Mar.–Jun. 1964
	General K.S. Thimayya (India)	Jun. 1964–Dec. 1965
	Brigadier A.J. Wilson (United Kingdom) (Acting)	Dec. 1965–May 1966
	Lieutenant-General I.A.E. Martola (Finland)	May 1966–Dec. 1969
	Lieutenant-General Dewan Prem Chand (India)	Dec. 1969–Dec. 1976
	Major-General J.J. Quinn (Ireland)	Dec. 1976–Feb. 1981
	Major-General G.G. Greindl (Austria)	Mar. 1981 to date

Contributors		*Duration*	*Contribution*
	Australia	25 May 1964 to date	Civilian police
	Austria	14 Apr. 1964–27 Jul. 1977	Civilian police
		17 May 1964–Oct. 1973	Field hospital and personnel
		Oct. 1973–Apr. 1976	Medical centre
		25 Apr. 1972 to date	Infantry
	Canada	13 Mar. 1964 to date	Infantry
		Apr. 1976 to date	Medical centre
	Denmark	22 May 1964 to date	Infantry
		25 May 1964–4 Jun. 1975	Civilian police
	Finland	28 Mar. 1964–31 Oct. 1977	Infantry
		31 Oct. 1977 to date	Staff officers, military police
	Ireland	28 Mar. 1964–31 Oct. 1973	Infantry
		31 Oct. 1973 to date	Staff officers
	New Zealand	22 May 1964–28 Jun. 1967	Civilian police
	Sweden	28 Mar. 1964 to date	Infantry
		5 May 1964 to date	Civilian police
	United Kingdom	27 Mar. 1964 to date	Infantry, logistics, air unit
		Apr. 1976 to date	Medical centre

Other contributions (without cost to UN)	Australia	Basic salaries, overseas allowances, travel outside Cyprus, uniforms and equipment initially brought from Australia, compensation
	Austria	Domestic salaries of medical and police contingents
	Canada	Contingent costs
	Denmark	Salaries of service personnel
	Finland	Pay of professional personnel
	Ireland	Pay and allowances, including overseas and *per diem* allowances, supplies and equipment
	Italy	Airlift

Other contributions (without cost to UN) (cont.)	New Zealand	Pay, overseas allowances, equipment, arms, ammunition and travel outside Cyprus for its police contingent
	Sweden	Airlift, pay to professional personnel, staff contributions, arrangements for staff, remuneration to administrative personnel and other expenditures in Sweden
	United Kingdom	Airlift, contingent costs and those of UNFICYP headquarters personnel
	United States	Airlift

United Nations Security Force in West New Guinea (West Irian)

Authorization:	General Assembly resolution 1752(XVII) of 21 September 1962
Function:	To maintain peace and security in the territory under the United Nations Temporary Executive Authority (UNTEA) established by agreement between Indonesia and the Netherlands
Location:	West New Guinea (West Irian)
Headquarters:	Hollandia [now Jayaphra]
Duration:	3 October 1962–30 April 1963
Maximum strength:	1,500 infantry personnel and 76 aircraft personnel
Strength at withdrawal:	1,500 infantry personnel and 76 aircraft personnel
Fatalities:	None
Method of Financing:	The Governments of Indonesia and the Netherlands paid full costs in equal amounts
Commander:	Major-General Said Uddin Khan (Pakistan)

Contributors:

	Duration	*Contribution*
Pakistan	3 Oct. 1962–30 Apr. 1963	Infantry
Canada	3 Oct. 1962–30 Apr. 1963	Supporting aircraft and crews
United States	3 Oct. 1962–30 Apr. 1963	Supporting aircraft and crews

(From 18 August to 21 September 1962, the Secretary-General's Military Adviser, Brigadier-General Indar Jit Rikhye (India), and a group of 21 military observers assisted in the implementation of the agreement of 15 August 1962 between Indonesia and the Netherlands on cessation of hostilities. The military observers were provided by Brazil, Ceylon, India, Ireland, Nigeria and Sweden.)

Maps

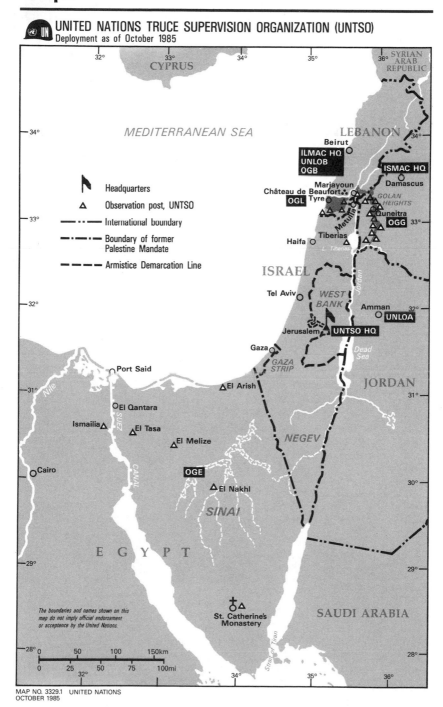

UNITED NATIONS TRUCE SUPERVISION ORGANIZATION (UNTSO)
Deployment as of October 1985

CYPRUS

MEDITERRANEAN SEA

SYRIAN ARAB REPUBLIC

LEBANON

Beirut

ILMAC HQ
UNLOB
OGB

ISMAC HQ

Damascus

Headquarters

Observation post, UNTSO

International boundary

Boundary of former Palestine Mandate

Armistice Demarcation Line

Château de Beaufort

OGL

Marjayoun

Tyre

GOLAN HEIGHTS

Quneitra

OGG

Metulla

Haifa

Tiberias

L. Tiberias

ISRAEL

Tel Aviv

WEST BANK

Amman

UNLOA

Jordan

Jerusalem

UNTSO HQ

Gaza

GAZA STRIP

Dead Sea

Port Said

Nile

El Arish

JORDAN

El Qantara

Ismailia

El Tasa

SUEZ

NEGEV

El Melize

Cairo

CANAL

OGE

El Nakhl

SINAI

EGYPT

St. Catherine's Monastery

SAUDI ARABIA

The boundaries and names shown on this map do not imply official endorsement or acceptance by the United Nations.

| 0 | 50 | 100 | 150km |
| 0 | 25 | 50 | 75 | 100mi |

Strait of Tiran

THE UNITED NATIONS EMERGENCY FORCE (UNEF I)

Deployment as of August 1957

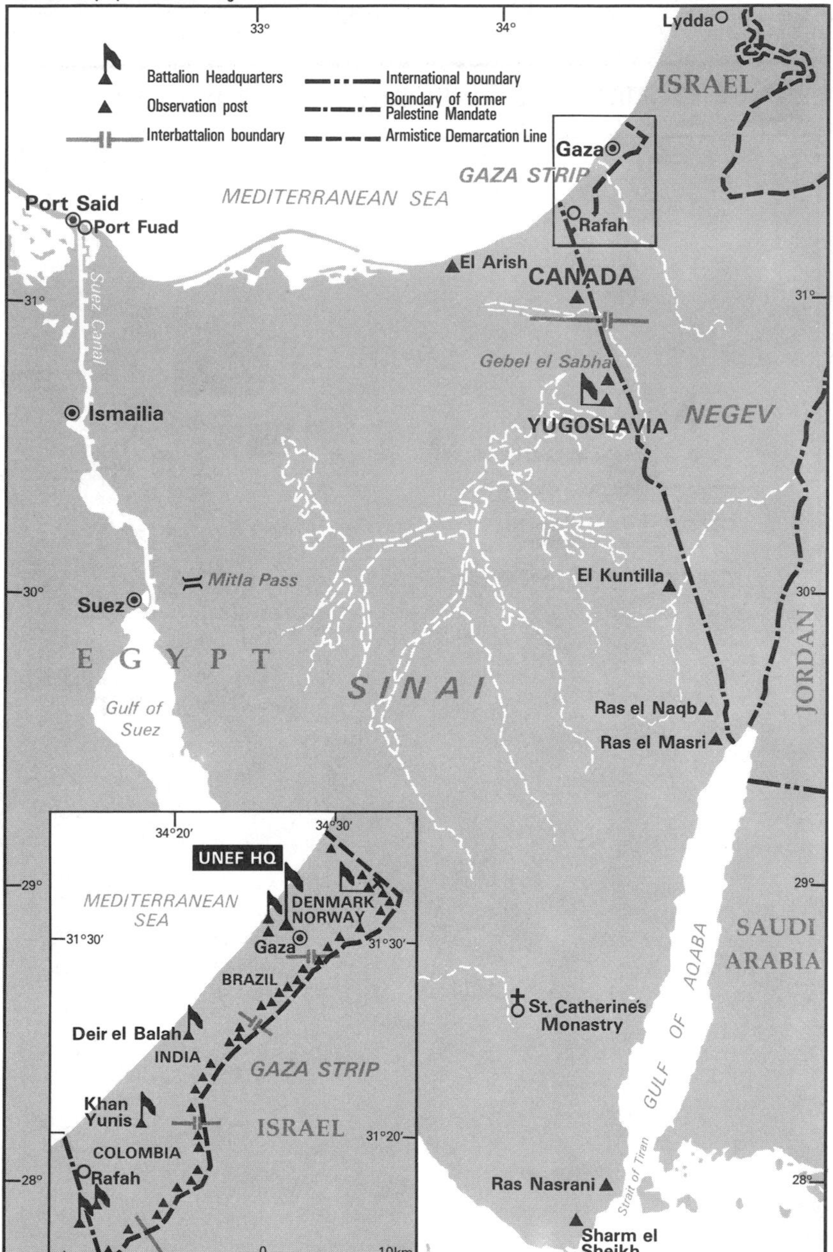
Battalion Headquarters
Observation post
Interbattalion boundary
International boundary
Boundary of former Palestine Mandate
Armistice Demarcation Line
Lydda
ISRAEL
Gaza
GAZA STRIP
Rafah
MEDITERRANEAN SEA
Port Said
Port Fuad
Suez Canal
El Arish
CANADA
Gebel el Sabha
YUGOSLAVIA
NEGEV
Ismailia
Mitla Pass
El Kuntilla
Suez
EGYPT
SINAI
JORDAN
Gulf of Suez
Ras el Naqb
Ras el Masri
UNEF HQ
MEDITERRANEAN SEA
DENMARK
NORWAY
Gaza
BRAZIL
Deir el Balah
INDIA
GAZA STRIP
Khan Yunis
ISRAEL
COLOMBIA
Rafah
FINLAND
CANADA
SAUDI ARABIA
GULF OF AQABA
St. Catherine's Monastry
Strait of Tiran
Ras Nasrani
Sharm el Sheikh
RED SEA
The boundaries and names shown on this map do not imply official endorsement or acceptance by the United Nations.
33°
34°
35°
31°
30°
29°
28°
34°20′
34°30′
31°30′
31°20′
0 10km
0 6mi
0 25 50 75 100km
0 20 40 60mi

MAP NO. 3329.2 UNITED NATIONS
JUNE 1985

THE SECOND UNITED NATIONS EMERGENCY FORCE (UNEF II)
Deployment as of May 1979

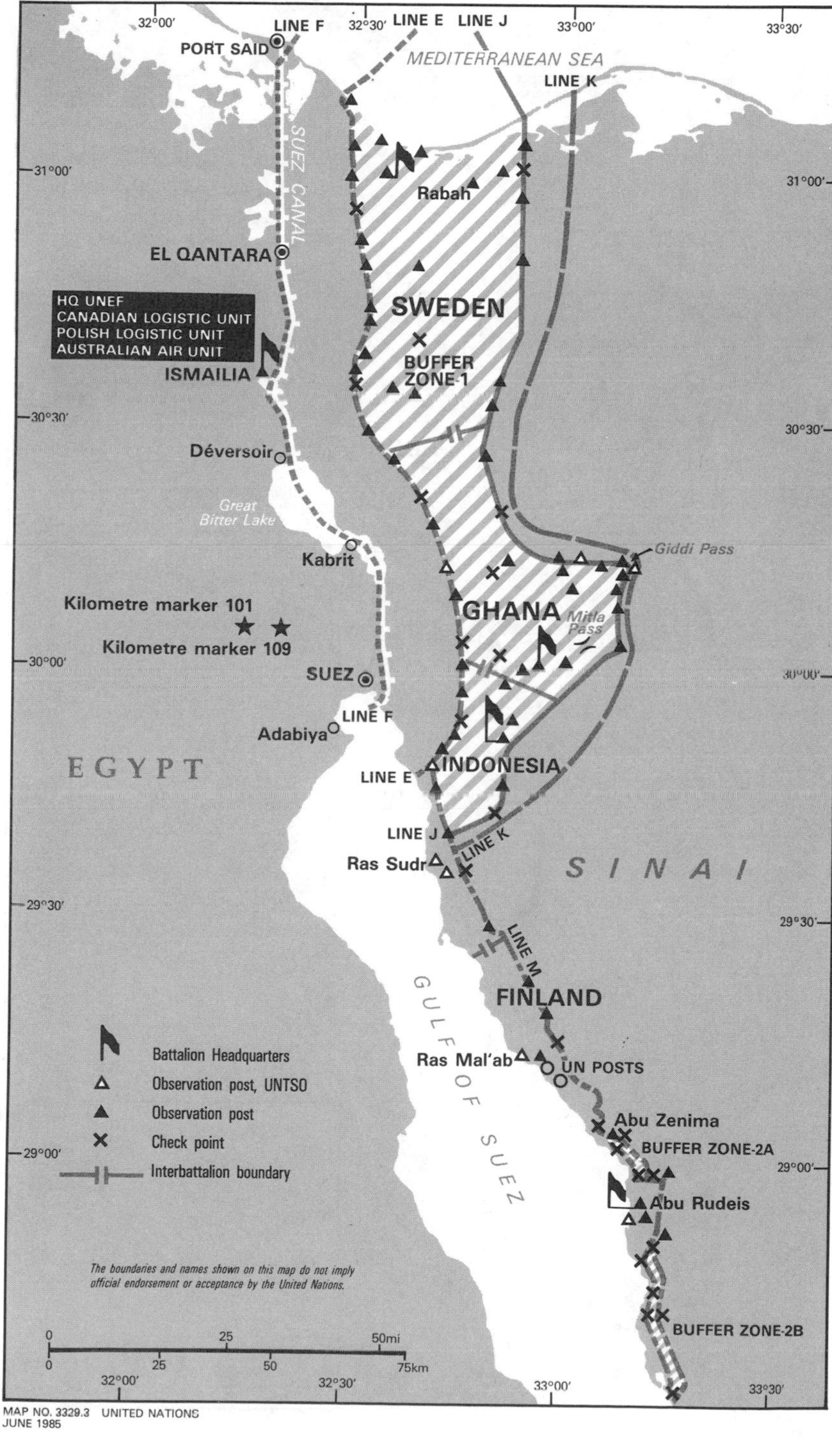

LINE F
LINE E   LINE J
PORT SAID
MEDITERRANEAN SEA
LINE K

32°00'   32°30'   33°00'   33°30'

31°00'   31°00'

Rabah

SUEZ CANAL

EL QANTARA

SWEDEN

HQ UNEF
CANADIAN LOGISTIC UNIT
POLISH LOGISTIC UNIT
AUSTRALIAN AIR UNIT

BUFFER
ZONE-1

ISMAILIA

30°30'   30°30'

Déversoir

Great
Bitter Lake

Giddi Pass

Kabrit

Kilometre marker 101

GHANA   Mitla
Pass

Kilometre marker 109

30°00'   30°00'

SUEZ

LINE F

Adabiya

EGYPT

LINE E   INDONESIA

LINE J   LINE K

Ras Sudr

S I N A I

29°30'   29°30'

LINE M

FINLAND

G U L F   Battalion Headquarters

Ras Mal'ab   UN POSTS

△   Observation post, UNTSO

O F   ▲   Observation post

Abu Zenima
BUFFER ZONE-2A

✕   Check point

S U E Z   Interbattalion boundary

29°00'   29°00'

Abu Rudeis

The boundaries and names shown on this map do not imply
official endorsement or acceptance by the United Nations.

0   25   50mi
0   25   50   75km

BUFFER ZONE-2B

32°00'   32°30'   33°00'   33°30'

MAP NO. 3329.3   UNITED NATIONS
JUNE 1985

UNITED NATIONS DISENGAGEMENT OBSERVER FORCE (UNDOF)

Deployment as of October 1985

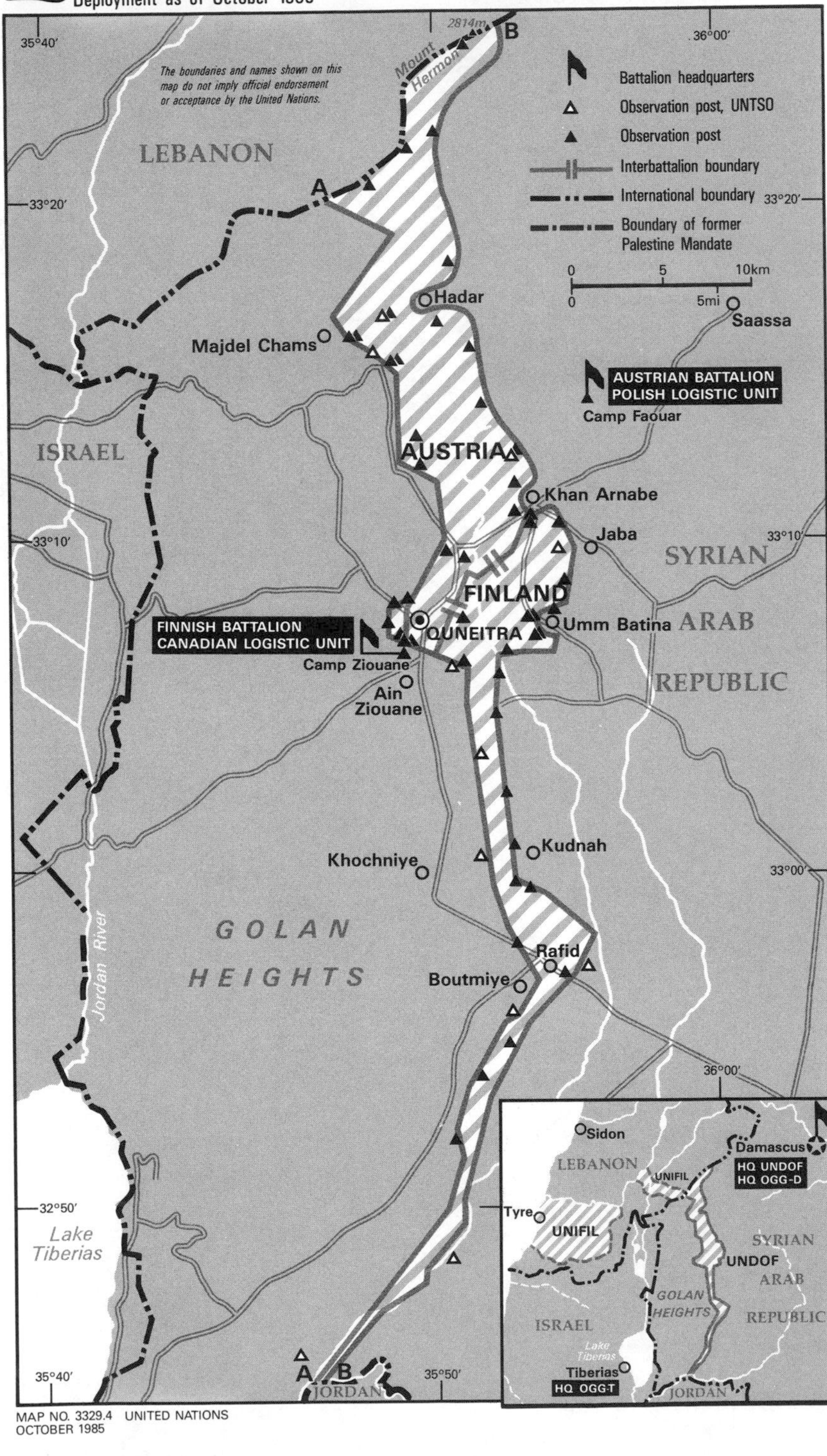

The boundaries and names shown on this map do not imply official endorsement or acceptance by the United Nations.
Battalion headquarters
Observation post, UNTSO
Observation post
Interbattalion boundary
International boundary
Boundary of former Palestine Mandate
0 5 10km
0 5mi
LEBANON
ISRAEL
SYRIAN ARAB REPUBLIC
GOLAN HEIGHTS
JORDAN
Jordan River
Lake Tiberias
Mount Hermon
2814m
AUSTRIA
FINLAND
AUSTRIAN BATTALION
POLISH LOGISTIC UNIT
Camp Faouar
FINNISH BATTALION
CANADIAN LOGISTIC UNIT
Camp Ziouane
Hadar
Majdel Chams
Saassa
Khan Arnabe
Jaba
QUNEITRA
Umm Batina
Ain Ziouane
Kudnah
Khochniye
Rafid
Boutmiye
35°40′
35°50′
36°00′
33°20′
33°10′
33°00′
32°50′
A
B
Sidon
Damascus
HQ UNDOF
HQ OGG-D
UNIFIL
Tyre
UNDOF
Tiberias
HQ OGG-T

MAP NO. 3329.4 UNITED NATIONS
OCTOBER 1985

UNITED NATIONS INTERIM FORCE IN LEBANON (UNIFIL)
Deployment as of October 1985

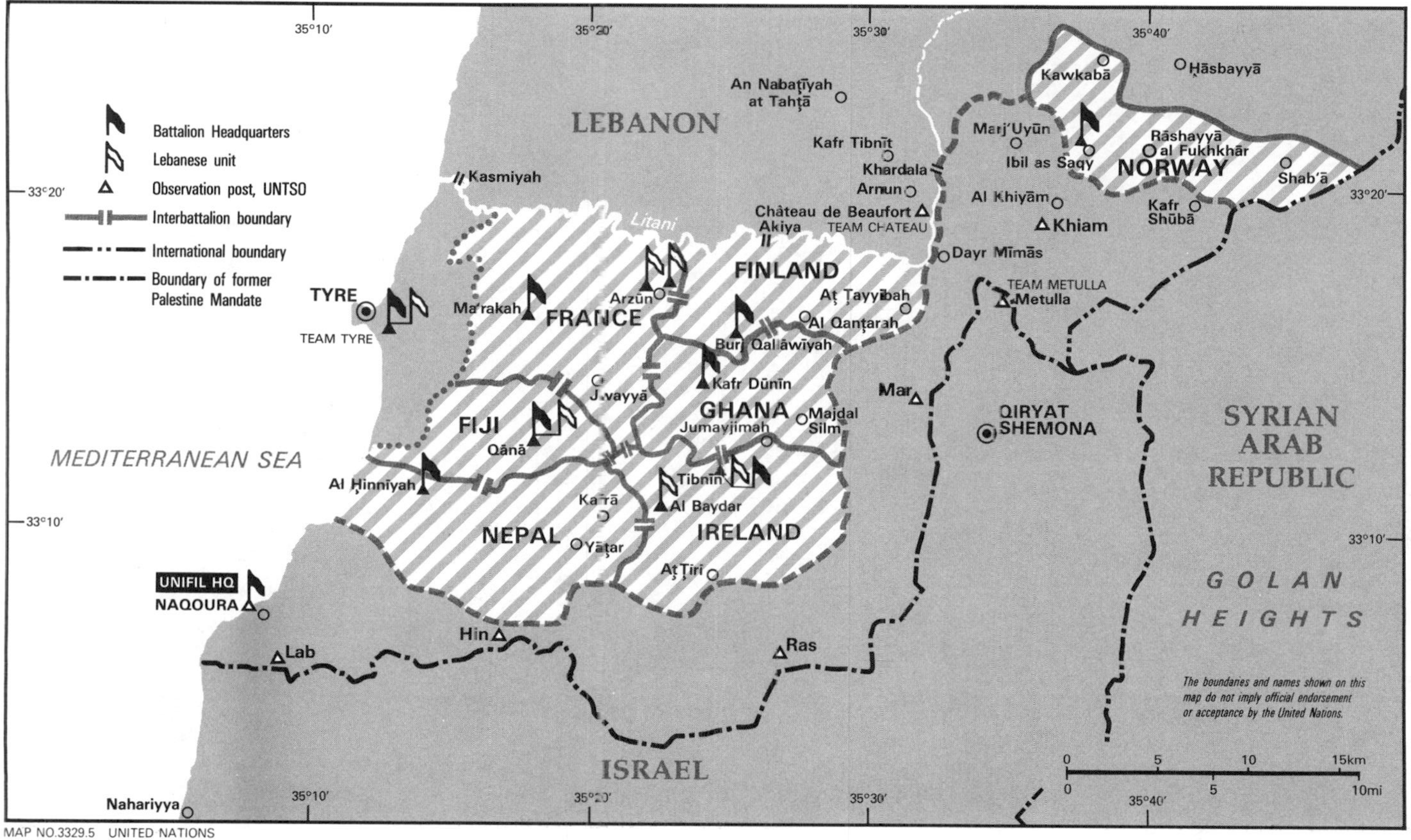

Legend:
- Battalion Headquarters
- Lebanese unit
- Observation post, UNTSO
- Interbattalion boundary
- International boundary
- Boundary of former Palestine Mandate

MEDITERRANEAN SEA

LEBANON

SYRIAN ARAB REPUBLIC

GOLAN HEIGHTS

ISRAEL

NORWAY

FINLAND

FRANCE

GHANA

IRELAND

FIJI

NEPAL

Shab'ā

Hāsbayyā

Rāshayyā al Fukhkhār

Kafr Shūbā

Kawkabā

Merj'Uyūn

Ibil as Saqy

Al Khiyām

Khiam

Dayr Mimās

TEAM METULLA

Metulla

QIRYAT SHEMONA

An Nabaţīyah at Tahţā

Kafr Tibnīt

Khardala

Arnūn

Château de Beaufort
Akīya   TEAM CHÂTEAU

At Tayyibah

Al Qanţarah

Mar

Ras

Burj Qallāwiyah

Kafr Dūnīn

Majdal Silm

Jumayjimah

Tibnīn

Al Baydar

Aţ Ţīrī

Arnūn

J. vayyā

Kafrā

Yāţar

Hin

Lab

Marrakah

Qānā

Al Hinnīyah

TEAM TYRE

TYRE

Litani

Il Kasmiyah

UNIFIL HQ
NAQOURA

Nahariyya

MAP NO. 3329.5   UNITED NATIONS
OCTOBER 1985

33°20'
35°40'
33°20'
35°30'
35°20'
35°10'
33°10'
35°10'
35°30'
33°10'
35°25'

15km
10
5
0
10mi
5
0

The boundaries and names shown on this map do not imply official endorsement or acceptance by the United Nations.

UNITED NATIONS MILITARY OBSERVER GROUP IN INDIA AND PAKISTAN
Deployment as of October 1985 (UNMOGIP)

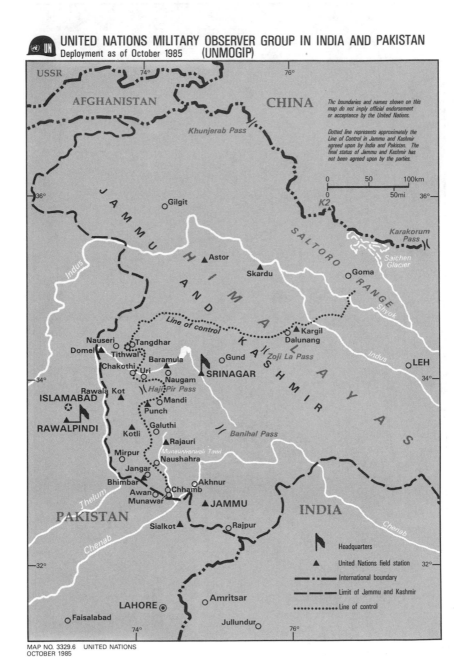

The boundaries and names shown on this map do not imply official endorsement or acceptance by the United Nations.

Dotted line represents approximately the Line of Control in Jammu and Kashmir agreed upon by India and Pakistan. The final status of Jammu and Kashmir has not been agreed upon by the parties.

0	50	100km	
0		50mi	

USSR

AFGHANISTAN

CHINA

Khunjerab Pass

Gilgit

Astor

Skardu

K2

Karakorum Pass

Saichen Glacier

Goma

Shyok

Kargil
Dalunang

Nauseri
Domel
Tangdhar
Tithwal
Baramula
Chakothi
Uri
Naugam
Rawala Kot
Haji Pir Pass

Gund
Zoji La Pass
SRINAGAR

LEH

Indus

ISLAMABAD
RAWALPINDI

Mandi
Punch

Galuthi
Kotli

Rajauri
Banihal Pass

Mirpur
Naushahra
Munawwarwali Tawi

Jangar
Bhimbar
Akhnur
Awan
Munawar
Chhamb

JAMMU

INDIA

Thelum

PAKISTAN

Sialkot
Rajpur

Chenab

Chenab

LAHORE
Faisalabad
Amritsar
Jullundur

Headquarters

▲ United Nations field station

━ ⋅ ━ International boundary

━ ━ Limit of Jammu and Kashmir

• • • • Line of control

J A M M U & H I M A L A Y A S K A S H M I R

SALTORO RANGE

MAP NO. 3329.6 UNITED NATIONS
OCTOBER 1985

UNITED NATIONS OBSERVATION GROUP IN LEBANON (UNOGIL)
Deployment as of July 1959

The boundaries and names shown on this map do not imply official endorsement or acceptance by the United Nations.

35°30'
36°
36°30'

Arida
Chadra
Aziziyé
Notre-Dame du-Fort
Halba
Beino
34°30'

Munié
Koussair
Tripoli
Sir Danié
Hermel
El Kah

Amioun
Ehden
Zabboud
Râs Baalbek
Hadeth Jobbé
El Laboué
Arsal
Aïnata
Yammouné

MEDITERRANEAN SEA

Btedaï

LEBANON
Baalbek
34°

UNOGIL HQ
Dhour Choueir
A.U.E.F.
BEIRUT
Rayak
Maarboûn
Chtaura
Zahlé
Jennta

Deïr el Kamar
Barouk
UNITED ARAB
REPUBLIC
(SYRIA)
Aïn Zebdé
Masnaa
Aïta el Foukhar
Aïn Arab
Deïr el Aachäyer
Sidon
Kfar Mechki
Jezzine
Station
33°30'
Sub-station
El Haouch
Hasbaya
Observation post and Traffic check post
Marjayoûn
Chebaa
Station Boundary
Tyre
Deïr Mimass
International boundary
Kherouia
Boundary of former Palestine Mandate

BEKAA VALLEY

Awwali
Hasbani
Litani

0   10   20   30   40   50km
0   10   20   30mi

ISRAEL
35°30'
36°

UNITED NATIONS YEMEN OBSERVATION MISSION (UNYOM)
1963-1964

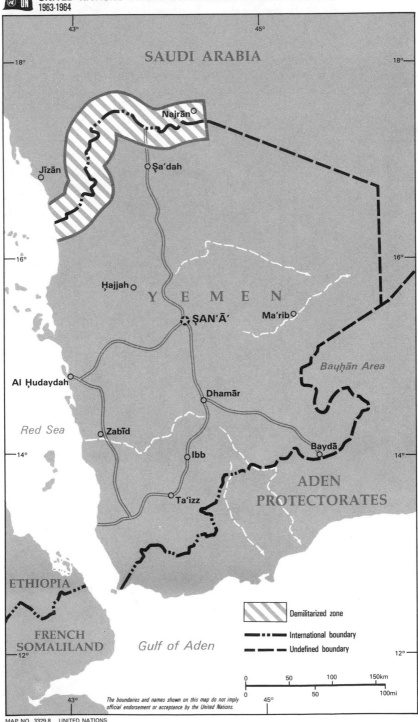

SAUDI ARABIA

18°   43°   45°   18°

Najrān○

Jīzān○

○Şa'dah

16°   16°

Ḥajjah○   Y E M E N

◌ŞAN'Ā'   Ma'rib○

Bayḥān Area

Al Ḥudaydah○

Dhamār○

Red Sea   Zabīd○

Baydā○

14°   Ibb○   14°

ADEN
PROTECTORATES

Ta'izz○

ETHIOPIA

FRENCH
SOMALILAND   Gulf of Aden

12°   12°

```
▨  Demilitarized zone
━··━··  International boundary
━ ━ ━  Undefined boundary
```

0   50   100   150km
0   50   100mi

43°   45°

The boundaries and names shown on this map do not imply
official endorsement or acceptance by the United Nations.

MAP NO. 3329.8   UNITED NATIONS
JUNE 1985